# How to have your cake and eat it, too!

# How to have your cake and eat it, too!

Diet Cooking for the Whole Family:
Diabetic — Hypoglycemic — Low Cholesterol
Low Fat / Low Salt / Low Calories

*Revised Edition*

## Norma M. MacRae, R.D.

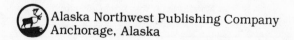 Alaska Northwest Publishing Company
Anchorage, Alaska

Library of Congress cataloging in publication data:
MacRae, Norma M., 1924-
    How to have your cake and eat it, too!
    "New recipes, plus natural sweetening directions."
    Bibliography: p.
    Includes index.
    1. Sugar-free diet — Recipes.    2. Low-cholesterol diet
— Recipes.    3. Low-fat diet — Recipes.    4. Salt-free diet
— Recipes.    5. Low-calorie diet — Recipes.    I. Title.
RM237.85.M3  1982        641.5'63        82-8682
ISBN 0-88240-226-9              AACR2

Design and layout by Jon.Hersh
Illustrations by Cheri Vigna
Alaska Northwest Publishing Company

Printed in U.S.A.

## For Robert Hardin Williams, M.D.

*In grateful appreciation of his friendly support over the years and his faith in the capabilities of the skinny young redhead he hired.*

# Contents

# Foreword

The public is very fortunate to have this book available. It was written by a dietitian who had splendid training at the Johns Hopkins Hospital. She then had magnificent additional training and experience as the head dietitian on the research ward of Harvard Medical School, at the Thorndike Laboratory. Thereafter, she worked in my metabolic research laboratory for three years, thereby acquiring an excellent understanding of metabolic and nutritional problems and appropriate diets. Subsequently, while serving twenty years as a consultant dietitian, she formulated an increasing variety of tasty and practical diets best suited to the patient's problems. The fact that she developed such an excellent private practice in dietetics is testimony to the great faith and appreciation by physicians, patients and others.

As clinical research has progressed, it has become evident that we do not need to restrict carbohydrates as vigorously for diabetics as in the past. Thus, Miss MacRae's recipes allow the diabetic to enjoy almost the same good things as everyone else, although they are lower in free sugar. The diet provides for food that is appetizing to the patient's family. Moreover, many diets are suitable to serve guests because they have relatively good taste appeal.

This is the first cookbook that provides for the needs of patients with sodium, cholesterol, and triglyceride restrictions, made necessary by various types of alteration in the blood fats. There are tasty recipes for pickles, soups, casseroles and all types of desserts, including low-cholesterol and low-sugar ice cream. There are also directions for canning and freezing fruits, suggestions for low-Calorie dips and nibbling foods. There are a number of tables and charts that help the patients when they eat at picnics, restaurants and elsewhere.

The chapter on replacements and substitutions has material that has not been presented in previous diet cookbooks. The recipes are original and were developed to fit the needs of individual patients.

Moreover, there are explanations of why the various diets are provided. The basic rules are presented simply and clearly. Each recipe gives the content of protein, fat, carbohydrate and Calories, along with the cholesterol level per serving, and the sodium content.

In conclusion, this book is a magnificent one dealing with diets for patients with diabetes, hypoglycemia, excess cholesterol and triglyceride, obesity, and salt and water retention.

*Robert H. Williams, M.D.*
*Professor of Medicine*
*University of Washington, and*
*Head, Diabetes Research Center*

# The Author

Norma M. MacRae was one of the first full-time consulting dietitians in the United States. For more than twenty-five years she has had a busy practice in Seattle, with offices both downtown and in the Northgate medical complex.

During her years of practice the need for a cookbook such as this became apparent. As a result of requests from patients and physicians she has developed many special recipes; until now they have never been put together in book form. Thus this cookbook is the result of many years' experience, and the recipes have been used and approved by her patients. She is constantly experimenting with new products to develop tastier foods for dieters.

The author is a native of Detroit, Michigan. She is a graduate of Alma College (St. Thomas, Ontario), Michigan State College, and the Johns Hopkins School of Dietetics in Baltimore. She is a Registered Dietitian.

At Johns Hopkins she did research in the laboratories of the biochemists who discovered vitamins A and D, Dr. and Mrs. Elmer V. McCollum. She was later employed by Harvard University Medical School as the dietitian for the Fourth Harvard Medical Service at Thorndike Memorial Laboratory. There, she was dietitian for Dr. Robert H. Williams, one of the world's foremost endocri-

nologists, and accompanied him to the University of Washington in Seattle to work in metabolic research.

She has been president of both the Seattle and Washington State Dietetic Associations and has served as a national committee chairman for the American Dietetic Association. She has been a panelist on medical forums and is in demand as a speaker.

Along with her love of cooking and good food, the author likes to fish, raises orchids and has Norwegian elkhounds. She loves the Northwest life and spends much of her free time at a cabin on Camano Island in Puget Sound, where most of the experimental work for this book was done.

# 1 Why Did I Write This Cookbook?

When a patient is told to limit sugar, cholesterol and Calories* the common reaction is, "What's left?" As you'll see in the recipe sections, there's plenty left.

When I'm seeing patients for dietary consultation, I like to be able to recommend one or more cookbooks for their use. But after telling several new patients that I knew of no recipe book for limiting sugar, cholesterol, fat *and* salt, I realized that many patients had these combined dietary limits, and that a recipe book was needed. So I prepared this book for them. Diabetics, hypoglycemics, persons on hyperlipoproteinemia (Fredrickson) diets of types 3, 4 and 5 (low-sugar, low-cholesterol) and those with sodium or salt restrictions will find this book useful.

Variety is the key to being able to stay on a restricted diet for a long time. Now that recipes for tasty, appetizing foods are available, there is no excuse for not making diet meals attractive and palatable.

Hypoglycemia has become a popular subject for diet articles in the last few years (diabetes has been recognized for centuries). Physicians are diagnosing hypoglycemia in more patients, and the public is aware of the disease and of the dietary problems it involves. Although the problems of hypoglycemia and

diabetes are quite different (insulin excess versus insulin shortage), the two conditions have some points of relationship, and the diet plans are similar.

Most recipes in this cookbook are designed for both diabetics and hypoglycemics. This, of course, presumes use in reasonable quantities. Too many dietetic cookies — too many anythings, dietetic or not — will cause problems. Used as directed, these recipes offer a safe diet that is anything but dull. And the desserts fill the cravings to

---

*The food Calorie is the kilocalorie (1,000 x calorie). It is written with a capital C in this book.

1

which people with these metabolic disorders are prone.

I recognize how frustrating it is for the good cook to find that one of the family must be on a restricted diet and cannot eat the usual meals. This cookbook should help the one doing the food preparation to plan attractive meals and to prevent monotony and lack of appeal for the dieter.

Unfortunately not all foods can be modified to fit into a low-sugar diet, or a low-cholesterol diet, or a low-saturated-fat diet. So some food items are missing from this cookbook.

Because there has been so much controversy over the use of saccharin and cyclamate sweeteners, we have modified as many recipes as possible using *natural sweetening directions.* However, when some foods are naturally sweetened, their sugar content becomes too high to be eaten by hypoglycemics and diabetics. This is noted in these recipes. And, too, some foods cannot be made sweet enough without either sugar or artificial sweeteners. This fact is also noted where indicated.

The dessert recipes are especially numerous. Most dieters will watch the rest of what they eat if they can have a nice dessert to end the meal. Some of the combinations of ingredients may seem odd to the person just learning how to adapt recipes, but the important thing is that the recipes do work. The food is tasty and attractive to the dieter.

For the person wanting to reduce his weight, these recipes are lower in Calories than the same items made with sugar, cream or added eggs. Just the same, too many servings means too many Calories just as any other food would. Let the dieter beware of eating too much of the pie or too many of the cookies. Although they are prepared dietetically, they are still not free of Calories!

I hope you will experiment with these recipes and come up with some of your own as well. A good cook will always be challenged by a change in meal plans; these suggestions should show the way.

Dieting needn't be dull — use your imagination and *enjoy* food.

# 2 General Information on Diets

## Blood Fats: Cholesterol and Triglycerides

Most people do not realize that fats are perfectly normal parts of human blood. They are found largely in the serum, not in the blood cells, and they have specific functions in the chemistry of the body. It is only when the body manufactures too many of these fats, so that the blood becomes overloaded with them, that we have to worry about it.

The best-known blood fat is *cholesterol.* This substance is an important source from which the body manufactures several hormones, vitamin D and other body chemicals. Cholesterol is normally found in the liver, in nerve tissue and in gallstones. The hormones produced by the adrenals and the various sex glands are also related to cholesterol.

As much as 75 percent of the body's cholesterol has been manufactured from other materials, including fats.

The average American eats about 40 percent of his daily Calories as fat. Almost half of this fat is saturated because the main sources are meat, eggs, cheese, cream, whole milk,

butter and other dairy foods. These saturated fats tend to increase the level of cholesterol in the blood; the unsaturated fats (polyunsaturated and monounsaturated) tend to lower the level of cholesterol in the blood.

It has recently been discovered that cholesterol exists in more than one

form. HDL (high density lipoprotein) cholesterol seems to be a helpful fellow, rather than a bad actor. LDL (low density lipoprotein) seems to be the offender that leads to artery disease. By separating out the blood cholesterol into the different types, it can be found whether the body is

3

keeping its defense mechanism in good working order by making ample HDL or is forming artery fatty "sludge" with excessive levels of LDL. This now explains why some people can have very high cholesterol levels in the blood and not show any signs of artery disease or other vascular problems. Probably they have high levels of HDL cholesterol! Average levels for males are 40 to 50; for premenopause females, 50 to 60; for post-menopause females, same as males, 40 to 50.

People have been told about saturated and polyunsaturated fats for several years. Few understand what they are. In general, the saturated fats are those that are solid at body temperature. One exception is coconut oil, a very saturated fat but liquid at 98 degrees. The unsaturated fats are mostly those that stay liquid at body temperature.

These adjectives describe the chemical structure of the fats. Because of their structure, saturated fats may attach themselves to the artery walls, in a sludgelike deposit, unless the blood flow is able to carry them along. Most are found in the high-cholesterol foods and in the so-called "nondairy creamers," which are usually coconut oil. Avoiding excessive amounts of the saturated fats helps prevent fat deposits in the arteries and the narrowing of the channel. Instead of forming sludge deposits in the arteries, the unsaturated fats tend to carry the

sludge along with them, thus helping prevent accumulation on the artery wall.

More simply — think of the saturated fats as lazy, sludge-forming materials and the unsaturated fats as scrubbing brushes: The monounsaturated fat has only two scrubbing surfaces while the

polyunsaturated fat may have fourteen or more. Obviously, the polyunsaturated fats do a better job of acting as detergents because they have a larger capacity. These polyunsaturated fats are found in fish (oils), walnuts, corn oil, soybean oil and safflower oil.

The monounsaturated fats are found in poultry, olives, other nuts (except coconut) and cottonseed oil. Many foods contain small amounts of these substances, but only those listed have enough to be effective.

4

Polyunsaturated fats, eaten in reasonable amounts, apparently tend to lower the blood levels of cholesterol and triglycerides and may also help remove the fat already deposited, provided that fat has not been hardened by the addition of calcium by the body. The ratio of unsaturated to saturated fats found effective for controlling fatty deposits is at least two to one.

Any human body will make cholesterol if given excess Calories. The Calories do not have to be from any specific food. Whenever a person is gaining weight, he is making extra cholesterol, and he is making other blood fats, too. Which of the blood fats will be increased the greatest amount depends on the metabolic balance and chemistry of the individual. Some persons make extra cholesterol only; others make that plus extra triglycerides. Either of these can cause artery and heart damage.

Changing your diet can usually control the total amount of cholesterol in the blood, but as we just mentioned, that is not the only concern. If cholesterol is low and HDL is also low, the risk is still great. Diet change alone does not seem to make the HDL increase. The only thing that

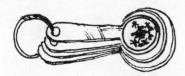

seems to do that is increased exercise. Three hours weekly (one hour, three times) is normally enough *hard* exercise to raise the HDL. Of course, additional time exercising might do even more, so don't stop with three hours if you can manage to do extra.

The other big factor in lowering both cholesterol and triglycerides is getting down to a normal weight, as this rids the body of fat both in the tissues and in the blood.

To do this cut down (or stop) eating foods high in cholesterol. These foods include egg yolk, liver and glandular meats, milk fat, meat fat and some shellfish, especially shrimp. Coconut oil (highly saturated) turns into cholesterol very readily, so this should be avoided, too. The fats eaten should be primarily from the polyunsaturated (vegetable) groups. By switching the fat intake in this manner, the body is encouraged to reduce the cholesterol deposits and to no longer manufacture it in increased amounts.

*Triglycerides* are also fats that are found in the blood serum. They are also manufactured in the body, but the sources are sugars, excessive amounts of starch and alcohol. Persons with diabetes or hypoglycemia often have high triglyceride levels since the metabolic upset caused by these diseases tends to make the body manufacture them. These excess fats can then be deposited in the arteries — which may lead to heart attacks and strokes.

Many physicians place diabetics on fat-restricted diets in an attempt to prevent the development of this secondary artery problem. Diabetics tend to develop heart and artery problems earlier than and at a rate many times higher than average. Control of diabetes helps prevent the development of these related vascular diseases.

When the blood sugar is in balance, the sugar is used for energy and heat with only the excess going to storage. If the metabolic balance is off, the body tends to produce excess cholesterol and triglycerides. These are mostly made in the liver and then distributed throughout the body and blood.

The rules for prevention of high cholesterol and triglyceride levels are similar; combined, there are eight rules on which the recipes in this cookbook are based:

1. Lose weight until a normal level is reached. This is necessary for control of both cholesterol and triglycerides.

2. Avoid free sugar and limit natural sugars in order to reduce triglycerides.

3. Avoid or limit the intake of high-cholesterol foods. This means cut out animal fats and limit red meats to three meals per week — no more — and eliminate milk fat and coconut fat entirely (including nondairy creamers). Use fish, poultry, low-fat cheese and cottage cheese to supply most of the diet protein.

4. Include unsaturated fats in the diet (soybean oil, safflower oil or corn oil) to help desludge cholesterol and triglyceride deposits. The polyunsaturated fats do not produce excess fat in the blood unless overeaten.

5. Limit or avoid the use of alcohol. This will have to be decided by your doctor on the basis of your blood content of triglycerides. Be sure to discuss this frankly with your physician. Diet control in every aspect but this one may cause you to still manufacture excess triglycerides and therefore develop vascular disease.

6. Limit food intake to give *no excess* over the body's needs. This is necessary for control of both cholesterol and triglycerides.

7. Limit caffeine to reasonable amounts (one cup per meal or less). It has been observed that very high levels of triglycerides are sometimes due to high caffeine intake and will drop rapidly when caffeine is removed from the daily diet.

8. Increase exercise to a minimum of one hour (or more) three times weekly if your HDL blood levels are lower than average.

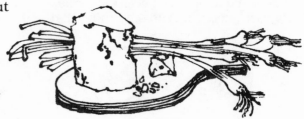

# Diabetes versus Hypoglycemia

*Diabetes mellitus* is caused by a shortage of insulin, a hormone needed to regulate the use of sugar in the body. This disease has been recognized since ancient times. The Egyptians and Greeks were known to have suffered from it, and the symptoms we see are the same as described by ancient physicians.

Those who cannot control diabetes by just watching what they eat, must have medicine to supply the insulin they lack. No human can live without insulin. Either it must be made by the body in adequate amounts, or it must be given in the form of drugs, which extend the body's own insulin, or as injected insulin. There is no alternative substance to fill this need.

Without insulin, the uncontrolled blood sugar goes higher and higher, causing unquenchable thirst (some diabetics drink gallons of liquids each day), unsatisfiable hunger (at the end of a huge meal they still feel hungry), and then frequent urination from all the liquid taken in. Failure to heal may also be a sign of a high blood sugar level: lingering vaginal and bladder infections in women are often indications of diabetes.

Among the serious problems which diabetes may lead to are heart attacks and strokes. Kidney disease with eventual kidney failure and blindness are also long-term developments of the poorly controlled diabetic. Forty percent of the blind in the state of Washington are blind from diabetes; undoubtedly this figure is the same in other areas.

*All sugars* (natural in food and refined) and *all starches* require treatment by insulin before the body can use their energy content for heat and/or work. Starches convert to sugar when digested, but the coarse, high-fiber starches digest and convert much more slowly, so they are handled best. But even these must still be spread throughout the day to avoid overloading at any one time.

Losing weight will help bring the blood sugar into control. An overweight body has more cells using insulin, so the insulin need increases with weight gain. It is also believed that fat cells use insulin less efficiently than muscle cells, thus an overweight person has a doubly increased need. So, the pounds you

lose might be enough to let you control diabetes by diet alone: NO SHOTS! Doesn't that give you an incentive for sticking to your diet and losing weight?

When first developing diabetes, many persons have symptoms of both low sugar and high sugar at varying times. (The damaged pancreas's insulin-making cells first overproduce, then underproduce.) Both conditions have similar symptoms, so only a blood test can tell if the body needs food (sugar) or insulin.

How can this double problem be controlled? By following the guidelines for hypoglycemia as given on pages 9 and 10.

Hypoglycemia is a more recently recognized disease. It is frequently found in families where there is diabetes and may be an early or pre-diabetic condition. As we mentioned before, it is often difficult to determine whether a person is suffering from diabetes or hypoglycemia, or both!

True hypoglycemia is the overproduction of insulin. This leads to lowering of the blood sugar and subsequent cell starvation. Headaches, forgetfulness, dizziness, nausea, anxiety, heart palpitations, excessive fatigue and shakiness may all be symptoms of this disease. Much of this is due to lack of adequate sugar supply for the brain. (Most parts of the body are able to convert nonsugar foods into the energy they need, but the brain has difficulty doing this.) Persons who suffer from hypoglycemia frequently show personality changes that are quite violent. (Perhaps Dr. Jeckyll/Mr. Hyde suffered from this disease!)

It seems logical that persons with hypoglycemia would need only to eat sugar often to control their low blood sugar. Not so. Eating sugar stimulates the production of still more insulin, with the result that the blood sugar goes even lower. The only way we know to prevent excess insulin production in hypoglycemics is to eliminate from the diet those foods that directly stimulate this overproduction.

Obesity makes hypoglycemia harder to control, and yet hypoglycemia may be the basis for the weight gain in the first place. The constant, unsatisfied hunger caused by hypoglycemia makes people crave food, eat, and gain weight. The weight gain places the insulin balance under greater stress, and the hypoglycemia becomes more severe as a result. This is a vicious circle for many people.

Items that may cause severe problems for the hypoglycemic (and the diabetic with hypoglycemic periods) include *caffeine,* and items that contain it, and the sweeteners *sorbitol* and *mannitol,* and foods that contain them.

Caffeine stresses the hypoglycemic just as sugar does. It temporarily raises the blood sugar so the person feels good. Then the sugar level drops sharply and the hypoglycemic symptoms promptly start to appear: irritability, forgetfulness, headache, anxiety, nausea, etc. Caffeine is not only found in foods, but in many drugs and you should check out any new drug to be sure it does not contain this substance.

Sorbitol and mannitol are sugarlike alcohols that give a sweet taste to many dietetic foods. For the hypoglycemic, these alcohols mean trouble. They are apt to cause the same reaction that eating sugar does, and may also cause diarrhea. Read labels carefully and avoid any products that contain these sweeteners.

Caffeine is not the only substance that can cause hypoglycemic reactions. Many over-the-counter drugs contain caffeine, but also may contain forms of Adrenaline, which have an affect similar to caffeine — and sometimes even more severe. When your doctor prescribes a new drug, you may need to remind him of your sugar intolerance. Many drugs are sugar-coated or contain sugar in some form; usually there is an alternate drug that does not have this sugar content, so check these out with your pharmacist. After all, having a hypoglycemic reaction won't help you recover from whatever else you may be suffering from!

Although diabetes and hypoglycemia are different in cause and effect, their dietary treatment is much the same. The main difference is that the hypoglycemic must eat small, frequent meals with protein at each, while the diabetic usually needs only three normal meals and a bedtime snack. Recipes that are suitable for one are usually suitable for the other, unless the carbohydrate content is too high for the hypoglycemic to handle.

There are nine rules for dietary control of diabetes and hypoglycemia. The first six apply to both disorders:

1. Avoid concentrated sugars (sugar, molasses, syrup, etc.).

2. Eat natural sugars and starches sparingly, and spread the amounts throughout the day in order to moderate blood sugar level and insulin demand.

3. Include coarse grains and cereals in your diet at every meal. The presence of fiber in the intestine has been shown to help regulate insulin production. Eat vegetables and fruits with skins and fibers, and avoid quickly digested white flour items.

4. Maintain normal weight for your body size. Excess fat increases the need for insulin in diabetics and increases the strain on insulin production in hypoglycemics. In either case, it makes the disease harder to control.

5. Exercise to keep your body firm and muscular. Exercise helps the body utilize food with less insulin needed.

6. Count Calories. Total Calories must not exceed the amount needed to maintain normal body weight and supply fuel for usual activities.

Three additional rules apply to help the control of hypoglycemia:

7. Avoid caffeine. This means coffee, strong tea, most cola drinks,

the majority of headache and cold remedies and some prescription drugs. Check before you take any drug.

8. Avoid or drastically limit alcohol. For many people with hypoglycemia, alcohol acts similar to sugar, and the reaction is as bad but slower occurring.

9. Eat protein foods (meat, fish, poultry, eggs, cheese) every few hours. The exact plan of the diet should depend on the results of the glucose tolerance tests: mealtimes must be planned to prevent low blood sugar levels.

Nobody should self-diagnose medical problems. If you think you may have either diabetes or hypoglycemia, be sure to have a doctor test you. In the case of diabetes, a simple blood test may be enough, or the doctor may want to do a glucose tolerance test. In the case of hypoglycemia, a longer glucose tolerance test (at least five hours), preceded by a diet high in sugar and starch for three days, is the only accurate test. These tests show the level of insulin production.

There is some disagreement about the interpretation of data found in these five-hour tests. Generally it is agreed that the following results indicate hypoglycemia: a level of 50-milligrams percent at any point; levels below 100 milligrams during the first two hours; and failure to have a rise in blood sugar above 100 at any time during the test

(continuous excess insulin production has kept the blood sugar down). Some persons will have severe symptoms at levels above 50 if the sugar has

dropped very suddenly. The severe development of symptoms is also the basis for a diagnosis of hypoglycemia.

People can bring on hypoglycemia by the way they live and eat. This may not be a true hypoglycemia, but may be as serious a problem. Excess use of caffeine and alcohol (many who cannot handle alcohol are actually undiagnosed hypoglycemics), unwise dieting and eating only junk foods with little protein can produce the same symptoms as metabolic hypoglycemia. If you think this may be your problem, try drinking decaffeinated coffee (or none), and drastically limiting the alcohol you drink; avoid junk foods (which are little more than sugar), and eat at least three meals per day — at regular intervals — being sure to have some meat or other protein food, fruit or vegetables and bread or other starch at each feeding. After two weeks you should be able to tell whether the problem is of your own making or not. While this change in diet will help the true hypoglycemic, it will not completely eliminate the symptoms. If you still feel bad, you need further help.

# Salt and Sodium

There is a lot of difference between the food that is low-salt and that which is low-sodium. Everyone involved in the care of patients requiring diets low in salt should clearly understand the differences between the two and know what changes to make in the food allowed.

In some areas water may have such a high sodium content that anyone on a low-sodium diet should drink and cook with distilled water. (You can find out how high the sodium in your water is by calling your local health department. They will know if there is any problem in your area.)

Table salt is sodium chloride. It is the *sodium* part of the formula that is the troublemaker. Sodium is also found in baking soda (sodium bicarbonate), in monosodium glutamate and in baking powder (mostly disodium phosphate).

Sodium eaten in food stimulates the body to hold water in its tissues. This extra water makes additional work for the heart and kidneys. It can cause high blood pressure, heart failure and even strokes. So you can understand that when the doctor decides that a patient must limit salt intake, it is a serious matter. The strictness of the limitation depends upon how badly that person is holding water in his body. If he has only a slight problem, perhaps a low-salt diet is enough cutting down; if he has a major problem, a low-sodium diet may be needed. The difference between these two diets is a matter of how strict you must be in avoiding foods with salt.

The first level (low salt) omits free (added) salt and any foods prepared with large amounts of salt, such as bacon, ham, frankfurters and lunch meats, pickles and olives; and all canned soups, canned vegetables, and canned meats, fish and poultry, unless the label is marked "Salt-free" or "No added salt."

The second level (low sodium) omits all of these, *plus* limits foods that are naturally high in salt, such as celery, dark green leafy vegetables, beets, carrots and shellfish.

On both levels, salt, soda, monosodium glutamate and regular baking powder are forbidden. You

11

may use a salt substitute for flavoring, but use sparingly: too much will give an unpleasant taste.

The Salt-Free Herb Seasoning Mix recipe, page 240, can be used in place of commercial salt substitute to greatly improve the taste of foods cooked without salt.

The usual American diet contains 8 to 15 grams of salt a day. Forty percent of the salt molecule is sodium. Multiply the salt figures by 0.4 to get the sodium value.

The low-salt diet contains 3 to 4 grams of salt, or 1.25 to 1.5 grams of sodium. The low-sodium diet contains 1 to 2 grams of salt, or .4 to .8 grams of sodium. This comes from naturally occurring sodium in foods, not from anything added in processing. If all of

your food, including salt-free bread and margarine, is prepared without salt, and you limit milk (or milk products) to a cup a day or less, you will be following a low-sodium diet.

If your doctor wants you to follow a very strict low-sodium diet, you will not be able to use some of the recipes in this book. If the recipe is labeled "This recipe cannot be made low in salt," don't try to eat it. The other

recipes give the amount of sodium when made according to the low-salt directions. A reasonable rule is do not use anything with more than 30 milligrams of sodium in a serving of vegetable or dessert, and 70 to 80 milligrams of sodium for a main dish selection if you are on a low-sodium diet.

If such a rigid diet is required, purchase a low-sodium cookbook. There are several good ones in print. If you can't find one, ask your local Heart Association which ones they recommend. Recipes in these books will not be low in sugar, and if you have diabetes or hypoglycemia along with the salt problem, you will have to be careful what you make from such a cookbook. The recipe may be low enough in salt but too high in sugar and starch for your diet.

If you don't understand or can't remember your diet prescription, recheck with your doctor. If possible, have a registered dietitian explain the diet limits and help you plan your meal pattern. Write down what the doctor and dietitian tell you. It is confusing when two diets sound so much alike, yet are so different in foods allowed.

The following may help you to distinguish between these diets:

The *low-salt diet* is 1,250 to 1,500 milligrams of sodium a day. Omit all free salt; omit all salt in cooking; avoid excessively salty foods such as bacon, ham, lunch meat, pickles, olives, salted nuts or salted crackers.

The *low-sodium diet* is 400 to 800 milligrams of sodium a day. Avoid all the items omitted for the low-salt diet plus the following additional restrictions: Limit milk and milk products to 1 cup (240 mL) a day or less. Avoid all canned or processed food unless it is diet-packed without salt. Omit beets and beet greens, carrots, spinach, kale, chard, celery and turnips.

If your doctor orders this strict a diet, you must have a diet plan for your meals and a low-sodium cookbook for recipes.

*Salt-free* is a rather vague term, and not a definite diet level. It usually means a low-sodium diet, but with no limit on the amounts of foods eaten (such as milk) as long as the items are prepared without added salt.

Fast-food restaurants are bad places to eat when trying to follow a low-salt diet. A regular chicken dinner or a deluxe burger may contain up to 2,000 milligrams of sodium —without counting what is in the French fries, relishes, etc. For this reason, if you do eat out, pick a good restaurant. Ask to have your meat or other entree cooked without added salt, have a baked potato and a salad with oil/vinegar dressing. This will be the best you can do. Better yet, plan to eat at home!

# Do's and Don'ts for Dieting

## Do's

Do be home for as many meals as possible. It is better not to struggle with meals out when they can be avoided.

Do take a snack with you when you know you may be delayed. This is the easiest way to say no to temptation.

Do expect to be able to follow your diet most places. The chapter on eating out (page 275) has tips that make it less complicated than you might think.

Do remember that if you have one bad day with dieting, the next day you have a new chance. Because you blew it once doesn't give you a corner on doing it again. If you do, it is because you want to go off your diet.

## Don'ts

Don't go shopping when you are angry, you'll be apt to buy goodies to make yourself feel better. In the long run, you'll end up feeling worse!

Don't go shopping when you are hungry. You will buy all sorts of goodies and then they will be there to tempt you. A good rule is not to shop more than an hour and a half after a meal.

Don't go to a party so hungry that you eat (and drink) everything you see. Have something to eat before you go — perhaps your usual nighttime snack if you are having a late dinner.

Don't have several drinks and then expect your will power to work when the food comes. Alcohol not only adds Calories, it relaxes your will to control what you eat. It's double dynamite.

Don't stock up on goodies for visitors. The only person who will end up enjoying them is you.

Don't think, "I'll have just one bite." It won't work. You will end up eating what you know you shouldn't. The food-aholic has to learn what the alcoholic does, namely that the first bite (drink) is the fatal one.

Don't make everyone miserable by talking about your diet all the time. Show people results and they will do the talking, and the compliments will be music to your ears. Save your energy for working at your diet instead of wearing out your tongue (and your friends' ears).

Don't set yourself up for temptation. If you deliberately put yourself in a situation where you can't follow your diet, then take the consequences without complaining.

## Remember

People find time and opportunity for things they really want to accomplish. If they want to find excuses to fail, that is easy enough. The really hard job is to stick with it and prove that your brain is boss, not your stomach.

# 3 A Little Home Chemistry

## How to Read a Label and Understand What It Says

Most people can't interpret a label — whether they're on a diet or not. Our new labeling laws will make this simpler, but it still can require a mathematics degree to figure out the food values in some cases. Try following the tips given here and see how easy it is once you know how to do it.

### What Does a Label Tell You?

Many people don't know that the federal rules regarding the labeling of products apply only to products that cross state lines. Products made and sold within a state are subject only to the laws of that state. It is the products made in one state and sold in another that come under federal law.

Some products, such as mayonnaise, peanut butter and many others, are not required to have ingredients listed on the label as long as they meet federal standards. The U.S. government's *Code of Federal Regulations, Foods & Drugs,* available in most public libraries, will tell you what ingredients are allowed

in these foods, but you still might not know whether those ingredients are there. The product might have all the allowed items, some of them or none of them; you have no way of knowing for sure. You must assume that all the allowed ingredients are there. If sugar is one of the allowed items, you will have to skip that product or buy one labeled "No Sugar Added" or "Dietetic — No Sugar." Dietetic products must list the nutritional breakdown (protein, fat and carbohydrate) and other information on the label. Our new laws on labeling dietetic foods make it much easier for a person to read and interpret data.

The following rules will make it easier for you to read a label and know what you are reading:

1. Look to see whether it is a local product. Local products will be covered by state laws which probably do not require that the contents be labeled. If there are no food values given, do not use it. Buy a brand that is labeled, so you know what you are getting.

2. Ingredients are listed in the order of amount in a product. If wheat is the main ingredient, it is listed first; the other ingredients are listed in descending order. Many of the ingredients at the bottom of the list represent such a very tiny amount that they don't matter.

3. If the ingredient you want to avoid (for example, sugar) is one of the first three ingredients on a label, DO NOT USE IT. If it is listed fourth, consider how sweet the product is. If it is a sweet product (or salty, or whatever you want to avoid) then still don't use it. After the fourth-listed ingredient, however, there is not enough to matter, and you may use the food. However, a person on a low-sodium diet is an exception to this rule.

If you aren't sure about the sugar content of a variety of bread — try toasting it. If it browns quickly it has a fairly high sugar content. If it browns very slowly it has less sugar and is a better choice for the diabetic or hypoglycemic.

4. These words mean sugar: dextrose, sucrose, glucose, fructose, maltose, lactose, malt, corn syrup, corn solids, sugar, honey, invert sugars, molasses.

The sweeteners sorbitol and mannitol, both sweet-tasting alcohols, may cause trouble, too. Persons who must limit sugar should avoid using these. Like sugar, they will cause a reaction in persons with hypoglycemia, but it will occur more

slowly. You'll be wise to avoid foods containing these alcohols.

5. If you really want to know more about a product that you would like to use, write to the manufacturer and ask for information. Give specific data from the label so that the reply can be specific in answering your questions. Most large manufacturers are prepared for consumers to consult them about their products, and they employ home economists for just this purpose.

6. If you want information and don't know where to write, call a library and ask them to look up the company's business address. Address your letters to the company's Customer Relations Department.

If you want to look up the allowed ingredients of products in the government's standard of identity booklets, go to your public library and ask for the *Code of Federal Regulations, Foods & Drugs.* Most large libraries will have them for you to use.

# Now That You Have Read the Label, What Does It Mean?

Perhaps you wonder what the percent figures on the label mean in food amounts. The following will give you some means to judge whether the food is worth what it has to replace.

## Percents

The percent figures given on the labels of prepared foods (% protein, % fat, and % carbohydrates) also express the number of grams of protein, fat, or carbohydrate found in 100 grams of the product. Since 100 grams is slightly less than 1/2 cup, or 20 teaspoons, percentage on the label divided by 20 equals the number of grams in 1 teaspoon.

---

For example:

Diet jelly = 20% carbohydrate, 1% protein, 0% fat

$\frac{20}{20}$ = 1 gram carbohydrate in 1 teaspoon of jelly

$\frac{1}{20}$ = .05 gram protein in 1 teaspoon of jelly (which is too little to count)

---

No replacement is needed for 1 to 2 grams per meal of protein, fat or carbohydrate. Therefore, 1 teaspoon of this diet jelly could be used without giving up any other food.

## To Figure Portions

You can figure the nutritional value per serving from the package weight and the number of servings using this formula:

---

$\frac{\text{\% (on label) x package weight}}{100}$ = grams protein/fat/carbohydrate per package

$\frac{\text{grams protein/fat/carbohydrate per package}}{\text{number of servings}}$ = grams per serving

---

For example, if a package of diet pudding weighs 2.5 ounces, will make 8 servings and contains 8% protein, 0% fat and 68% carbohydrate, you can figure the grams of protein, fat and carbohydrate per serving by using this formula:

---

1 ounce = 30 grams, thus 30 x 2.5 = 75 grams in the package

$\frac{\text{8\% protein x 75}}{100}$ = 6 grams protein per package

$\frac{\text{6 grams/package}}{\text{8 servings}}$ = .75 gram per serving

Three-fourths of a gram can be ignored.

---

To figure the grams of carbohydrates per serving, use the same formula:

$$\frac{68\% \text{ carbohydrate} \times 75}{100} = 51 \text{ grams carbohydrate per package}$$

$$\frac{51 \text{ grams/package}}{8 \text{ servings}} = 6.5 \text{ grams per serving, which cannot be ignored.}$$

To find a food of equal value, use Table III on pages 291-295. The replacement could be 1/2 serving of fruit (1/2 fruit exchange), which equals 5 grams of carbohydrate. (Remember that within 2 grams you don't have to replace any group.)

### Calories

When only Calories are given, assume that they are whatever you are avoiding, whether sugar or starch. A gram of carbohydrate contains 4 Calories. Calories ÷ 4 = grams of carbohydrate; up to 2 grams may be used at a meal without replacement. For example, dietetic pop may contain 2 Calories per 8 ounces. Carbohydrate per bottle is 2 Calories ÷ 4 Calories per gram = .5 gram, so you could consume three bottles in a day without replacement.

All dietetic foods will fit into one of three categories: calculated by teaspoons, by portions, or by Calories. As labels improve, you will have less trouble figuring them out. Keep a card file (like a recipe file) of information about replacements for the dietetic foods you use. Then when you buy a new supply you will only have to check to be sure the label is the same; you won't have to refigure the product. You might cut out the original label and stick it on the back of the card. Write on the card the substitute for one serving and your future meal planning will be easy.

# Substitutions and Equivalents

Balancing the flavorings and seasonings in dietetic recipes makes them appeal to everyone. Don't be afraid to experiment with new combinations; use your imagination to give new touches to common dishes.

## The Salt Substitutes

Most salt substitutes are potassium forms of the items they replace.

The commonest is potassium chloride (instead of table salt which is sodium chloride) and this may be mixed with other potassium and ammonium compounds. Potassium chloride has a much more biting taste than salt and must be used with caution. Many persons find these substitutes objectionable and avoid using them altogether. You can reduce the amount you use to get seasoning without bitterness, or you can combine lemon, vinegar, garlic, onion and pepper for other acceptable nonsalt taste combinations.

You might also like some of the recently marketed combined herb/salt substitute mixtures — onion salt substitute, garlic salt substitute, seasoned salt substitute. Try them as indicated in our low-salt directions or in your own recipes.

A good rule to follow with any substitute is to underuse it until you are sure you like it and the level is correct. You can add more, but you can't take out the excess! *Note:* The best salt substitute we have found is HealthLine Salt Replacement, available from Johnny's Enterprises, Inc., Tacoma, Washington 98421. Use as you would salt, in moderation.

Herbs also add good flavor to saltless dishes. The recipe for Salt-Free Herb Seasoning Mix on page 240 is a good replacement and is excellent in any entree or vegetable dish.

## The Sugar Substitutes

A new food ingredient, *polydextrose,* is almost indigestible in the human stomach. Because of this, it contains only 1 Calorie per gram, compared to 4 Calories per gram in sugar and starch. Food manufacturers are beginning to use it as a bulking agent in making Calorie-reduced foods, so you may find it in low-Calorie baking mixes, chewing gum, candy, salad dressings, gelatins,

frozen desserts and puddings. Despite the *-ose* ending, this is not a sugar! Actually, adding polydextrose to a product allows the sugar and fat content to be reduced as much as one-third, while keeping the product tender and soft.

Testing foods with polydextrose content has shown that it is safe for use by diabetics as it does not cause a significant rise in blood sugar. Whether it is safe for hypoglycemics to use remains to be proven. Our recommendation for this is the old adage, "When in doubt — do without!" That way you won't get into problems.

Should you or shouldn't you use saccharin? Laboratory testing on rats has shown that when massive doses of saccharin were given to several generations of rats, a few in the second generation developed bladder cancer. However, saccharin has been in general use for more than 80 years and there has not been a single case where it has been shown to be the cause of this (or any other) form of cancer in humans. Recent research at Johns Hopkins and other medical centers has shown no link between use of saccharin and the occurrence of bladder cancer in all the patients seen in these institutions during the last 20 years. So, rats and men do differ!

You will have to make up your own mind about using replacements. We have given you an alternative with the natural sweetening directions. Not all recipes can be naturally sweetened without sucrose (sugar) or sugar substitute. If you have diabetes mellitus, hypoglycemia or if the triglycerides in your blood are too high, *you should not use sugar.* Naturally sweetening some foods may make them too high in sugar for hypoglycemics (and possibly for diabetics), leaving you little choice: use the saccharin-based substitutes or don't eat the food.

## Types of Sugar Substitutes

*1. Nonsucrose sugars* — Fructose is still a sugar, although it is not table sugar (sucrose). It can cause hypoglycemics to have a reaction, although it may be slower to occur. DO NOT USE fructose if you are eliminating sugar from your diet.

*2. Saccharin-containing* — Available in liquid, tablets and granular forms. These granular forms are diluted with other material to reduce the concentration and make them easier to sprinkle on food. Unfortunately, the product used to dilute the saccharin is often a sugar! The most available granular substitute (the pink envelopes you find in many restaurants) contains dextrose as its main ingredient. This is the quickest-absorbed sugar and the worst for hypoglycemics to use. So BEWARE of this product.

If you can find a granular substitute that is diluted with dextrin (a starch product) or lactose (a slower-absorbed sugar which does not directly stimulate insulin), you will be wise to use these. They still have approximately 4 Calories per tablespoon (carbohydrate), so they cannot be used in large amounts without replacement. On the other hand, the liquid and tablet forms have no Calories and can be used without counting.

**3. Nonsaccharin-containing —** Products containing other natural sweetening agents are now available. Aspartame has just been approved for use and probably other similar products will be approved in the near future.

Aspartame is a combination of two amino acids (protein) which has sweetening capacity. Unfortunately, it cannot be used in cooked foods or it loses its taste. This will limit its usefulness for the cook.

Like other protein, this product contains about 4 Calories per gram and must be counted in when calculating the food value of the cooked item.

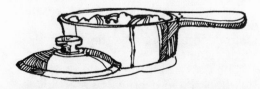

## How to Use These Substitutes

*Nonsucrose Sugars —* Fructose contains fewer calories than sugar for the same level of sweetening: 1 teaspoon fructose = 11 Calories, 1 teaspoon sugar = 18. It is claimed that you can use about two-thirds the volume of fructose, compared to

sugar for the same sweetening. For those who are merely counting Calories, fructose would be an acceptable product. For diabetics, hypoglycemics and those with high triglycerides, *Beware!*

*Liquid saccharin products —* Most liquid sweeteners are concentrated so that 1/4 teaspoon = 1 teaspoon sugar. This can vary with brands, so be sure you read the label to find out exactly how much *is* needed to replace 1 teaspoon of sugar. Then multiply this by 3, the amount to replace 1 tablespoon. Use less than the recipe calls for by at least one-fifth or one-fourth. (If the recipe calls for 1 teaspoon liquid sweetener to replace the sugar in the recipe, then use 3/4 or at the most 4/5 teaspoon. You can always add more if it isn't sweet enough.)

*Tablet-form products —* Saccharin comes in at least two tablet sizes: .25-grain and .5-grain; the .25-grain tablet is expected to sweeten similar to 1 teaspoon of sugar. Be very careful which strength you buy. Too much will give a very bitter taste, but used at the right level, it will be acceptable.

*Granular-form products —* There is more variance between products in this form of sweetener than in the previous types. The amounts needed to equal 1 teaspoon sugar vary from as little as 1/5 teaspoon to 1/2 teaspoon. Don't believe the package directions and use just as you would sugar — you wouldn't want to eat the result. Check the package to see what is recommended, then use one-third as much. Taste, and add more if necessary. (If you do use too much, add some lemon juice to cut the excess sweetness.)

Baked goods made with granular-type substitutes have a better texture and are somewhat lighter than those made with liquids or tablets. Dissolve tablets in a little warm water before using in baked or mixed dishes. Add last whenever possible. Both liquid and granular sweetening agents are capable of making foods taste sweet, but they vary in their capacity to make a product with satisfactory texture and appearance.

*Saccharin* — The most common basis of substitute sweeteners is saccharin. A derivative of coal, it is a totally non-Caloric substance.

Saccharin may change taste when subjected to high temperatures. It should be added at the end of cooking, so that it does not change taste due to prolonged heating. Of course, this cannot be done with baked goods or foods that are cooked in sealed containers (jam, canned fruits). Again, always add saccharin as late in a recipe as you can — after removing from the heat is the best time.

Concentrated soluble saccharin powder used in commercial canning has virtually no aftertaste; about 1 teaspoon equals 5 pounds of sugar. This concentrated form is not usually available to the householder;

saccharin for domestic use is all cut with an inert substance.

Each package label will tell how much sweetening is in a measured portion of the contents. Usually it will show how many drops (or what volume) is required to replace 1 teaspoon of sugar. There are 48 level teaspoons in 1 cup. If you change brands, be sure you check the strength of the new product as there may be a difference. (Some of the cheaper products are not good bargains because they contain less sweetening and you have to use more.)

When you start using sugar substitutes, you will notice that it is hard to get enough sweetening without having a bitter or strong aftertaste. The trick is to undersweeten and use other things to enhance the sweetness. Try using less sugar substitute than you think you want. Soon your taste for sugar will decrease, the less-sweet items will taste good to you, and there will be no aftertaste.

The Calories in the basic recipes in this book have been calculated for granular substitutes. Using a totally non-Caloric sweetener will drop the food value about 3 Calories per serving. If you are watching Calories closely enough for that difference to matter, use the liquid sweeteners, but remember while foods prepared with liquid sweeteners will have fewer Calories, their texture and appearance will be not as close to the real thing as those made with the granular products.

If you remove the sugar from a recipe and do not use anything to replace the carbohydrate, the appearance of the food will be different. It may fail to brown satisfactorily, and if sugar was a major ingredient in the recipe, the food made without it will be heavier in texture.

*Date sugar* — This is simply ground-up dates. Date sugar may be used for sweetening and is particularly good in baked items. For the person who has not used sugar for some time, the replacement is: 2-1/2 teaspoons = 1 tablespoon of sugar in sweetening capacity. 1 tablespoon of date sugar = about 10 grams of carbohydrate and 40

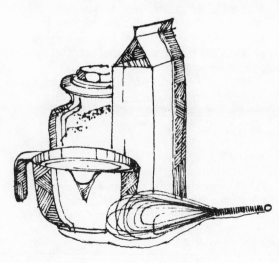

Calories. This value must be added into any recipe when substituting date sugar for a saccharin-based product.

*Fruit juices* — 1 tablespoon of concentrated apple juice, or 2 tablespoons of white grape juice = 1 teaspoon of sugar (5 grams of carbohydrate). You must omit liquid in a recipe equal in volume to the amount of juice used.

## Sodium-Free Baking Powder

You can buy sodium-free baking powder or you can make your own; see recipe on page 241. Potassium bicarbonate is available in many pharmacies. Substitute in an equal amount for regular double-acting baking powder.

## Milk Substitutions

*Whole milk* — Use equal volume skim milk plus 2 teaspoons oil per cup. Add oil with other liquid ingredients. One to two drops of butter flavoring added to the oil will give the flavor which skim milk lacks.

*Evaporated milk (2%)* — To substitute for evaporated 2% milk, use an equal volume skim milk plus 2 teaspoons oil per cup. (Add oil to other liquids in recipe.) To substitute for evaporated whole milk, use equal volume milk but add 4 teaspoons oil per cup.

*Half-and-half* — Use 1 cup skim milk plus 3 tablespoons oil. Put this in the blender and blend at top speed for about 1 minute until the oil is homogenized into the milk. This will be approximately 18 percent fat, equal to the fat content of half-and-half. It will stay homogenized for several hours and may be reblended.

*Powdered milk* — Use 1/3 cup dry skim milk for each cup of whole milk in recipe. Then add 1 cup (less 1 tablespoon) of water to the other liquid ingredients. This is the same as using liquid skim milk.

*Cream* — The so-called nondairy creamers are frequently mixtures of coconut oil and corn solids (syrup); unless the label specifically says otherwise, don't use them. The first item contributes to the forming of cholesterol and the second (sugar) may add to the blood triglycerides. Those made with soybean oil will still have the undesirable sugar content.

These cream substitutes are not only empty Calories which give only fuel, but they also do harm by contributing to the formation of blood fats. It is better to use skim milk, evaporated skim milk or even small amounts of whole milk; these would at least provide some vitamins and minerals along with the protein.

## Eggs and Substitutes

For 1 egg use 2 egg whites plus 1-1/4 teaspoons (6.3 mL) oil and 6 drops of yellow food coloring. Add oil with coloring to other liquid ingredients. Add the egg whites as directed for whole eggs.

Most liquid egg substitutes call for 2 ounces per medium egg. Read the package directions for the amount to use. Use the substitute as you would fresh eggs. If the recipe calls for separating the egg yolk and white, use 1 fresh egg white, 2/3 ounce of egg substitute and 1/4 teaspoon oil or melted margarine. Add the oil to the egg substitute. Use the white separately as the recipe directs.

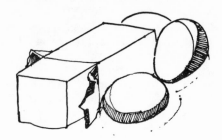

Watch the sodium content of egg substitutes. Those currently on the market run from 100 milligrams to almost 250 milligrams in sodium content. The higher ones cannot be used on a low-sodium diet and must be limited on any sodium restriction. (1 whole egg contains about 61 milligrams of sodium.) You can make your own egg substitute using the recipe on page 241, which was adapted from a patient's recipe.

## Flours

Flour measurements in the first edition of this book were for instant (Wondra) flour. To substitute whole-wheat or whole-grain flour in those recipes, just sift the flour twice before measuring.

Unbleached flour may be used in all recipes, and you can make any of them higher in fiber by using 1/2 unbleached flour and 1/2 whole-wheat flour, or 3/4 unbleached flour and 1/4 wheat germ or wheat bran.

Most whole-wheat flour sold in grocery stores does not contain the entire wheat kernel. (The wheat germ and part of the bran have been removed.) If you want whole-grain wheat flour, you will have to buy the grain and grind your own. If you decide to do this, buy hard winter wheat for the highest protein content and most nourishment.

To lighten baked items made without sugar, always sift flour twice before you measure it and then again before adding to the mixture.

*Oat flour* — Do not substitute any other flour for oat flour. The result will be unsatisfactory. Oat flour may be made by putting old-fashioned oats in a blender and running it for a minute at top speed. Put the result into a sieve; the fine matter that goes through the mesh is oat flour. Or put the oats through a food mill; whatever part goes through the mill is usable as oat flour.

## Fats

*Margarine* — Never use soft margarine unless a recipe calls for that type. Use the cube variety (one that is high in unsaturated fat).

To select the margarine highest in polyunsaturated fats, be sure that liquid oil is the first ingredient listed. This ensures that the product is high in unsaturated fats; those with partially hydrogenated (or hardened) oils are less desirable, as the treatment with hydrogen converts some of the scrubbers to inactive fats.

To use margarine in a recipe that calls for butter, be sure to add a little extra flour (1 teaspoon per cup) or the dough will be too soft.

*Oil* — Use oil only if the recipe calls for it. Don't use oil to replace butter or margarine in a recipe in which you are also using a sugar substitute. The use of oil requires extra sugar for satisfactory texture. There is no way to correct this in a dietetic recipe.

## Flavorings

As a general rule, food sweetened artificially needs a little more of whatever other flavoring is called for in the recipe. For instance, if vanilla is the other flavoring, it might need to be increased from 1/2 teaspoon (2.5 mL) to 3/4 teaspoon (3.8 mL).

Use combinations of flavorings to get interesting results. Try less vanilla and more almond, black walnut, maple, rum and even anise extract. Use any flavoring you have not tried before sparingly, because some have a stronger flavor than vanilla. To start, substitute half vanilla and half (or slightly less) another flavoring. Adjust to taste with each change of flavoring.

## Citrus Rind and Juice

You may substitute any of the following for 1 teaspoon (1.5 grams) of grated lemon rind:
1 teaspoon (1.5 grams) grated orange rind
2/3 teaspoon (1 gram) grated grapefruit rind

1/2 teaspoon (.8 gram) dried lemon rind
2 tablespoons (30 mL) lemon juice

Since lemon and other fresh citrus fruits give out their oils gradually, the flavor will become stronger as the product stands. If you make something ahead of time, use a little less rind or it may prove too strong-tasting when you serve it. See the recipe for drying your own rind on page 237.

## Sweetening with Natural Fruits

Concentrated fruit juices, whole fresh or dried fruits, date sugar and lemon juice may all be used to sweeten foods. However, with none of

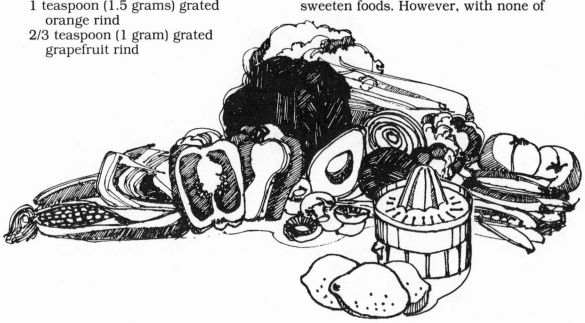

26

these is it as simple as replacing the sugar amount for amount. With fruit juices, you must omit the volume of liquid elsewhere in the recipe; with applesauce or pineapple you must compensate for the liquid content, and that is hard to do in most baked goods. Although date sugar does not cause problems with liquids, it does not act exactly like sugar. Date sugar is quite acidic and using it in a baked product will require the addition of a small amount of lemon juice for flavor and/or baking soda to neutralize the acid. Date sugar must be counted as part of the fruit allowed and may be used in small amounts by diabetics and hypoglycemics.

Wherever possible, the directions for naturally sweetening the recipes have been included. It may be that using the fruit for sweetening will increase the carbohydrate and Calorie count beyond what you can fit into your diet. In this case, use the recipe with the sugar substitute sweetening.

Combinations of tart fruits and naturally sweet ones give an end product that requires less artificial sugar substitute. Adding lemon juice also brings out the natural sweet flavor in fruit. Try using 1 teaspoon (5 mL) of lemon juice per cup of fruit and taste before adding any sweetener.

Two fruits that are difficult to sweeten alone are rhubarb and lemon. Both can be sweetened by combining with sweeter fruits such as apples or berries. Try a proportion of half each, and then add more of the tarter fruit until you find out what proportion is best.

Dried fruits, such as raisins or dates, may furnish all the sweetening needed in some combinations.

Don't be afraid to use your imagination when trying different fruit mixtures. Very few fruits fail to blend well with others, however unlikely some combinations may seem.

# Food Values

No dietetic cookbook would be complete without some chart showing approximate food values and replacements. These are given in the least complicated form possible. So many factors are involved in the growing and processing of foods that there are great variations in the values. For this reason, it is ridiculous to try to measure food to the fraction of the gram. The measurements used in this book are fully as accurate as the foods themselves. The current trend is away from dwelling on detailed weighing, emphasizing instead the planning of meals that approximate each other in food content and volume. This makes it much easier to live comfortably with one's family.

See Table II, Average Food Values, beginning on page 287.

# Weights and Measures

The metric weights used in this book were determined by actually weighing the ingredients and then averaging the weights of three samples. In addition to these actual weights, we used two publications from the Agricultural Research Service, U.S. Department of Agriculture: *Average Weight of a Measured Cup of Various Foods* (ARS 61-1, February 1969), and *Nutritive Value of American Foods in Common Units* (Agricultural Handbook 456, November 1975).

The value for 1 pound used in this book is 454 grams; for 1 ounce, 28.5 grams, as found in these two references. The figure used for 1 liquid ounce is 30 mL as accepted in diabetic calculations.

# 4 Recipes

# Breads

Most breads contain a small amount of sugar or malt to provide food for rapid yeast growth. This sugar is converted into gas (carbon dioxide) and is part of what causes the dough to rise. Breads made without refined sugar will take longer to rise and are likely to be heavier and less browned than those made with sugar.

None of the bread and biscuit recipes in this section are sweet-tasting except the sweet rolls. If you wish a sweeter taste, use additional fruit or sugar substitute. Excess sugar substitute often produces a bitter taste, so be conservative in your use of substitutes, and the results will be excellent.

# White Bread

*This recipe is not for hypoglycemics.*
* Makes two 18-slice loaves, 1 pound (454 grams) each
* 1 slice contains 81 Calories (P3, F1, C15), no cholesterol
* 1 slice = 1 bread exchange

**Skim milk**    1 cup (240 mL)
**Hot water**    1 cup (240 mL)
**Salt**    2-1/2 teaspoons (15 grams)
**Margarine**    3 tablespoons (42 grams); use corn-oil, soybean-oil or safflower-oil
    margarine
**Yeast**    1 cake (18 grams) or 1 scant tablespoon (9 grams) of dry yeast
**Warm water**    1/2 cup (120 mL), at 85°F (30°C)
**Brown-type granular sugar substitute**    3 tablespoons (18 grams); or substitute
    equal to 6 tablespoons (73.2 grams) of sugar
**Unbleached flour**    6-1/2 cups (754 grams), sifted; or 5 cups (580 grams) sifted
    unbleached flour and 1-1/2 cups (144 grams) wheat germ or 1-1/2 cups (120
    grams) raw bran

Scald milk; add the hot water, salt and margarine. Put the yeast in the warm water, add the sugar substitute and stir to dissolve. Let stand 10 minutes. Add flour gradually, beating after each addition. Divide dough in half. Knead on lightly floured board until texture is smooth and elastic. Round dough into balls, grease with vegetable oil, cover with a towel and put in a warm place to rise.

When the dough has doubled in size, knead again until all bubbles are out; shape. Grease again with oil and put in bread pans to rise. When dough has doubled in size again, place in a cool oven. Set the oven at 400°F (204°C). After 15 minutes, reduce temperature to 350°F (177°C) and bake 25 minutes longer. Remove bread from pans and place on a rack to cool.

*Natural sweetening directions:*
* No change in nutritional value.
Omit sugar substitute; use 2 teaspoons (8 grams) of diastatic malt. Diastatic malt is a natural yeast food made from sprouted grain. It can be purchased where wine-making supplies are sold, or in health food stores. It may be used in low-salt recipes as it has a very low sodium content.

*For low-salt diet:*
* 1 slice contains 4 mg of sodium
Omit salt, use 2 teaspoons (8 grams) of salt substitute. Use salt-free margarine.

# Light Wheat Bread

- Makes two 18-slice loaves, about 1 pound (454 grams) each
- 1 slice contains 94 Calories (P3, F2, C16), 7 mg of cholesterol if made with egg, no cholesterol if made with egg substitute
- 1 slice = 1 slice of bread + 1/2 teaspoon of fat (1 bread exchange + 1/2 fat exchange)

**Yeast**   2 cakes (36 grams) or 2 scant tablespoons (18 grams) of dry yeast
**Warm water**   1/2 cup (120 mL), at 85°F (30°C)
**Brown-type granular sugar substitute**   2 tablespoons (12 grams); or substitute equal to 1/4 cup (48.8 grams) of sugar
**Skim milk**   2 cups (480 mL)
**Soft margarine**   1/3 cup (75 grams); use corn-oil, soybean-oil or safflower-oil margarine
**1 large egg**   (57 grams) or 2 ounces (60 mL) liquid egg substitute
**Salt**   1-1/2 teaspoons (9 grams)
**Unbleached flour**   5-1/2 cups (638 grams), sifted
**Whole-wheat flour**   1 cup (137 grams), unsifted
**Unsweetened wheat germ**   3 tablespoons (18 grams)

Put yeast in warm water, add 1 teaspoon of sugar substitute and stir to dissolve. Let stand 10 to 15 minutes. Scald milk, add margarine and set aside to cool to 85°. Add milk mixture to yeast, then add egg, salt and remainder of sugar substitute. Save 1/2 cup (58 grams) of the unbleached flour for the board. Combine wheat germ with flour and add gradually. Knead on lightly floured board until texture is even. Form two loaves. Grease with vegetable oil. Cover with a towel and put in warm place to rise.

When loaves have doubled in size, knead again on lightly floured board until all bubbles are gone and dough has an even, elastic texture. Grease bread pans with vegetable oil. Put shaped dough into pans; oil sides and top, as before. Allow to double in size. Put pans in a cool oven. Set it at 400°F (204°C). After 15 minutes, lower temperature to 350°F (177°C). Bake 25 to 30 minutes more, until well-browned. Remove loaves; grease tops sparingly with margarine. Place loaves on a rack to cool.

### Natural sweetening directions:
- 1 slice contains 98 Calories (P3, F2, C17), no change in cholesterol
- 1 slice of bread + 1/2 teaspoon of fat = 1 bread exchange + 1/2 fat exchange

Omit sugar substitute. Substitute 1/2 cup (120 mL) apple juice for the water. Add 2 teaspoons (8 grams) of diastatic malt. Follow the rest of the directions as given.

### For low-salt diet:
- 1 slice contains 10 mg of sodium

Omit salt; use 1 teaspoon (4 grams) of salt substitute. Use salt-free margarine.

# Whole-Wheat Bread

- Makes 1 loaf, 18 thin slices
- 1 slice contains 81 Calories (P3, F1, C15), no cholesterol
- 1 slice = 1 bread exchange

**Warm water**    1 cup (240 mL), at 85°F (30°C)
**Yeast**    1 cake (18 grams) or 1 tablespoon (9 grams) of dry yeast
**Salt**    1 teaspoon (6 grams)
**Brown-type granular sugar substitute**    1-1/2 tablespoons (9 grams); or substitute equal to 3 tablespoons (36.5 grams) of sugar
**Melted margarine**    1 tablespoon (15 mL); use corn-oil, soybean-oil or safflower-oil margarine
**Whole-wheat flour**    3 cups (381 grams), sifted

*Optional:*
**Molasses**    1 tablespoon (15 mL)

Place water, yeast, and sugar substitute in a large bowl. Mix well and allow to stand until the yeast has worked and the mixture shows bubbles. Add margarine, salt, molasses and enough flour to make a soft dough. Put on a floured board and knead until smooth and elastic. Form into a ball, oil and place in a warm place to rise. When doubled in size, knead again until all bubbles are out. Shape into loaf form. Oil dough again and place in bread pan. When dough has again doubled in size, place in a cool oven. Set it at 400°F (204°C). After 15 minutes, reduce temperature to 350°F (177°C) and bake 25 minutes, or until well-browned. Remove bread from pan and place on a rack to cool.

### Natural sweetening directions:

- 1 slice contains 81 Calories (P3, F1, C15), no cholesterol or increased sodium
- 1 slice = 1 bread exchange

Omit sugar substitute. Reduce water to 3/4 cup (180 mL) and add 1/4 cup (60 mL) apple juice. Add 1 teaspoon (4 grams) of diastatic malt and do use the molasses. Follow directions as given.

### For low-salt diet:

- 1 slice contains 2 mg of sodium

Omit salt; use 1 teaspoon (4 grams) of salt substitute. Use salt-free margarine.

# Bran Breakfast Bars

- Makes 24 squares
- 2 squares contain 122 Calories (P1, F6, C16), no cholesterol
- 2 squares = 1 slice of bread + 1 teaspoon of fat (1 bread exchange + 1 fat exchange)

**Oatmeal**  1 cup (72 grams)
**Pure bran**  1-1/2 cups (120 grams)
**Whole-wheat flour**  1/2 cup (68.5 grams), unsifted
**Salt**  1/2 teaspoon (3 grams)
**Brown-type granular sugar substitute**  3 tablespoons (18 grams); or substitute equal to 6 tablespoons (73.2 grams) of sugar
**Raisins**  1/3 cup (54 grams), chopped; or 8 medium dates (64 grams), diced
**Boiling water**  1 cup (240 mL)
**Oil**  1/3 cup (80 mL); use corn, soybean or safflower oil

Pour boiling water over diced fruit. Allow to stand at least 20 minutes. Combine dry ingredients in a large mixing bowl. Drain fruit, add boiling water to make 1 cup (240 mL) with what drains off fruit and place in blender with oil. Blend 1 minute. Immediately pour into dry ingredients and mix well. Add fruit, remix. Place batter in a nonstick oblong, 8x10 (20x25 cm) baking dish. Level with fingers or spatula and then mark for cutting: 4 squares the narrow way, 6 squares the long way. Bake in a preheated oven at 375°F (191°C) for 22 minutes; cool on a rack. Refrigerate or freeze if keeping more than 2 days, as these tend to mold quickly. *Note:* Do not eat too many as these are quite laxative. Each square represents 1 tablespoon of pure bran. For most people, two in place of breakfast toast will serve as an excellent laxative.

### Natural sweetening directions:
- 1-1/2 squares contain 105 Calories (P1, F5, C14)
- 1-1/2 squares = 1 slice of bread + 1 teaspoon of fat (1 bread exchange + 1 fat exchange)

Omit sugar substitute; use 3 tablespoons (30 grams) of date sugar.

### For low-salt diet:
- 2 squares contain 1 mg of sodium

Omit salt; substitute 1/2 teaspoon (2 grams) salt substitute.

# Baking Powder Biscuits / *Plain and Herbed*

- Makes 12 biscuits
- 1 biscuit contains 117 Calories (P3, F5, C15), no cholesterol
- 1 biscuit = 1 slice of bread + 1 teaspoon of fat (1 bread exchange + 1 fat exchange)

**Unbleached flour**   2 cups (252 grams), unsifted; or 2 cups (254 grams) whole-wheat flour, sifted. *Note: Hypoglycemics use whole-wheat flour only.*
**Double-acting baking powder**   1 tablespoon (12 grams)
**Salt**   1/2 teaspoon (3 grams)
**Soft margarine**   1/3 cup (75 grams); use corn-oil, soybean-oil or safflower-oil margarine
**Skim milk**   3/4 cup (180 mL)

*Optional:*
**Chives**   1 tablespoon (3 grams), diced fine
**Oregano**   1/2 teaspoon (1.5 grams)
**Thyme**   1/4 teaspoon (.8 gram)
**Parsley**   1 teaspoon (1.5 grams); if using fresh, dice fine

Sift dry ingredients together. Cut in margarine with pastry blender. Add milk to make a soft dough. Sprinkle herbs over the dough, spreading evenly through the mixture. Roll out dough 1/2-inch (1.3 cm) thick on a lightly floured board. Cut into 12 parts, or use a 2-inch (5 cm) round cutter. Place biscuits on an oiled pan. Bake at 450°F (232°C) for 12 to 15 minutes until brown.

**Natural sweetening directions:**
- Not needed.

**For low-salt diet:**
- 1 biscuit contains 10 mg of sodium
Omit salt; use 1/2 teaspoon (2 grams) of salt substitute. Use 1 tablespoon (12 grams) of sodium-free baking powder. Use salt-free margarine. All pure, dried herbs are low in salt, so you may use them.

# Sweet Rolls with Raisins

- Makes 36 rolls
- 1 roll contains 102 Calories (P3, F2, C18), no cholesterol
- 1 roll = 1 slice of bread + 1/2 teaspoon of fat + 1/4 cup of fruit (1 bread exchange + 1/2 fat exchange + 1/2 fruit exchange)

---

**Recipe for White Bread, page 31.** *Note: Hypoglycemics use whole-wheat bread recipe, page 33.*
**Margarine**   4 tablespoons (56.5 grams); use corn-oil, soybean-oil or safflower-oil margarine
**Brown-type granular sugar substitute**   1 cup (96 grams); or substitute equal to 2 cups (390 grams) of sugar
**Cinnamon**   1/2 teaspoon (1.5 grams)
**Raisins**   1/2 cup (72 grams), soaked in hot water, then drained

---

Follow the bread recipe to the point of dividing dough in half. With a rolling pin, roll out dough about 1/2-inch (1.3 cm) thick. Try to make it rectangular, so it can be made into an even roll. Spread dough with softened margarine, leaving edges ungreased. Mix sugar substitute and cinnamon; sprinkle over margarine. Scatter drained raisins over sugared area.

Roll from one of the long sides to make a long, narrow roll. Dampen edges with warm water and seal. Cut roll into 3/4-inch (2 cm) slices. Place slices on greased cookie sheet and let rise until doubled in size. Bake in preheated oven at 425°F (218°C) 15 to 18 minutes, until brown. Remove rolls from sheet and put on a rack to cool.

---

*Natural sweetening directions:*
- 1 roll contains 118 Calories (P3, F2, C22), no change in cholesterol or sodium
- 1 roll = 1-1/2 slices of bread (1-1/2 bread exchanges)

Make bread using natural sweetening directions. Omit sugar substitute; replace with 3/4 cup (120 grams) of date sugar. Follow directions as given.

*For low-salt diet:*
- 1 roll contains 5 mg of sodium

Make bread using low-salt directions. Use salt-free margarine for filling.

# Scotch Scones with Raisins

- Makes 12 scones
- 1 scone contains 112 Calories (P3, F4, C16), no cholesterol
- 1 scone = 1 slice of bread + 1 teaspoon of fat (1 bread exchange + 1 fat exchange)

**Unbleached flour**   2 cups (252 grams), unsifted; or 2 cups (254 grams) sifted whole-wheat flour. *Note: Hypoglycemics use whole-wheat flour only.*
**Double-acting baking powder**   1 tablespoon (12 grams)
**Salt**   1/2 teaspoon (3 grams)
**Margarine**   1/4 cup (56 grams); use corn-oil, soybean-oil or safflower-oil margarine
**Skim milk**   2/3 cup (160 mL)
**Brown-type granular sugar substitute**   1-1/2 teaspoons (3 grams); or substitute equal to 1 tablespoon (12.2 grams) of sugar
**Raisins**   2 tablespoons (18 grams) soaked in hot water and drained

Sift dry ingredients together. Cut in margarine as if for pie crust, using pastry blender or fork. Add skim milk and sugar substitute and mix well. Drain raisins, add to dough and mix again. Knead lightly on floured board. Divide in half.

Roll each half into a circle about 1/2-inch (1.3 cm) thick. Cut into 6 wedges, as if cutting a pie. Place on nonstick baking sheet or sheet sprayed with nonstick coating. Bake at 425°F (218°C) for 15 to 18 minutes, until browned.

**Natural sweetening directions:**
- 1 scone contains 125 Calories (P3, F5, C17), no change in cholesterol or sodium
- 1 scone = 1 slice of bread + 1 teaspoon of fat (1 bread exchange + 1 fat exchange)

Omit sugar substitute. Replace skim milk with 1/3 cup (80 mL) evaporated skim milk and 1/3 cup (80 mL) apple juice. Follow directions as given.

**For low-salt diet:**
- 1 scone contains 9 mg of sodium

Omit salt; use 1/2 teaspoon (2 grams) salt substitute. Use 1 tablespoon (12 grams) of sodium-free baking powder. Use salt-free margarine.

# Old-Fashioned Dumplings

- Makes 8 medium dumplings or 12 small dumplings
- 1 medium dumpling contains 98 Calories (P3, F2, C17), no cholesterol
- 1 medium dumpling = 1 slice of bread + 1/2 teaspoon of fat (1 bread exchange + 1/2 fat exchange)
- 1 small dumpling contains 67 Calories (P2, F1, C11), no cholesterol
- 1 small dumpling = 2/3 slice of bread + 1/4 teaspoon of fat (2/3 bread exchange + 1/4 fat exchange)

**Unbleached flour**   2 cups (252 grams), unsifted; or 2 cups (254 grams) unsifted whole-wheat flour. *Note: Hypoglycemics use whole-wheat flour only.*
**Double-acting baking powder**   4 teaspoons (16 grams)
**Salt**   1/2 teaspoon (3 grams)
**Margarine**   1-1/2 tablespoons (21 grams); use corn-oil, soybean-oil or safflower-oil margarine
**Skim milk**   1/2 cup (120 mL)
**Water**   1/4 cup (60 mL)

Sift dry ingredients together. Cut in margarine with a pastry blender, as for pie crust. Combine liquids; add slowly to flour mixture and mix gently. Put on a lightly floured board, and roll or pat into about 1/2-inch (1.3 cm) thickness. To make 8 dumplings, cut with a 2-inch (5 cm) biscuit cutter; to make small dumplings, divide dough in 12 parts (about 3 tablespoons per serving). Drop dough into boiling stew or soup. Cover and cook 12 to 15 minutes, until cooked through.

*Natural sweetening directions:*
- Not needed.

*For low-salt diet:*
- 1 medium dumpling contains 7 mg of sodium
- 1 small dumpling contains 5 mg of sodium

Omit salt; use 1/2 teaspoon (2 grams) of salt substitute. Use 4 teaspoons (16 grams) of sodium-free baking powder. Use salt-free margarine.

# Basic Pancake and Waffle Mix

- Makes 5 cups (655 grams)
- 1 cup (131 grams) contains 495 Calories (P13, F19, C68), no cholesterol

**Instant dry milk powder**   1 cup (75 grams)
**Unbleached flour**   3-1/2 cups (441 grams), unsifted; or 3-1/2 cups (445 grams) whole-wheat flour, sifted. *Note: Hypoglycemics use whole-wheat flour only.*
**Double-acting baking powder**   1-1/2 tablespoons (18 grams)
**Salt**   3/4 teaspoon (4.5 grams)
**Brown-type granular sugar substitute**   1 tablespoon (6 grams); or substitute equal to 2 tablespoons (24.4 grams) of sugar
**Margarine**   1/2 cup (113 grams); use corn-oil, soybean-oil or safflower-oil margarine

Mix dry ingredients thoroughly. With pastry blender, cut in margarine until mixture is like fine corn meal. Put in tight container and store in a cool place.

### Natural sweetening directions:
- No change in nutritional values.

Omit sugar substitute. Add 1 tablespoon (10 grams) of date sugar. Follow directions as given.

### For low-salt diet:
- 1 cup contains 69 mg of sodium

Omit salt; use 3/4 teaspoon (3 grams) salt substitute. Use 1-1/2 tablespoons (18 grams) of sodium-free baking powder. Use salt-free margarine.

# Pancakes

- Makes 8 pancakes, about 5-1/2 inches (13.75 cm) round
- 1 pancake contains 101 Calories (P4, F3, C17), 32 mg of cholesterol if made with egg, no cholesterol if made with egg substitute
- 1 pancake = 1 slice of bread + 1/2 teaspoon of fat (1 bread exchange + 1/2 fat exchange)

**Recipe for Basic Mix, page 39**   2 cups (262 grams)
**Water**   1-1/2 cups (360 mL)
**1 large egg**   (57 grams); or 2 ounces (60 mL) of liquid egg substitute

Combine ingredients; stir until moistened well and free of lumps. Do not beat. Bake on a griddle sprayed with nonstick coating or lightly brushed with vegetable oil. Have griddle hot, but not smoking. Cook until bubbles form on top. Turn and brown on other side. Serve with dietetic jam or sauce (see recipes on pages 250-261).

*Natural sweetening directions:*
- Not needed. See Basic Mix recipe, page 39.

*For low-salt diet:*
- 1 pancake contains 36 mg of sodium
Make Basic Mix, page 39, according to salt-free directions.

# Waffles

- Makes 4 waffles
- 1 square contains 142 Calories (P5, F6, C17), 32 mg of cholesterol if made with egg, no cholesterol if made with egg substitute
- 1 square = 1 slice of bread + 1/2 teaspoon of fat + 1/2 ounce of meat (1 bread exchange + 1/2 fat exchange + 1/2 meat exchange)

**Water**   1-1/2 cups (360 mL)
**1 large egg**   (57 grams), beaten; or 2 ounces (60 mL) of liquid egg substitute
**2 egg whites**   (66 grams)
**Vegetable oil**   1 teaspoon (5 mL)
**Recipe for Basic Mix, page 39**   2 cups (262 grams)

*Optional:*
**Blueberries**   1/2 cup (73 grams)

Combine beaten egg, water and oil. Gradually add to Basic Mix, stirring to remove lumps. Add blueberries. Beat egg whites until dry and fluffy, then gently fold into the batter, being careful not to overmix. Bake in a hot waffle iron that has been oiled or sprayed with nonstick coating, on medium setting until brown. Serve with dietetic jam or sauce (see recipes on pages 250-261).

*Suggestions:*
Waffles are good when they contain fresh fruit for variety. You may add 1/2 cup (73 grams) of blueberries just before you fold in the egg whites. Follow the other directions and bake as usual. If adding blueberries, allow 1 tablespoon fruit for each waffle square eaten.

*Natural sweetening directions:*
- Not needed.

*For low-salt diet:*
- 1 square contains 36 mg of sodium; with 1/4 cup (60 mL) sauce or 2 tablespoons (36 grams) of jam, 37 mg of sodium

Make Basic Mix, page 39, according to low-salt directions. Use 3 ounces (90 mL) of liquid egg substitute and only 1 egg white (33 grams).

# Terry's Pancakes *(All-in-One Breakfast!)*

- Makes 1 serving
- 1 serving contains 249 Calories (P13, F7, C37), 10 mg of cholesterol if made with egg substitute
- 1 serving = 1 slice of bread + 1 ounce of meat + 1/2 cup of fruit + 1/2 cup of milk (1 bread exchange + 1 meat exchange + 1 fruit exchange + 1/2 milk exchange)

**Unbleached flour**   2-1/2 tablespoons (20 grams), unsifted; or 2-1/2 tablespoons (24 grams) whole-wheat flour, sifted. *Note: Hypoglycemics use whole-wheat flour only.*
**Double-acting baking powder**   1/4 teaspoon (1 gram)
**Salt**   sprinkle
**1 medium egg**   (50 grams), beaten; or 2 ounces (60 mL) of liquid egg substitute
**Plain yogurt**   1/2 cup (120 mL)
**Raisins**   2 tablespoons (18 grams)

Sift dry ingredients together. Add beaten egg and yogurt. Mix well, adding raisins evenly through mixture. Spray nonstick coating on skillet. Heat until a drop of water turns to steam when dropped on the hot pan. Drop batter by tablespoonfuls onto pan. Turn when bubbles form. Serve immediately with small amount of dietetic jam (see recipes on pages 250-261), instead of syrup.

*Natural sweetening directions:*
- Not needed.

*For low-salt diet:*
- Total recipe contains 118 mg of sodium
Omit salt; use salt-free baking powder.

# Homemade Graham Crackers

- Makes about 12 dozen
- 5 crackers contain 112 Calories (P3, F4, C16), no cholesterol
- 5 crackers = 1 slice of bread + 1 teaspoon of fat (1 bread exchange + 1 fat exchange)

**Whole-wheat flour**   2-3/4 cups (377 grams), unsifted
**Wheat germ**   1/2 cup (48 grams)
**Wheat bran**   1/4 cup (20 grams)
**Double-acting baking powder**   1 teaspoon (4 grams)
**Baking soda**   1/2 teaspoon (2 grams)
**Salt**   1/2 teaspoon (3 grams)
**Soft margarine**   1/2 cup (113 grams); use corn-oil, soybean-oil or safflower-oil margarine
**Brown-type granular sugar substitute**   5 to 6 tablespoons (30 to 36 grams); or substitute equal to 2/3 cup (130 grams) sugar
**Skim milk**   1/2 cup (120 mL)
**Water**   1/2 cup (120 mL)

Combine dry ingredients. Cream margarine in bowl, add sugar substitute/flour mixture gradually, alternating with liquids. Be sure mixture is well-stirred to evenly distribute wheat germ and bran. Chill dough for several hours. Divide dough into four parts. Roll each part as thin as possible on greased cookie sheet or on sheet of foil which you then transfer to cookie sheet. Prick all over with a fork. Mark into 1-inch (2.5 cm) squares. Bake in a preheated oven at 375°F (191°C) 13 to 15 minutes, until brown.

*Suggestions:*
Sprinkle crackers with cinnamon, or with a mixture of 1 teaspoon (3 grams) cinnamon and 1 tablespoon (6 grams) brown-type granular sugar substitute before baking.

*Natural sweetening directions:*
- 4 crackers contain 99 Calories (P2, F3, C16), no cholesterol
- 4 crackers = 1 slice of bread + 1/2 teaspoon of fat (1 bread exchange + 1/2 fat exchange)
Omit sugar substitute. Omit water. Add 1/2 cup (120 mL) concentrated apple juice. Follow the directions as given, using plain cinnamon for the topping, if desired.

*For low-salt diet:*
- 5 crackers contain 4 mg of sodium
Omit salt; use 1/2 teaspoon (2 grams) salt substitute. Omit baking soda; substitute same amount of potassium bicarbonate. Use Sodium-Free Baking Powder (see recipe on page 241). Use salt-free margarine.

# Soups

Soups are a good way to use leftovers economically. They are nutritious and appealing when well prepared and seasoned. When you have a dab of leftover vegetable, don't throw it away — make soup! For example, you can substitute almost any vegetable for the cauliflower in the Cream of Cauliflower Soup, page 53.

The recipes in this chapter are planned for quick preparation, but they still have the good flavor and appeal of the old-style, long-cooked soup pot.

Experiment with seasonings and herbs to suit your taste. Learn to use herbs freely. They help to bring out flavors and enhance the appetizing aroma of hot soup.

Note that a few of these recipes— Cream of Tomato Soup, page 56, Northwest Fish Soup, page 57, and Oyster Chowder à la Maryland, page 60 — cannot be adapted for a low-salt diet.

# Basic Chicken Broth

- Makes about 5 cups (1.2 L)
- 1 cup contains 17 Calories (P2, F2, C0), 5 mg of cholesterol
- 1 cup = 1/3 ounce of meat (1/3 meat exchange)

**Chicken**   3 pounds (1,362 grams), necks and backs
**Onion**   1 large slice (15 grams), chopped
**Celery**   1 large stalk (70 grams), with leaves, chopped
**Garlic**   1 small clove (1 gram)
**Bay leaf**   1 (1 gram)
**Boiling water**   7 cups (1.7 L)
**Salt**   1/2 teaspoon (3 grams)
**Pepper**   1/8 teaspoon (.5 gram)

Bake chicken in roasting pan at 450°F (232°C) for 45 to 60 minutes. Remove to large soup kettle; discard fat. Add vegetables, bay leaf and water. Simmer, covered, 3-1/2 to 4 hours, until meat falls from bones. Strain; add seasonings to liquid; taste and adjust to suit. Line sieve with a white disposable tissue; strain liquid. (Tissue works well as a filter and is cheaper and easier to get than filter paper.) Pour strained liquid into jars and allow to stand at room temperature until completely cool. Refrigerate until liquid is jelled. Discard any fat from top. Use jellied liquid in any recipe that requires chicken broth or as a clear soup. Pick all the lean meat from sieved solids; use in any recipe calling for cooked chicken or add to broth to make a heartier soup. (Allow for at least 1 ounce (28.5 grams) of meat serving per cup if you add the shredded meat.)

*Natural sweetening directions:*
- Not needed.

*For low-salt diet:*
- 1 cup contains 36 mg of sodium

Omit salt; use 1/2 to 3/4 teaspoon (2 to 3 grams) of salt substitute. You can also add 1/4 to 1/2 teaspoon (.8 to 1.5 grams) Salt-Free Herb Mix (see recipe on page 240).

# Jo's Brown Beef Broth

- Makes about 8 cups (1.92 L)
- 1 cup (240 mL) contains 36 Calories (P5, F1, C2), 5 mg of cholesterol
- 1 cup (240 mL) = 1/2 ounce of meat (1/2 meat exchange)

**Beef bones**   4 pounds (1,816 grams), cut into pieces
**Yellow onion**   1 large (200 grams), including skin, chopped
**Celery**   2 large stalks (140 grams), with leaves, chopped
**Parsley**   1 small bunch chopped or 1 tablespoon (5 grams) dry
**Carrot**   1 medium (60 grams), sliced
**Potato**   1 small (120 grams), cut in small cubes
**Garlic**   1/2 clove (.5 gram), chopped fine
**Boiling water**   10 cups (2.4 L)
**Salt**   2/3 teaspoon (4 grams)
**Pepper**   1/8 teaspoon (.5 gram)

Place bones and onion in roasting pan; bake 45 to 60 minutes at 450°F (232°C), until bones are brown. Drain off fat. Place bones and onions in a deep soup pot; add remaining ingredients. Cover and cook about 4 hours. About every half-hour, skim off the gray scum that forms on the surface. Keep covered between skimmings. Remove from heat; pour though a colander to separate solids from liquids. Strain liquid through a sieve, using a white disposable tissue for a filter. (A tissue works well and is cheaper and easier to get than filter paper.) Pour strained liquid into jars; cool completely; place in refrigerator. After broth is chilled, remove any fat congealed on the surface. Use in any recipe that calls for beef broth.

*Suggestions:*
This is a pleasant, mild-flavored broth that blends well with other recipes. You can make it a stronger-flavored soup by adding herbs or more garlic or onion.

*Natural sweetening directions:*
- Not needed.

*For low-salt diet:*
- 1 cup (240 mL) contains 40 mg of sodium
Omit salt; use 2/3 teaspoon (2.5 grams) of salt substitute near the end of the cooking process. You can also add 1/4 to 1/2 teaspoon (.8 to 1.5 grams) Salt-Free Herb Mix (see recipe on page 240).

# Tomato Madrilene / *Bouillon*

- Makes 4 servings, about 3/4 cup (180 mL) each
- 1 serving contains 24 Calories (P2, F0, C4), 2 mg of cholesterol
- 1 serving = 1/3 slice of bread or 1/2 vegetable serving (1/3 bread exchange or 1/2 vegetable exchange)

**Beef broth**   10-1/2 ounces (315 mL); use fat-free canned, or make Jo's Brown Beef Broth, page 46
**Tomato juice**   10-1/2 ounces (315 mL)
**Bay leaf**   1 (1 gram); use 2 (2 grams) if you like it spicy
**Lemon juice**   1 tablespoon (15 mL)
**Parsley sprig**   (5 grams), finely chopped
**Tabasco**   4 to 6 drops
**Salt and pepper**   to taste
**Cloves**   4 (1 gram)
**Lemon**   4 thin slices (40 grams)

Combine broth, tomato juice and bay leaf; simmer about 1 hour: Then add enough water to replace evaporation loss until you have 21 ounces (630 mL) total. Add lemon juice, parsley and Tabasco; simmer for 30 minutes. Add salt and pepper to taste. Remove bay leaf; insert clove at angle in each lemon slice; serve soup with lemon slice on top.

**Suggestions:**
If you want this to really warm the throat as it goes down, cook for 2 hours with the bay leaf, then add twice as much Tabasco. This is an excellent soup to start a heavy dinner, because it is light and refreshing and does not take away the appetite for other food.

**Natural sweetening directions:**
- Not needed.

**For low-salt diet:**
- 1 serving contains 14 mg of sodium
Omit salt; use salt substitute. Add 1/2 teaspoon (1.5 grams) dried sweet basil. Use salt-free tomato juice. Use homemade chicken or beef broth made without salt and skimmed of all fat (see recipes on pages 45 and 46).

# Quick Chicken Soup

- Makes 6 servings
- 1 serving contains 162 Calories (P16, F6, C11), 49 mg of cholesterol
- 1 serving = 2/3 slice of bread + 2 ounces of meat (2/3 bread exchange + 2 meat exchanges)

**Chicken broth**  10-1/2 ounces (315 mL), fat-free. (Chill can before opening, so you can remove any fat — it sticks to lid when cold!)
**Chicken or turkey**  6 ounces (168 grams), cooked, trimmed of all fat and skin
**Water**  7 ounces (210 mL)
**Onion or chives**  1/2 teaspoon (1.7 to 1.5 grams), diced
**Celery**  1/4 cup (30 grams), diced
**Carrot**  1 small (50 grams), peeled and diced
**Bay leaf**  1 large or 2 small (1 to 2 grams)
**Skim milk powder**  1/2 cup (37.5 grams)
**Unbleached flour**  2 tablespoons (16 grams)
**Salt**  1/2 teaspoon (3 grams)
**Pepper**  1/4 teaspoon (1 gram)
**Water**  to make 1 to 1-1/2 quarts (960 mL to 1.4 L) final volume

*Optional:*
**Onion powder**  to taste

Remove any fat from chilled chicken broth. Blend chicken, broth and water on puree setting for 1 minute. Cook diced vegetables and bay leaf in water to cover, until soft but not mushy. Combine with chicken puree. Add milk powder; stir to dissolve completely. Make a thin paste with flour and a little cold water (or use instant flour, which will dissolve by itself). Add flour paste to chicken-vegetable mixture; stir well. Cook until slightly thickened. Add salt and pepper; mix well. Taste and add more seasonings if desired; add onion powder if you want the onion flavor stronger; remove bay leaf. Add water to bring total volume to 1-1/2 quarts (1.4 L). Heat and serve.

**Suggestions:**
This is a good way to serve some of the leftover holiday fowl. You can make it a vegetable-chicken soup by doubling the vegetable amounts given. The additions won't increase the food value enough to change what must be given up for a serving of soup.

**Natural sweetening directions:**
- Not needed.

**For low-salt diet:**
- 1 serving contains 48 mg of sodium
Omit salt; use salt substitute to taste. Omit canned chicken broth; use 3 cups (720 mL) of chicken broth made without salt (see recipe on page 45). Be sure the chicken or turkey has been cooked without salt; do not use canned or smoked poultry.

# Vegetarian Vegetable Soup

- Makes 5 servings, about 7 ounces (210 mL) each
- 1 serving contains 68 Calories (P4, F0, C13), no cholesterol
- 1 serving = 1 slice of bread (1 bread exchange)

**Celery**  1/4 cup (30 grams)
**Green pepper**  1/4 cup (37.5 grams), chopped
**Carrot**  1/2 cup (72 grams), diced
**Potato**  1/2 cup (78.5 grams), diced; or 1/8 cup (17 grams) macaroni
**Onion**  1 medium (150 grams), diced
**Parsley**  1 teaspoon (1.5 grams), chopped
**Canned tomatoes**  2 cups (480 mL)
**Consommé**  10-1/2-ounce can (315 mL); or 2 beef bouillon cubes (8 grams) and
   10-1/2 ounces (315 mL) water
**Salt**  1 teaspoon (6 grams); reduce to 1/2 teaspoon (3 grams) if using bouillon
   cubes
**Pepper**  1/4 teaspoon (1 gram)
**Tabasco**  3 to 6 drops
**Water**  to make 5 cups (1.2 L) total

*Optional:*
**Garlic**  1 clove (2 to 3 grams)
**Turnip**  1/2 cup (63.5 grams), diced

Combine prepared vegetables, except tomatoes; cover with water; simmer until tender. Chop tomatoes and add. Add consomme and seasonings to taste. Heat to blend flavors; add hot water to adjust volume. Serve with toast cubes or oyster crackers, if you have an additional bread serving.

**Suggestions:**
This soup can be varied endlessly by adding any leftover vegetables. Keep a pot of soup in the refrigerator, add leftovers, and adjust the seasonings when soup is heated for serving. Add consommé or bouillon cubes and water to increase the liquid, if needed.

**Natural sweetening directions:**
- Not needed.

**For low-salt diet:**
- 1 serving contains 33 mg of sodium

Omit salt; use 1 teaspoon (4 grams) of salt substitute. Use fresh or diet-pack tomatoes. If using fresh tomatoes, drop into boiling water for about 30 seconds to loosen skin, then peel, chop and measure. Omit consommé; use 2 cups (480 mL) of unsalted, fat-free beef broth (see recipe on page 46).

# Chinese Chicken Vegetable Soup

- Makes 4 servings
- 1 serving contains 36 Calories (P2, F0, C7), 5 mg of cholesterol
- 1 serving = 1 vegetable serving (1 vegetable exchange)
- With chicken, 1 serving contains 151 Calories (P15, F7, C7), 41 mg of cholesterol
- With chicken, 1 serving = 2 ounces of meat + 1 vegetable serving (2 meat exchanges + 1 vegetable exchange)

**Chicken broth**  10-1/2-ounce can (315 mL); chill before opening
**Water**  10-1/2 ounces (315 mL)
**Bay leaf**  1 (1 gram)
**Whole-wheat noodles**  2 tablespoons (14 grams), broken into small pieces
**Celery**  1 large stalk (70 grams), sliced thin diagonally
**Bok choy or Napa cabbage**  1 large stalk (70 grams), sliced thin diagonally
**Frozen peas**  1/4 cup (36 grams)
**Mushrooms**  1/4 cup (21.5 grams), sliced thin
**Green onions**  2 (10 grams), including tops, chopped fine
**Salt**  1/4 teaspoon (1.5 grams)
**Sweet basil**  1/4 teaspoon (.8 gram), dried
**White pepper**  1/8 teaspoon (.5 gram)

*Optional:*
**Chicken**  8 ounces (227 grams), with skin and bones removed, sliced diagonally

Combine broth and water; add bay leaf
and noodles; cover and simmer for 5
minutes. Add sliced celery and bok choy;
cook covered another 3 minutes. For
milder flavor, remove the bay leaf. Add
remaining ingredients, including sliced
chicken. Cook until peas are tender.
Serve immediately.

### Natural sweetening directions:
- Not needed.

### For low-salt diet:
- 1 serving contains 45 mg of sodium
- With chicken, 1 serving contains 81 mg of sodium

Omit salt; use 1/2 teaspoon (2 grams) of salt substitute. Use homemade chicken broth made according to low-salt directions (see recipe on page 45). Use fresh mushrooms only. If adding chicken or turkey be sure it was cooked without salt.

# Mock Pea Soup

- Makes 6 servings
- 1 serving contains 28 Calories (P1, F0, C6), no cholesterol
- 1 serving = 1/2 slice of bread *or* 1 vegetable serving (1/2 bread exchange *or* 1 vegetable exchange)

**Zucchini**   2-1/2 cups (450 grams), sliced thin
**Carrot**   1 medium (60 grams), sliced thin
**Celery**   1 large stalk (70 grams), sliced thin
**Onion**   1 small (120 grams), diced
**Bay leaf**   1 (1 gram)
**Water**   1 quart (960 mL)
**Sage**   1/4 teaspoon (.8 gram); use 1/8 teaspoon (.4 gram) if you prefer less sage flavor
**Garlic salt**   1/2 teaspoon (2.5 grams)
**Sweet basil**   1/4-plus teaspoon (.8 gram)
**Pepper**   1/8 teaspoon (.5 gram)
**Chicken broth**   1-1/2 cups (360 mL); see recipe on page 45

Combine vegetables and bay leaf in saucepan; add water; simmer until very tender. Remove bay leaf; put vegetables in blender with enough liquid to make blending easy; blend at top speed for about 1 minute, until no pieces of vegetable are visible. Return mixture to pan; add other seasonings and chicken broth; add enough vegetable liquid to make consistency of pea soup. Add extra water if needed for desired consistency. Heat thoroughly; taste; add more seasonings if desired.

### Suggestions:
Add small pieces of lean ham or lean ground beef that has been browned and drained well to remove fat. Use 6 ounces (171 grams) of meat in all and allow 1 ounce (28.5 grams) of meat per serving of soup in addition to equivalent in bread or vegetable.

### Natural sweetening directions:
- Not needed.

### For low-salt diet:
- 1 serving contains 14 mg of sodium

Substitute garlic powder for garlic salt. Use chicken broth made without salt and with all fat removed. Do not add ham or ground beef. Add 1/2 teaspoon (2 grams) of salt substitute.

# Connors' Onion and Carrot Puree / *Hot or Chilled*

- Makes 5 cups (1.2 L)
- 1 6-ounce (180 mL) serving contains 53 Calories (P3, F1, C9), no cholesterol
- 1 serving = 1/2 slice of bread *or* 1 vegetable serving (1/2 bread exchange *or* 1 vegetable exchange)

**Onion**   1-1/2 cups (240 grams), chopped
**Carrots**   3/4 cup (108 grams), peeled and chopped
**Garlic**   1 small clove (1 gram), minced
**Hot water**   1 cup (240 mL)
**Chicken broth**   3 cups (720 mL)
**Cream of Wheat or Farina**   1 tablespoon (11 grams). *Note: Do not use the instant kind.*
**Salt**   1/2 teaspoon (3 grams); use more if using unsalted broth
**Pepper**   1/8 teaspoon (.5 gram)
**Sweet basil**   2 large pinches
**Tabasco**   4 to 6 drops
**Plain low-fat yogurt**   1/4 cup (60 mL)

Place chopped vegetables in deep kettle; add the water; cover and cook over low heat about 20 minutes. Add chicken broth; cover and simmer 40 minutes more, until vegetables are very soft. Add Cream of Wheat; stir to mix; cook uncovered about 15 minutes, until slightly thickened. Remove from heat; add seasonings; taste and adjust to suit. Dilute with hot water to total volume of 4-3/4 cups (1.14 L). Whip in the yogurt; blend thoroughly. Serve hot immediately, or chill and serve as cold soup. Garnish with shredded fresh or dried parsley.

**Suggestions:**
For those who don't care much for onion, this will be a pleasant surprise. The onion flavor is subtle, despite the amount used. If you wish an even milder onion flavor, use 3/4 cup (120 grams) of onion and 1-1/2 cups (216 grams) of carrots.

**Natural sweetening directions:**
- Not needed.

**For low-salt diet:**
- 6 ounces (180 mL) contain 36 mg of sodium
Omit salt; use 3/4 teaspoon (3 grams) of salt substitute. Use salt-free chicken broth (see recipe on page 45), or use 3 salt-free bouillon cubes (12 grams) and 3 cups (720 mL) of hot water.

# Cream of Cauliflower Soup / *Basic Creamed Vegetable Soup*

- Makes 3 servings
- 1 serving contains 52 Calories (P4, F0, C9), 2 mg of cholesterol
- 1 serving = 1/2 slice of bread (1/2 bread exchange)

**Skim milk**    1 cup (240 mL)
**Hot water**    3/4 cup (180 mL)
**Onion**    1/4 teaspoon (1 gram), dried and minced; or 3/4 teaspoon (2.5 grams) fresh onion, chopped fine
**Salt**    1/2 teaspoon (3 grams)
**Pepper**    1/4 teaspoon (1 gram)
**Parsley flakes**    1/4 teaspoon (.5 gram)
**Celery salt**    sprinkle
**Bay leaf**    1/2 small (.5 gram)
**Butter flavoring**    4 to 6 drops
**Unbleached flour**    1-1/4 tablespoons (10 grams) plus 1/4 cup (60 mL) cold water
**Cauliflower**    1 cup (180 grams) mashed or pureed; or other vegetable

*Optional:*
**Tabasco**    2 drops

Make a paste of flour and cold water. Combine milk and hot water; add seasonings and simmer about 3 minutes. Remove bay leaf; add butter flavoring and flour; stir until smooth. Return to heat and cook until slightly thick. Add mashed or pureed vegetable. Heat 1 minute to combine seasonings. Taste and add salt if needed.

**Suggestions:**
For celery soup, dice 1 cup (120 grams) of celery, cover with water and cook until tender. Save liquid and use as part of liquid in soup. For cabbage or broccoli soup, use 1/4 teaspoon (.8 gram) of dry mustard in place of celery salt and bay leaf. If using fresh vegetables (not leftovers), chop, cover with water and cook until tender. This basic vegetable soup recipe can be used for almost any vegetable normally eaten. If you wish to use mixed vegetables, cook them and add them whole in place of the mashed vegetable.

**Natural sweetening directions:**
- Not needed

**For low-salt diet:**
- 1 serving contains 49 mg of sodium

Omit salt and celery salt; use 1/2 teaspoon (2 grams) of salt substitute. Be sure to use fresh vegetables cooked in unsalted water, or diet-pack canned vegetables. Do not use frozen mixed vegetables, as they are salted in their preparation. Do not use celery.

# Cream of Potato Soup

- Makes 3 servings
- 1 serving contains 138 Calories (P5, F6, C15), 2 mg of cholesterol
- 1 serving = 1 slice of bread + 1/2 ounce of meat + 1 teaspoon of fat (1 bread exchange + 1/2 meat exchange + 1 fat exchange)

**Onion**   2 tablespoons (20 grams), diced; or 1 tablespoon (10 grams) diced onion and 1 tablespoon (3 grams) diced chives
**Celery**   2 tablespoons (15 grams) diced
**Celery leaves**   1 teaspoon (2 grams) diced
**Parsley**   1 teaspoon (1.5 grams) fresh, minced
**Margarine**   1 tablespoon (14 grams); use corn-oil, soybean-oil or safflower-oil margarine
**Unbleached flour**   1-1/2 tablespoons (12 grams)
**Skim milk**   1 cup (240 mL)
**Mashed potatoes**   3/4 cup (155 grams)
**Salt**   1/4 teaspoon (1.5 grams). Use 1/2 teaspoon (3 grams) if potato was not salted in cooking
**Pepper**   1/8 teaspoon (.5 gram)

Cover raw vegetables with just enough water to simmer them in, about 1/2 cup (120 mL); cover and cook until tender. Make a roux by melting the margarine and stirring in the flour. Add milk gradually, stirring to avoid lumps. Cook over low heat until slightly thickened. Add potatoes and cooked vegetables with liquid. Add salt and pepper; mix well; add enough hot water to make 2-1/2 cups (600 mL). Heat, stirring constantly, about 1 minute to blend seasonings. Serve immediately.

**Suggestions:**
This is an excellent soup for the dab of leftover mashed potatoes that isn't enough for anything else. You may extend leftovers with instant dry potato flakes. Just make up the needed amount according to the recipe on the package, then use like fresh potato.

**Natural sweetening directions:**
- Not needed.

**For low-salt diet:**
- 1 serving contains 56 mg of sodium

Omit salt; use 1/2 teaspoon (2 grams) of salt substitute. Be sure potato is cooked in unsalted water; do not use instant potatoes. Use salt-free margarine. Omit diced celery; use only celery leaves. Increase the parsley to 1-1/2 teaspoons (2.3 grams) for additional flavor.

# Cream of Asparagus Soup

- Makes 3 servings
- 1 serving contains 113 Calories (P5, F5, C12), 2 mg of cholesterol
- 1 serving = 1 slice of bread + 1/2 ounce of meat + 1/2 teaspoon of fat (1 bread exchange + 1/2 meat exchange + 1/2 fat exchange)

**Margarine**   1 tablespoon (14 grams); use corn-oil, soybean-oil or safflower-oil margarine
**Unbleached flour**   3 tablespoons (24 grams)
**Skim milk**   1 cup (240 mL)
**Salt**   1/3 teaspoon (2 grams)
**Pepper**   1/16 teaspoon (.3 gram)
**Chives**   2 teaspoons (2 grams), chopped; or 1 teaspoon (3.3 grams) diced onion
**Liquid**   1 cup (240 mL) combined asparagus liquid and water
**Cut asparagus**   8-ounce can (224 grams); or 1 cup (181 grams) asparagus ends cooked with 1/4 teaspoon (1.5 grams) salt

Melt margarine; stir in flour to make roux. Add milk gradually, stirring to keep mixture smooth. Add salt, pepper and chives. Cook over low heat in double boiler, stirring often, until thickened. Using part of liquid, puree asparagus in blender for about 30 seconds. Add pureed asparagus and remaining liquid to milk mixture. Cook 3 to 5 minutes to blend flavors and bring to serving temperature. Taste; adjust seasonings to suit.

**Suggestions:**
When asparagus is in season, cook the tips to serve as a vegetable and save the coarser stems for soup. Chop stems, cover with water and cook until tender. Process in blender until smooth, then strain to remove any tough fibers. This gives you asparagus for two meals at the price of one.

**Natural sweetening directions:**
- Not needed.

**For low-salt diet:**
- 1 serving contains 45 mg of sodium

Omit salt; use 1/3 teaspoon (1.3 grams) of salt substitute. Use fresh asparagus cooked without salt, or diet-pack asparagus. Use salt-free margarine.

# Cream of Tomato Soup

- Makes 5 servings
- 1 serving contains 123 Calories (P7, F3, C17), 3 mg of cholesterol
- 1 serving = 1 slice of bread + 1/2 ounce of meat (1 bread exchange + 1/2 lean meat exchange)

**Water**   1 cup (240 mL)
**Onion**   1 tablespoon (10 grams), grated
**Salt**   2/3 teaspoon (4 grams)
**Brown-type granular sugar substitute**   2/3 teaspoon (1.3 grams); or substitute equal to 1-1/2 teaspoons (9 grams) of sugar
**Bay leaf**   1/2 (.5 gram)
**Cloves**   2 (.5 gram)
**Peppercorns**   2 (.4 gram); or 1/8 teaspoon (.5 gram) pepper
**Unbleached flour**   2-1/2 tablespoons (20 grams)
**Margarine**   1 tablespoon (14 grams); use corn-oil, soybean-oil or safflower-oil margarine
**Butter flavoring**   6 drops
**Baking soda**   1/16 teaspoon (.3 gram)
**Tomato puree**   2 cups (480 mL); or 1 cup (240 mL) tomato paste plus 1 cup (240 mL) water
**Skim milk powder**   2/3 cup (50 grams)
**Skim milk**   1 cup (240 mL)

Put 3/4 cup (180 mL) water in a pan; add onion, salt, sugar substitute, bay leaf, cloves and peppercorns. Simmer slowly for 5 to 10 minutes, but no longer. Remove bay leaf, cloves and peppercorns. Combine flour with 1/4 cup (60 mL) water to make a paste. Gradually add to first mixture, stirring to prevent lumps. Cook over slow heat until mixture thickens slightly. Add margarine and butter flavoring; cook 1 to 2 minutes longer, stirring often. Add baking soda to tomato puree; stir to dissolve. Add to thickened vegetable and spice mixture. Stir to mix well. Dissolve dry milk in liquid milk, beating to be sure all is in solution; warm slightly, but do not boil. Add warm water mixture to previous combination, stirring to avoid curdling; taste and add more seasonings if you wish. Heat to serving temperature; serve at once.

### Suggestions:
If you want a bulkier soup, use half canned tomatoes and half puree.

### Natural sweetening directions:
- 1 serving contains 123 Calories (P7, F3, C17), 3 mg of cholesterol
- 1 serving = 1 slice of bread + 1/2 ounce of meat (1 bread exchange + 1/2 lean meat exchange)
Omit sugar substitute. Add 2 tablespoons (32 grams) unsweetened applesauce. Increase baking soda to 1/8 teaspoon (.5 gram). Follow directions as given.

### For low-salt diet:
*This recipe cannot be made low in salt.*

# Northwest Fish Soup

- Makes 5 cups (1.2 L)
- 1 7-ounce (210 mL) serving contains 60 Calories (P8, F2, C2), 34 mg of cholesterol
- 1 7-ounce (210 mL) serving = 1 ounce of meat (1 meat exchange)

**Carrots**   2 cups (288 grams), peeled and sliced
**Onion**   1 tablespoon (10 grams) chopped
**Garlic**   1 small clove (1 to 2 grams), diced
**Margarine**   1 tablespoon (14 grams); use corn-oil, soybean-oil or safflower-oil
   margarine
**Boiling water**   1-1/2 cups (360 mL)
**Skim milk**   1 cup (240 mL)
**Parsley**   1/4 teaspoon (.5 gram), dried
**Sweet basil**   1/16 teaspoon (.2 gram), dried
**Tarragon or oregano**   1/16 teaspoon (.2 gram), dried
**Tabasco**   2 to 3 drops
**Salt**   3/4 teaspoon (4.5 grams)
**Pepper**   1/8 teaspoon (.5 gram)
**Halibut**   1 cup (170 grams), cooked and finely shredded
**Water**   to bring volume to 5 cups (1.2 L)

*Optional:*
**Cumin**   1/16 teaspoon (.2 gram)

In soup kettle, combine carrots, onion, garlic, margarine and boiling water. Cover and cook over low heat about 1 hour or until tender. Place in blender; blend until quite smooth. Return to kettle; add milk and seasonings. Heat gently to blend flavors. Taste and add more seasonings if desired. (Remember, there's fish to add, so you don't want it weakly seasoned at this stage.) Add shredded fish; heat over low temperature about 5 minutes; dilute to 5 cups (1.2 L) in all. Taste; add more seasonings if necessary. Serve immediately.

**Suggestions:**
Any white fish — sole, snapper or cod — or a combination of these will work well. Cook until tender in a minimum amount of liquid. Cool and shred. You could use leftovers — or use crab for the protein if you don't have to watch your cholesterol and saturated fat.

**Natural sweetening directions:**
- Not needed.

**For low-salt diet:**
*Do not use on 1-gram sodium diet. This recipe cannot be made very low in salt.*
- 1 serving contains 96 mg of sodium
Omit salt; use 3/4 to 1 teaspoon (3 to 4 grams) of salt substitute instead. Cook fish in unsalted water. Substitute 1 cup (240 mL) of diet-pack stewed tomatoes for the cup of carrots.

# Salmon Bisque / *Cream of Salmon Soup*

- Makes 8 servings, about 3/4 cup (180 mL) each
- 1 serving contains 149 Calories (P20, F5, C6), 30 mg of cholesterol
- 1 serving = 1/2 slice of bread + 3 ounces of meat (1/2 bread exchange + 3 meat exchanges)

**Salmon**   1-1/2 pounds (681 grams), cooked
**Celery**   1/4 cup (30 grams), diced
**Onion**   1/4 cup (40 grams), diced
**Parsley**   2 teaspoons (3 grams), chopped
**Sweet basil, rosemary, thyme**   2 pinches each
**Salt**   1 teaspoon (6 grams); use less if using canned salmon
**Pepper**   1/4 teaspoon (1 gram)
**Tabasco**   2 to 4 drops
**Skim milk**   4 cups (960 mL) plus 3 tablespoons (24 grams) unbleached flour
**Water**   1 to 1-1/2 quarts (960 mL to 1.4 L)

Drain salmon and pick over to remove skin and bones. Flake fish with fork. Simmer vegetables in 1 cup (240 mL) water until tender; remove from heat; add seasonings; place in blender to smooth if you wish. Make a paste of the skim milk and flour and add to the vegetable mixture; cook over low heat until thickened slightly, stirring frequently to avoid lumping or sticking. Add fish; mix well. Thin with water to desired consistency. One quart of water will make it a thick soup (3/4 cup (180 mL) equals 1 serving); 1-1/2 quarts (1.4 L) of water will make it thin (1-1/4 cups (300 mL) equal 1 serving). Taste; add more seasonings if desired. If you have used fresh fish, you may want more salt. You may want to increase the pepper or Tabasco, or add some onion powder. Heat to serving temperature and serve.

*Suggestions:*
For a filling and welcome change, serve this as a luncheon dish on a cold day. You may add a small potato and reduce flour to 1-1/2 tablespoons (12 grams). If you do this, mince the potato and add with the other vegetables. The food value will not change. You may substitute plain white fish for the salmon.

*Natural sweetening directions:*
- Not needed.

*For low-salt diet:*
- 1 serving contains 65 mg of sodium
Omit salt; use 3/4 to 1 teaspoon (3 to 4 grams) of salt substitute. Use fresh fish that has been cooked without added salt. Decrease skim milk to 2 cups (480 mL); add 2 cups (480 mL) more water.

# Halibut Chowder

- Makes 6 servings, about 1-1/2 cups (360 mL) each
- 1 serving contains 172 Calories (P25, F4, C9), 34 mg of cholesterol
- 1 serving = 1/2 slice of bread + 3 ounces of meat (1/2 bread exchange + 3 meat exchanges)

**Halibut or other white fish**   1-1/2 pounds (681 grams), fresh
**Hot water**   2 cups (480 mL)
**Bay leaf**   1 or 2 (1 to 2 grams)
**Onion**   2-1/2 tablespoons (25 grams), minced
**Parsley**   1 teaspoon (1.5 grams), diced
**Potato**   1 cup (157 grams), cubed
**Celery**   1/4 cup (30 grams), diced
**Water**   1-1/2 quarts (1.4 L)
**Unbleached flour**   2 tablespoons (16 grams)
**Margarine**   1 tablespoon (14 grams); use corn-oil, soybean-oil or safflower-oil margarine
**Salt**   2 teaspoons (12 grams)
**Pepper**   to taste, but use at least 1/4 teaspoon (1 gram)

Simmer fish in hot water with bay leaf until fish flakes easily. Drain (save liquid) and cool. Cook vegetables in 1 quart (960 mL) of water until barely tender. Flake fish; discard skin and bones. Combine remaining 2 cups (480 mL) of water with fish liquid. Add the flour, stirring to prevent lumping. Cook until thickened. Combine thickened liquid with vegetables in their liquid; add flaked fish. Add margarine, salt and pepper; heat thoroughly for about 1 minute; taste; add more salt and pepper if desired. Serve immediately.

*Suggestions:*
If you prefer more bay and less fish taste, cook a bay leaf with the vegetables as well as with the fish. Discard the leaves when you combine the ingredients for final heating.

*Natural sweetening directions:*
- Not needed.

*For low-salt diet:*
- 1 serving contains 86 mg of sodium

Omit salt; use 2 teaspoons (8 grams) of salt substitute. Use salt-free margarine. Be sure the fish has never been frozen. Some frozen fish is packed in brine, which greatly increases the sodium content.

# Oyster Chowder à la Maryland

- Makes 4 servings
- 1 serving contains 128 Calories (P13, F4, C10), 60 mg of cholesterol
- 1 serving = 1/2 slice of bread + 2 ounces of meat (1/2 bread exchange + 2 meat exchanges)

**Fresh oysters**    1 pint (480 mL)
**Carrots**    1/4 cup (29 grams), julienne
**Celery**    1/4 cup (30 grams), julienne
**Green pepper**    1/8 cup (12 grams), julienne
**Onion**    1 teaspoon (3.3 grams), diced
**Parsley**    1/4 teaspoon (.5 gram), chopped
**Salt**    1/2 teaspoon (3 grams)
**Pepper**    1/4 teaspoon (1 gram)
**Margarine**    1 teaspoon (4.7 grams); or 4 to 6 drops of butter flavoring; use corn-oil, soybean-oil or safflower-oil margarine

Cover oysters with water; bring to boil and cook until edges curl; set aside. Cut vegetables in julienne strips; combine with seasonings, except margarine or butter flavoring; cook in 1 cup (240 mL) water until barely tender. Combine vegetables and margarine or butter flavoring with oysters and add water to make 1 quart (960 mL). Taste; add seasonings to suit. Heat to serving temperature, about 2 minutes. Serve at once.

**Suggestions:**

- 1 serving thickened soup = 1 slice of bread + 2 ounces of meat (1 bread exchange + 2 meat exchanges)

For a slightly thicker soup, drain cooked oysters and vegetables and thicken the liquid with 2 tablespoons (16 grams) of unbleached flour. Cook until clear and slightly thick, then add oysters and vegetables and proceed with recipe. This type of chowder could be made with clams, shrimp or even white fish.

**Natural sweetening directions:**
- Not needed.

**For low-salt diet:**
This recipe cannot be made low in salt.

# Easy Corn Chowder

*This recipe is not for hypoglycemics.*
- Makes 4 servings
- 1 serving conta̶ ̶s 156 Calories (P4, F4, C26), 1 mg of cholesterol (This is no recipe for a low-Calorie diet!)
- 1 serving = 1-1/2 slices of bread + 1 teaspoon of fat (1-1/2 bread exchanges + 1 fat exchange)

**Whole-kernel corn**   #303 can (482 grams)
**Water**   1 can (482 mL)
**Salt**   1/2 teaspoon (3 grams)
**Pepper**   1/8 teaspoon (.5 gram)
**Tabasco**   3 to 4 drops
**Onion**   1 tablespoon (10 grams), diced; double this (20 grams) if you like onion flavor
**Parsley**   1 teaspoon (1.5 grams), chopped
**Unbleached flour**   1 tablespoon (8 grams) plus 1/4 cup (60 mL) cold water
**Evaporated skim milk**   1/4 cup (60 mL)
**Margarine**   1 tablespoon (14 grams); use corn-oil, soybean-oil or safflower-oil margarine

Put half the corn and all the corn liquid and water in a blender; blend on "chop" 1 to 2 minutes. Pour into a saucepan; add seasonings, onion, parsley and remaining corn. Simmer, uncovered, about 15 minutes. When onion seems quite soft, remove pan from heat. Make a paste of flour and cold water and add to mixture; stir to prevent lumping. Return to heat and cook slowly about 5 minutes. Add milk and margarine; heat thoroughly, about 1 minute; taste, and adjust seasonings if necessary. Serve immediately.

**Suggestions:**
For a more colorful soup, add 1-1/2 tablespoons (14 grams) of chopped green pepper and 1 tablespoon (13 grams) chopped pimento when you add the corn.

*Natural sweetening directions:*
- Not needed.

*For low-salt diet:*
- 1 serving contains 12 mg of sodium

Omit salt; use 1/2 teaspoon (2 grams) of salt substitute. Use salt-free margarine. Use fresh or diet-pack canned corn. If using fresh corn, use 1-1/2 cups (248 grams) of kernels and cook in unsalted water until tender.

# Salads

If the salad is attractive, the entire meal is more appealing. These recipes are unusual combinations that will add greatly to your mealtime pleasure.

Try the dressings on your favorite green salads — even lettuce becomes more appealing. You may find you like a change.

For a really spicy, nippy taste, try the Vinaigrette Dressing, page 83. Your palate will certainly stand up and take notice!

# Cabbage Fruit Salad

- Makes lots — enough for the whole family! You may want to cut the recipe in half
- 2/3 cup contains 48 Calories (P2, F1, C10), no cholesterol
- 2/3 cup = 1/2 cup of fruit (1 fruit exchange)

**Cabbage**   1 head, about 2 pounds (908 grams)
**Carrot**   1 small (50 grams), peeled and grated
**Celery**   1/2 cup (60 grams), diced
**Pimento**   2 tablespoons (26 grams), minced
**Plain low-fat yogurt**   1/4 cup (60 mL)
**White vinegar**   1 tablespoon (15 mL)
**Crushed pineapple**   8-ounce can (228 grams), diet-pack
**Salt**   1/2 teaspoon (3 grams)

*Optional:*
**Celery seed**   1 teaspoon (3 grams)

Put cabbage through old-fashioned meat grinder, using coarse blade. Grate or grind carrot. Combine cabbage, carrot, diced celery and pimento; mix well. Combine yogurt, vinegar, celery seed and salt; mix well. Add dressing to vegetables; mix thoroughly. Add pineapple; mix again; if too dry, add a small amount of juice from the pineapple. Taste; add more salt if needed.

**Suggestions:**
This salad may be made ahead of time and stored in the refrigerator. It will keep 24 hours or more without changing texture. It is a good salad to take on a picnic.

**Natural sweetening directions:**
- Not needed.

**For low-salt diet:**
- No change in nutritional values.
- 1 cup contains 48 mg of sodium

Omit salt; use 1/2 teaspoon (2 grams) of salt substitute. Omit celery, celery seed and pimento. Use 1/4 cup (37.5 grams) of diced green pepper to restore volume, and 1/2 teaspoon (1.5 grams) of unsalted poppy or caraway seeds for texture.

# Coleslaw

- Makes about 3 cups
- 1 cup contains 45 Calories (P3, F1, C6), 1 mg of cholesterol
- 1 cup = 1/2 slice of bread *or* 1 vegetable serving (1/2 bread exchange *or* 1 vegetable exchange)

**Cabbage**   2 cups (122 grams), shredded
**Parsley**   1 tablespoon (5 grams), chopped
**Onion**   2 teaspoons (6.6 grams), chopped

*Optional:*
**Green pepper**   1 tablespoon (9 grams), minced

*Dressing:*
**Plain low-fat yogurt**   1/2 cup (120 mL); or use buttermilk
**Dry mustard**   1/8 teaspoon (.6 gram); or 1/6 teaspoon (.4 gram) of mustard seed
**Salt**   1/2 teaspoon (3 grams)
**Coarse pepper**   1/8 teaspoon (.5 gram)
**Cider vinegar**   1 tablespoon (15 mL)
**Granular sugar substitute**   1-1/2 teaspoons (3 grams); or substitute equal to 1 tablespoon (12.2 grams) of sugar

Combine cabbage, parsley, onion and green pepper; mix. Combine dressing ingredients; taste; add more vinegar if you want if tarter, more sugar substitute if you want it sweeter. Combine vegetables and dressing; mix well. Let stand at least 30 minutes so vegetables will absorb dressing flavor.

*Warning:*
Do not make this far ahead of serving time, or it may separate because it has nothing to bind the dressing to the vegetables.

*Natural sweetening directions:*
- 1 cup contains 49 Calories (P3, F1, C7)
- 1 cup = 1/2 slice of bread *or* 1 vegetable serving (1/2 bread exchange *or* 1 vegetable exchange)
Omit sugar substitute in dressing. Add 2 tablespoons (32 grams) sieved applesauce or blended diet-pack pineapple.

*For low-salt diet:*
- 1 cup contains 52 mg of sodium
Omit salt; use 1/2 teaspoon (2 grams) of salt substitute. Omit yogurt or buttermilk; use 1/2 cup (120 mL) of evaporated skim milk plus 1 tablespoon (15 mL) more vinegar. Add vinegar to milk and allow to stand about 5 minutes to thicken slightly.

# Three-Bean Salad / *With and Without Tuna*

- Makes about 7 cups
- 1/2 cup contains 90 Calories (P2, F6, C7), no cholesterol
- 1/2 cup = 1 vegetable serving + 1 teaspoon of fat (1 vegetable exchange + 1 fat exchange)

**Oil**   1/3 cup (80 mL); use corn, soybean or safflower oil
**White vinegar**   1/2 cup (120 mL)
**Granular sugar substitute**   1/3 cup (32 grams); or substitute equal to 2/3 cup (130 grams) of sugar
**Bean sprouts**   2 cups; or #303 can (482 grams), drained
**Green beans**   2 cups; or #303 can (482 grams), julienne
**Yellow wax beans**   2 cups; or #303 can (482 grams)
**Celery**   1/2 cup (60 grams), diced
**Onion**   1/4 cup (40 grams), diced
**Green pepper**   1/4 cup (37.5 grams), diced
**Pimento**   1/8 cup (26 grams), minced; or 1/8 cup (24 grams) tomato, diced

### *With Tuna:*

- Add a 6.5-ounce (185 grams) can of **water-packed tuna**
- 1 cup contains 174 Calories (P8, F10, C13), 16 mg of cholesterol
- 1 cup = 1 slice of bread + 1 ounce of meat + 1 teaspoon of fat (1 bread exchange + 1 meat exchange + 1 fat exchange)

Prepare marinade from first three ingredients. Drain canned vegetables; save juices for soup. Combine beans and chopped vegetables; mix well. Pour marinade over vegetables; stir so all will be well covered with liquid. Let stand at least 2 hours, stirring occasionally. Chill; serve on lettuce leaf.

*Suggestions:*
This salad improves with age, so double the recipe and use it over a week or more.

### *Natural sweetening directions:*

- 1/2 cup contains 94 Calories (P2, F6, C8)
- 1/2 cup = 1/2 slice of bread + 1 teaspoon of fat *or* 1 vegetable serving (1/2 bread exchange + 1 fat exchange *or* 1 vegetable exchange)

Omit sugar substitute; add 1/3 cup (80 mL) concentrated apple juice. Increase vinegar by 1-1/2 teaspoons (7.5 mL). Follow directions as given.

### *For low-salt diet:*

*Do not use tuna on a 1-gram sodium diet.*
- 1 serving without tuna contains 6 mg of sodium
- 1 serving with tuna contains 114 mg of sodium

Use diet-pack vegetables, or fresh vegetables cooked without salt. Cook until barely done, as a crisp texture is more appealing. Omit celery; use 1/2 cup (75 grams) green pepper and 1/2 cup (80 grams) onion. Omit pimento; use tomato for color. If using tuna, use water-packed and rinse with hot water before using to remove some of the salt.

# Pear Waldorf Salad

- Makes 2 cups
- 1/2 cup contains 108 Calories (P1, F8, C8), 7 mg of cholesterol
- 1/2 cup = 1/2 cup of fruit + 1-1/2 teaspoons of fat (1 fruit exchange + 1-1/2 fat exchanges)

**Red apples**    1/2 cup (55 grams), diced, with skins
**Canned pears**    1/2 cup (113 grams), diet-pack, drained and diced
**Celery**    1/2 cup (60 grams), diced
**Walnuts**    2 tablespoons (15 grams), chopped

*Dressing:*
**Mayonnaise**    2 tablespoons (28 grams)
**Sour half-and-half**    2 tablespoons (30 mL)
**Juice from pears**    1/2 tablespoon (7.5 mL)
**Lemon juice**    1 teaspoon (5 mL)
**Lemon rind**    1/5 teaspoon (.3 gram), grated
**Ground ginger**    1/12 teaspoon (.3 gram)
**Lettuce**    4 large leaves (40 grams)

Combine dressing ingredients. Refrigerate while preparing fruit. Place fruit, celery and nuts in mixing bowl. Pour dressing over top, and mix well. Chill at least 30 minutes before serving to allow flavors to blend. Serve on lettuce leaves.

*Natural sweetening directions:*
- 1/2 cup contains 116 Calories (P1, F8, C10), no change in cholesterol or sodium
- 1/2 cup = 1/2 cup of fruit + 1-1/2 teaspoons of fat (1 fruit exchange + 1-1/2 fat exchanges)
Use pears canned in natural juice. Drain well.

*For low-salt diet:*
- 1/2 cup contains 23 mg of sodium
Use salt-free mayonnaise.

# Hot Potato Salad

- Makes 3 servings
- 1 serving contains 129 Calories (P3, F5, C18), no cholesterol
- 1 serving = 1 slice of bread + 1 teaspoon of fat (1 bread exchange + 1 fat exchange)

**Potatoes**    1 to 2 (235.5 grams); 1-1/2 cups (360 mL) diced potatoes after cooking
**Onion**    1 tablespoon (10 grams), diced
**Celery**    2 tablespoons (15 grams), diced
**Green pepper**    1 tablespoon (9 grams), diced
**Oil**    1 tablespoon (15 mL); use corn, soybean or safflower oil
**Hot water**    2-1/2 tablespoons (37.5 mL)
**Cider vinegar**    2 tablespoons (30 mL)
**Granular sugar substitute**    1/6 teaspoon (.3 gram); or substitute equal to 1/3 teaspoon (1.3 grams) of sugar
**Salt**    1/4 teaspoon (1.5 grams)
**Pepper**    1/8 teaspoon (.5 gram)
**Dry mustard**    1/8 teaspoon (.4 gram)
**Imitation bacon bits**    1 teaspoon (4 grams)
**Parsley**    1 teaspoon (1.5 grams), chopped
**Dill pickle**    2 tablespoons (18 grams), diced

*Optional:*
**Celery seed**    1/4 teaspoon (.8 gram)

Cook potatoes (do not overcook); peel, dice, measure 1-1/2 cups (360 mL) and keep hot in covered pan. Sauté onion, celery and green pepper in oil until slightly brown, stirring to prevent overcooking. To vegetables, add hot water, vinegar, sugar substitute and seasonings, then bacon bits and remaining ingredients. Heat to boiling but do not recook. Combine with hot potato; toss with fork to mix gently but well; serve immediately in preheated bowl.

*Suggestions:*
This salad is a good complement for leftover cold meat. It does not reheat well, so plan to use it all at one meal or serve later as a cold salad.

**Natural sweetening directions:**
- No change in nutritional values.
Omit sugar substitute. Add 1-1/2 teaspoons (7.5 mL) apple juice. Follow directions as given.

**For low-salt diet:**
- 1 serving contains 12 mg of sodium
Omit salt; use 1/3 teaspoon (1.3 grams) of salt substitute. Omit imitation bacon bits, which are very high in salt. Omit dill pickle; use 1/2 teaspoon (1.5 grams) of dill weed. Omit celery seed. Cook potatoes in unsalted water.

# Vegetable Potpourri

- Makes 6 cups of vegetables
- 1 cup contains 48 Calories (P2, F0, C10), no cholesterol
- 1 cup vegetables = 1 vegetable serving (1 vegetable exchange)
- 1 cup vegetables with dressing = 1 vegetable serving + 1 teaspoon of fat
   (1 vegetable exchange + 1 fat exchange)

**Bean sprouts**  1 cup (142 grams) canned, drained
**Carrots**  1 cup (159 grams) canned, drained
**Green peas**  1 cup (172 grams) canned, drained
**Green beans**  1 cup (142 grams) regular-cut canned, drained
**Sliced beets**  1 cup (176 grams) canned, drained
**Asparagus spears**  #1 can (454 grams), drained

### Dressing:
- Makes 5-1/2 tablespoons
- 1/6 recipe contains 36 Calories (P0, F4, C0)

**Mayonnaise**  2 tablespoons (28 grams)
**Skim milk**  1-1/2 tablespoons (22.5 mL)
**White vinegar**  1-1/2 teaspoons (7.5 mL)
**Granular sugar substitute**  1/2 teaspoon (1 gram); or substitute equal to
   1 teaspoon (4 grams) of sugar
**Pimento or sweet pepper**  1 teaspoon (4.2 grams), minced

Chill vegetables well before opening cans. Drain; arrange on a large platter, interspersing colors; refrigerate until serving time. Combine dressing ingredients; taste; add more sugar substitute if you like a sweet dressing on vegetable salad. Serve with dressing separate — perhaps in a small bowl in middle of platter.

### Suggestions:
This is an attractive platter for a buffet luncheon. Other vegetables, such as Mexican-style corn or packaged mixed vegetables, may be used, but if so, the food value would be increased by at least half, so adjust portions accordingly.

### Natural sweetening directions:
- No change in nutritional values.
Omit sugar substitute; add 1-1/2 tablespoons (24 grams) sieved diet-pack applesauce. Follow directions as given.

### For low-salt diet:
- 1 serving of vegetables contains 28 mg of sodium
- 1 serving of dressing contains 4 mg of sodium
Use diet-pack vegetables or fresh vegetables cooked without salt. (Do not overcook as they are better when crisp.) Omit sliced beets; substitute raw cherry tomatoes cut in half (190 grams). Use salt-free mayonnaise (purchased or homemade, see recipe on page 84) in dressing. Omit pimento.

# Tasty Sauerkraut Slaw

- Makes 4 servings, 3/4 cup each
- 1 serving contains 28 Calories (P1, F0, C6), no cholesterol
- 1 serving = 1 vegetable serving (1 vegetable exchange)

**Sauerkraut**   1 cup (142 grams), drained and chopped coarsely
**Cabbage**   1 cup (61 grams), shredded
**Parsley**   2 tablespoons (10 grams), minced
**Onion**   1/4 cup (40 grams), minced
**Green pepper**   1/4 cup (37.5 grams), minced

*Dressing:*
**Apple juice**   1/4 cup (60 mL)
**Lemon juice**   1 tablespoon (15 mL)
**Water**   2 tablespoons (30 mL)
**Arrowroot flour**   1/2 teaspoon (1.5 grams)
**Dry mustard**   1/4 teaspoon (.8 gram)
**Celery seed**   1/2 teaspoon (1.5 grams)
**Salt**   1/8 teaspoon (.6 gram)

Combine dressing ingredients in a small
saucepan. Simmer until slightly
thickened. Cool. Prepare vegetables; place
in a mixing bowl and cover with cooled
dressing. Toss to mix thoroughly.
Refrigerate before serving.

*Natural sweetening directions:*
No changes needed. Just be sure that the sauerkraut you buy does not contain sugar.

*For low-salt diet:*
- 1/4 cup contains 12 mg of sodium
Omit sauerkraut; use 2 cups (122 grams) shredded cabbage. Omit salt in dressing; use 1/4 teaspoon (1 gram)
salt substitute, or increase lemon juice to 1-1/2 tablespoons (22.5 mL).

# Jellied Citrus Salad

- Makes 7 servings
- 1 serving contains 52 Calories (P2, F0, C11), no cholesterol
- 1 serving = 1/2 cup of fruit (1 fruit exchange)

**Unflavored gelatin**   1 tablespoon (7 grams)
**Cold water**   1/4 cup (60 mL)
**Fruit juice**   1-3/4 cups (420 mL); use frozen orange or grapefruit juice mixed according to directions
**Lemon juice**   1-1/2 tablespoons (22.5 mL)
**Salt**   sprinkle
**Yellow food coloring**   2 to 4 drops
**Granular sugar substitute**   1-1/2 tablespoons (9 grams); or substitute equal to 3 tablespoons (36.6 grams) sugar
**Grapefruit sections**   3/4 cup (150 grams), diet-pack or fresh
**Orange sections**   3/4 cup (150 grams), diet-pack or fresh

Dissolve gelatin in water; let stand 5 minutes; if necessary, heat slightly to dissolve gelatin completely. Add juice, food coloring, lemon juice, salt and sugar substitute; stir to blend well. Chill until slightly thicker than unbeaten egg whites. Add well-drained fruits. If using individual molds, arrange fruits on bottom of mold to form a design. Return to refrigerator and chill until very firm. Serve individually on a lettuce leaf with 1 teaspoon (4.7 grams) of mayonnaise on top (see recipe on page 84). Count 1 fat serving for the mayonnaise.

***Suggestions:***
To enhance the design on the bottom of the mold, you can add dietetic maraschino cherries, cut in half. Use only 3-1/2 (26.3 grams), and you need not count them as food value.

***Natural sweetening directions:***
- 1 serving contains 56 Calories (P2, F0, C12), no change in cholesterol or sodium
- 1 serving = 1/2 cup of fruit (1 fruit exchange)
Omit sugar substitute. Add 4 tablespoons (60 mL) finely blended diet-pack pineapple. Increase lemon juice by 1/2 teaspoon (2.5 mL). Follow directions as given.

***For low-salt diet:***
- 1 serving contains 3 mg of sodium
Omit salt; use salt substitute.

# Cranberry Salad

- Makes 6 servings
- 1 serving contains 52 Calories (P2, F0, C11), no cholesterol
- 1 serving = 1/2 cup of fruit (1 fruit exchange)

**Fresh cranberries**   2 cups (190 grams)
**Orange**   1 large (180 grams)
**Granular sugar substitute**   1-1/2 teaspoons (3 grams); or substitute equal to
   1 tablespoon (12.2 grams) sugar
**Diet gelatin**   1 package (9 grams), orange or raspberry
**Boiling water**   1 cup (240 mL)
**Orange juice**   1/2 cup (120 mL), fresh or frozen
**Lemon juice**   1 teaspoon (5 mL)
**Salt**   sprinkle

Put cranberries and orange through a grinder, using the coarse blade. Add sugar substitute and mix well. Dissolve gelatin in water; stir well. Add cold juices and salt. Refrigerate until almost set. Remove from refrigerator; fold in ground fruit and pour into a large fruit mold or ring, or into six individual molds. Refrigerate until firm. Unmold onto lettuce; serve with mayonnaise (see recipe on page 84) or cooked salad dressing (see recipe on page 76).

*Suggestions:*
This is a good holiday salad that will take the place of cranberry sauce for dieting diners. If made in individual molds, it can be dressed and served individually, thus giving complete control of each portion.

*Natural sweetening directions:*
- 1 serving contains 80 Calories (P2, F0, C18)
- 1 serving = 1 cup of fruit (2 fruit exchanges)

Omit sugar substitute. Reduce boiling water to 1/2 cup (120 mL). Add 1/2 cup (120 mL) concentrated apple juice. Omit diet gelatin; use 1/3 package (2 grams) unsweetened orange drink powder. Add 1 envelope, or 1 tablespoon (7 grams), plain gelatin. Dissolve gelatin and fruit powder in boiling water. Add apple juice with other juices as directed.

*For low-salt diet:*
- 1 serving contains 3 mg of sodium

Omit salt; use sprinkle of salt substitute. Use unsalted diet gelatin; check label to be sure.

71

# Vinaigrette Molded Salad

- Makes 6 servings
- 1 serving contains 52 Calories (P6, F0, C7), no cholesterol
- 1 serving = 1/2 ounce of lean meat + 1 vegetable serving (1/2 meat exchange + 1 vegetable exchange)

**Unflavored gelatin**  2 tablespoons (14 grams)
**Lemon juice**  2 tablespoons (30 mL)
**Cider vinegar**  2-1/2 tablespoons (37.5 mL)
**Salt**  1/2 teaspoon (3 grams)
**Granular sugar substitute**  2 tablespoons (12 grams); or substitute equal to 1/4 cup (48.8 grams) sugar
**Carrots**  1 cup (108 grams), shredded
**Celery**  3/4 cup (90 grams), diced
**Green peas**  3/4 cup (129 grams), cooked and well-drained
**Pimento or sweet red pepper**  2 tablespoons (26 or 18 grams)
**Green pepper**  1 small (90 grams), chopped
**Dietetic Ginger Ale or Fresca**  2 cups (480 mL), well-chilled

Soak gelatin in 1/4 cup (60 mL) of cold water for 5 minutes then dissolve in 1/3 cup (80 mL) boiling water; if necessary, heat mixture to dissolve gelatin completely. Add lemon juice, vinegar, salt and sugar substitute, mix to blend. Chill until almost set; chill vegetables also. Add Ginger Ale or Fresca and vegetables. Pour into a ring mold or 6 individual molds; chill until very firm. Serve on a bed of lettuce or on a lettuce leaf, if using individual molds.

*Suggestions:*
For a more colorful salad, add yellow food coloring, but the interesting color combination of the vegetables shows off well if no color is added.

*Natural sweetening directions:*
- 1 serving contains 68 Calories (P6, F0, C11), no cholesterol
- 1 serving = 1/2 ounce of meat + 1/2 cup of fruit (1/2 meat exchange + 1 fruit exchange)
Omit sugar substitute. Omit dietetic soft drink; substitute 1-1/4 cups (300 mL) water, 3/4 cup (180 mL) apple juice and add 1/8 (.4 gram) teaspoon ground ginger and 1 extra teaspoon (5 mL) lemon juice.

*For low-salt diet:*
- 1 serving contains 27 mg of sodium
Omit salt; use 1/3 teaspoon (1.3 grams) of salt substitute. Omit celery, substitute 3/4 cup (46 grams) of finely chopped cabbage.

# New Orleans Vegetable Aspic

- Makes 6 servings
- 1 serving contains 20 Calories (P2, F0, C3), no cholesterol
- 1 serving = 1/2 slice of bread *or* 1 vegetable serving (1/2 bread exchange *or* 1 vegetable exchange)

**Unflavored gelatin**   1 tablespoon (7 grams)
**Cold water**   1-3/4 cups (420 mL)
**White vinegar**   3 tablespoons (45 mL)
**Granular sugar substitute**   2 tablespoons (12 grams); or substitute equal to 1/4 cup (48.8 grams) of sugar
**Tabasco**   1/8 teaspoon (.6 gram)
**Salt**   1/4 teaspoon (1.5 grams); use 2/3 teaspoon (4 grams) if all vegetables are fresh
**Yellow or green food coloring**   4 drops
**Celery**   1/2 cup (60 grams), finely diced
**Carrot**   1/4 cup (27 grams), grated
**Canned okra**   1/2 cup (80 grams), diced; or 1/2 cup (68.5 grams) French-cut green beans
**Pimento or sweet red pepper**   1/4 cup (52 or 37.5 grams), chopped

Dissolve gelatin in water; stir well; heat slightly if necessary to complete dissolving. Add vinegar, seasonings and food coloring; stir thoroughly. Mix vegetables together. (Be sure to drain any canned vegetables well before adding them.) Pour into 6 individual molds and refrigerate until firm; or pour into a large mold and divide when serving. Serve on lettuce leaf with cooked salad dressing (see recipe on page 76) for topping.

*Suggestions:*
Substitute tomato juice for 1 cup (240 mL) of water and omit the food coloring. This will not increase the food value enough to change the replacement required.

*Natural sweetening directions:*
- 1 serving contains 36 Calories (P2, F0, C7), no change in cholesterol or sodium
- 1 serving = 1 vegetable serving (1 vegetable exchange)
Omit sugar substitute. Reduce water to 1 cup (240 mL); add 3/4 cup (180 mL) apple juice plus 1 tablespoon (15 mL) lemon juice. Follow directions as given.

*For low-salt diet:*
- 1 serving contains 10 mg of sodium
Omit salt; use 1/2 teaspoon (2 grams) of salt substitute. Omit celery; use 1/2 cup (44.5 grams) finely chopped cabbage. Use diet-pack green beans and omit okra. Omit pimento; use a small tomato, diced very fine and drained of liquid and seeds.

# Submarine Salad

- Makes 4 servings
- 1 serving contains 65 Calories (P6, F1, C8), 3 mg of cholesterol
- 1 serving = 1 ounce of meat + 1/2 cup of fruit (1 meat exchange + 1 fruit exchange)

**Dietetic lime gelatin**   1 package (9 grams)
**Boiling water**   1-1/2 cups (360 mL)
**Pear juice**   1/2 cup (120 mL)
**Salt**   1/4 teaspoon (1.5 grams)
**White vinegar**   2/3 teaspoon (3.3 mL)
**Ground ginger**   1/8 teaspoon (.4 gram)
**Dietetic pears**   1 cup (215 grams), sliced
**Low-fat cottage cheese**   4 ounces (120 mL), well-washed and drained

Mix gelatin with water; stir well to dissolve. Add pear juice, salt, vinegar and ginger. Put 1/3 of this mixture into mold and chill until firm. Place sliced pears on top of firm gelatin in mold. When it is almost set, beat half of the remaining gelatin to the consistency of egg whites; pour over sliced pears; refrigerate until firm. Add cottage cheese to remaining gelatin; beat until smooth; pour on top of two previously set layers; allow to set until very firm. Serve on lettuce with mayonnaise topping (see recipe on page 84); white layer (with cottage cheese) should be on the bottom, so it will look as if pears are on the bottom of the ocean. (Now you know why it is called Submarine Salad!)

*Suggestions:*
This is a sweet salad, so serve it with tart or spicy vegetable and meat dishes.

## Natural sweetening directions:
- 1/4 recipe contains 89 Calories (P6, F1, C14), 3 mg of cholesterol, 98 mg of sodium*
- 1/4 recipe = 1 ounce of meat + 3/4 cup of fruit (1 meat exchange + 1-1/2 fruit exchanges)
- 1/6 recipe contains 61 Calories (P4, F1, C9), 2 mg of cholesterol, 65 mg of sodium*
- 1/6 recipe = 1/2 ounce of meat + 1/2 cup of fruit (1/2 meat exchange + 1 fruit exchange)

Omit dietetic gelatin; add 1 tablespoon (7 grams) plain gelatin and 1/3 package (2 grams) lime-flavored drink mix. Reduce water to 3/4 cup (180 mL) and add 3/4 cup (180 mL) apple juice plus 1-1/4 teaspoons (6.3 mL) lemon juice. Follow directions as given.

## *For low-salt diet:
- 1/4 recipe contains approximately 98 mg of sodium. This salad should not be used in a 1-gram salt diet, even though you wash the cottage cheese well. Washing the cottage cheese removes only the salt added in preparation, not the natural salt.

Omit salt; use 1/4 teaspoon (1 gram) of salt substitute. Wash cottage cheese thoroughly by placing it in a colander and running cold water through it until the water runs clear. Stir as you wash it to eliminate all the salt you can.

# Molded Beet Salad

- Makes 4 servings
- 1 serving contains 45 Calories (P3, F1, C6), no cholesterol
- 1 serving = 1/2 slice of bread *or* 1 vegetable serving (1/2 bread exchange *or* 1 vegetable exchange)

**Dietetic lemon gelatin**   1 package (9 grams)
**Cold water**   1-1/4 cups (300 mL)
**Beet liquid**   3/4 cup (180 mL)
**Salt**   1/4 teaspoon (1.5 grams)
**White vinegar**   1-1/2 tablespoons (22.5 mL)
**Tabasco**   4 drops
**Worcestershire sauce**   1 teaspoon (5 mL)
**Beets**   1-1/2 cups (245 grams), diced
**Celery**   1/2 cup (60 grams), diced
**Onion**   1 teaspoon (3.3 grams), grated or minced

*Optional:*
**Horseradish**   1 teaspoon (5 grams)

Dissolve gelatin in water; heat slowly to complete dissolving. Add beet liquid and seasonings; mix well. Combine beets, celery and onion with gelatin mix; stir well. Refrigerate until almost set; stir to distribute vegetables evenly; return to refrigerator and allow to set until firm. Cut into squares and serve on lettuce leaf; or, if made in individual molds, unmold onto lettuce leaf. Top with 1 teaspoon (5 mL) of cooked salad dressing or mayonnaise (see recipes on pages 76 and 84).

**Suggestions:**
This salad gives a cheerful color to a meal. If you like salad vinegary, use an extra 1-1/2 teaspoons (7.5 mL) of white vinegar. It will almost bite back!

**Natural sweetening directions:**
- 1 serving contains 69 Calories (P3, F1, C12), no cholesterol
- 1 serving = 1/2 ounce of meat + 1/2 cup of fruit (1/2 meat exchange + 1 fruit exchange)
Omit dietetic gelatin. Add 1 tablespoon (7 grams) plain gelatin and 1/3 package (2 grams) unsweetened lemon-flavored drink mix. Reduce water to 1/2 cup (120 mL). Add 3/4 cup (180 mL) apple juice plus 1 teaspoon (5 mL) lemon juice. Follow directions as given.

**For low-salt diet:**
*This recipe cannot be made low in salt because of the beets and celery.*

# Cooked Salad Dressing

- Makes 1-1/2 cups (360 mL)
- 1 tablespoon (15 mL) contains 4 Calories (P0, F0, C1), no cholesterol
- 3 tablespoons (45 mL) contain 12 Calories
- 3 tablespoons = 1/4 slice of bread (1/4 bread exchange)

**Cornstarch**    2 tablespoons (16 grams)
**Salt**    1 teaspoon (6 grams)
**Dry mustard**    1/2 teaspoon (1.5 grams)
**Granular sugar substitute**    2 teaspoons (4 grams); or substitute equal to
    1-1/2 tablespoons (18.3 grams) of sugar
**Cider vinegar**    3/4 cup (180 mL)
**Water**    1/3 cup (80 mL)
**Liquid egg substitute**    4 ounces (120 mL). Use 2 whole eggs (114 grams) for a
    regular diet

In saucepan, combine cornstarch, salt, mustard and sugar substitute. Stir in vinegar and water to make a smooth paste. Cook over low heat, stirring frequently, until boiling; cook about 3 minutes more. Gradually add egg substitute or beaten whole eggs, stirring constantly to avoid curdling. Cool and refrigerate in covered container.

**Suggestions:**
Substitute white vinegar for cider vinegar for a milder flavor.

### Natural sweetening directions:
- No change in nutritional values.
Omit sugar substitute. Omit water. Add 1/3 cup (80 mL) apple juice plus 1/2 teaspoon (2.5 mL) lemon juice. Follow directions as given.

### For low-salt diet:
- 1 tablespoon (15 mL) contains 6 mg of sodium
Omit salt; use 1 teaspoon (4 grams) of salt substitute.

# Eggless Salad Dressing

- Makes 3 cups (720 mL)
- 1 tablespoon (15 mL) contains 89 Calories (P1, F9, C1), no cholesterol
- 1 tablespoon = 2 teaspoons of fat (2 fat exchanges)

**Skim milk powder**   1/3 cup (25 grams)
**Salt**   1-1/2 teaspoons (9 grams)
**Dry mustard**   1-1/2 teaspoons (4.5 grams)
**Granular sugar substitute**   1 tablespoon (6 grams); or substitute equal to
   2 tablespoons (24.4 grams) of sugar
**Water**   1/3 cup (80 mL)
**Oil**   2 cups (480 mL); use corn, soybean or safflower oil
**Cider vinegar**   1/2 cup (120 mL)

With rotary beater or wire whip, beat together dry milk, salt, mustard, sugar substitute and water. Add half the oil, 1/4 cup (60 mL) at a time, beating smooth after each addition; add vinegar; beat until smooth and thick; add remainder of oil gradually. Cover and store in refrigerator.

**Suggestions:**
If you like a spicy salad dressing, add 1/2 to 3/4 teaspoon (1.5 to 2.3 grams) of Salt-Free Herb Mix (see page 240). A small amount of sweet basil or oregano is also compatible with the other ingredients.

*Natural sweetening directions:*
- No change in nutritional values.
Omit sugar substitute. Omit water. Add 1/3 cup (80 mL) apple juice plus 1 teaspoon (5 mL) lemon juice. Follow directions as given.

*For low-salt diet:*
- 1 tablespoon (15 mL) contains 2 mg of sodium
Omit salt; use 1-1/2 teaspoons (6 grams) of salt substitute.

# Easy French Dressing

- Makes about 2-1/2 cups (600 mL)
- 1 tablespoon (15 mL) contains 54 Calories (P0, F6, C0), no cholesterol
- 1 tablespoon = 1 teaspoon of fat (1 fat exchange)

**Oil**   1 cup (240 mL); use corn, soybean or safflower oil
**Cider vinegar**   1/2 cup (120 mL)
**Tomato paste**   1/4 cup (64.5 grams) + 1/4 cup (60 mL) water
**Granular sugar substitute**   1/2 teaspoon (1 gram); or substitute equal to
   1 teaspoon (4 grams) of sugar
**Paprika**   1/2 teaspoon (1.5 grams)
**Dry mustard**   1/2 teaspoon (1.5 grams)
**Garlic**   1/4 clove (.5 gram), mashed
**Egg white**   1 (33 grams)
**Salt**   1/2 teaspoon (3 grams) or more
**Unflavored gelatin**   1/2 tablespoon (3.5 grams)
**Water**   1/2 cup (120 mL)

Combine all ingredients except gelatin and water in blender jar. Blend until smooth. Combine gelatin and water; heat slowly to dissolve; cool slightly. Add gelatin to blended ingredients and blend for 1 minute. Store in refrigerator, covered, until needed; then allow to stand at room temperature until oil loses its cloudiness. Shake well before using.

*Suggestions:*
This is not a thick dressing but the consistency is good on green salads. Dressing will not separate when poured on vegetables. It can be used for marinating chicken or fish before cooking.

*Natural sweetening directions:*
- 1 tablespoon contains 58 Calories (P0, F6, C1), no cholesterol
- 1 tablespoon = 1 teaspoon of fat (1 fat exchange)
Omit sugar substitute. Reduce water to 1/4 cup (60 mL). Add 1/4 cup (60 mL) concentrated apple juice plus 1 teaspoon (5 mL) lemon juice. Follow directions as given.

*For low-salt diet:*
- 1 tablespoon contains 2 mg of sodium
Omit salt; use 1/2 teaspoon (2 grams) of salt substitute. Use salt-free tomato paste, or tomato puree (be sure it says salt-free on the label); or if you make your own using canned salt-free tomatoes, use 1/2 cup (120 mL) and omit water.

# Italian Dressing

- Makes 1 cup (240 mL)
- 1 tablespoon (15 mL) contains 45 Calories (P0, F5, C0), no cholesterol
- 1 tablespoon = 1 teaspoon of fat (1 fat exchange)

**Salt**   1/2 teaspoon (3 grams)
**Pepper**   1/4 teaspoon (1 gram)
**Garlic powder**   1/8 teaspoon (.4 gram)
**Onion powder**   1/8 teaspoon (.4 gram)
**Paprika**   1/8 teaspoon (.4 gram)
**Red wine vinegar**   1/3 cup (80 mL)
**Water**   1/3 cup (80 mL)
**Oil**   1/3 cup (80 mL); use corn, soybean or safflower oil

Mix dry ingredients. In glass jar with tight lid, add water to vinegar; add dry ingredients. Add oil; cover and shake well. Keep refrigerated. Before using, allow to stand at room temperature until oil loses cloudiness; shake well.

**Suggestions:**
In place of garlic powder add a piece of garlic clove, and in place of onion powder, use a section of fresh onion. Dressing will absorb the flavors during storage. Don't do this unless you really love garlic!

**Natural sweetening directions:**
- Not needed.

**For low-salt diet:**
- 1 tablespoon contains less than 1 mg of sodium
Omit salt; use 1/2 teaspoon (2 grams) of salt substitute. Add 1/2 teaspoon (1.5 grams) Salt-Free Herb Mix (page 240) for added flavor.

# Oil-Free Italian Dressing

- Makes 5-1/2 ounces (165 mL)
- This recipe contains no Calories (P0, F0, C0), no cholesterol
- No replacements are needed

**Red wine vinegar**    1/3 cup (80 mL)
**Water**    1/3 cup (80 mL)
**Garlic powder**    1/16 teaspoon (.2 gram)
**Onion powder**    1/8 teaspoon (.4 gram)
**Pepper**    1/16 teaspoon (.3 gram), coarse-ground
**Paprika**    1/16 teaspoon (.2 gram)

*Optional:*
**Salt-Free Herb Mix**    1/2 teaspoon (1.5 grams) (see recipe on page 240)

Combine all ingredients and mix well.

**Suggestions:**
In place of garlic powder, add a piece of garlic clove, and in place of onion powder, use a section of fresh onion. Dressing will absorb the flavors during storage. This is an excellent marinade for fish or chicken.

**Natural sweetening directions:**
- Not needed.

**For low-salt diet:**
- 1 ounce contains less than 1 mg of sodium

# Creamy Salad Dressing

- Makes 3 cups (720 mL)
- 2 tablespoons (30 mL) contain 17 Calories (P1, F1, C1), 1 mg of cholesterol
- No replacements are needed

**Buttermilk**   1-1/8 cups (270 mL)
**Low-fat cottage cheese**   1-1/2 cups (352.5 grams)
**Cider vinegar**   1-1/4 teaspoons (6.3 mL)
**Garlic powder**   1-1/2 teaspoons (4.8 grams)
**Onion powder**   1-1/2 teaspoons (4.8 grams)
**Dry mustard**   1/4 teaspoon (.8 gram)
**Pepper**   1/4 teaspoon (1 gram)
**Tabasco**   8 to 10 drops

*Optional:*
Use only one of the following:
**Sweet basil**   2 teaspoons (6 grams)
**Dill weed**   1-1/4 teaspoons (4.5 grams)
**Italian Herb Mix**   1-1/2 teaspoons (4.5 grams)

Place all ingredients in a blender and
blend until smooth. Taste and adjust
spices to suit your taste.

**Natural sweetening directions:**
- Not needed.

**For low-salt diet:**
*This recipe cannot be made lower in salt. It is too high for a low-sodium diet.*
- 2 tablespoons contain 62 mg of sodium

# Salt-Free, Oil-Free Italian Dressing

- Makes 12 ounces (360 mL)
- 2 tablespoons (30 mL) contain 2 Calories (P0, F0, C.5), no cholesterol
- No replacements are needed

**Salt-free tomato juice**    1 cup (240 mL)
**Red wine vinegar**    1/2 cup (120 mL)
**Garlic powder**    1/8 teaspoon (.4 gram)
**Onion powder**    1/8 teaspoon (.4 gram)
**Pepper**    1/8 teaspoon (.5 gram)
**Paprika**    1/8 teaspoon (.4 gram)
**Brown-type granular sugar substitute**    1/2 teaspoon (1 gram); or substitute equal
    to 1 teaspoon (4 grams) of sugar

Combine all ingredients and mix well.

**Suggestions:**
In place of garlic powder, add a piece of garlic clove, and in place of the onion powder, use a slice of fresh onion. Dressing will absorb the flavors during storage. This is an excellent marinade for chicken or fish.

*Natural sweetening directions:*
- No change in nutritional values.
Omit sugar substitute. Add 1 tablespoon (15 mL) concentrated apple juice plus 1/4 teaspoon (1.3 mL) lemon juice. Follow directions as given.

*For low-salt diet:*
- 1 tablespoon contains less than 1 mg of sodium
- No changes necessary

# Vinaigrette Dressing

- Makes about 3-3/4 cups (900 mL)
- 1-1/2 tablespoons (22.5 mL) contain 36 Calories (P0, F4, C0), no cholesterol
- 1-1/2 tablespoons = 1 teaspoon of fat (1 fat exchange)

**Water**   1-1/2 cups (360 mL)
**Cider vinegar**   5/8 cup (150 mL)
**Red wine vinegar**   5/8 cup (150 mL)
**Oil**   3/4 cup (180 mL); use corn, soybean or safflower oil
**Green pepper**   1/4 (32.5 grams)
**Pimento**   2 teaspoons (8.7 grams)
**Garlic**   2 cloves (4 grams)
**Parsley**   1-1/2 tablespoons (7.5 grams)
**Salt**   1 tablespoon (18 grams)
**Pepper**   1/4 teaspoon (1 gram)
**Granular sugar substitute**   2 teaspoons (4 grams); or substitute equal to
   4 teaspoons (16 grams) of sugar

*Optional:*
**Cayenne**   1/8 teaspoon (.5 gram)

Combine liquids. Grind, or blend on coarse-chop setting, green pepper, pimento, garlic and parsley. Combine with liquids, seasonings and sugar substitute; mix well. Refrigerate, tightly covered; before using, let stand at room temperature until oil loses cloudiness; shake well.

**Suggestions:**
This is a very tangy dressing, excellent on dandelion greens, beet greens and spinach.

**Natural sweetening directions:**
- No change in nutritional values.
Omit sugar substitute. Reduce water to 1-1/4 cups (300 mL). Add 1/4 cup (60 mL) apple juice plus 1 teaspoon (5 mL) lemon juice. Follow directions as given.

**For low-salt diet:**
- 1 tablespoon contains 1 mg of sodium
Omit salt; use 1 tablespoon (12 grams) of salt substitute. Omit pimento; use 1/4 teaspoon (.8 gram) of paprika for color.

# Low-Cholesterol Mayonnaise

- Makes 2-1/2 cups (600 mL)
- 1 tablespoon (15 mL) contains 58 Calories (P0, F6, C1), no cholesterol
- 1 tablespoon = 1 teaspoon of fat (1 fat exchange)

**Unbleached flour**   1/3 cup (42 grams), unsifted
**Salt**   1 teaspoon (6 grams)
**Dry mustard**   1/3 teaspoon (1 gram)
**Granular sugar substitute**   1/2 teaspoon (1 gram); or substitute equal to
   1 teaspoon (4 grams) of sugar
**Water**   3/4 cup (180 mL)
**Cider vinegar**   1/3 cup (80 mL)
**Egg whites**   3 (99 grams); or 3 ounces (90 mL) of liquid egg substitute
**Oil**   1 cup (240 mL); use corn, soybean or safflower oil
**Yellow food coloring**   2 to 6 drops

Make a paste with flour, salt, mustard, sugar substitute, water and vinegar; stir constantly as you add liquids. Cook in a double boiler, stirring constantly until thick, boiling at least 1 minute. Remove from heat and cool slightly. Beat egg whites with rotary beater, wire whip or mixer; add to cooked mixture, beating as you add. (Be sure cooked material is cool enough that egg whites do not curdle.) Add oil gradually, beating after each addition to be sure all oil is absorbed. Add enough food coloring to give the creamy yellow color of mayonnaise. Cover and store in refrigerator until needed.

**Suggestions:**
Add more sweetenings or seasonings if you wish, though proportions given are those for real mayonnaise — normally a rather bland mixture.

**Natural sweetening directions:**
- No change in nutritional values.
Omit sugar substitute. Add 1 tablespoon (15 mL) apple or white grape juice plus 1/4 teaspoon (1.3 mL) lemon juice. Increase flour by 1/4 teaspoon (.7 gram). Follow directions as given.

**For low-salt diet:**
- 1 tablespoon contains 4 mg of sodium
Omit salt; use 1 teaspoon (4 grams) of salt substitute.

# Extended Mayonnaise
## *How to Stretch Mayonnaise*

- Makes 1/2 cup (120 mL)
- 1 tablespoon (15 mL) contains 62 Calories (P1, F6, C1), 63 mg of cholesterol
- 1 tablespoon = 1-1/2 teaspoons of fat (1-1/2 fat exchanges)

**Pure mayonnaise**   4 tablespoons (56 grams)
**Evaporated skim milk**   3 tablespoons (45 mL)
**Cider vinegar**   1 tablespoon (15 mL)
**Liquid sweetener**   3 drops; or substitute equal to 1/2 teaspoon (2 grams) of sugar
**Salt, pepper and onion powder**   to taste

*Optional:*
**Paprika**   sprinkle

Put mayonnaise, milk and vinegar in a bowl and mix well; let stand for 15 minutes. Add liquid sweetener and seasonings to taste; mix well. Refrigerate.

**Suggestions:**
If your diet allows very little mayonnaise, try stretching it with this. This works well for sandwiches and salads. You can use 7 tablespoons (105 mL) of low-fat yogurt for the milk and mayonnaise; the dressing will be thinner, but not significantly different in food value.

**Natural sweetening directions:**
- No change in nutritional values.
Omit liquid sweetener. Add 1-1/2 teaspoons (7.5 mL) apple or white grape juice plus 1/4 teaspoon (1.3 mL) lemon juice. Follow directions as given.

**For low-salt diet:**
- 1 teaspoon contains 9 mg of sodium
Omit salt; use sprinkle of salt substitute. Use salt-free mayonnaise.

# The Main Course

### Meats

To keep lean meats from becoming dry and unappetizing, without adding fat, requires effort. Spiced marinades and slow, low-temperature cooking help tenderize these dishes.

### Casseroles

Never hurry a mixed dish as you will lose much of the expected taste and texture. Using very dry wine in recipes improves taste and tenderness. The alcohol evaporates during cooking so the Calories do not have to be counted.

### Vegetables

Vegetables are your most useful foods for making meals both filling and eye-catching. A little variety in taste and appearance does wonders for preventing boredom in a diet. When you have tried the vegetable combinations given here, experiment to see what other dishes you can come up with.

### Sauces

Most conventional main course sauces contain either cream or fat. Sauce recipes in this cookbook are low in saturated fats (butter and eggs). Use them to make meals more appetizing, to give a change of appearance when you have leftovers or to lend elegance to your meal. Pamper your palate and dieting will be much easier.

86

# Beef Stew with Vegetables

- Makes 5 servings
- 1 serving contains 219 Calories (P22, F7, C17), 64 mg of cholesterol
- 1 serving = 3 ounces of meat + 1 slice of bread + 1/2 vegetable serving (3 meat exchanges + 1 bread exchange + 1/2 vegetable exchange)

**Lean beef** 1 pound (454 grams), cubed; buy a little extra and trim off the fat
**Oil** 1 tablespoon (15 mL); use corn, soybean or safflower oil
**Potatoes** 3 small (360 grams), peeled and cut into 5 pieces each
**Carrots** 3 medium (180 grams), peeled and cut into pieces. Try to have 10 or 15 pieces for easy division.
**Onion** 1 medium (150 grams), peeled and cut into 5 pieces
**Celery** 2 large stalks (140 grams), cut into 2-inch pieces
**Salt** 1/2 teaspoon (3 grams)
**Pepper** 1/8 teaspoon (.5 gram)
**Unbleached flour** 1 tablespoon (8 grams)
**Cold water** 1/4 cup (60 mL)

*Optional:*
**Green pepper** 1/4 (32.5 grams), cut into small pieces
**Garlic** 1/2 clove (.5 gram)
**Tabasco** 3 to 4 drops

Trim all fat from beef; weigh to make sure you have 1 pound. In a pressure cooker, brown beef cubes in oil, turning cubes to brown all surfaces and to prevent sticking; keep heat low enough to prevent oil from smoking. Arrange vegetables on top of browned beef cubes; pour 1-1/2 cups (360 mL) water over vegetables and add seasonings. Close pressure cooker and cook at 10 pounds of pressure for 20 minutes from time pressure indicator starts to jiggle. Remove cooker from heat; hold under cold water to reduce pressure quickly. Remove lid; drain liquid into a bowl; retain solids in colander. Return liquid to cooker; add 1/2 cup (120 mL) hot water. Make a paste of flour and cold water; add to liquid, stirring to prevent lumps. Cook until slightly thick. Add more salt and pepper and Tabasco, if you wish. Add drained vegetables and meat to gravy and reheat quickly. Serve immediately, dividing into 5 equal portions.

***Natural sweetening directions:***
- Not needed.

***For low-salt diet:***
- 1 serving contains 94 mg of sodium
Omit salt; use 1/2 teaspoon (2 grams) of salt substitute. Add 1/2 teaspoon (1.5 grams) Salt-Free Herb Mix (page 240) for added flavor.

# Burger Chop Suey

- Makes 3 servings
- 1 serving contains 154 Calories (P19, F6, C6), 53 mg of cholesterol
- 1 serving = 3 ounces of lean meat + 1/2 slice of bread (3 lean meat exchanges + 1/2 bread exchange)

**Very lean ground beef**   1/2 pound (227 grams)
**Onion**   3 tablespoons (30 grams), diced
**Oil**   1 teaspoon (5 mL); use corn, soybean or safflower oil
**Beef bouillon cube**   1 (4 grams)
**Boiling water**   1 cup (240 mL)
**Brown-type granular sugar substitute**   1/2 teaspoon (1 gram); or substitute equal to 1 teaspoon (4 grams) of sugar
**Soy sauce**   1 teaspoon (5 mL)
**Tabasco**   2 drops
**Bean sprouts**   1 cup fresh (105 grams), or 1 cup canned and drained (142 grams). If using fresh sprouts, blanch with boiling water.
**Celery**   1/2 cup (60 grams), diced
**Unbleached flour**   1 tablespoon (8 grams)

*Optional:*
**Mushrooms**   1/2 cup (43 grams), sliced
**Water chestnuts**   1/2 cup (65 grams), sliced

Sauté beef and onion in oil until brown. Dissolve bouillon cube in boiling water; add to beef and onion; add sugar substitute, soy sauce and Tabasco; mix well. Add vegetables, then cover and cook slowly until vegetables are just tender; add more water if necessary. Drain liquid into separate pan; add water to flour to make about 2/3 cup (160 mL); stir in and cook until thick. Add sauce to vegetables in original pan; heat thoroughly; serve immediately over rice or noodles. (Allow 1 slice of bread for each 1/2 cup of cooked rice or noodles.)

### Natural sweetening directions:
- No change in nutritional values.

Omit sugar substitute; add 1 tablespoon (15 mL) apple or white grape juice plus 1/2 teaspoon (2.5 mL) lemon juice. Follow directions as given.

### For low-salt diet:
- 1 serving contains 47 mg of sodium

Omit soy sauce; use 1/2 teaspoon (2 grams) of salt substitute; or use 1 teaspoon salt-free soy sauce. Omit bouillon cube and water; use homemade, salt-free broth (see recipe on page 46) or use 1 salt-free bouillon cube with water. Omit water chestnuts; use 1 cup (86 grams) fresh mushrooms. Omit celery; increase fresh bean sprouts to 1-1/2 cups (157.5 grams). Be sure to use fresh bean sprouts, as canned sprouts are high in salt.

# Meat Loaf

- Makes 5 servings
- 1 serving contains 141 Calories (P21, F5, C3), 63 mg of cholesterol
- 1 serving = 3 ounces of meat (3 lean meat exchanges)

**Egg white**    1 (33 grams)
**Extra-lean, coarse-ground beef**    1 pound (454 grams)
**Sauerkraut**    1/2 cup (71 grams), washed and chopped
**Onion**    2 tablespoons (20 grams), diced
**Green pepper**    2 tablespoons (18 grams), diced
**Sage or poultry seasoning**    1/2 teaspoon (1.5 grams)
**Salt**    1/2 teaspoon (3 grams)
**Pepper**    1/4 teaspoon (1 gram)
**Quick-cooking oatmeal**    1/4 cup (18 grams)

Beat egg white slightly. Add beef, sauerkraut, onion and green pepper; mix well. Sprinkle seasonings evenly over mixture; add oatmeal and mix well. Form into a loaf; use a few drops of warm water if it feels dry. Place loaf in open roasting pan, on a rack so drippings will collect in pan and not be reabsorbed by the loaf. Bake at 325°F (163°C) about 1 hour, until outside crust is well browned.

**Suggestions:**
This makes good hamburgers, too! Make 5 equal patties from raw mixture; brown in nonstick pan. To change the taste completely, add 2 tablespoons (30 grams) of horseradish and omit sauerkraut and sage or poultry seasoning. Use leftover meat loaf cold for sandwich filling, or make it for use in sandwiches. For variety, form raw mixture into meatballs.

**Natural sweetening directions:**
- Not needed.

**For low-salt diet:**
- 1 serving contains 101 mg of sodium

Omit salt; use 1/2 teaspoon (2 grams) of salt substitute. Replace sauerkraut with an extra 1/2 teaspoon (1.5 grams) of sage and 1/8 teaspoon (.4 gram) of dry mustard mixed into the meat before the other ingredients are added.

# Poor Man's Stroganoff

- Makes 5 servings
- 1 serving contains 174 Calories (P23, F6, C7), 78 mg of cholesterol
- 1 serving = 3 ounces of meat + 1/2 slice of bread (3 lean meat exchanges + 1/2 bread exchange)

**Extra-lean ground beef**   1 pound (454 grams)
**Onion**   1 small (120 grams), diced
**Garlic**   1/2 clove (.5 gram)
**Celery and celery leaves**   1/4 cup (27 grams), diced
**Oil**   1 teaspoon (5 mL); use corn, soybean or safflower oil
**Beef or chicken bouillon cubes**   2 (8 grams)
**Hot water**   1 cup (240 mL)
**Dry white wine**   1 cup (240 mL)
**Mock sour cream**   1/2 cup (120 mL) (see recipe on page 239); or 1/2 cup (120 mL) plain low-fat yogurt
**Unbleached flour**   2 tablespoons (16 grams), plus 2 tablespoons (30 mL) cold water
**Pepper**   1/4 teaspoon (1 gram)

*Optional:*
**Tabasco**   6 to 8 drops

Sauté beef, onion, garlic and celery in oil until vegetables are tender. Dissolve bouillon cubes in hot water; pour over meat mixture. Cook slowly until all liquid is evaporated. Pour wine over meat mixture and simmer, covered, until half the wine is evaporated. Add sour cream, cold water and flour mixture, and seasonings; mix well. Cook until mixture is thick and smooth, about 5 minutes. Pour over cooked whole-wheat noodles and serve. (Add a little hot water if it gets too thick to pour easily.) Allow 1 slice bread for each 1/2 cup noodles.

*Suggestions:*
Add 1/2 cup (43 grams) sliced mushrooms. Cook only enough to heat them through. No replacements are necessary.

***Natural sweetening directions:***
- Not needed.

***For low-salt diet:***
- 1 serving contains 65 mg of sodium

Omit salt; use fresh, homemade, unsalted beef broth (see recipe on page 46); use 1/2 teaspoon (2 grams) of salt substitute. Do not use canned mushrooms. Cook fresh mushrooms in unsalted liquid, or add sliced mushrooms just before simmering the mixture.

# Stuffed Steak

- Makes 5 servings
- 1 serving contains 196 Calories (P22, F8, C9), 63 mg of cholesterol
- 1 serving = 3 ounces of meat + 1/2 slice of bread (3 lean meat exchanges + 1/2 bread exchange)

**Top-round steak**    1 pound (454 grams), thin-sliced; or use 1 pound (454 grams) flank steak. Trim off fat before weighing.
**Poultry stuffing**    1/2 recipe, page 102

Pound steak with a mallet to tenderize and flatten it evenly. Prepare poultry stuffing. Place flattened steak on board; spread on dressing, leaving edges bare. Roll; tie with string at ends and 1 or 2 places midway. Place on rack in roasting pan; cover with foil or lid. Bake at 300°F (149°C) for about 1-1/2 hours; uncover for last 15 to 20 minutes to brown.

*Suggestions:*
For a different flavor, add sliced mushrooms to stuffing. If you wish, make a thin gravy from the fat-free drippings. It will taste like gravy from a stuffed turkey or chicken.

*Natural sweetening directions:*
- Not needed.

*For low-salt diet:*
- 1 serving contains 73 mg of sodium
Follow low-salt directions given in Poultry Stuffing recipe. Do not use canned mushrooms. Slice and steam fresh mushrooms in a covered pan before adding them to the stuffing.

# Dieter's Homemade Sausage
*(Yes, you can have this sausage!)*

- Makes 8 2-ounce (57 grams) patties
- 1 patty contains 102 Calories (P11, F6, C1), 40 mg of cholesterol
- 1 patty = 1-1/2 ounces of meat (1-1/2 lean meat exchanges)

Because you probably can't buy lean enough ground pork and beef, you will have to grind your own. Buy lean beef and lean pork steak; trim off all fat and discard any portion of the meat that looks fatty. Chop the meat into small pieces to avoid clogging your grinder; coarse-grind the pork and beef; grind the potato last. *Warning:* If you use a food processor, be sure to not grind the meat too fine — sausage is supposed to have pieces the size you get with an old-fashioned meat-grinder's coarse blade!

**Very-lean ground beef**   1/2 pound (227 grams)
**Very lean ground pork**   1/2 pound (227 grams)
**Ground sage**   2/3 to 1 teaspoon (2 to 3 grams)
**Salt**   1 teaspoon (6 grams)
**Pepper**   2/3 teaspoon (2.7 grams)
**Marjoram**   1/4 teaspoon (.8 gram)
**Thyme**   1/4 teaspoon (.8 gram)
**Garlic powder**   1/4 teaspoon (.8 gram)
**Sweet basil**   1/2 teaspoon (1.5 grams)
**Nutmeg**   1/8 teaspoon (.4 gram)
**Onion powder**   1/4 teaspoon (.8 gram)
**Lemon juice**   2 teaspoons (10 mL)
**Potato**   1 cup (157 grams), raw and ground fine. You can leave the skin on — it gives good nutritional value and will not change the texture.

Place ground meat in a bowl, sprinkle with spices and seasonings and lemon juice. Mix well with your hands. Add raw potato and remix. Shape into two rolls about 2-1/2 inches (6.25 cm) wide. Wrap in foil and chill. Slice 4 patties from each roll; flatten patties if you want them thinner. Freeze, or cook on a nonstick griddle, turning once to brown both sides.

*Natural sweetening directions:*
- Not needed.

*For low-salt diet:*
- 1 patty contains 85 mg of sodium
Omit salt; add 1 teaspoon (4 grams) salt substitute. Add 1 teaspoon (5 mL) more lemon juice.

# American Lamb Stew

- Makes 9 cups (2.2 L)
- 1/7 recipe contains 312 Calories (P30, F12, C21), 68 mg of cholesterol
- 1/7 recipe = 4 ounces of meat + 1 slice of bread + 1 vegetable serving (4 lean meat exchanges + 1 bread exchange + 1 vegetable exchange)

**Boned lamb shoulder**   1-1/2 pounds (681 grams), cubed
**Unbleached flour**   3 tablespoons (24 grams) plus sprinkle each salt and pepper
**Bacon**   4 strips (92 grams)
**Potatoes**   3 medium (410 grams), peeled and quartered
**Carrots**   6 medium (360 grams), scrubbed and cut into 3/4-inch pieces
**Onions**   6 tiny, whole (180 grams)
**Celery**   2 large stalks (140 grams), cut into 3/4-inch pieces
**Green pepper**   3 tablespoons (27 grams), chopped
**Mushrooms**   4 ounces (114 grams), bits and pieces, drained
**Canned tomatoes**   1-1/2 cups (360 mL), drained and chopped
**Rosemary**   1/2 teaspoon (1.5 grams)
**Marjoram**   1/4 teaspoon (.8 gram)
**Bay leaf**   1 (1 gram), broken in quarters
**Lemon juice**   2 tablespoons (30 mL)
**Salt**   1 teaspoon (6 grams)
**Pepper**   1/8 teaspoon (.5 gram)

Roll lamb cubes in seasoned flour to coat well, saving unused flour for thickening at the end. Chop bacon into small pieces and brown until quite crisp. Remove bacon bits and sauté lamb in remaining fat. When browned, put lamb in deep stew pot or Dutch oven. Add vegetables and all other ingredients, except the leftover seasoned flour. Add enough water to cover, at least 1-1/2 cups (360 mL). Cover and cook until vegetables are done; at least 1 hour on low heat. Make a paste with leftover seasoned flour and add to stew liquid to thicken. Adjust seasonings to taste.

***Natural sweetening directions:***
- Not needed.

***For low-salt diet:***
- 1/7 recipe contains 107 mg of sodium

Omit salt; use 1 teaspoon (4 grams) of salt substitute and 1 tablespoon (15 mL) lemon juice; or increase other herbs to suit your taste. Omit bacon; use 1-1/4 tablespoons (19 mL) oil plus 4 drops liquid smoke flavoring. Use fresh mushrooms. Use salt-free canned tomatoes.

# Barbecued Lamb or Veal Chops or Cutlets

- Makes 4 servings
- 1 serving contains 217 Calories (P24, F11, C3), 80 mg of cholesterol for lamb; 102 mg cholesterol for veal
- 1 serving = 3 ounces of meat (3 meat exchanges)

**Lamb or veal cutlets, or lamb shoulder chops**   1 pound (454 grams), trimmed of fat and cut into four pieces

*Barbecue Sauce:*
**Tomato paste**   1/4 cup (64.5 grams)
**Water**   1/4 cup (60 mL)
**Onion**   1-1/2 tablespoons (15 grams), chopped
**Green pepper**   1-1/2 tablespoons (13.5 grams), chopped
**Celery**   1-1/2 tablespoons (11.3 grams), chopped
**Worcestershire sauce**   1 teaspoon (5 mL)
**White vinegar**   1-1/2 tablespoons (22.5 mL)
**Brown-type granular sugar substitute**   1-1/2 teaspoons (3 grams); or substitute equal to 1 tablespoon (12.2 grams) of sugar
**Dry mustard**   1/8 to 1/4 teaspoon (.4 to .8 gram); use less for milder sauce
**Salt**   1/4 teaspoon (1.5 grams)
**Pepper**   sprinkle

Combine sauce ingredients and simmer about 10 minutes. Brown cutlets in a nonstick pan, turning to brown evenly. Place in a greased or sprayed baking dish; cover with sauce. Bake in a preheated 350°F (177°C) oven for 45 minutes until sauce is slightly browned. Serve immediately.

*Natural sweetening directions:*
- 1 serving contains 235 Calories (P30, F11, C4), 80 mg of cholesterol for lamb; 102 mg of cholesterol for veal

Omit sugar substitute; use 1-1/2 tablespoons (22.5 mL) concentrated apple juice.

*For low-salt diet:*
- 1 serving contains 78 mg of sodium

Omit Worcestershire sauce; use 4 to 6 drops Tabasco. Use salt-free tomato paste, or 1/2 cup (120 mL) pureed salt-free tomatoes and omit water.

# Chicken Italienne

- Makes 4 to 6 servings
- 4-1/2-ounce serving contains 182 Calories (P21, F10, C2), 90 mg of cholesterol
- 4-1/2-ounce serving = 3 ounces of meat (3 lean meat exchanges)

**Lemon juice**   1/2 to 2/3 cup (120 to 160 mL)
**Italian dressing**   1 to 1-1/2 cups (240 to 360 mL), low-Calorie; see recipe on
    page 79
**Chicken fryer**   1-1/2 to 2 pounds (681 to 908 grams), cut up
**Paprika**

Combine lemon juice and Italian dressing; marinate chicken in this for at least 2 hours, turning frequently to keep meat covered. Broil chicken in oven or table-top broiler; use marinade to baste chicken as it cooks, basting with pastry brush to be sure you cover it well. Sprinkle both sides of chicken with paprika the first time you turn it. Serve portion as permitted on your diet; allow at least 4-1/2 ounces, including skin and bone, for each 3 ounces of meat permitted.

**Suggestions:**
Cook more than you need for one meal. It's a wonderful leftover for a cold lunch and a good picnic dish.

**Natural sweetening directions:**
- Use Italian Dressing recipe, page 79.

**For low-salt diet:**
- 1/6 recipe contains 68 mg of sodium
Use Salt-Free Italian Dressing; see recipe on page 82.

# Chicken Salad with Green Grapes

- Makes 3 cups
- 1 cup contains 216 Calories (P16, F12, C11), 62 mg of cholesterol
- 1 cup = 2 ounces of meat + 1 teaspoon of fat + 1/2 cup of fruit (2 meat exchanges + 1 fat exchange + 1 fruit exchange)

**Cooked chicken or turkey**   1 cup (134 grams), diced
**Celery**   6 tablespoons (45 grams), diced
**Onion**   2 tablespoons (20 grams), minced
**Parsley**   1-1/2 teaspoons (2.5 grams), chopped fine
**Canned mushrooms**   1/4 cup (21.5 grams) bits and pieces, drained
**Seedless green grapes**   3/4 cup (128 grams), halved

*Dressing:*
**Diet mayonnaise**   6 tablespoons (90 mL)
**Prepared mustard**   1/4 teaspoon (1.3 mL)
**Grated lemon rind**   1/4 teaspoon (.4 gram)
**Paprika**   1/8 teaspoon (.4 gram)
**Pepper**   1/16 teaspoon (.3 gram)

Prepare dressing and refrigerate. Put first
six ingredients in a bowl; pour dressing
on top and toss to mix well. Chill for at
least 30 minutes before serving on a
lettuce leaf.

*Natural sweetening directions:*
- Not needed.

*For low-salt diet:*
- 1 cup contains 38 mg of sodium
Use salt-free mayonnaise. Use fresh mushrooms.

# Ginger Baked Chicken *(Good cold, too!)*

- Makes 6 servings, 1/2 breast each
- 1 serving contains 145 Calories (P24, F5, C1), 54 mg of cholesterol
- 1 serving = 3 ounces of meat (3 lean meat exchanges)

**Whole chicken breasts**   3 (564 grams), split in half
**Soy sauce**   1/3 cup (80 mL)
**Dry white wine**   2/3 cup (160 mL)
**Brown-type granular sugar substitute**   1 tablespoon (6 grams); or substitute
   equal to 2 tablespoons (24.4 grams) of sugar
**Garlic**   1 to 2 cloves (2 to 4 grams), minced; use 2 for stronger flavor
**Ginger root**   1 tablespoon (12 grams), grated; or 1 teaspoon (3 grams) dry ground
   ginger. *Note: Ginger root can be kept frozen and grated without thawing.*
**White pepper**   1/4 teaspoon (1 gram)
**Onion powder**   1/4 teaspoon (.8 gram)

Wash and dry chicken breasts, removing
any fat. Mix marinade, add to chicken
and marinate at least 2 hours. Drain;
place in baking dish and bake 50 minutes
at 350°F (177°C), basting with the
marinade every 15 minutes.

### Natural sweetening directions:
- 1 serving contains 153 Calories (P24, F5, C3), 54 mg of cholesterol
Omit sugar substitute; use 3 tablespoons (45 mL) concentrated apple juice.

### For low-salt diet:
*This recipe cannot be made low in sodium due to the soy sauce.*

# Crunchy Chicken Loaf

- Makes 8 servings
- 1 serving contains 129 Calories (P15, F7, C2), 59 mg of cholesterol
- 1 serving = 2 ounces of meat + 1/2 vegetable serving (2 lean meat exchanges + 1/2 vegetable exchange)

**Chicken fryer**   or Cornish game hen; 2 pounds (908 grams)
**Bay leaf**   1 (1 gram)
**Garlic**   1/2 clove (.5 gram)
**Celery**   1 large stalk (70 grams), coarsely chopped
**Water**   1-1/2 quarts (1.4 L), or enough to cover 2/3 of the chicken
**Parsley**   1 tablespoon (5 grams), chopped
**Celery**   1/4 cup (30 grams), diced
**Onion**   1-1/2 tablespoons (15 grams), diced
**Green pepper**   1 tablespoon (9 grams), diced
**Pimento**   3 tablespoons (39 grams), diced; or 3 tablespoons (27 grams) sweet red pepper diced; or 3 tablespoons (36 grams) diced tomato with seeds removed
**Bean sprouts**   1 cup (105 grams), coarsely chopped
**Salt**   1 teaspoon (6 grams)
**Pepper**   1/8 teaspoon (.5 gram)
**Tabasco**   4 drops

*Optional:*
**Olives**   5 large (23 grams), green or black, diced
**Plain gelatin**   1 to 2 tablespoons (7 to 14 grams). *Note: The gelatin makes slicing the loaf easier. If making this in warm weather, use 2 tablespoons of gelatin.*

Put poultry in Dutch oven or stew kettle; add bay leaf, garlic, coarsely chopped celery and water; cook 3 to 3-1/2 hours, until meat falls off the bone, adding liquid as needed to keep poultry at least half-covered during cooking; turn about midway in cooking, if you wish, to get uniform doneness. Remove from heat; drain liquid and store in jars. (Do not refrigerate while liquid is still warm, or it will make a cloudy gelatin.) Pick meat from bones and skin, shredding so no piece is larger than 1/2 inch; discard skin, bones, fat and any connective tissue; set aside to cool completely. When liquid is cold, remove fat from top and discard; place 2 cups of the liquid in saucepan. Add vegetables including bean sprouts, if fresh, to chicken liquid and simmer until slightly soft, about 5 minutes; if using canned bean sprouts, add them now; add olives. If liquid did not make a firm gel, add gelatin; add seasonings; taste; add more seasonings if needed. Combine gelatin mixture and minced poultry. Spray loaf pan with nonstick coating; pour in mixture; chill until firm.

***Natural sweetening directions:***
- Not needed.

***For low-salt diet:***
- 1 serving contains 53 mg of sodium

Omit salt; use 1 teaspoon (4 grams) of salt substitute. Use fresh bean sprouts. Omit olives.

# Chicken Bavarian

- Makes 4 servings
- 1 serving contains 177 Calories (P21, F9, C3), 90 mg of cholesterol
- 1 serving = 3 ounces of meat + 1/2 vegetable serving (3 lean meat exchanges + 1/2 vegetable exchange)

**Water**   3 ounces (90 mL)
**Tomato paste**   3 ounces (90 mL)
**Italian dressing**   6 ounces (180 mL), low-Calorie; or make your own from recipe on page 79
**Sauerkraut**   1/2 cup (71 grams)
**Whole chicken breasts**   2 medium-size (376 grams), cut in half

Combine tomato paste, water, Italian dressing and sauerkraut for marinade. Wash chicken; drain dry; place in bowl and cover with marinade; let stand at least 2 hours. Remove chicken from marinade; arrange in nonstick baking dish or dish sprayed with nonstick coating. With slotted spoon, take sauerkraut from marinade and spread evenly over chicken parts; spoon liquid over garnished chicken. Bake uncovered at 325°F (163°C) 1-1/4 to 1-1/2 hours, until chicken looks brown and dry. Discard liquid when serving, or spoon 1 to 2 tablespoons (15 to 30 mL) over each piece of chicken to moisten.

**Natural sweetening directions:**
- Not needed.

**For low-salt diet:**
This recipe cannot be made low in salt because of the dressing and the sauerkraut.

99

# Baked Turkey Loaf

- Makes 6 servings
- 1 serving contains 149 Calories (P14, F9, C3), 87 mg of cholesterol if made with egg; 45 mg of cholesterol if made with egg substitute
- 1 serving = 2 ounces of lean meat + 1/2 teaspoon of fat (2 lean meat exchanges + 1/2 fat exchange)

**Raw ground turkey**   1 pound (454 grams)
**Egg**   1 large (57 grams), well-beaten; or 2 ounces (60 mL) egg substitute
**Onion**   1/4 cup (40 grams), chopped fine
**Parsley**   2 tablespoons (10 grams), fresh, minced
**Oatmeal**   1/4 cup (18 grams)
**Lemon juice**   1 tablespoon (15 mL)
**Salt**   1 teaspoon (6 grams)
**Pepper**   1/4 teaspoon (1 gram)

*Optional:*
**Sage or poultry seasoning**   1/2 teaspoon (1.5 grams)

Place ground turkey in a bowl; add beaten
egg or egg substitute and mix well. Add
remaining ingredients and remix. Place in
a greased loaf pan and bake at 325°F
(163°C) about 1 hour, until loaf is
well-browned on top.

*Natural sweetening directions:*
- Not needed.

*For low-salt diet:*
- 1 serving contains 41 mg of sodium
Omit salt; use 1 teaspoon (4 grams) of salt substitute. Use poultry seasoning. Do not use egg substitute.

# Chicken/Turkey Newburg

- Makes 5 servings
- 1 serving contains 213 Calories (P24, F9, C9), 125 mg of cholesterol
- 1 serving = 3 ounces of meat + 1/2 slice of bread (3 lean meat exchanges + 1/2 bread exchange)

**Margarine**   4 teaspoons (18.8 grams); use corn-oil or soybean-oil or safflower-oil margarine
**Unbleached flour**   3 tablespoons (24 grams)
**Skim milk**   1 cup (240 mL)
**Onion or chives**   1 tablespoon (10 grams), minced
**Butter flavoring**   4 drops
**Salt**   1/2 teaspoon (3 grams)
**Pepper**   1/8 teaspoon (.5 gram)
**Dry white wine**   1/4 cup (60 mL); or 1/2 teaspoon (2.5 mL) sherry flavoring plus 1/4 cup (60 mL) water
**Chicken or turkey**   2-1/2 cups (335 grams), diced
**Mushrooms**   1 cup (86 grams), sliced and cooked

*Optional:*
**Yellow food coloring**   3 drops

Melt margarine; stir in flour to make smooth paste; gradually add milk, stirring to keep smooth. Add onion or chives, butter flavoring and food coloring. Cook slowly, stirring constantly, about 5 minutes until thickened. Add seasonings, chicken or turkey, and mushrooms. Heat, stirring to prevent sticking, but do not cook. Serve over rice, biscuits or toast. Allow 1 slice of bread serving for whatever you use, in addition to food value given.

*Suggestions:*
Add 2 tablespoons (26 grams) of chopped pimento or 2 tablespoons (18 grams) sweet red pepper for additional color. Use equal parts turkey and ham (trimmed of all fat).

*Natural sweetening directions:*
- Not needed.

*For low-salt diet:*
- 1 serving contains 105 mg of sodium
Omit salt; use 1/2 teaspoon (2 grams) of salt substitute. Cook chicken or turkey without salt. Use salt-free margarine. Use fresh mushrooms and cook without salt.

# Poultry Stuffing

- Makes about 4 cups, enough to stuff a 3- to 4-pound (1.4 Kg to 1.8 Kg) chicken
- 1 serving contains 82 Calories (P3, F2, C13), no cholesterol
- 1 serving = 1 slice of bread + 1/2 teaspoon of fat (1 bread exchange + 1/2 fat exchange)

**Bread crumbs**   4 cups (180 grams), firmly packed
**Celery**   1/4 cup (30 grams), diced
**Celery leaves**   2 tablespoons (12 grams), diced
**Onion**   1/4 cup (40 grams), chopped
**Melted margarine**   4 teaspoons (20 mL); use corn-oil, soybean-oil or safflower-oil margarine
**Salt**   1 teaspoon (6 grams)
**Pepper**   1/4 teaspoon (1 gram)
**Poultry seasoning or sage**   1-1/2 teaspoons (4.5 grams). Use 2 teaspoons (6 grams) if you like strong seasonings.
**Hot water**   3 to 5 tablespoons (45 to 75 mL)

*Optional:*
**Imitation bacon bits**   1 tablespoon (12 grams)

Sauté diced vegetables in margarine; after browning lightly, cover and allow to steam. Put bread crumbs in a large bowl. Mix seasonings together and sprinkle over crumbs, mixing well. Add margarine-vegetable mixture to bread-spice mixture; blend well. Add enough hot water to make mix stick together, but not be heavy; add bacon bits. Clean out body cavity of chicken; wipe it dry; stuff; skewer opening closed. In roasting pan, bake chicken as directed for any roast fowl, until skin is crisp and well-browned — 20 to 25 minutes per pound at 325°F (163°C). Remove any leftover stuffing from cavity and reheat before serving. NEVER leave leftover dressing in carcass to eat later.

**Suggestions:**
This stuffing is a sure-fire favorite. Use under chicken breasts, in stuffed flank steak or as a side dish with other entrees.

***Natural sweetening directions:***
- Not needed.

***For low-salt diet:***
- 1 serving contains 23 mg of sodium
Omit salt; use 1 teaspoon (4 grams) of salt substitute. Make bread crumbs from salt-free bread. Use salt-free margarine. Do not use poultry seasoning as it may contain salt; use pure sage. Do not use bacon bits.

# Sole Vichy

- Makes 3 servings
- 1 serving contains 162 Calories (P23, F6, C4), 80 mg of cholesterol
- 1 serving = 3 ounces of meat + 1/4 slice of bread (3 lean meat exchanges + 1/4 bread exchange)

**Fillet of sole**   1 pound (454 grams)
**Margarine**   4 teaspoons (18.8 grams); use corn-oil, soybean-oil or safflower-oil margarine
**Lemon juice**   1/3 cup (80 mL)
**Dry white wine**   1/3 cup (80 mL). Use a Chablis, Rhine or mountain white wine.
**Celery leaves**   1-1/2 tablespoons (9 grams), chopped
**Parsley**   1 tablespoon (5 grams) fresh, chopped
**Thyme**   2 pinches
**Rosemary**   1 pinch
**Lemon-pepper mix**   1/4 teaspoon (1 gram)
**Salt**   1/2 teaspoon (3 grams)
**Lemon**   3 paper-thin slices (30 grams)

Wash and dry sole; cut into 3 equal pieces. Melt margarine in lemon juice; add wine, herbs and seasonings. Simmer about 5 minutes over low heat; bruise herbs with bowl of spoon to release their flavor. Pour over fish pieces, covering well; let stand to marinate. Spray baking dish, 8 to 9 inches (20 to 22.5 cm) square, with nonstick coating, or oil lightly with vegetable oil. Place fish in pan; pour on marinade slowly, so herbs are on fish rather than dish; place a lemon slice on top of each piece of fish. Bake, uncovered, at 375°-400°F (191°-204°C) for about 20 minutes. If you want the fish browner, baste with the marinade after 15 minutes. Turn on broiler; place dish close enough to heat element to brown fish slowly. Serve with lemon slice on top; spoon on enough marinade to moisten.

***Natural sweetening directions:***
- Not needed.

***For low-salt diet:***
- 1 serving contains 92 mg of sodium
Omit salt; use salt substitute. Use fresh fish, as frozen fish is sometimes brined. Use salt-free margarine. Use only 1 tablespoon (5 grams) celery leaves, and fork them aside when eating fish. Omit lemon-pepper mix; use 1/8 teaspoon (.5 gram) black pepper plus 1/4 teaspoon (.4 gram) grated lemon rind.

# Oven-Poached Halibut

- Makes 5 servings
- 1 serving contains 128 Calories (P21, F4, C2), 58 mg of cholesterol
- 1 serving = 3 ounces of meat (3 lean meat exchanges)

**Halibut or other white fish fillet**   1 pound (454 grams), cut in 5 equal pieces
**Skim milk**   2/3 cup (160 mL)
**Hot water**   2/3 cup (160 mL)
**Onion**   5 large slices (75 grams)
**Margarine**   5 teaspoons (23.5 grams); use corn-oil, soybean-oil or safflower-oil
   margarine
**Celery leaves**   1 tablespoon (6 grams), chopped
**Chives or parsley**   1 tablespoon (3 or 5 grams), chopped
**Salt**   1/2 teaspoon (3 grams)
**Pepper**   1/4 teaspoon (1 gram)

Wash and dry halibut pieces; place in deep baking dish, 8 or 9 inches (20 or 22.5 cm) square, sprayed with nonstick coating or lightly greased with vegetable oil. Add milk and water, mixed. This should come about even with the top of the fish but not cover it. Place slice of onion on each piece; put 1 teaspoon (4.7 grams) of margarine on each onion slice; sprinkle on chopped celery and chives or parsley. Season with salt and pepper. Bake, uncovered, at 375°F (191°C) for about 25 minutes. Spoon some of the liquid over the top of fish; place under broiler; allow to brown about 5 minutes. Discard cooking liquid. About half the margarine will be thrown away, too, so you don't have to count it.

*Suggestions:*
This method of cooking can be used for any mild fish. If the pieces are thick, use additional skim milk and water to come to the top of fish, but not to cover it. If fish is more than 1 inch thick, allow more baking time.

*Natural sweetening directions:*
- Not needed.

*For low-salt diet:*
- 1 serving contains 68 mg of sodium
Omit salt; use 1/2 teaspoon (2 grams) of salt substitute. You can also add 1/4 teaspoon (.8 gram) Salt-Free Herb Mix (see recipe on page 240), for more flavor. Use salt-free stick margarine. Use fresh fish only, as frozen fish is brined in the freezing process.

# Barbecued Salmon/Halibut/Lake Trout

- Makes 8 servings or more
- 1 serving contains 309 Calories (P21, F25, C0), 63 mg of cholesterol
- 1 serving = 3 ounces of meat + 1-1/2 teaspoons of fat for salmon; 1/2 teaspoon of fat for halibut and lake trout (3 lean meat exchanges + 1-1/2 fat exchanges — 1/2 fat exchange for halibut/lake trout)

**Lemon juice**   1/4 cup (60 mL)
**Paprika**   1/2 teaspoon (1.5 grams)
**Salt**   1 teaspoon (6 grams)
**Pepper**   1/4 teaspoon (1 gram)
**Salmon, halibut or lake trout**   2-1/2 pounds (1,135 grams) fresh
**Garlic powder**   1/8 teaspoon (.4 gram)
**Ketchup**   1/2 cup (120 mL); see recipe on page 272
**Vegetable oil**   1/3 cup (80 mL)

Make a marinade of lemon juice, paprika, salt and pepper and brush on fish, covering thoroughly; let stand for 2 hours, brushing often with marinade. Combine garlic powder, ketchup and oil with remainder of marinade; coat fish well with this sauce. Preheat oven to 325°F (163°C), bake fish on rack, uncovered, about 1 hour, basting frequently with barbecue sauce.

*Suggestions:*
This marinade/barbecue sauce and style of cooking are good with large fresh-water fish, such as lake trout, or you can use halibut. It's especially good cooked outdoors on a large barbecue. Put grill far enough above the coals to avoid burning the fish. Use the recipe for Ketchup on page 272, or combine 1/4 cup (60 mL) of tomato paste plus 1/4 cup (60 mL) of water, 1 tablespoon (10 grams) diced onion, 1/2 clove (.5 gram) of minced garlic and 1-1/2 teaspoons (7.5 mL) of vinegar.

*Natural sweetening directions:*
- Not needed.

*For low-salt diet:*
- 1 serving contains 54 mg of sodium
Omit salt; use 1 teaspoon (4 grams) of salt substitute. Use the above ingredients for the ketchup replacement, using salt-free tomato paste.

# Oven-Baked Fish with Lemon Sauce

- Makes 4 servings
- 1 serving contains 144 Calories (P23, F4, C4), 85 mg of cholesterol
- 1 serving = 3 ounces of meat + 1 vegetable serving (3 lean meat exchanges + 1 vegetable exchange)

**Halibut, snapper or cod fillets**   1 pound (454 grams) fresh, cut into 4 equal pieces
**Lemon juice**   2-1/2 tablespoons (37.5 mL)
**Vinegar**   1 tablespoon (15 mL)
**Salt**   1/4 teaspoon (1.5 grams)
**Italian Herb Mix**
**Pepper**

*Sauce:*
**Water**   1/2 cup (120 mL)
**Lemon juice**   1-1/2 tablespoons (22.5 mL)
**Cornstarch**   2-1/2 teaspoons (6.7 grams)
**Margarine**   2-1/4 teaspoons (10.5 grams); use corn-oil, soybean-oil or safflower-oil margarine
**Parsley**   1 tablespoon (5 grams), minced
**Lemon rind**   1/4 teaspoon (.4 gram), grated
**Salt**   1/8 teaspoon (.8 gram)
**Pepper**   1/16 teaspoon (.3 gram)

*Optional:*
Use only one:
**Yellow food coloring**   3 drops
**Cumin**   1 pinch

Make a marinade with the 2-1/2 tablespoons (37.5 mL) of lemon juice, 1 tablespoon (15 mL) of vinegar and 1/4 teaspoon (1.5 grams) of salt; pour over fish and marinate for at least 1 hour. Drain fish and discard the liquid. Place fish on a greased, or nonstick, baking sheet. Sprinkle liberally with Italian Herb Mix and pepper. Bake at 400°F (204°C) (204°C) for 20 to 25 minutes. Prepare lemon sauce by making a paste with the water and cornstarch; add the remaining ingredients, except the food coloring, and cook over low heat, stirring frequently, until thickened. Remove from heat and add coloring. Serve about 2-1/2 tablespoons (37.5 mL) over each piece of fish.

*Natural sweetening directions:*
- Not needed.

*For low-salt diet:*
- 1 serving contains 64 mg of sodium
Omit salt; use salt substitute. Use salt-free margarine.

# Tuna-Noodle-Mushroom Hot Dish

- Makes 4 servings
- 1 serving contains 214 Calories (P23, F6, C17), 30 mg of cholesterol
- 1 serving = 3 ounces of meat + 1 slice of bread (3 lean meat exchanges + 1 bread exchange)

**Dry, whole-wheat noodles**   about 3 ounces (85.5 grams), broken into small pieces
**Skim milk**   1 cup (240 mL)
**Unbleached flour**   1-1/2 tablespoons (12 grams)
**Butter flavoring**   6 drops
**Tuna**   6.5-ounce can (195 grams), water-packed. *Note: If you don't have salt-free tuna, use 1 cup (85 grams) of any cooked white fish and add 1 tablespoon (15 mL) lemon juice just before putting it into a loaf pan.*
**Low-fat cottage cheese**   1/2 cup (117.5 grams)
**Dried onion**   1 tablespoon (4 grams)
**Mushrooms**   1/2 cup (43 grams), sliced
**Sweet basil**   1/4 teaspoon (.8 gram), dried
**Parsley**   1/2 teaspoon (.8 gram), dried
**Pimento**   1 tablespoon (13 grams), or 1 tablespoon (9 grams) sweet red pepper, chopped
**Salt**   1/4 teaspoon (1.5 grams)
**Pepper**   1/16 teaspoon (.3 gram)

*Optional:*
**Yellow food coloring**   3 drops. Do not use if butter flavoring is colored.

Cook noodles in salted water until tender; drain well. Meanwhile, prepare sauce. Make paste with part of milk and flour; thin with remaining milk. Add butter flavoring and coloring; cook in double boiler until thickened; stir often to prevent lumping. Drain tuna well; flake fine; combine with cottage cheese, mushrooms, onion and herbs. Combine all ingredients except sauce; mix well; add sauce; mix again. Spray loaf pan with nonstick coating, or oil lightly with vegetable oil. Fill loaf pan with mixture; sprinkle top lightly with paprika for color. Bake at 325°F (163°C) about 40 minutes, until top is browned.

**Natural sweetening directions:**
- Not needed.

**For low-salt diet:**
- 1 serving contains 120 mg of sodium

Omit salt; use 1/2 teaspoon (2 grams) of salt substitute. Cook noodles in unsalted water. Use water-pack tuna, with no salt added; be sure to check label. Run water over cottage cheese, at least 2 minutes, until water runs clear; stir to wash thoroughly. Use fresh mushrooms.

# White Fish with Herb Sauce

- Makes 3 servings
- 1 serving contains 139 Calories (P24, F3, C4), 113 mg of cholesterol
- 1 serving = 3 ounces of meat + 1/2 vegetable serving (3 lean meat exchanges + 1/2 vegetable exchange)

**White fish**    1 pound (454 grams). Use cod, halibut, sole or snapper.
**Lemon juice**    1/3 cup (80 mL)
**Water**    1 cup (240 mL)
**Skim milk**    1/4 cup (60 mL)
**Unbleached flour**    1 tablespoon (8 grams)
**Oil**    1 teaspoon (5 mL); use corn, soybean or safflower oil
**Tarragon**    1 tablespoon (4 grams) fresh, minced; or 2/3 teaspoon (2 grams) dried
**Chives**    1 tablespoon (3 grams) fresh, minced; or 1-1/2 teaspoons (5 grams) minced onion
**Sweet basil**    1 sprig or generous pinch
**Rosemary**    1/2 teaspoon (1.5 grams)
**Salt**    1/4 teaspoon (1.5 grams)
**Pepper**    1/16 teaspoon (.3 gram)
**Tabasco**    3 drops

*Optional:*
**Yellow food coloring**    2 drops

Marinate fish in lemon juice at least 30 minutes, turning often so it is well covered at all times. Put fish in steamer; add water; cook about 15 minutes, until done. Drain liquid and save 3/4 cup (180 mL); cover fish and put in a warm place to stay hot until sauce is done. Add milk to saved liquid; add flour; stir to smooth; add oil. Cook sauce over low heat until slightly thickened, stirring often. Add herbs; cook 5 minutes longer; remove from heat. Add seasonings and food coloring; stir well. Pour sauce over fish portions; serve immediately.

**Suggestions:**
If there is any of this left, put in a covered casserole and save. It is excellent reheated.

**Natural sweetening directions:**
- Not needed.

**For low-salt diet:**
- 1 serving contains 100 mg of sodium
Omit salt; use 1/4 teaspoon (1 gram) of salt substitute. Be sure to use fresh fish; frozen or brined fish has a high sodium content.

# Salmon Loaf / *Tasty Fish Loaf*

- Makes 5 servings
- 1 serving contains 128 Calories (P20, F4, C3), 46 mg of cholesterol
- 1 serving = 3 ounces of meat + 1/4 slice of bread (3 lean meat exchanges + 1/4 bread exchange)

---

**Pink salmon**   16-ounce can (454 grams); or 2 cups (340 grams) cooked white fish
**Salt**   1/2 teaspoon (3 grams). Omit if you like less-salty foods.
**Pepper**   1/4 teaspoon (1 gram)
**Parsley**   1 teaspoon (1.5 grams), dried
**Sweet basil**   1/4 teaspoon (.8 gram), dried
**Thyme**   pinch, dried
**Onion**   2 tablespoons (20 grams), finely chopped
**Egg whites**   2 (66 grams), slightly beaten
**Toasted whole-wheat bread crumbs**   1/2 cup (35 grams); or 1/2 cup (35 grams) rye or whole-wheat cracker crumbs

Break salmon or fish into small pieces, removing skin and bones. Add seasonings, onion and slightly beaten egg whites; mix well. Stir in crumbs. If mixture seems dry, add about 2 tablespoons of hot water. Spray loaf pan with nonstick coating or oil lightly with vegetable oil. Form fish into loaf; place in pan. Bake at 325°F (163°C) for 1 hour.

*Suggestions:*
This is good with Spanish Barbecue Sauce; see recipe on page 271. Heat the sauce and pour it over slices of the salmon/fish loaf.

---

*Natural sweetening directions:*
- Not needed.

*For low-salt diet:*
- 1 serving contains 62 mg of sodium

Omit salt; use 1/2 teaspoon (2 grams) of salt substitute. If you use barbecued fish, omit the salt substitute, too. Use fresh-cooked salmon, or leftovers from barbecued salmon if made by a low-salt recipe. Use salt-free bread crumbs, or 1/4 cup (18 grams) of rolled oats, chopped fine in a blender.

# Seafood Spaghetti

- Makes 3 servings
- 1 serving contains 246 Calories (P23, F10, C16), 38 mg of cholesterol
- 1 serving = 3 ounces of meat + 1 slice of bread (3 lean meat exchanges +
    1 bread exchange)

**Dry whole-wheat spaghetti**   about 3 ounces (85.5 grams); makes 1-1/2 cups
    (195 grams) cooked
**Onion**   1/4 cup (40 grams), diced
**Oil**   1 tablespoon (15 mL); use corn, soybean or safflower oil
**Tomato paste**   1/2 cup (120 mL) plus 1/2 cup (120 mL) water
**Green pepper**   2 tablespoons (18 grams), diced
**Mushrooms**   1/2 cup (43 grams), sliced
**Garlic**   1/2 clove (.5 gram), minced
**Cider vinegar**   2 teaspoons (10 mL)
**Tabasco**   2 to 4 drops
**Salt**   1/3 teaspoon (2 grams)
**Pepper**   1/8 teaspoon (.5 gram)
**Tuna**   6.5-ounce can (185 grams), water-pack; or 1 cup (170 grams) cooked
    white fish

*Optional:*
**Oregano**   1/16 teaspoon or more (.2 gram +)

Cover spaghetti with boiling water; cook
until tender; drain. Sauté onion in oil; add
tomato paste, green pepper, mushrooms,
seasonings and 1/2 cup (120 mL) of
water. Simmer, covered, about 10
minutes, until green pepper is tender.
Flake tuna fairly fine; add to sauce; mix
well; heat to serving temperature. Divide
cooked spaghetti into 3 half-cup portions;
cover each with 1/3 of sauce.

**Suggestions:**
If there is no cholesterol problem, shrimp
is a delicious substitute for tuna, but the
recipe would then be higher in both
cholesterol and sodium content; 1 serving
would contain 176 Calories.

**Natural sweetening directions:**
- Not needed.

**For low-salt diet:**
- 1 serving contains 39 mg of sodium
Omit salt; use 1/3 teaspoon (1.3 grams) of salt substitute. Cook spaghetti in unsalted water. Use water-pack
tuna with no added salt; check label; if using cooked white fish, add 1/2 teaspoon (2.5 mL) of lemon juice.

# Finnan Haddie Supreme

- Makes 3 servings
- 1 serving contains 165 Calories (P25, F5, C5), 60 mg of cholesterol
- 1 serving = 3 ounces of meat + 1/3 slice of bread (3 lean meat exchanges + 1/3 bread exchange)

**Finnan haddie**   1/2 pound (227 grams)
**Skim milk**   1/2 cup (120 mL)
**Margarine**   1 teaspoon (4.7 grams); use corn-oil, soybean-oil or safflower-oil margarine
**Unbleached flour**   1 tablespoon (8 grams) plus 1/4 cup (60 mL) water
**Butter flavoring**   4 drops
**Celery**   1 teaspoon (2.5 grams) chopped
**Parsley**   1/2 teaspoon (.8 gram) fresh, finely chopped
**Onion**   1/2 to 1 tablespoon (5 to 10 grams), chopped
**Salt**   1/3 teaspoon (2 grams)
**Pepper**   2 sprinkles
**Prepared mustard**   1/8 teaspoon (.6 mL)
**Egg white**   1 (33 grams)
**Low-fat cottage cheese**   1/2 cup (117.5 grams)

*Optional:*
**Yellow food coloring**   3 drops. Omit if butter flavoring is colored.

Cover fish with cold water; bring to a slow boil. Discard the water; cover fish with fresh boiling water and cook until very tender. Drain and cool fish; flake into fine pieces. To make cream sauce, melt margarine in milk and stir in flour-water paste. Cook until slightly thickened. Remove from heat; add butter flavoring, food coloring, seasonings and lightly beaten egg white. Combine cottage cheese and flaked fish; mix well; pour on sauce and mix again. Spray baking dish with nonstick coating, or oil lightly with vegetable oil. Put mixture in baking dish; bake at 350°F (177°C) 40 to 45 minutes, until nicely browned on top.

*Suggestions:*
For a more spicy and interesting casserole, add a pinch of sweet basil or dill weed, or a tiny pinch of cumin. Adding 1/2 cup (43 grams) of fresh, sliced mushrooms will vary the texture and give more volume without altering the food value.

***Natural sweetening directions:***
- Not needed.

***For low-salt diet:***
*This recipe cannot be made low in salt because it uses cured fish, which has been processed in brine.*

# New England Fishcakes

- Makes 12 cakes
- 2 cakes contain 170 Calories (P20, F6, C9), 94 mg of cholesterol if made with egg, 55 mg of cholesterol if made with egg substitute
- 2 cakes = 3 ounces of meat + 1/2 slice of bread (3 lean meat exchanges + 1/2 bread exchange)

**Salted cod**   3/4 pound (340.5 grams); or 1 pound (454 grams) white fish plus 1/2 teaspoon (3 grams) salt
**Mashed potatoes**   4 cups (828 grams)
**Egg**   1 large (57 grams), well-beaten; or 2 ounces (60 mL) liquid egg substitute
**Onion**   1/4 cup (40 grams), minced
**Pepper**   1/4 teaspoon (1 gram)
**Oil or melted margarine**   2 tablespoons (30 mL); use corn-oil, soybean-oil or safflower-oil margarine

*Optional:*
**Tabasco**   3 to 4 drops

Cover salted fish with cold water and allow to stand for at least 3 hours. Discard water, add fresh water and simmer until fish is tender. If using fresh fish, cover with cold water and salt and simmer until fish is tender. Cool and flake fish in a large bowl. Add mashed potatoes. Mix egg with remaining ingredients and stir into fish/potato mixture; mix well. Using a 1/2-cup scoop, form into balls or cakes. Place on a nonstick baking sheet and bake at 450°F (232°C) for 20 minutes, turning once to brown cakes evenly on both sides, or fry until crusty brown in a skillet that has been lightly greased or sprayed with a nonstick coating. *Note:* These fishcakes can be made ahead and frozen, either cooked or raw. Allow to thaw for at least 1 hour before cooking. If cooked, reheat at 300°F (149°C) for 10 minutes.

### Natural sweetening directions:
- Not needed.

### For low-salt diet:
- 2 cakes contain 55 mg of sodium

Use fresh white fish and omit salt; use 1/2 teaspoon (2 grams) of salt substitute plus 1/2 teaspoon (1.5 grams) of Salt-Free Herb Mix (page 240), plus 1 tablespoon (15 mL) of lemon juice. Cook potatoes in unsalted water.

# Patrick's Shrimp Dish

- Makes 3 servings
- 1 serving contains 172 Calories (P19, F4, C15), 104 mg of cholesterol
- 1 serving = 2 ounces of meat + 1 slice of bread (2 lean meat exchanges + 1 bread exchange)

**Fresh mushrooms**    1/2 cup (43 grams), cut in pieces
**Margarine**    2 teaspoons (9.3 grams); use corn-oil, soybean-oil or safflower-oil margarine
**Unbleached flour**    1-1/2 tablespoons (12 grams)
**Water**    1/2 cup (120 mL)
**Frozen string beans**    10-ounce package (285 grams), French-cut
**Shrimp**    8 ounces (227 grams), cooked and deveined
**Salt, pepper**    to taste

Sauté mushrooms in margarine until brown, stirring often. Stir in flour, mixing well; thin with water until mixture is runny. Steam string beans until tender; drain well. Set 1/4 of the beans aside to use in another recipe. Add the remaining beans to the shrimp; pour on the mushroom sauce; toss to coat. Season with salt and pepper. Heat and serve.

**Suggestions:**
For added flavor, use a little of your favorite herb. A small pinch of rosemary or sweet basil blends well here.

### Natural sweetening directions:
- Not needed.

### For low-salt diet:
*This recipe cannot be made low in salt because of the natural salt in the shrimp.*
- 1 serving contains 119 mg of sodium

*Many people want to reduce the amount of meat they eat. These recipes contain no meat, but do contain eggs and cheese. This makes them higher in cholesterol than most of the recipes in this book. If you are supposed to limit cholesterol, use these foods only occasionally.*

# Dinner Cheese Soufflé

- Makes 4 servings
- 1 serving contains 276 Calories (P19, F16, C15), 94 mg of cholesterol if made with egg and egg substitute
- 1 serving = 2 ounces of meat + 1 slice of bread + 2 teaspoons of fat (2 lean meat exchanges + 1 bread exchange + 2 fat exchanges)

**Whole-wheat bread**    3 slices (84 grams)
**Margarine**    4 teaspoons (18.7 grams); use corn-oil, soybean-oil or safflower-oil margarine
**Sharp cheddar cheese**    1 cup (111 grams), grated and loosely packed
**Eggs**    3 large or 4 medium (171 or 200 grams); or 1 large egg (57 grams) + 1/3 cup (80 mL) liquid egg substitute
**Skim milk**    1-1/2 cups (360 mL)
**Salt**    1/3 teaspoon (2 grams)
**White pepper**    2 sprinkles

*Optional:*
**Onion powder**    1/8 teaspoon (.4 gram)

Spread margarine on bread. Place eggs and milk in a blender (or large bowl, if you are using an egg beater), and blend until well-mixed. Oil or grease soufflé baking dish. Preheat oven to 375°F (191°C). Add bread, seasoning, and cheese to blender mixture and mix about 1 minute, until smooth. (If you are using a hand mixer, allow bread to soften before beating.) Pour mixture into soufflé dish and bake for 25 to 30 minutes until it is brown and has puffed. Serve immediately.

**Natural sweetening directions:**
- Not needed.

**For low-salt diet:**
*This recipe cannot be made low in salt due to the high sodium content of the sharp cheese, milk and eggs.*

# Zucchini-Rice Casserole

- Makes 4 servings
- 1 serving contains 230 Calories (P15, F10, C20), 23 mg of cholesterol if made with skim milk and egg substitute.
- 1 serving = 2 ounces of meat + 1 slice of bread + 1 teaspoon of fat + 1 vegetable serving (2 lean meat exchanges + 1 bread exchange + 1 fat exchange + 1 vegetable exchange)

**Celery**   3 tablespoons (22.5 grams), chopped
**Onion**   3 tablespoons (30 grams), chopped
**Water**   3/4 cup (180 mL)
**Whole-wheat flour**   1-1/4 tablespoons (12 grams)
**Evaporated skim milk**   3/4 cup (180 mL)
**Salt**   1/2 teaspoon (3 grams)
**Prepared mustard**   1/4 teaspoon (1.2 mL)
**Pepper**   1/8 teaspoon (.5 gram)
**Lemon rind**   1/4 teaspoon (.4 gram), grated
**Zucchini**   1-1/2 cups (225 grams), grated
**Eggs**   2 large (114 grams), well beaten; or 4 ounces (120 mL) egg substitute
**Cooked brown rice**   1 cup (180 grams)
**Sharp cheddar cheese**   3/4 cup (83.3 grams), grated and loosely packed
**Lemon juice**   1-1/2 tablespoons (22.5 mL)
**Sweet basil**   to sprinkle as topping

Simmer water, celery and onion in a saucepan for 5 minutes. Make a paste of the flour with some of the milk; add paste and seasonings to the vegetables and cook over low heat until slightly thickened. Remove from heat and add remaining ingredients. Pour into a 1-1/2- or 2-quart (1.5- or 2-liter) casserole. Sprinkle the top with sweet basil. Bake at 350°F (177°C) for 50 minutes until top is nicely browned.

*Natural sweetening directions:*
- Not needed.

*For low-salt diet:*
- 1 serving contains 105 mg of sodium

Omit salt and prepared mustard; use 1/2 teaspoon (2 grams) of salt substitute and 1/8 teaspoon (.4 gram) dry mustard. Cook brown rice in unsalted water. Use salt-free cheese. Do not use egg substitute.

# Cheese and Mushroom Pie

- Makes 6 servings
- 1 serving contains 262 Calories (P16, F14, C18), 115 mg of cholesterol
- 1 serving = 2 ounces of meat + 1 slice of bread + 1-1/2 teaspoons of fat + 1 vegetable serving (2 lean meat exchanges + 1 bread exchange + 1-1/2 fat exchanges + 1 vegetable exchange)

**Eggs**   2 large separated (114 grams); or 2 ounces (60 mL) of liquid egg substitute + 2 egg whites (66 grams)
**Whole-wheat flour**   1 cup (137 grams), unsifted
**Salt**   1/2 teaspoon (3 grams)
**Pepper**   1/8 teaspoon (.5 gram)
**Skim milk**   1-1/2 cups (360 mL)
**Water**   1/4 cup (60 mL)
**Sharp cheddar cheese**   1-1/2 cups (166.5 grams), grated
**Mushrooms**   1 cup (86 grams), chopped
**Oil**   1 tablespoon (15 mL); use corn, soybean or safflower oil
**Onion**   1 tablespoon (10 grams), grated
**Parmesan cheese**   1/4 cup (26.5 grams), grated, for topping

Separate eggs; beat yolks well. Stir in flour and seasonings, alternating with milk/water and beating after each addition. Sauté the mushrooms in oil for 2 minutes. Cool slightly. Add cheddar cheese, onion and add to flour/egg mixture, mixing well. Fold in stiffly beaten egg whites. Pour into a greased 9-inch (22.5 cm) pie plate. Sprinkle Parmesan cheese on top and bake at 425°F (218°C) for 30 to 35 minutes until well-browned. Cut into six wedges and serve.

*Natural sweetening directions:*
- Not needed.

*For low-salt diet:*
- 1 serving contains 187 mg of sodium
Omit salt; use salt substitute. Use fresh eggs, not egg substitute.

# Italian-Style Baked Beans

- Makes 6 cups (1.4 L). This recipe doubles easily.
- 1 cup (240 mL) contains 196 Calories (P14, F8, C17), 2 mg of cholesterol per cup with cheese
- 1 serving = 2 ounces of meat + 1 slice of bread + 1/2 teaspoon of fat (2 lean meat exchanges + 1 bread exchange + 1/2 fat exchange)

**Soybeans**   1 cup (210 grams), soaked overnight
**Onion**   1/2 cup (80 grams), chopped
**Celery**   1/4 cup (30 grams), chopped
**Green pepper**   1/4 cup (37.5 grams), chopped
**Garlic**   1/2 large clove (1.5 grams)
**Oil**   1-1/2 teaspoons (7.5 mL); use corn oil or soybean oil.
**Parsley**   1 tablespoon (5 grams), minced
**Canned tomatoes**   2 cups (476 mL), chopped, with juice
**Mushrooms**   1 cup (86 grams), sliced
**Salt**   1/2 teaspoon (3 grams)
**Pepper**   1/8 teaspoon (.5 gram)
**Sweet basil**   1/4 teaspoon (.8 gram)
**Thyme**   1/16 to 1/8 teaspoon (.2 to .4 gram) ground
**Oregano**   1/8 teaspoon (.4 gram) ground
**Boiling water**   to cover

*Optional:*
**Dry white wine**   1/4 cup (60 mL)
**Parmesan cheese**   1/8 cup (13 grams) for topping

Drain soaked soybeans. Add fresh water and cook, covered, about 2-1/2 hours, until tender. Drain and discard liquid. Sauté garlic and onion in oil until lightly browned. Combine all ingredients in a bean pot or large casserole; cover with boiling water. Bake, covered, at 300°F (149°C) for 8 hours, adding water as needed to keep beans covered. Cook beans longer if you want them more tender — they will not get too soft. Sprinkle with Parmesan cheese as you serve the beans. **Note:** You may use pinto beans in recipe, with no change in directions. 1 cup contains 90 Calories (P9, F2, C9), 2 mg cholesterol with cheese. 1 serving = 1 ounce of meat + 1/2 slice of bread (1 lean meat exchange + 1/2 bread exchange).

*Natural sweetening directions:*
- Not needed.

*For low-salt diet:*
- 1 cup contains 18 mg of sodium
Omit salt; use equal amount of salt substitute. Use salt-free canned tomatoes, or fresh. Omit Parmesan cheese.

117

# Mushroom-Vegetable Pie

- Makes 3 large servings, 6 pieces
- 1 serving (1/3 recipe) contains 206 Calories (P15, F10, C14), 180 mg of cholesterol; or 6 mg of cholesterol if made with egg substitute and skim milk cheese
- 1 serving = 2 ounces of meat + 1 slice of bread + 1/2 teaspoon of fat (2 lean meat exchanges + 1 bread exchange + 1/2 fat exchange)

**Mushrooms**   3/4 cup (64.5 grams), sliced
**Zucchini**   1 cup (150 grams), chopped fine
**Tomato**   1/2 cup (95 grams), chopped fine
**Onion**   1/4 cup (40 grams), chopped fine
**Swiss cheese**   1-1/2 cups (166.5 grams), coarsely grated. Use skim milk cheese for low-cholesterol diet.
**Skim milk**   1/2 cup (120 mL)
**Eggs**   2 large (114 grams); or 4 ounces (120 mL) liquid egg substitute
**Whole-wheat flour**   1/3 cup (45.7 grams)
**Baking powder**   1-1/2 teaspoons (6 grams)
**Shortening**   1-1/2 tablespoons (21 grams), at room temperature
**Salt**   1/2 teaspoon (3 grams)
**Pepper**   1/8 teaspoon (.5 gram)
**Sweet basil**   1/3 teaspoon (1 gram), dried
**Italian Herb Mix**   for topping

Grease or spray a 9-inch (22.5 cm) pie plate. Mix together onion, zucchini, and tomato and spread over bottom of plate. Cover with chopped mushrooms, then grated cheese. Place remaining ingredients in a blender and run for 1 minute. Pour over vegetable/mushrooms in the pie plate. Sprinkle Italian Herb Mix on top. Bake at 400°F (204°C) for 30 minutes, or until a silver knife comes out clean when inserted in the middle of the pie. Let stand 5 minutes before serving. Cut into 6 pieces; serving 2 for each person.

### Natural sweetening directions:
- Not needed.

### For low-salt diet:
- 1 serving contains 107 mg sodium

Omit salt and baking powder; use equal amounts of salt substitute and low-salt baking powder. Use salt-free cheese. Increase amount of sweet basil to 1/2 teaspoon (1.5 grams).

# Double Cheese Macaroni

- Makes 6 cups (1.4 L)
- 1 cup (240 mL) contains 206 Calories (P15, F10, C14), 29 mg of cholesterol
- 1 cup = 2 ounces of meat + 1 slice of bread + 1/2 teaspoon of fat (2 meat exchanges + 1 bread exchange + 1/2 fat exchange)

**Whole-wheat macaroni**   about 5 ounces (138.5 grams)
**Onion**   1/4 cup (40 grams), diced
**Green pepper**   1/4 cup (37.5 grams), diced
**Celery**   1/4 cup (30 grams), diced
**Oil**   1 tablespoon (15 mL); use corn oil or soybean oil.
**Mushrooms**   1-1/2 cups (129 grams), sliced
**Small-curd cottage cheese**   1 cup (235 grams), drained
**Sharp cheddar cheese**   1 cup (111 grams), grated
**Margarine**   1/2 tablespoon (7 grams)
**Whole-wheat flour**   1 tablespoon (9 grams)
**Skim milk**   3/4 cup (180 mL)
**Salt**   1/2 teaspoon (3 grams)
**Pepper**   2 sprinkles

*Optional:*
**Imitation bacon bits**   1-1/2 tablespoons (18 grams), for topping

Cook macaroni in boiling water for 10 minutes; drain. Sauté vegetables in oil until limp. Place margarine in a pan, melt; stir in flour. Gradually add milk, stirring to prevent lumps. Add salt and pepper and cook for 2 minutes. Stir in both cheeses; heat 2 to 3 minutes until melted. Combine all ingredients except bacon bits. Place in a greased 2-quart (2-liter) casserole. Crush bacon bits with a rolling pin and sprinkle on top. Bake at 350°F (177°C) for 30 minutes.

***Natural sweetening directions:***
- Not needed.

***For low-salt diet:***
*This recipe cannot be made low in salt due to the cottage cheese and sharp cheddar cheese.*

# Baked Seafood Pie

- Makes 6 wedges, 3 servings of 2 wedges each
- 2 wedges contain 235 Calories (P14, F11, C20), 73 mg of cholesterol
- 2 wedges = 2 ounces of meat + 1 slice of bread + 1 teaspoon of fat + 1 vegetable
  serving (2 lean meat exchanges + 1 bread exchange + 1 fat exchange +
  1 vegetable exchange)

**Cooked white fish**   3/4 cup (127.5 grams), flaked. Use snapper or sole, etc.
**Mushrooms**   1 cup (86 grams), sliced
**Margarine**   1-1/2 tablespoons (21 grams), plus 2 tablespoons (28 grams); use
   corn-oil, soybean-oil or safflower-oil margarine
**Evaporated skim milk**   1-1/2 cups (360 mL)
**Eggs**   2 large (114 grams), well-beaten; or 1 egg (57 grams) plus 2 ounces (60 mL)
   of liquid egg substitute
**Whole-wheat flour**   2 tablespoons (18 grams)
**Salt**   1/2 teaspoon (3 grams)
**Pepper**   1/8 teaspoon (.5 gram)
**Onion**   1 tablespoon (10 grams)
**Garlic clove**   1/2 large (1.5 grams), minced
**Whole-wheat bread**   4 slices (112 grams), plus 1/4 cup (11.3 grams) bread crumbs
**Lemon-pepper mix**   for topping

Grease a 9-inch (22.5 cm) pie plate. Spread the 2 tablespoons (28 grams) of margarine on the bread; cut the bread in strips and fit it into the pie plate to make a crust; use the bread crumbs to fill in any spaces left between the strips. Bake at 400°F (204°C) for 15 minutes. Let cool and prepare the filling. Sauté mushrooms in remaining margarine for 5 minutes. Set aside. Make a paste with the flour and milk; add the beaten eggs and seasonings. Stir in mushrooms and flaked fish; pour into the pie shell. Sprinkle lemon-pepper mix on top and bake at 450°F (232°C) for 20 to 25 minutes, until filling is cooked; a silver knife blade will come out clean when filling is done.

### Natural sweetening directions:
- Not needed.

### For low-salt diet:
*Do not eat on a 400-mg or 1-gram sodium diet.*
- 2 wedges contain 243 mg of sodium

Omit salt; replace with salt substitute. Omit lemon-pepper mix; use Salt-Free Herb Mix (see recipe, page 240). Use eggs, not liquid egg substitute. Use salt-free bread, bread crumbs and margarine.

# Vegetarian Cheese Strata

- Makes 5 servings
- 1 serving contains 297 Calories (P23, F13, C22), 39 mg of cholesterol if made with egg substitute and low-fat cottage cheese
- 1 serving = 3 ounces of lean meat + 1 slice of bread + 1 teaspoon of fat (3 lean meat exchanges + 1 bread exchange + 1 fat exchange)

**Margarine**   2 tablespoons (28 grams); use corn-oil, soybean-oil or safflower-oil margarine
**Whole-wheat bread**   5 slices (140 grams), toasted
**Sharp cheddar cheese**   1-1/2 cups (166 grams), grated
**Tomato**   1 medium (150 grams), chopped
**Onion**   1 small (120 grams), chopped
**Green pepper**   1/2 cup (75 grams), chopped
**Broccoli**   1 cup (155 grams), chopped. You can use frozen broccoli.
**Eggs**   3 large (171 grams), or 4 medium (200 grams), beaten; or use 6 ounces (180 mL) egg substitute
**Skim milk**   2 cups (480 mL)
**Low-fat, small-curd cottage cheese**   1/2 cup (117.5 grams)
**Prepared mustard**   1/4 teaspoon (1.3 mL)
**Salt**   1/2 teaspoon (3 grams)
**Pepper**   1/16 teaspoon (.3 gram)

Grease an 8-inch (20 cm) square baking dish with small amount of margarine. Spread the remaining margarine on the bread slices. Line baking dish with 3 slices of bread. Cut remaining slices into cubes and set aside. Sprinkle half of the grated cheese over the bread in the bottom of the dish. Combine all the remaining ingredients, including the cubed bread; allow to stand a few minutes to soften the bread. Pour over cheese in casserole; let stand for at least 30 minutes so bread will soak up all the liquid. Bake at 350°F (177°C) for 50 minutes until nicely browned. Serve at once.

*Natural sweetening directions:*
- Not needed.

*For low-salt diet:*
*This recipe cannot be made low in salt due to the high sodium content in the eggs, cheese, milk and cottage cheese.*

# Vegetable Protein

## How to Use Vegetable Protein Products

Soy protein is available in three general forms: soybeans (whole and broken into grits), soy granules and spun soy products that imitate various meat forms. The latter two are called textured vegetable protein (TVP) and are available in a dehydrated form in grocery stores. Freeze-dried and frozen TVP are also now available on the wholesale and retail markets.

These imitation meat products are made by a complicated process. First the soybean is separated into soy flour and soybean oil. The flour is then spun (extruded) into protein fibers or woven into a meatlike product. This is then fortified with natural nutrients similar to the product it is imitating, and finally it is given a meatlike flavor — beef, chicken, ham or tuna. Many of these textured vegetable protein products are used in the prepared foods you buy in the grocery store. For example, imitation bacon pieces have been treated to look, taste and even smell like bacon.

The soy granules may be added to any mixed dish, such as meat loaf, fish loaf, meat or fish patties and meat sauces. They are used to stretch the meat or fish with which they are used. You can substitute soy protein for up to half of the protein and still have an acceptable product if you use seasonings and flavorings in the right amounts.

The imitation protein products (spun protein derivatives) can be used in part or alone to replace the meat, fish or poultry they copy. When used alone, 1/3 cup (85 grams) reconstituted substitutes for each 1 ounce (28.5 grams) of meat in the recipe.

## How to Reconstitute Protein Granules

For 1-1/2 ounces of granules (3 ounces, 90 mL volume in a measuring cup), add 5 ounces (150 mL) of boiling water, mix well

and allow to stand for at least 20 minutes. You may want to add a few drops of red food coloring to match the color of the meat to which you plan to add the granules. Allow to cool. Mix with 1/2 pound (227 grams) of meat for a final volume of 3/4 pound (340.5 grams). Form into loaf or patties, or add to sauce as recipes require.

## How to Reconstitute Spun Protein Products

Place 1-1/2 ounces (3 ounces, 90 mL volume in a measuring cup) in a large pan. Add 1 quart (960 mL) of water and 1/2 teaspoon of salt (3 grams) or salt substitute (2 grams). Bring to a boil and cook for 7 to 8 minutes, until tender. Drain and cool. This amount will make 1 cup of meat substitute.

**Note:** Once they are cooked, treat these products just as you would fresh meat. Refrigerate if you are not going to use them immediately.

Be sure to season these products adequately. Onion, green pepper, spices and herbs will help disguise the substitution. The spun soy derivatives need fewer additions than the plain granules.

---

Note the difference in food values in the following comparison of reconstituted soy protein and Hamburger Helper:

Reconstituted soy protein, either type
- 1/3 cup contains 50 Calories (P7, F0, C4.5), no cholesterol
- 1/3 cup + 1 teaspoon of fat = 1 ounce of meat + 1/3 slice of bread
    (1 meat exchange + 1/3 bread exchange)

Hamburger Helper, made with meat according to package directions
- 1 cup contains 238 Calories (P16, F6, C30), 30 grams of carbohydrate,
    approximately 25 mg of cholesterol
- 1 cup = 2 ounces of meat + 2 slices of bread (2 lean meat exchanges +
    2 bread exchanges)

---

# Imitation Goulash

- Makes 2 servings
- 1 serving contains 226 Calories (P19, F2, C33), 8 mg of cholesterol
- 1 serving = 2 ounces of meat + 2 slices of bread (2 lean meat exchanges + 2 bread exchanges)

**Beef-flavor TVP**    1-1/2 ounces (90 mL)
**Whole-wheat macaroni**    1-1/2 ounces (42.3 grams)
**Salt**    1 teaspoon (6 grams)
**Water**    1 quart (960 mL)
**Onion**    1/4 cup (40 grams), diced
**Green pepper**    1-1/2 tablespoons (13.5 grams)
**Tomatoes**    1-1/2 cups (360 mL), canned and chopped
**Pepper**    1/16 teaspoon (.3 gram)
**Sweet basil or oregano**    1/8 to 1/4 teaspoon (.4 to .8 gram), dried
**Low-fat cheese**    1 ounce (28.5 grams); 5% butterfat or less

Place soy TVP, macaroni, half of salt and
the water in large pot; bring to boil and
cook 7 minutes; drain. Combine onion
and green pepper with tomatoes; add
seasonings. Mix drained beef substitute,
vegetables and seasonings. Place in
casserole or baking dish that has been
sprayed with a nonstick coating or lightly
oiled. Chop or grate cheese; sprinkle over
top of mixture. Bake at 350°F (177°C) for
50 minutes; serve immediately.

***Natural sweetening directions:***
- Not needed.

***For low-salt diet:***
*Due to the sodium added in processing soy TVP, it should not be used on a sodium-restricted diet.*

# Soy and Beef Hamburgers

- Makes 6 patties
- 1 patty contains 95 Calories (P14, F5, C4.5), 15 mg of cholesterol
- 1 patty = 2 ounces of meat + 1/3 slice of bread (2 lean meat exchanges +
  1/3 bread exchange)

**Dry soy granules**   1-1/2 ounces (90 mL); 3 ounces measured in cup
**Boiling water**   5 ounces (150 mL)
**Red food coloring**   3 to 4 drops; or use liquid from cooked beets in place of boiling
water and omit food coloring
**Onion**   1 to 2 tablespoons (10 to 20 grams), diced
**Lean ground beef**   1/2 pound (227 grams)
**Salt**   1/2 teaspoon (3 grams), or to taste
**Pepper**   to taste

Place soy granules in mixing bowl; mix boiling water and food coloring; add to soy and allow to stand at least 20 minutes. Mix granules well so the coloring is even throughout. Add onion to ground beef; add cooled granules and seasonings to beef/onion mixture; work with hands until evenly blended (you should not be able to detect the granules).

Mold into 6 patties; place on wax paper and refrigerate or freeze until ready to cook. Cook as you normally do meat patties, turning to be sure both sides are equally done; serve immediately. For meatballs or meat loaf: Use same directions, making 2 balls per patty. Add usual other ingredients to meat loaf. Bake or cook as you would all meat items.

*Natural sweetening directions:*
- Not needed.

*For low-salt diet:*
*Due to the sodium added in processing soy granules, they should not be used on a sodium-restricted diet.*

# Imitation Ham Omelette

- Makes 1 serving
- 1 serving contains 228 Calories (P21, F14, C4.5), no cholesterol
- 1 serving = 3 ounces of meat + 1/3 slice of bread + 1 teaspoon of fat (3 lean meat exchanges + 1/3 bread exchange + 1 fat exchange)

**Skim milk**   1 tablespoon (15 mL)
**Liquid egg substitute**   4 ounces (120 mL)
**Onion**   1 teaspoon (3.3 grams), diced
**Green pepper**   1 teaspoon (3 grams), diced
**Ham-flavored TVP**   1/3 cup (85 grams), reconstituted
**Salt**   1/4 teaspoon (1.5 grams)
**Pepper**   sprinkle
**Oil**   1 teaspoon (5 mL); use corn, soybean or safflower oil

Add skim milk to egg substitute; mix well. Add vegetables with ham substitute to egg mixture. Season with salt and pepper as you would for normal omelette (use more if you wish). Place oil in heavy iron skillet or nonstick pan; use a brush or your fingers to spread it around the pan; heat pan until the oil is hot but not smoking. (Never cook at a heat level that causes fat to smoke.) Add egg mixture and cook, turning edges to form omelette and cooking all sides. Serve immediately.

***Natural sweetening directions:***
- Not needed.

***For low-salt diet:***
*Due to the sodium added in processing TVP, it should not be used on a sodium-restricted diet.*

# Carrots Viennese

- Makes 3 servings
- 1 serving contains 59 Calories (P1, F3, C7), no cholesterol
- 1 serving = 1 vegetable serving + 1/2 teaspoon of fat (1 vegetable exchange + 1/2 fat exchange)

**Carrots**   1-1/3 cups (169 grams), peeled and sliced 1/4-inch thick
**Margarine**   2 teaspoons (9.3 grams); use corn-oil, soybean-oil or safflower-oil margarine
**Lemon juice**   1 tablespoon (15 mL)
**Granular sugar substitute**   1-1/2 teaspoons (3 grams); or substitute equal to 1 tablespoon (12.2 grams) of sugar
**Parsley**   1/4 teaspoon (.5 gram), chopped

Cook carrots in lightly salted water until tender. Drain off all but about 2 tablespoons (30 mL) of liquid (save for soup). Add margarine, lemon juice, sugar substitute and parsley. Heat on low, stirring gently to mix ingredients well. Do not overcook.

*Suggestions:*
This can be prepared ahead of time and reheated in a covered casserole.

*Natural sweetening directions:*
- 1 serving contains 87 Calories (P1, F3, C14), no change in cholesterol
- 1 serving = 1 slice of bread + 1/2 teaspoon of fat (1 bread exchange + 1/2 fat exchange)
Omit sugar substitute. Add 2 tablespoons (30 mL) concentrated apple juice plus 1 teaspoon (5 mL) lemon juice. Follow directions as given.

*For low-salt diet:*
*Do not use on a low-sodium diet because of the natural salt in carrots.*
- 1 serving contains 62 mg of sodium
Use fresh carrots only; cook carrots in unsalted water. Use salt-free margarine.

# Don's Favorite Lancastershire Vegetable

- Makes 4 servings
- 1 serving contains 50 Calories (P1, F2, C7), no cholesterol
- 1 serving = 1 vegetable serving + 1/2 teaspoon of fat (1 vegetable exchange + 1/2 fat exchange)

**Carrots**   1 cup (127 grams), peeled and sliced
**Rutabagas**   1 cup (139 grams), peeled and diced
**Margarine**   2 teaspoons (9.3 grams); use corn-oil, soybean-oil or safflower-oil margarine
**Salt**   1/4 teaspoon (1.5 grams)
**Pepper**   1/16 teaspoon (.3 gram)

Put carrots in saucepan; add enough water — about 1/2 cup (120 mL) — to prevent burning; cover and cook until tender. Cook rutabagas the same way. Drain both vegetables; discard liquids or save for soup. Combine vegetables; mash thoroughly with potato masher. Blend in margarine, salt and pepper; taste; add seasonings if desired. Serve immediately.

**Suggestions:**
This can be made early and kept covered in the oven for 20 to 30 minutes without changing flavor.

**Natural sweetening directions:**
- Not needed.

**For low-salt diet:**
- 1 serving contains 17 mg of sodium

Omit salt; use 1/4 teaspoon (1 gram) of salt substitute plus 1 teaspoon (5 mL) of lemon juice.

# Harvard Beets

- Makes 2 servings
- 1 serving contains 93 Calories (P1, F5, C11), no cholesterol
- 1 serving = 1 vegetable serving + 1 teaspoon of fat (1 vegetable exchange + 1 fat exchange)

**Beets**   1 cup (176 grams), canned, sliced and drained (save liquid)
**Liquid from beets**   plus enough water to equal 1/2 cup (120 mL)
**Granular sugar substitute**   1 tablespoon (6 grams); or substitute equal to 2 tablespoons (24.4 grams) of sugar
**Cornstarch**   1/2 tablespoon (4 grams)
**Salt**   1/8 teaspoon (.8 gram)
**Margarine**   2 teaspoons (9.3 grams); use corn-oil, soybean-oil or safflower-oil margarine
**Cloves**   4 (1 gram)
**Cider vinegar**   1-1/2 tablespoons (22.5 mL)

Combine all ingredients except beets. Cook in double boiler over low heat, stirring frequently to prevent lumps, until liquid turns somewhat clear and thick. Add beets; stir gently to coat all slices. Keep warm over hot water at least 15 minutes before serving to allow flavors to penetrate beets.

**Suggestions:**
This recipe can be served cold as an appetizer. Drain off most of the liquid before serving. Tiny whole beets can be used as a finger food.

*Natural sweetening directions:*
- 1 serving contains 113 Calories (P1, F5, C16), no cholesterol, no change in sodium
- 1 serving = 1 slice of bread + 1 teaspoon of fat (1 bread exchange + 1 fat exchange)
Omit sugar substitute; use 2-1/2 tablespoons (37.5 mL) concentrated apple juice plus 1 teaspoon (5 mL) lemon juice. Increase cornstarch to 3/4 tablespoon (6 grams). Follow directions as given.

*For low-salt diet:*
*This recipe cannot be made low in salt because of the high natural sodium in beets.*

# Quick Scalloped Potatoes

- Makes 3 servings
- 1 serving contains 103 Calories (P3, F3, C16), 1 mg of cholesterol
- 1 serving = 1 slice of bread + 1/2 teaspoon of fat (1 bread exchange + 1/2 fat exchange)

**Potatoes**   2 small (240 grams)
**Onion**   1/4 small (30 grams)
**Margarine**   2 teaspoons (9.3 grams); use corn-oil, soybean-oil or safflower-oil margarine
**Skim milk**   1/2 cup (120 mL)
**Butter flavoring**   4 drops
**Salt**   1/3 teaspoon (2 grams)
**Pepper**   1/8 teaspoon (.5 gram)
**Unbleached flour**   1 scant tablespoon (7 grams) plus 1/4 cup (60 mL) cold water

Pare and slice potatoes and onion thin. Cover with boiling water and let stand about 5 minutes. Melt margarine in milk. Add flour to water to make a paste, stir into milk mixture. Add flavoring and seasonings; stir and cook about 1 minute, until slightly thickened. Drain potatoes and onions (save the water for the soup pot!); pour sauce over potatoes and onions, tossing to coat well. Place in a nonstick or lightly oiled baking dish and bake at 400°F (204°C) for 30 minutes, or until potatoes are fork-tender.

*Suggestions:*
If diet permits, sprinkle potatoes lightly with grated cheese before baking. If you use about 1 tablespoon (7 grams) of cheese, you won't have to count its food value. For variety, add 1 tablespoon (12 grams) of imitation bacon bits to potato slices just before adding the sauce. This will make a surprising change in looks and flavor, but not in food value.

*Natural sweetening directions:*
- Not needed.

*For low-salt diet:*
- 1 serving contains 29 mg of sodium
Omit salt; use 1/3 teaspoon (1.3 grams) of salt substitute. Cook potatoes and onion in unsalted water. Use salt-free margarine. Do not add grated cheese or imitation bacon bits.

# Mexican Tomatoes with Celery

- Makes 5 servings
- 1 serving contains 40 Calories (P2, F0, C8), no cholesterol
- 1 serving = 1/2 slice of bread *or* 1 vegetable serving (1/2 bread exchange *or* 1 vegetable exchange)

**Canned tomatoes**   2 cups (476 grams)
**Celery**   1 cup (121 grams), diced medium-sized
**Green pepper**   1/3 cup (50 grams), diced
**Onion**   1/4 cup (40 grams), diced
**Salt**   1/4 teaspoon (1.5 grams)
**Tabasco**   4 to 6 drops
**Granular sugar substitute**   1/2 teaspoon (1 gram); or substitute equal to 1 teaspoon (4 grams) of sugar

*Optional:*
**Cayenne pepper**   1/8 teaspoon (.5 gram)

Drain juice from tomatoes. Add to celery, green pepper and onions. Simmer in covered pan until vegetables are tender; add water if needed. Combine vegetables with tomato solids; add salt, Tabasco, sugar substitute and cayenne. Heat through to blend flavors. Serve immediately.

**Suggestions:**
This can be simmered until thick, then used on scrambled eggs for a tasty luncheon dish.

### Natural sweetening directions:
- 1 serving contains 44 Calories (P2, F0, C9), no cholesterol
- 1 serving = 1/2 slice of bread (1/2 bread exchange)
Omit sugar substitute; add 1 tablespoon (15 mL) concentrated apple juice plus 1/4 teaspoon (1.3 mL) lemon juice. Follow directions as given.

### For low-salt diet:
*This recipe cannot be made low in salt because of the high natural salt in celery.*

# Pennsylvania Dutch Green Beans

- Makes 4 servings
- 1 serving contains 59 Calories (P2, F3, C6), no cholesterol
- 1 serving = 1 vegetable serving + 1/2 teaspoon of fat (1 vegetable exchange + 1/2 fat exchange)

**Frozen green beans**   10-ounce package (285 grams), French-cut
**Onion**   2 tablespoons (20 grams), diced
**Oil**   2 teaspoons (10 mL); use corn, soybean or safflower oil
**White vinegar**   1 tablespoon (15 mL)
**Granular sugar substitute**   1-1/2 teaspoons (3 grams); or substitute equal to
    1 tablespoon (12.2 grams) of sugar
**Salt**   1/4 teaspoon (1.5 grams)
**Imitation bacon bits**   1 teaspoon (4 grams)

Steam green beans with a minimum amount of water until almost tender. Drain, but leave about 3 tablespoons (45 mL) of liquid. Sauté onion in oil until slightly brown; cool a little. Add vinegar, sugar substitute, salt and bacon bits. Add mixture to green beans; toss to mix well. Reheat to serving temperature in tightly covered pan. Time your cooking schedule so beans are still hot when the onion-seasoning mixture is added. Reheating can then be avoided and vegetables kept crisp.

**Suggestions:**
If you plan to reheat this dish, save a little cooking liquid from the beans to add then. Do not cook long enough so that the beans lose their crispness.

### Natural sweetening directions:
- 1 serving contains 67 Calories (P2, F3, C8), no change in cholesterol or sodium
- 1 serving = 1/2 slice of bread *or* 1 vegetable serving + 1/2 teaspoon of fat (1/2 bread exchange *or* 1 vegetable exchange + 1/2 fat exchange)

Omit sugar substitute; add 2 tablespoons (30 mL) of concentrated apple juice plus 1 teaspoon (5 mL) lemon juice. Follow directions as given.

### For low-salt diet:
- 1 serving contains 4 mg of sodium

Omit salt; use 1/3 teaspoon (1.3 grams) of salt substitute. Omit imitation bacon bits, as they are very high in salt. Use diet-pack green beans, or fresh beans cooked (not overcooked) in unsalted water.

# Rice Curry/Rice Pilaf

- Makes 6 servings
- 1 serving contains 103 Calories (P2, F3, C17), no cholesterol
- 1 serving = 1 slice of bread + 1/2 teaspoon of fat (1 bread exchange + 1/2 fat exchange)

**Rice**   2/3 cup (132 grams), uncooked
**Margarine**   4 teaspoons (18.7 grams); use corn-oil, soybean-oil or safflower-oil margarine
**Hot water**   2 cups (480 mL)
**Chicken bouillon**   1 cube (4 grams)
**Salt**   1/4 teaspoon (1.5 grams)
**Mild curry powder**   2/3 teaspoon (2 grams)

*Optional:*
**Mushrooms**   1/2 cup (43 grams), uncooked

Stir and brown rice in margarine. Add water, bouillon cube and seasonings. Cover and cook over low heat about 20 minutes, until all liquid is absorbed and rice is done. Add mushrooms; reheat.

*Suggestions:*
If you like a stronger curry flavor, use more, or use a stronger curry. If you omit the curry powder, you have rice pilaf.

*Natural sweetening directions:*
- Not needed.

*For low-salt diet:*
- 1 serving contains 3 mg of sodium
Omit salt; use 1/2 teaspoon (2 grams) of salt substitute. Instead of bouillon cube and water, use 2 cups (480 mL) of fat-free chicken broth, homemade without salt (see recipe on page 45). Add 1 tablespoon (15 mL) lemon juice to broth. Use fresh mushrooms; slice and steam them without salt. Use salt-free margarine.

# Spanish Baked Eggplant

- Makes 6 to 8 servings
- 1/6 recipe contains 40 Calories (P2, F0, C8), no cholesterol
- 1/6 recipe = 1/2 slice of bread *or* 1 vegetable serving (1/2 bread exchange *or* 1 vegetable exchange)

**Whole stewed tomatoes**   #303 can (454 grams), with onion and green pepper; or use 1 can (454 grams) whole tomatoes, 1/4 cup (37.5 grams) diced green pepper + 1/4 cup (40 grams) diced onion + 1/4 teaspoon (1.5 grams) of salt
**Chili powder**   1/2 teaspoon (1.5 grams) or more, to taste
**Cumin**   small pinch
**Butter flavoring**   6 drops
**Eggplant**   1 medium, about 1 pound (454 grams)
**Whole-wheat toast**   1/2 slice (14 grams), crumbled

If not using canned tomatoes stewed with pepper and onion, combine pepper, onion and salt with whole tomatoes; add 1/4 cup (60 mL) water; simmer until raw vegetables are tender. Add chili powder, cumin and butter flavoring to tomatoes. Wash eggplant; peel if you want to and slice as for frying. Cover with boiling water and cook for 5 minutes; drain well. Place eggplant slices in a greased casserole; pour hot tomato mixture over slices and top with bread crumbs. Bake at 375 °F (191 °C) about 1-1/4 hours, until eggplant is tender.

*Suggestions:*
Use zucchini or yellow summer squash for this recipe if you prefer; food values remain the same. This dish can be reheated, but vegetables will get mushy if overcooked.

*Natural sweetening directions:*
- Not needed.

*For low-salt diet:*
- 1/6 recipe contains 15 mg of sodium
Omit salt; use 1/2 teaspoon (2 grams) of salt substitute. Use fresh or diet-pack tomatoes. If fresh, dip in boiling water for about 30 seconds to make them easier to peel; chop. Use 1-1/2 to 2 cups (360 to 480 mL) of tomatoes, including liquid. Use salt-free bread or 2 salt-free crackers for the crumb topping.

# Stuffed Bell Peppers

- Makes 4 servings
- 1 serving contains 114 Calories (P5, F2, C19), no cholesterol
- 1 serving = 1 slice of bread + 1/2 ounce of meat + 1/2 vegetable serving (1 bread exchange + 1/2 meat exchange + 1/2 vegetable exchange)

**Green peppers**   4 medium (520 grams)
**Poultry stuffing**   1/2 recipe, page 102
**Mushroom pieces**   1 cup (86 grams), cooked and drained

Core and seed green peppers; blanch in boiling water about 5 minutes; drain and cool. Prepare poultry stuffing without bacon bits; mix in mushrooms. Stuff peppers full; put in a greased baking pan. Bake at 350°F (177°C) about 20 minutes until top of dressing is brown and peppers are soft.

**Suggestions:**
Serve in place of potato or rice as your starch. Omit the mushrooms and use ordinary poultry seasoning, with or without bacon bits.

**Natural sweetening directions:**
- Not needed.

**For low-salt diet:**
- 1 serving contains 31 mg of sodium

Make poultry stuffing by low-salt directions. Use fresh mushrooms; sauté without salt in a nonstick pan; cover and cook slowly until tender.

# Mixed Vegetables with Green Grapes

- Makes 3 servings
- 1 serving contains 75 Calories (P2, F3, C6), 1 mg of cholesterol
- 1 serving = 1 vegetable serving + 1/2 teaspoon of fat (1 vegetable exchange + 1/2 fat exchange)

**Zucchini**   1 cup (130 grams), sliced 1/3-inch thick
**Cauliflower**   1 cup (83 grams), flowerettes sliced 1/3-inch thick
**Boiling water**   1/2 cup (120 mL)
**Salt**   1/4 teaspoon (1.5 grams)
**Margarine**   1-1/2 teaspoons (7.1 grams); use corn-oil, soybean-oil or safflower-oil margarine
**Green grapes**   1/4 cup (42.8 grams), halved
**Pimento**   1 tablespoon (13 grams), chopped fine
**Bacon bits**   1-1/2 tablespoons (18 grams)
**Pepper**   2 sprinkles

Place prepared vegetables in a saucepan with water and salt. Cook about 7 minutes, until just tender. Remove from heat and drain. Add margarine, bacon bits and pimento; stir to mix. Add grapes; sprinkle with pepper and serve.

*Natural sweetening directions:*
- Not needed.

*For low-salt diet:*
- 1 serving contains 20 mg of sodium

Omit salt, bacon bits and pimento. Use salt-free margarine. Add 1/8 teaspoon (.4 gram) onion powder when adding margarine.

# Zucchini Casserole

- Makes 6 servings
- 1 serving contains 48 Calories (P2, F0, C10), no cholesterol
- 1 serving = 1/2 slice of bread *or* 1 vegetable serving (1/2 bread exchange *or* 1 vegetable exchange)

**Zucchini**   2 cups (260 grams), sliced medium thick
**Canned tomatoes**   2 cups (476 grams), drained
**Onion**   1 tablespoon (10 grams), diced
**Pepper**   1/16 teaspoon (.3 gram)
**Tabasco**   2 to 4 drops
**Sauerkraut**   1 cup (142 grams)
**Whole-wheat toast**   1 slice (28 grams), cubed small

*Optional:*
**Green pepper**   1 tablespoon (9 grams), diced

Cover zucchini with water and boil 5 minutes; drain; place slices in lightly oiled baking dish. Combine tomatoes, onion, green pepper, pepper and Tabasco. Drain and wash sauerkraut; add to tomatoes and stir; pour over zucchini; or layer sauerkraut over zucchini, then pour on tomato mixture. Top with toast cubes. Bake at 350°F (177°C) about 1 hour and 10 minutes, until zucchini is soft.

**Natural sweetening directions:**
- Not needed.

**For low-salt diet:**
- 1 serving contains 5 mg of sodium

Use fresh or salt-free canned tomatoes. If fresh, dip for 30 seconds in boiling water to loosen skin; peel and chop. Omit sauerkraut; add 3 tablespoons (45 mL) of white vinegar (less if you prefer) to tomato mixture when you add onion and pepper. Add 1/2 teaspoon (2 grams) of salt substitute to tomato mixture. Use 5 salt-free crackers crumbled, or cube 1 slice of salt-free bread for topping.

# Chili

- Makes 4 servings
- 1 serving contains 103 Calories (P4, F3, C15), no cholesterol
- 1 serving = 1 slice of bread + 1/2 teaspoon of fat (1 bread exchange + 1/2 fat exchange)

**Pinto or red kidney beans**   3/4 cup (144 grams), uncooked
**Onion**   1/4 cup (40 grams), chopped
**Garlic**   1/2 clove (.5 gram), minced
**Oil**   1 tablespoon (15 mL); use corn, soybean or safflower oil
**Canned tomatoes**   2 cups (476 grams)
**Tomato liquid**   1 cup (240 mL)
**Oregano**   1/8 teaspoon (.4 gram)
**Cumin**   1/16 teaspoon (.2 gram)
**Bay leaf**   1/2 (.5 gram)
**Salt**   1/2 teaspoon (3 grams)
**Chili powder**   1 to 2 teaspoons (3 to 6 grams), to taste
**Granular sugar substitute**   1-1/2 teaspoons (3 grams); or substitute equal to 1 tablespoon (12.2 grams) of sugar

*Optional:*
**Tabasco**   1/8 teaspoon (.6 mL)
**Red food coloring**

Soak beans overnight in cold water. Simmer until soft, adding water to cover as needed. Sauté onion and garlic in oil. Add the tomatoes, tomato liquid, seasonings and sugar substitute. Combine with 2 cups (480 mL) of cooked and drained beans; simmer for at least 40 minutes to blend the flavors. If mixture cooks down too much, add hot water to thin; if mixture is too pale, add food coloring. Taste; add more salt and chili powder if desired. Serve very hot.

### Natural sweetening directions:
- 1/4 recipe contains 111 Calories (P4, F3, C17)
- 1/4 recipe = 1 slice of bread + 1/2 teaspoon of fat (1 bread exchange + 1/2 fat exchange)

Omit sugar substitute; add 2 tablespoons (30 mL) concentrated apple juice plus 1 teaspoon (5 mL) lemon juice. Follow directions as given.

### For low-salt diet:
- 1/5 recipe contains 5 mg of sodium

Omit salt; use 1/2 teaspoon (2 grams) of salt substitute. Cook beans in unsalted water. Use fresh or diet-pack salt-free tomatoes. Dip fresh tomatoes in boiling water for 30 seconds to loosen skins, peel and chop. Omit Tabasco; add 1/16 teaspoon (.4 gram) cayenne pepper if you want hot chili.

# Chili with Beef

- Makes 5 servings
- 1 serving contains 213 Calories (P20, F9, C13), 68 mg of cholesterol
- 1 serving = 3 ounces of meat + 1 slice of bread (3 lean meat exchanges + 1 bread exchange)

**Lean ground beef**   1 pound (454 grams)

Brown the beef until well cooked; drain on paper to remove fat. Add to beans with tomatoes, and follow directions as given for chili.

**Suggestions:**
This chili reheats well, but may taste too spicy with the bay leaf left in, so remove it after the first serving.

### Natural sweetening directions:
- 1/5 recipe contains 217 Calories (P20, F9, C14)
- 1/5 recipe = 3 ounces of meat + 1 slice of bread (3 lean meat exchanges + 1 bread exchange)

Omit sugar substitute; add 2 tablespoons (30 mL) concentrated apple juice plus 1 teaspoon (5 mL) lemon juice. Follow directions as given.

### For low-salt diet:
- 1/6 recipe contains 49 mg of sodium

Omit salt; use 1/2 teaspoon (2 grams) of salt substitute. Cook beans in unsalted water. Use fresh or diet-pack salt-free tomatoes. Dip fresh tomatoes in boiling water for 30 seconds to loosen skins, peel and chop. Omit Tabasco; add 1/16 teaspoon (.4 gram) cayenne pepper if you want hot chili.

# Cranberry Sauce

- Makes about 6 cups (1.4 L)
- 6 tablespoons (90 mL) contain 36 Calories (P0, F0, C9), no cholesterol
- 6 tablespoons = 1/2 cup of fruit (1 fruit exchange)
- You can use 2 tablespoons (30 mL) of this sauce without counting it in your diet!

**Plain gelatin**   1 tablespoon (7 grams)
**Water**   1-3/4 cups (420 mL)
**Raw cranberries**   4 cups (380 grams), washed and sorted
**Granular sugar substitute**   8 tablespoons (48 grams); or substitute equal to 1 cup (195 grams) of sugar
**Lemon juice**   2 tablespoons (30 mL)
**Liquid sweetener**   1/2 teaspoon (2.5 mL)
**Dietetic applesauce**   1/2 cup (128 grams), sweetened
**Salt**   2 sprinkles

Dissolve gelatin in 1/4 cup (60 mL) of water. Cook berries in 1-1/2 cups (360 mL) water until they are very soft; mash them with a potato masher to open all berries. Remove from heat; add gelatin mixture to hot berries and stir well to dissolve. Add all other ingredients and mix thoroughly. Pour into sterile jars, cover and refrigerate or freeze, or pour into canning jars, seal and process in hot water bath about 20 minutes.

**Suggestions:**
Pour into individual molds and serve on lettuce as a salad. This can be stored in the refrigerator up to 10 days.

**Natural sweetening directions:**
- 6 tablespoons (90 mL) contain 44 Calories (P0, F0, C11), no change in cholesterol or sodium
- 6 tablespoons = 1/2 cup of fruit (1 fruit exchange)
Omit liquid sweetener and sugar substitute. Reduce water to 3/4 cup (180 mL). Add 1 cup (240 mL) white grape juice plus 1-1/2 tablespoons (15 grams) of date sugar; increase lemon juice by 1-1/2 teaspoons (7.5 mL). Follow directions as given. *Note:* This will be tart.

**For low-salt diet:**
- 2 tablespoons (30 mL) contain 2 mg of sodium
Omit salt; use sprinkle of salt substitute.

140

# Mock Hollandaise Sauce

- Makes about 1 cup (240 mL)
- 1/3 cup (80 mL) contains 81 Calories (P2, F5, C7), 1 mg of cholesterol
- 1/3 cup = 1/2 slice of bread + 1 teaspoon of fat (1/2 bread exchange + 1 fat exchange)

---

**Water**   1/2 cup (120 mL)
**Lemon juice**   1 tablespoon (15 mL)
**Margarine**   1 tablespoon (14 grams); use corn-oil, soybean-oil or safflower-oil margarine
**Unbleached flour**   2 tablespoons (16 grams)
**Salt**   1/3 teaspoon (2 grams)
**Paprika**   1/8 teaspoon (.4 gram)
**Dry mustard**   1/4 teaspoon (.8 gram)
**Granular sugar substitute**   1-1/2 teaspoons (3 grams); or substitute equal to 1 tablespoon (12.2 grams) of sugar
**Butter flavoring**   8 drops
**Cumin or saffron**   sprinkle; or 4 drops yellow food coloring. Omit if butter flavoring is colored.
**Nutmeg**   sprinkle
**Plain yogurt**   1/2 cup (120 mL)

Combine first 8 ingredients; mix well. Cook over low heat until thickened, stirring often to prevent lumps or sticking. Remove from heat and add butter flavoring and food coloring, nutmeg and yogurt. Blend well. Serve on vegetables and steamed fish.

*Suggestions:*
To vary the thickness of this sauce, use more or less water. The food value of the total recipe will remain the same, so allow 1/3 of the total volume for 1 serving.

---

*Natural sweetening directions:*
- 1/3 (80 mL) cup contains 93 Calories (P2, F5, C10), no change in cholesterol or sodium
- 1/3 cup = 1 teaspoon of fat + 1/2 cup of fruit (1 fat exchange + 1 fruit exchange)
Omit sugar substitute. Reduce water to 1/4 cup (60 mL); add 1/4 cup (60 mL) apple juice and increase the amount of lemon juice by 1/2 teaspoon (2.5 mL). Follow directions as given.

*For low-salt diet:*
- 1/3 cup (80 mL) contains 40 mg of sodium
Omit salt; use 1/3 teaspoon (1.3 grams) of salt substitute. Use salt-free margarine.

# Cream Sauce

- Makes 1 cup (240 mL)
- 1/4 cup (60 mL) contains 50 Calories (P2, F2, C6), 2 mg of cholesterol
- 1/4 cup = 1/3 slice of bread + 1/2 teaspoon of fat (1/3 bread exchange + 1/2 fat exchange)

**Margarine**   2 teaspoons (9.3 grams); use corn-oil, soybean-oil or safflower-oil margarine
**Unbleached flour**   1-1/2 tablespoons (12 grams)
**Skim milk**   1 cup (240 mL)
**Salt**   1/4 teaspoon (1.5 grams)
**Pepper**   sprinkle

Melt margarine; stir in flour and gradually add milk, stirring constantly. Cook in double boiler until thick. Add seasonings and mix well. Cook about 1 minute longer.

# Parsley Cream Sauce

**Parsley**   1 tablespoon (5 grams), minced
**Onion**   1/2 teaspoon (1.7 grams), minced

Add parsley and onion to cream sauce with the other seasonings. Vegetables can be a little crisp as they will cook more when the sauce is used.

# Herbed Cream Sauce

**Salt-Free Herb Mix**   1/3 to 1/2 teaspoon (1 to 1.5 grams); see recipe on page 240

Add Salt-Free Herb Mix to the cream sauce with the other seasonings at the end of the recipe.

### Natural sweetening directions:
- Not needed.

### For low-salt diet:
- 1/4 cup (60 mL) contains 33 mg of sodium
Omit salt; use 1/4 teaspoon (1 gram) of salt substitute. Use salt-free margarine.

# Fruit Dishes

Variety is the spice of life — and these fruit dishes are all spicy. Interesting combinations of fruits and different ways of combining them offer changes in taste and appearance. The following recipes are simple ways of varying your diet to avoid monotony and boredom and to increase palatability.

Apples have great sweetening capacity. You will find them included in most of the recipes in this section, either in the basic recipe or in the natural sweetening directions. Be careful, however, not to use too much or you may get an undesirable flavor.

Also try apples in some of your favorite recipes that you have been unable to adapt to your taste and dietary needs.

143

# Baked Apples

- Makes 6 servings, 1/2 apple each, plus juice
- 1/2 apple contains 48 Calories (P0, F0, C12), no cholesterol
- 1/2 apple = 1/2 cup fruit (1 fruit exchange)

**Apples**   3 large (690 grams)
**Strawberry-flavor dietetic soft drink**   12-ounce can (360 mL)
**Lemon juice**   1 tablespoon (15 mL)
**Lemon rind**   1/2 teaspoon (.8 gram), grated
**Salt**   sprinkle
**Cinnamon**   1/3 teaspoon (1 gram)

Cut apples in half lengthwise; core, remove stem and blossom end. Place apples, cut side down, in a 9-inch-square (22.5 cm) nonstick pan. Mix soft drink, lemon juice, lemon rind, cinnamon and salt and pour over apple halves. Bake at 325°F (163°C) about 1 hour, until apples wrinkle when touched. Serve hot or cool.

*Suggestions:*
For nondieters, serve apple half with cut side up and 1 tablespoon (8 grams) of vanilla ice cream in hollow.

*Natural sweetening directions:*
Omit diet soft drink; add 1-1/4 cups (300 mL) water plus 1/4 cup (60 mL) apple juice, plus an additional 1 teaspoon (5 mL) lemon juice. Follow directions as given.

*For low-salt diet:*
- 1/2 apple contains 11 mg of sodium
Omit salt; use sprinkle of salt substitute.

# Quick and Easy Applesauce

- Makes 7 or 8 cups (1.68 or 1.9 L)
- 1/2 cup contains 40 Calories (P0, F0, C10), no cholesterol
- 1/2 cup = 1/2 cup of fruit (1 fruit exchange)

**Apples**   8 large (1,840 grams) or 12 medium (2,160 grams)
**Water**   1/2 cup (120 mL)
**Lemon juice**   2 tablespoons (30 mL)
**Salt**   sprinkle
**Liquid sugar substitute**   1 to 2 tablespoons (5 to 10 mL); or substitute equal to
   1/2 to 1 cup sugar (87.5 to 195 grams)

*Optional:*
Use all of the following:
**Cinnamon**   1/2 teaspoon (1.5 gram)
**Nutmeg**   1/4 teaspoon (.8 gram)
**Ginger**   1/8 teaspoon (.4 gram)

Quarter apples; remove blossom and stem
ends. Place in deep kettle, add water and
cover and simmer until very soft; mash
with potato masher to break up any hard
pieces. Place in a food mill, sieve to
remove skins and seeds. Add lemon juice,
salt and sugar substitute to taste. To keep
more than a week, freeze or can,
according to directions.

### Natural sweetening directions:
- 1/2 cup (120 mL) contains 60 Calories (P0, F0, C15).
- 1/2 cup = 3/4 cup fruit (1-1/2 fruit exchanges)
- With date sugar: 1/2 cup contains 68 Calories (P0, F0, C17)
- With date sugar: 1/2 cup = 7/8 cup fruit (1-3/4 fruit exchange)
Omit sugar substitute. Omit water, and replace with concentrated apple juice. Increase lemon juice to
1-1/2 tablespoons (37.5 mL). If still not sweet enough, add 2 to 3 tablespoons (20 to 30 grams) of date sugar.
Stir to mix well.

### For low-salt diet:
- 1/2 cup (120 mL) contains 1 mg of sodium
Omit sprinkle of salt; use salt substitute.

# Spicy Baked Peaches

- Makes 3 servings
- 1 serving (2 halves) contains 88 Calories (P0, F4, C13), no cholesterol
- 1 serving = 1/2 cup of fruit + 1 teaspoon of fat (1 fruit exchange + 1 fat exchange)

**Peach halves**   6 with juice (546 grams), diet-pack
**Margarine**   1 tablespoon (14 grams); use corn-oil, soybean-oil or safflower-oil margarine
**Sherry or almond extract**   1/2 teaspoon (2.5 mL)
**Lemon or orange rind**   1 teaspoon (1.5 grams), grated
**Ground cloves**   sprinkle

Drain peach halves; save juice. Combine melted margarine, juice, flavoring and rind. Place peach halves in a nonstick pan or one that has been sprayed with nonstick coating or lightly oiled. Pour juice mixture over peaches so all are covered. Bake at 400°F (204°C) for about 10 minutes, until peaches are steaming hot. Sprinkle lightly with ground cloves and serve as a dessert or as a garnish with meat.

*Suggestions:*
Use pear halves and nutmeg instead of peaches and cloves. Add food coloring to fruit and juice. Allow to stand for several hours, so fruit will absorb some of the color, then cook as directed. Attractive and tasty!

*Natural sweetening directions:*
- Not needed.

*For low-salt diet:*
- 2 halves contain 2 mg of sodium
Use salt-free margarine.

# Stan's Spicy Applesauce

- Makes 7 cups (1.68 L)
- 1 serving contains 53 Calories (P0, F1, C11), no cholesterol
- 1 serving = 1/2 cup of fruit (1 fruit exchange)

**Apples**   8 large (1,840 grams); use Golden Delicious if available.
**Coriander seeds**   1/2 teaspoon (1.5 grams)
**Margarine**   1-1/2 teaspoons (7.1 grams); use corn-oil, soybean-oil or safflower-oil margarine
**Brown-type granular sugar substitute**   2-1/2 tablespoons (15 grams); or substitute equal to 1/3 cup (65 grams) of sugar
**Ginger**   1/2 teaspoon (1.5 grams)
**Nutmeg**   1/2 teaspoon (1.5 grams)
**Cinnamon**   1/2 teaspoon (1.5 grams)
**Salt**   sprinkle

Peel, core and dice apples. Crush coriander seeds and place in a spice bag; suspend in heavy saucepan. Place apples, margarine and sugar substitute in pot; sprinkle spices and salt over apples at regular intervals, so apples and spices are layered. Cover tightly and cook over very low heat without water, until apples are very soft. Remove spice bag; add enough water to make 7 cups (1.68 L) total. Cool, then refrigerate, or pack into pint containers and freeze for future use.

*Suggestions:*
If apples are quite hard, add 1/4 cup (60 mL) water before cooking. As a relish, this applesauce is a fine accompaniment for cold meat such as roast beef or lamb.

### Natural sweetening directions:
*This recipe is not for hypoglycemics.*
- 1 serving contains 65 Calories (P0, F1, C14), no change in cholesterol or sodium
- 1 serving = 3/4 cup fruit (1-1/2 fruit exchanges)
Omit sugar substitute; use 1/4 cup (40 grams) date sugar, plus 1 teaspoon (5 mL) lemon juice. Follow directions as given.

### For low-salt diet:
- 1 serving contains 1 mg of sodium
Omit salt; use sprinkle of salt substitute. Use salt-free margarine. Add 1 teaspoon (15 mL) lemon juice.

# Berry Applesauce

- Makes 11 servings, 1/2 cup (120 mL) each
- 1 serving contains 48 Calories (P0, F0, C12), no cholesterol
- 1 serving = 1/2 cup of fruit (1 fruit exchange)

**Green apples**   4 cups (480 grams), cored and quartered (6 or 7 small apples)
**Berries**   2 cups (340 grams), cleaned and sliced
**Lemon juice**   2 tablespoons (30 mL)
**Salt**   sprinkle
**Granular sugar substitute**   2 to 4 tablespoons (12 to 24 grams); or substitute
   equal to 1/4 to 1/2 cup (48.8 to 97.5 grams) of sugar

Put apples and 1-1/2 cups (360 mL) water in a saucepan. Cover and cook very slowly until tender, stirring occasionally to prevent sticking. Remove from heat; put apples through a food mill to remove any lumps or fibers. Set aside. Simmer berries in 1/3 cup (80 mL) of water until soft. Put through food mill to remove any large seeds or fibers. Combine apple and berry pulps. Heat to boiling point. Add lemon juice, salt and sugar substitute. To preserve for more than a few days, freeze or put into sterile jars and process by hot-water bath (see canning instructions pages 242-248).

*Suggestions:*
Use strawberries, raspberries or boysenberries for a delicious sauce. Taste before adding all the sugar substitute. Very sweet berries or very tart apples will require adjusting the amounts of sweetener and lemon juice.

*Natural sweetening directions:*
*This recipe is not for hypoglycemics.*
- 1 serving contains 64 Calories (P0, F0, C16), no change in cholesterol or sodium
- 1 serving = 1 slice of bread *or* 3/4 cup fruit (1 bread exchange *or* 1-1/2 fruit exchanges)
Omit sugar substitute. Cook apples in 1/3 cup (80 mL) concentrated apple juice. Increase lemon juice to 1-1/2 tablespoons (37.5 mL). Follow directions as given.

*For low-salt diet:*
- 1 serving contains 1 mg of sodium
Omit salt; use sprinkle of salt substitute.

# Rhubarb Applesauce

- Makes 2-1/2 quarts (2.4 L)
- 3/4 cup (180 mL) contains 44 Calories (P0, F0, C11), no cholesterol
- 3/4 cup = 1/2 cup of fruit (1 fruit exchange)

**Dried apple slices**   6-ounce package (170 grams)
**Rhubarb**   10 to 12 stalks, about 1 pound (454 grams), finely sliced
**Lemon juice**   4 to 6 teaspoons (20 to 30 mL)
**Salt**   sprinkle
**Granular sugar substitute**   1/3 to 1/2 cup (32 to 48 grams); or substitute equal to
   2/3 to 1 cup (130 to 195 grams) of sugar

Cover dried apples with water and soak overnight; if all water is absorbed, add more water to cover and allow to soak longer. Cook apples slowly in at least 1/2 cup (120 mL) of water until tender. Mash apple with potato masher; remove from heat. Add 2 tablespoons (30 mL) of water to rhubarb slices; cover and cook slowly until tender. Remove from heat; add a few drops of red food coloring if color is pale. Combine rhubarb and apples; add lemon juice, salt and sugar substitute to taste.

*Suggestions:*
This is delicious as a topping for plain yogurt, or on a biscuit as shortcake.

### Natural sweetening directions:
*This recipe is not for hypoglycemics.*
- 3/4 cup (180 mL) contains 60 Calories (P0, F0, C15), no change in cholesterol or sodium
- 3/4 cup = 3/4 cup of fruit (1-1/2 fruit exchanges)
Omit sugar substitute. Cook apples in 1/3 cup (80 mL) concentrated apple juice. Add 1/4 cup (40 grams) date sugar to cooked apples, stir and allow to stand for at least 5 minutes before combining with rhubarb. Add an additional 2 teaspoons (10 mL) of lemon juice. Follow directions as given.

### For low-salt diet:
- 3/4 cup (180 mL) contains 1 mg of sodium
Omit salt; use sprinkle of salt substitute. Use enough fresh apples to make 6 cups (1.4 L), sliced; core and remove blossom ends. Cook, covered, in 1 cup (240 mL) water over low heat until soft; put through a food mill to remove skin and fibers.

# Evelyn's Hot Fruit Compote

- Makes 8 servings, 3/4 cup (180 mL) each
- 3/4 cup (180 mL) contains 68 Calories (P1, F0, C16), no cholesterol
- 3/4 cup = 1 slice of bread *or* 3/4 cup of fruit (1 bread exchange *or* 1-1/2 fruit exchanges)

**Dried apple slices**    1 cup (86 grams), diet-pack or unsweetened
**Dried prunes**    4 medium (40 grams), halved and pitted
**Dried apricots**    8 halves (28 grams), pitted
**Frozen blueberries**    2/3 cup (110 grams), or 1 cup (123 grams) frozen raspberries
**Pineapple chunks**    1/2 cup (101 grams), diet-pack
**Orange rind**    1/4 teaspoon (.4 gram), grated
**Lemon rind**    1/2 teaspoon (.8 gram), grated
**Matzo meal**    3 tablespoons (13.5 grams), or 3 tablespoons (8.5 grams) whole-wheat bread crumbs
**Salt**    sprinkle
**Brown-type granular sugar substitute**    1/4 cup (24 grams); or substitute equal to 1/2 cup (97.5 grams) of sugar

Layer fruits so colors alternate; save all juices in a bowl. Mix rinds, crumbs, salt and sugar substitute; sprinkle on fruit. Pour juice over top; refrigerate for 24 hours. Bake at 250°F (121°C) for 2-1/2 hours. Serve hot.

**Suggestions:**
Serve this compote very hot. It can be reheated and is also good as a leftover. You can vary the fruits — peaches, pears, fruit cocktail, for example. Try adding 1/2 teaspoon (2.5 mL) of sherry flavoring to the fruit juice. For nondieters, serve with whipped cream topping.

**Natural sweetening directions:**
*This recipe is not for hypoglycemics.*
- 1 serving contains 72 Calories (P1, F0, C17), no change in cholesterol or sodium
- 1 serving = 1 slice of bread *or* 3/4 cup of fruit (1 bread exchange *or* 1-1/2 fruit exchanges)
Omit sugar substitute; add 1/4 cup (40 grams) of date sugar and 1 teaspoon (5 mL) of lemon juice. Follow directions as given.

**For low-salt diet:**
- 1 serving contains 3 mg of sodium
Omit salt; use sprinkle of salt substitute. Use salt-free crumbs.

# Fruit Medley

- Makes 5 cups (1.2 L)
- 1/2 cup (120 mL) contains 48 Calories (P0, F0, C12), no cholesterol
- 1/2 cup = 1/2 cup of fruit (1 fruit exchange)

**Fresh or frozen strawberries**   1 cup (144 grams), or 2/3 cup (110 grams)
   blueberries
**Diet pineapple chunks**   14-ounce can (398 grams), in juice
**Banana**   1 small (140 grams)
**Apple**   1 medium (180 grams)
**Cantaloupe**   1/2 small (477 grams), peeled and seeded

*Optional:*
Use one of the following:
**Fresh mint**   1 sprig
**Lemon rind, grated**   1/4 teaspoon (.4 gram)

Wash, hull and slice strawberries, or wash blueberries. Drain juice from pineapple chunks into large bowl. Slice banana into juice, stirring to coat all and avoid browning. Peel (if you wish), core and dice apple. Add apple to juice, again stirring to coat all and avoid fruit turning brown. Dice melon into 1/2-inch (1.25 cm) chunks; add to other fruit. Crush mint to release flavor and add to fruit, or sprinkle lemon rind over fruit and stir well. Refrigerate in covered plastic container (will keep for about 1 week); stir a few times each day to keep banana and apple coated. Serve chilled.

*Suggestions:*
You may substitute any fruits you wish, as long as you use the pineapple in juice for the basic ingredient. In winter, use frozen berries and substitute diet-pack fruit for the remainder. This is delicious as a fruit dish for Sunday brunch!

*Natural sweetening directions:*
- 1/2 cup (120 mL) contains 52 Calories (P0, F0, C12)
- 1/2 cup = 1/2 cup of fruit (1 fruit exchange)
Not really needed, but if you want the fruit a little bit sweeter, add 1 tablespoon (15 mL) concentrated apple juice plus 1/2 teaspoon (2.5 mL) lemon juice.

*For low-salt diet:*
- 1/2 cup (120 mL) contains 2 mg of sodium
No changes are needed.

# Desserts

Even if you are avoiding sugar or cholesterol, you can have good desserts. Try these and see for yourself. One word of warning, though: Don't change the ingredients, or you might have a flop.

Recipes can be made with sugar substitutes or without refined sugar by using natural sweeteners. Because some of these natural sweetenings will make the carbohydrate and Calorie contents too high for safe use by diabetics and/or hypoglycemics, you will have to eat much smaller portions or not eat the dessert at all.

## Cakes

Cakes and other baked goods made with sugar substitute (or egg substitute) tend to be heavier and coarser in texture than those made with usual ingredients. Unusual combinations make acceptable products not so readily compared with the usual cake or pudding-cake.

These desserts are tasty and acceptable in texture, but they will dry out quickly, so use them while fresh or freeze them.

## Dietetic Cookies

These dry out very fast. Store them in tight plastic containers and freeze or keep in a very cool place. Do not make large batches ahead.

Even though the cookies are dietetically prepared, they are not free of Calories or carbohydrates. So the "cookie-holic" has to watch the amount consumed. Look for the equivalent value at the top of the recipe and limit your eating accordingly.

Whole-wheat flour can be substituted in any recipe provided it is sifted twice before measuring and again as it is used in the recipe. This adjusts the volume and helps to lighten the texture of the product.

### Pies and Pie Fillings

Everyone in the family will eat dietetic pies. They're good. Plan to serve them whenever you want a special dessert.

The double-crust pies will freeze well, so you can make more than one at a time and freeze the extras, unbaked. For frozen double-crust pie, allow 20 minutes of baking time at 450°F (232°C), then 40 to 60 minutes more at 375°F (191°C) until the center of the pie crust is browned.

One-crust pies do not freeze well, but you can make the shells and freeze them for later use.

### Frozen Desserts

Commercially prepared dietetic iced desserts contain sorbitol and possibly fructose as the main sweeteners. Persons with hypoglycemia and with elevated triglycerides may find they do not tolerate these. Without sorbitol or any of the "fillers" used by creameries, frozen desserts tend to become grainy and unpleasant in texture. You will find that if the frozen desserts in this chapter are made exactly according to the recipe, this coarse graininess will not develop.

While an ice cream freezer is not essential for making these desserts, it makes an immensely better-textured product. If you are a real ice cream addict, you will probably find it worth the money to buy an electric freezer.

### Gelatin Desserts

The recipes for gelatin desserts in this cookbook are appetizing and contain so little of the forbidden Calories or other taboo items (salt, cholesterol) that they can be used frequently.

You can plan on serving the whole family these desserts, as there is nothing to indicate that they are different from the usual gelatin desserts.

### Puddings

These take a little more preparation than the gelatin desserts, but they are also much more filling for the hungry dieter. Whipped cream or ice cream may be added as topping for nondieters.

### Sauces

Most conventional dessert sauces are highly sugared. The two here, however, have no sugar, besides being low in saturated fats (butter and eggs). Use them to pamper your palate.

# Apple Crunch

- Makes 9 servings
- 1 serving contains 100 Calories (P1, F4, C15), no cholesterol
- 1 serving = 1 slice of bread + 1/2 teaspoon of fat *or* 3/4 cup of fruit +
  1/2 teaspoon of fat (1 bread exchange + 1/2 fat exchange *or* 1-1/2 fruit
  exchanges + 1/2 fat exchange)

**Apples**   4 medium (720 grams)
**Brown-type granular sugar substitute**   5 tablespoons (30 grams); or substitute
  equal to 2/3 cup (130 grams) of sugar
**Cinnamon**   1/2 teaspoon (1.5 grams)
**Nutmeg**   1/4 teaspoon (.8 gram)
**Ginger**   1/8 teaspoon (.4 gram)

*Topping:*
**Melted margarine**   3 tablespoons (45 mL); use corn-oil, soybean-oil or safflower-oil
  margarine
**Lemon juice**   3 tablespoons (45 mL)
**Brown-type granular sugar substitute**   5 tablespoons (30 grams); or substitute
  equal to 2/3 cup (130 grams) of sugar
**Cinnamon**   1/2 teaspoon (1.5 grams)
**Nutmeg**   1/4 teaspoon (.8 gram)
**Shredded wheat**   2 biscuits (50 grams), finely crushed
**Warm water**   1/4 cup (60 mL)

Peel apples and slice thin as you would for pie; place in bowl. Spray 9-inch (22.5 cm) pan with nonstick coating or use nonstick pan. Mix first set of dry ingredients and sift over apples; stir to coat all slices well. Arrange in pan.

Melt margarine; mix in lemon juice, sugar substitute and spices. Add crushed shredded wheat to margarine-spice mixture; mix well. Scatter topping evenly over apples. Pour in the warm water at sides of pan, without disturbing the topping. Bake at 350°F (177°C) for 1 hour; serve warm.

*Suggestions:*
If you like a strong lemon flavor, add 1/4 to 1/2 teaspoon (.4 to .8 gram) of grated lemon rind to topping mixture. This dessert can be made with diet-pack peaches or pears, or a mixture of diet-canned fruit for variety. The food value would be approximately the same.

*Natural sweetening directions:*
*This recipe is not for hypoglycemics.*
- 1 serving contains 124 Calories (P1, F4, C21), no cholesterol, 1 mg of sodium
- 1 serving = 1/2 slice of bread + 1 teaspoon of fat + 1/2 cup of fruit (1/2 bread exchange + 1 fat exchange + 1 fruit exchange)
In filling, omit sugar substitute; use 5 tablespoons (50 grams) of date sugar plus 3/4 teaspoon (1.2 grams) grated lemon rind. In topping, omit sugar substitute; use 5 tablespoons (50 grams) of date sugar and increase lemon juice to 3-1/2 tablespoons (52.5 mL).

*For low-salt diet:*
- 1 serving contains 2 mg of sodium
Use salt-free margarine.

# Bread Pudding / *with or Without Raisins*

- Makes 6 servings
- 1 plain serving contains 88 Calories (P6, F3, C9), 86 mg of cholesterol if made with egg, 2 mg of cholesterol if made with egg substitute
- 1 plain serving = 1 ounce of meat + 1/2 cup of fruit (1 meat exchange + 1 fruit exchange)
- 1 serving with raisins contains 107 Calories (P6, F3, C14)
- 1 serving with raisins = 1 slice of bread + 1 ounce of meat (1 bread exchange + 1 meat exchange)

**Skim milk**   2 cups (480 mL)
**Eggs**   2 large (114 grams); or 4 ounces (120 mL) of liquid egg substitute
**Whole-grain bread**   2 slices (56 grams)
**Margarine**   1 tablespoon (14 grams); use corn-oil, soybean-oil or safflower-oil margarine
**Butter flavoring**   6 drops
**Brown-type granular sugar substitute**   1/3 cup (32 grams); or substitute equal to 2/3 cup (130 grams) of sugar
**Salt**   1/2 teaspoon (3 grams)
**Vanilla**   1 teaspoon (5 mL)
**Cinnamon**   1/4 teaspoon (.8 gram)
**Nutmeg**   1/8 teaspoon (.4 gram)
**Ginger**   sprinkle
**Egg whites**   2 (66 grams)

*Optional:*
**Raisins**   4 tablespoons (36 grams), soaked in hot water and drained

Scald milk; set aside; when cool, add beaten egg. Spread bread with margarine; cube; add to other ingredients, except egg whites and raisins. Beat egg whites until stiff; fold into milk/bread mixture. Add raisins. Turn into nonstick pan or a pan sprayed with nonstick coating. Put pan in hot water; bake at 350°F (177°C) for about 1 hour and 15 minutes. Check by inserting silver knife in center of pudding. If knife comes out clean, pudding is done. Serve warm or cold.

### Suggestions:
For nondieters, serve warm pudding with a scoop of vanilla ice cream or cool pudding with whipped cream.

### Natural sweetening directions:
*This recipe is not for hypoglycemics.*
- 1 serving contains 140 Calories (P6, F4, C20), 97 mg of sodium, 4 mg of cholesterol
- 1 serving = 1/2 slice of bread + 1 ounce of meat + 1/2 cup of fruit (1/2 bread exchange + 1 meat exchange + 1 fruit exchange)
Omit skim milk; use 1 cup (240 mL) evaporated skim milk. Add 3/4 cup (180 mL) concentrated apple juice plus 1/4 cup (60 mL) water to make up the volume. Add 1/4 teaspoon (.4 gram) grated lemon rind with the other spices.

### For low-salt diet:
*Do not use on a 400-mg sodium or 1-gram salt diet.*
- 1 serving contains 88 mg of sodium
Omit salt; use 1/2 teaspoon (2 grams) of salt substitute. Use salt-free bread and margarine.

# Crunchy Banana Bread

- Makes 16 servings
- 1 serving contains 139 Calories (P3, F7, C16), 32 mg of cholesterol if made with egg, no cholesterol if made with egg substitute
- 1 serving = 1 slice of bread + 1 teaspoon of fat (1 bread exchange + 1 fat exchange)

**Margarine**   1/3 cup (75 grams); use corn-oil, soybean-oil or safflower-oil margarine

**Brown-type granular sugar substitute**   5 tablespoons (30 grams); or substitute equal to 2/3 cup (130 grams) of sugar

**Very ripe bananas**   1-3/4 cup (389 grams), mashed. *Note: Use only very ripe, almost black bananas. Much of the flavor and sweetening come from the bananas and unless they are quite ripe, the bread will be poor.*

**Eggs**   2 large (114 grams); or 4 ounces (120 mL) liquid egg substitute

**Unbleached or whole-wheat flour**   1-1/2 cups (174 or 190.5 grams), sifted. *Note: Hypoglycemics use whole-wheat flour only.*

**Salt**   1/2 teaspoon (3 grams)

**Double-acting baking powder**   2-1/2 teaspoons (10 grams)

**Baking soda**   1/2 teaspoon (2 grams)

**Shredded wheat**   1 cup (35 grams) crushed biscuits

**Vanilla**   1-1/4 teaspoon (6.3 mL)

**Water**   1-1/2 tablespoons (22.5 mL), or 1-1/2 tablespoons (22.5 mL) plain, low-fat yogurt

**Walnuts**   1/2 cup (60 grams), chopped

Cream margarine with sugar substitute and mashed bananas. Beat eggs; stir into creamed mixture. Sift flour, salt, baking powder and soda together. With rolling pin, roll shredded wheat biscuits until very fine; add to dry ingredients. Combine vanilla and water or yogurt; add alternately with dry ingredients to creamed mixture; mix thoroughly. Add chopped nuts; mix well. Turn into 9-inch-square (22.5 cm) nonstick pan or pan sprayed with nonstick coating. Bake at 350°F (177°C) for about 50 minutes. Cool on rack; then cut into 4 parts in each direction (16 total).

### Natural sweetening directions:

*This recipe is not for hypoglycemics.*
- 1 serving contains 151 Calories (P3, F7, C19), no cholesterol if made with egg substitute
- 1 serving = 1/2 slice of bread + 1 teaspoon of fat + 1/2 cup of fruit (1/2 bread exchange + 1 fat exchange + 1 fruit exchange)

Omit sugar substitute; use 5 tablespoons (50 grams) of date sugar plus 1/4 teaspoon (.4 gram) grated lemon rind. Increase baking soda to 3/4 teaspoon (3 grams).

### For low-salt diet:

- 1 serving contains 21 mg of sodium

Omit salt; use 1/2 teaspoon (2 grams) of salt substitute. Use 3 teaspoons (12 grams) of sodium-free baking powder instead of baking powder and soda. Use water instead of yogurt for liquid.

# Lemon Cake Custard

- Makes 4 servings
- 1 serving contains 97 Calories (P5, F5, C8), 3 mg of cholesterol if made with egg substitute
- 1 serving = 1 ounce of meat + 1/2 cup of fruit (1 meat exchange + 1 fruit exchange)

**Eggs**  2 large (114 grams), separated; or 2 ounces (60 mL) of liquid egg substitute + 2 egg whites (66 grams)
**Salt**  1/8 teaspoon (.8 gram)
**Lemon juice**  2-2/3 tablespoons (40 mL)
**Lemon rind**  1/8 teaspoon (.2 gram), grated
**Melted margarine**  1 tablespoon (15 mL); use corn-oil, soybean-oil or safflower-oil margarine
**Skim milk**  3/4 cup (180 mL)
**Unbleached flour**  2-1/4 tablespoons (18 grams)
**Brown-type granular sugar substitute**  2-1/2 tablespoons (15 grams); or substitute equal to 5 tablespoons (61 grams) of sugar
**Baking soda**  1/16 teaspoon (.3 gram)

Beat egg whites until very stiff. In a separate bowl beat yolks or liquid egg substitute, then gradually add remaining ingredients. Mix well. Stir a small amount of this mixture into egg whites, then fold all into remaining batter. Pour custard into a greased 1-quart (1 liter) casserole. Place casserole in a pan of hot water and bake at 350°F (177°C) for 1 hour and 10 minutes. Cool before serving.

### Natural sweetening directions:
- 1 serving contains 121 Calories (P5, F5, C14), 68 mg of sodium
- 1 serving = 1 slice of bread + 1 ounce of meat (1 bread exchange + 1 meat exchange)
Omit sugar substitute; use 2-1/2 tablespoons (25 grams) of date sugar. Increase lemon juice to 3 tablespoons (45 mL).

### For low-salt diet:
- 1 serving contains 69 mg of sodium, no change in cholesterol
Omit salt and baking soda; use 1/16 teaspoon (.3 gram) potassium bicarbonate instead of soda. Use fresh eggs, not egg substitute.

# Raisin-Applesauce Cake

- Makes 16 servings
- 1 serving contains 117 Calories (P3, F5, C15), 16 mg of cholesterol if made with egg, no cholesterol if made with egg substitute
- 1 serving = 1 slice of bread + 1 teaspoon of fat (1 bread exchange + 1 fat exchange)

**Soft margarine**   1/3 cup (75 grams); use corn-oil, soybean-oil or safflower-oil margarine
**Brown-type granular sugar substitute**   1/2 cup (48 grams; or substitute equal to 1 cup (195 grams) of sugar
**Egg**   1 large (57 grams); or 2 ounces (60 mL) of liquid egg substitute
**Plain low-fat yogurt**   2 tablespoons (30 mL)
**Unbleached flour**   2 cups (232 grams), sifted
**Baking soda**   1-1/2 teaspoons (6 grams)
**Salt**   1/3 teaspoon (2 grams)
**Ground cloves**   1/2 teaspoon (1.5 grams)
**Cinnamon**   1 teaspoon (3 grams)
**Nutmeg**   1/4 teaspoon (.8 gram)
**Raisins**   4 tablespoons (36 grams)
**Diet applesauce**   1 cup (256 grams) unsweetened. *Note: If you use Stan's Spicy Applesauce, page 147, cut the spices in half or omit and use only the vanilla.*
**Walnuts**   12 medium halves (66 grams), chopped

*Optional:*
**Vanilla**   1/2 teaspoon (2.5 mL)

Cream margarine with sugar substitute. Add beaten egg and yogurt; cream until very smooth and fluffy. Sift dry ingredients together. Cut each raisin in half; soak at least 5 minutes in hot water; drain well. Add dry ingredients and applesauce, alternately, a little at a time, to creamed mixture; mix well after each addition. Add vanilla, if desired, as it will blend nicely with the spices. Add raisins and chopped walnuts; mix thoroughly. Pour into 9-inch-square (22.5 cm) nonstick pan or a pan sprayed with nonstick coating. Bake at 350°F (177°C) for 50 minutes, or until toothpick stuck into the middle comes out clean. Cool on rack; serve warm or cold.

### Natural sweetening directions:
*This recipe is not for hypoglycemics.*
- 1 serving contains 137 Calories (P3, F5, C20), no cholesterol if made with egg substitute; 15 mg of sodium
- 1 serving = 1/2 slice of bread + 1 teaspoon of fat + 1/2 cup of fruit (1/2 bread exchange + 1 fat exchange + 1 fruit exchange)

Omit sugar substitute; use 1/2 cup plus 1 tablespoon (90 grams) of date sugar. Add 1/4 teaspoon (.4 gram) grated lemon rind. Use diet-pack applesauce.

### For low-salt diet:
- 1 serving contains 14 mg of sodium

Omit salt; use 1/3 teaspoon (1.3 grams) of salt substitute. Use 1-1/2 teaspoons (6 grams) of sodium-free baking powder in place of baking soda. Omit yogurt; use 2 tablespoons (30 mL) of skim milk. Use salt-free margarine.

# New England Flummery

- Makes 4 servings
- 1 serving contains 79 Calories (P1, F3, C12), no cholesterol
- 1 serving = 1/2 cup of fruit + 1/2 teaspoon of fat (1 fruit exchange + 1/2 fat exchange)

**Whole-wheat bread**    2 slices (56 grams)
**Margarine**    2 teaspoons (9.3 grams); use corn-oil, soybean-oil or safflower-oil margarine
**Blueberries**    1 cup (146 grams) fresh or frozen, unsweetened
**Lemon juice**    1 teaspoon (5 mL)
**Lemon rind**    1/4 teaspoon (.4 gram), grated. Use less if you are lukewarm about lemon.
**Brown-type granular sugar substitute**    1/4 cup (24 grams); or substitute equal to 1/2 cup (97.5 grams) of sugar
**Salt**    sprinkle
**Nutmeg**    2 sprinkles

Spread bread with margarine. Wash and sort berries; place in saucepan with 1-1/2 cups (360 mL) of water. Cook berries over low heat until soft, about 10 minutes. Remove from heat; add lemon juice, lemon rind, sugar substitute and salt. Mix well. Spray baking dish with nonstick coating or oil very lightly. Place bread slices in bottom of dish, cutting to fit evenly. Pour cooked berry mixture evenly over bread; sprinkle with nutmeg. Bake at 350°F (177°C) for about 15 minutes; serve hot or chilled.

*Suggestions:*
Flummery may be made with other berries, but the traditional New England dish is made with blueberries. If the diet allows, top it with 1 tablespoon (8 grams) of dietetic ice cream for extra-special flavor.

*Natural sweetening directions:*
*This recipe is not for hypoglycemics.*
- 1 serving contains 103 Calories (P1, F3, C18), no cholesterol, 6 mg of sodium
- 1 serving = 1/2 slice of bread + 1/2 teaspoon of fat + 1/2 cup of fruit (1/2 bread exchange + 1/2 fat exchange + 1 fruit exchange)

Omit sugar substitute. Reduce water to 1 cup (240 mL), substituting 1/2 cup (120 mL) concentrated apple juice for the other water. Add an additional 2 teaspoons (10 mL) of lemon juice.

*For low-salt diet:*
- 1 serving contains 6 mg of sodium

Omit salt; use sprinkle of salt substitute. Use salt-free bread and margarine.

# Ann Meerkerk's Zucchini Bread

- Makes 2 medium-sized loaves, 18 slices each
- 1 slice contains 114 Calories (P2, F6, C13), no cholesterol if made with egg substitute
- 1 slice = 1 slice of bread + 1 teaspoon of fat (1 bread exchange + 1 fat exchange)

**Zucchini**   3 cups (450 grams), grated coarsely
**Oil**   3/4 cup (180 mL); use corn, soybean or safflower oil
**Vanilla**   1 tablespoon (15 mL)
**Eggs**   3 large (171 grams); or 6 ounces (180 mL) of liquid egg substitute
**Apple juice**   1/4 cup (60 mL) concentrated
**Dates**   1/2 cup (87 grams), finely chopped
**Salt**   1 teaspoon (6 grams)
**Baking soda**   1 teaspoon (4 grams)
**Double-acting baking powder**   1 teaspoon (4 grams)
**Whole-wheat flour**   2 cups (254 grams), sifted
**Unbleached flour**   2 cups (252 grams), unsifted
**Cinnamon**   2 teaspoons (6 grams)
**Pumpkin pie spices**   2 teaspoons (6 grams); or 1 teaspoon (3 grams) **allspice** + 1/2 teaspoon (1.5 grams) **ginger** + 1/2 teaspoon (1.5 grams) **nutmeg**

Combine first 5 ingredients in a large bowl; beat until batter forms. Sift dry ingredients together in a separate bowl. Add dates, mixing them with flour so they will remain separate pieces. Gradually add to first batter, stirring well. Spray 2 loaf pans with nonstick coating.

Divide batter into halves and pour into pans. Bake at 350°F (177°C) for 1 hour and 15 minutes, until a toothpick comes out clean when inserted in the middle of the bread. Remove from pan and cool; do not slice until bread is completely cool.

*Natural sweetening directions:*
- Not needed.

*For low-salt diet:*
- 1 serving contains 7 mg of sodium

Omit salt, baking soda and baking powder; use same amounts of salt substitute, potassium bicarbonate and salt-free baking powder.

# Baked Custard

- Makes 8 servings
- 1 serving contains 92 Calories (P7, F4, C7), 8 mg of cholesterol if made with egg substitute and skim milk
- 1 serving = 1 ounce of meat + 1/4 cup of fruit (1 meat exchange + 1/2 fruit exchange)

**2% skim milk**   3 cups (720 mL)
**Eggs**   3 medium (150 grams); or 6 ounces (180 mL) of liquid egg substitute
**Brown-type granular sugar substitute**   1-1/2 tablespoons (9 grams); or substitute equal to 3 tablespoons (36.6 grams) of sugar
**Arrowroot flour**   1 teaspoon (3 grams)
**Vanilla**   1 teaspoon (5 mL)
**Salt**   sprinkle
**Nutmeg**

Combine sweetening with milk, vanilla and salt. Stir into flour, making a smooth paste; add remaining liquid and eggs. Pour into 8 individual cups or a 1-1/2-quart (1.5 L) casserole; sprinkle nutmeg on the top. Place custard cups or casserole in a pan of hot water, and bake at 350°F (177°C) for 50 to 60 minutes, until a silver knife comes out clean when inserted in the center. Do not overcook as this will cause the custard to become watery when it stands.

### Natural sweetening directions:
- 1 serving contains 104 Calories (P7, F4, C10), 82 mg of sodium, no change in cholesterol
- 1 serving = 1 ounce of meat + 1/2 cup of fruit (1 meat exchange + 1 fruit exchange)
Omit sugar substitute; use 4 tablespoons (60 mL) concentrated apple juice and an additional 1/2 teaspoon (2.5 mL) vanilla. Increase arrowroot flour to 1-1/3 teaspoons (4 grams).

### For low-salt diet:
- 1 serving contains 82 mg of sodium
Omit salt. Use fresh eggs, not egg substitute. Increase vanilla to 1-1/4 teaspoons (6.3 mL) for flavor.

# Date-Nut Cake

*This recipe is not for hypoglycemics.*
- Makes 16 pieces, 2 inches (5 cm) square
- 1 piece contains 132 Calories (P4, F4, C20), no cholesterol if made with egg substitute, 31 mg if made with eggs
- 1 piece = 1/2 slice of bread + 1/2 ounce of meat + 1/2 teaspoon of fat + 1/2 cup of fruit (1/2 bread exchange + 1/2 meat exchange + 1/2 fat exchange + 1 fruit exchange)

**Dates**   3/4 cup (131 grams), chopped
**Baking soda**   1 teaspoon (4 grams)
**Boiling water**   1-1/2 cups (360 mL)
**Margarine**   1-1/2 tablespoons (21 grams); use corn-oil, soybean-oil or safflower-oil margarine
**Brown-type granular sugar substitute**   1/4 cup (24 grams); or substitute equal to 1/2 cup (97.5 grams) of sugar
**Eggs**   2 large (114 grams), well beaten; or 4 ounces (120 mL) of liquid egg substitute
**Lemon rind**   3/4 teaspoon (1.2 grams), grated
**Whole-wheat flour**   1 cup (127 grams), sifted
**Unbleached flour**   1-1/2 cups (174 grams), sifted
**Double-acting baking powder**   1/2 teaspoon (2 grams)
**Salt**   1/4 teaspoon (1.5 grams)
**Walnuts**   1/2 cup (60 grams), chopped

Place chopped dates and soda in mixing bowl, add boiling water; allow to stand for at least 1 hour. Cream margarine and sugar substitute; add salt, lemon rind, beaten eggs and mix well. Sift together flours and baking powder and salt. Add nuts, stirring to coat with flour; add to date mixture, stirring well. Pour into an 8-inch-square (20 cm) pan or loaf pan; use a spatula to level top of batter. Bake at 325°F (163°C) for 40 to 45 minutes, until a toothpick comes out clean when inserted into the middle. Cool on a rack.

*Natural sweetening directions:*
- 1 piece contains 144 Calories (P4, F4, C23)
- 1 piece = 1 slice of bread + 1/2 ounce of meat + 1/2 teaspoon of fat + 1/2 cup of fruit (1 bread exchange + 1/2 meat exchange + 1/2 fat exchange + 1 fruit exchange)

Omit sugar substitute; use 1/4 cup (40 grams) of date sugar. Increase lemon rind to 1 teaspoon (1.5 grams).

*For low-salt diet:*
- 1 piece contains 8 mg of sodium

Omit salt; replace with salt substitute. Omit baking soda and baking powder; replace with same amounts of potassium bicarbonate and salt-free baking powder. Increase lemon rind to 1 teaspoon (1.5 grams).

# Fruit Betty

- Makes 4 servings
- 1 serving contains 97 Calories (P1, F5, C12), no cholesterol
- 1 serving = 1/2 cup of fruit + 1 teaspoon of fat (1 fruit exchange + 1 fat exchange)

**Crushed dietetic pineapple**   1 cup (254 grams); or other soft fruit, sliced
**Whole-wheat bread**   2 slices (56 grams), crumbled
**Brown-type granular sugar substitute**   3 to 4 tablespoons (18 to 24 grams); or substitute equal to 1/2 cup (97.5 grams) of sugar
**Nutmeg**   1/8 teaspoon (.4 gram)
**Lemon juice**   1 teaspoon (5 mL)
**Lemon rind**   1/4 teaspoon (.4 gram), grated. Use more if you like lemon.
**Melted margarine**   4 teaspoons (20 mL); use corn-oil, soybean-oil or safflower-oil margarine
**Salt**   sprinkle

Drain fruit; keep juice for other uses. Combine all other ingredients; mix well. Put fruit into nonstick baking dish or dish sprayed with nonstick coating. Cover with mixture. Bake at 400°F (204°C) about 20 minutes, until topping looks brown. Serve warm, plain or with milk.

**Suggestions:**
For nondieters, add a serving of vanilla ice cream or whipped cream on top.

### Natural sweetening directions:
*This recipe is not for hypoglycemics.*
- 1 serving contains 125 Calories (P1, F5, C19), no cholesterol, 2 mg of sodium
- 1 serving = 1 cup of fruit + 1 teaspoon of fat (2 fruit exchanges + 1 fat exchange)
Omit sugar substitute; use 3 tablespoons (30 grams) of date sugar plus 1 teaspoon (5 mL) lemon juice.

### For low-salt diet:
- 1 serving contains 7 mg of sodium
Omit salt; use sprinkle of salt substitute. Use salt-free margarine and salt-free bread for the crumbs. Use 1-1/2 teaspoons (7.5 mL) of lemon juice for increased flavor.

163

# Apple-Date Crisp

- Makes 7 servings
- 1 serving contains 139 Calories (P2, F3, C26), no cholesterol
- 1 serving = 1 slice of bread + 1/2 teaspoon of fat + 1/2 cup of fruit (1 bread exchange + 1/2 fat exchange + 1 fruit exchange)

**Apples**   2-1/2 cups (312.5 grams), peeled and sliced
**Unbleached or whole-wheat flour**   10 tablespoons (80 grams), sifted
**Date sugar**   1/2 cup (80 grams)
**Margarine**   2 tablespoons (28 grams); use corn-oil, soybean-oil or safflower-oil margarine
**Salt**   1/8 teaspoon (.8 gram)
**Cinnamon**   1/2 teaspoon (1.5 grams)
**Nutmeg**   1/4 teaspoon (.8 gram)
**Lemon rind**   3/4 teaspoon (1.2 grams)
**Lemon juice**   2 teaspoons (10 mL)

*Optional:*
**Ginger**   1/8 teaspoon (.4 gram)

Grease or spray with a nonstick coating a
6- or 7-inch (15 or 17.5 cm) baking dish
or pie plate. Place apple slices evenly in
bottom of dish. Mix remaining ingredients
in a bowl, stirring to mix evenly; mixture
should be crumbly. Sprinkle over the top
of the apples. Bake at 375°F (191°C) for
30 minutes.

### Natural sweetening directions:
- Not needed.

### For low-salt diet:
- 1 serving contains 1 mg of sodium
Omit salt; use salt substitute, or increase lemon juice to 2-1/4 teaspoons (11.3 mL). Use salt-free margarine.

# Semisweet Chocolate Sauce

* Makes about 2-1/2 cups (600 mL)
* 1/4 cup (60 mL) contains 33 Calories (P1, F1, C5), no cholesterol
* 1/4 cup = 1/4 cup of fruit (1/2 fruit exchange)

**Breakfast cocoa**    1-1/2 to 2-1/2 tablespoons (8.3 to 13.8 grams), depending how
  well you like chocolate
**Cornstarch**    1-1/4 tablespoons (10 grams)
**Salt**    1/8 teaspoon (.8 gram)
**Instant coffee granules**    1/4 teaspoon (.8 gram); use decaffeinated coffee, if you
  prefer. *Note: Hypoglycemics must use decaffeinated coffee.*
**Water**    1 cup (240 mL)
**Skim milk**    1 cup (240 mL)
**Vanilla**    2 teaspoons (10 mL)
**Brown-type granular sugar substitute**    1/2 cup (48 grams); or substitute equal to
  1-1/3 cups of sugar. Use 2/3 cup (130 grams) for each 2-1/2 tablespoons
  (13.8 grams) of cocoa.

*Optional:*
**Chocolate extract**    1/3 teaspoon (1.7 mL), unsweetened

In saucepan combine cocoa, cornstarch,
salt and coffee granules; gradually add
enough water to make a paste, then
remainder of water. Add milk; stir well.
Cook over low heat; stirring constantly
until thickened. Remove from heat; add
remaining ingredients; mix well. Serve
hot on pudding or dietetic ice cream, or
refrigerate for later use cold.

### Natural sweetening directions:
*This recipe is not for hypoglycemics.*
* 1/4 cup (60 mL) contains 53 Calories (P1, F1, C10), 13 mg of sodium
* 1/4 cup = 1/2 cup of fruit (1 fruit exchange)
Omit sugar substitute and water; use 1 cup (240 mL) white grape juice plus 2-1/2 tablespoons (25 grams) of
date sugar. Increase vanilla to 2-1/2 teaspoons (12.5 mL).

### For low-salt diet:
* 1/4 cup (60 mL) contains 17 mg of sodium
Omit salt; use 1/8 teaspoon (.5 gram) of salt substitute. Use old-fashioned plain cocoa, if you can find it; if
not, use breakfast cocoa powder, but not Dutch-process cocoa.

# Fruit Sauce

- Makes 1 cup (240 mL)
- 1/8 cup (30 mL) contains 20 Calories (P0, F0, C5), no cholesterol
- 1/8 cup = 1/4 cup of fruit (1/2 fruit exchange)

**Dietetic fruit juice**   1 cup (240 mL), blended from diet-pack peaches and pears
  and other fruits
**Cornstarch**   1 tablespoon (8 grams)
**Lemon juice**   3 tablespoons (45 mL)
**Salt**   sprinkle
**Lemon or orange rind**   1/4 teaspoon (.4 gram), grated
**Brown-type granular sugar substitute**   1 tablespoon (6 grams); or substitute
  equal to 2 tablespoons (24.4 grams) of sugar

*Optional:*
**Cinnamon**   1/4 teaspoon (.8 gram)

Save juice from canned dietetic peaches and pears until you have 1 cup (240 mL). Blend cornstarch with lemon juice to make a smooth paste; stir into fruit juice. Add salt. Cook in double boiler until mixture thickens and becomes somewhat clear, about 5 minutes. Cover and cook about 10 minutes more, stirring occasionally. Remove from heat; add lemon rind and sugar substitute and stir well. Serve hot on a biscuit or hot apple pie. For pie topping, add cinnamon.

***Natural sweetening directions:***
- 1/8 cup (30 mL) contains 28 Calories (P0, F0, C7)
- 1/8 cup = 1/4 cup of fruit (1/2 fruit exchange)
Omit sugar substitute. Include 1/3 cup (80 mL) apple or white grape juice in the 1 cup of juice combination. Increase lemon rind to 1/3 teaspoon (.5 gram).

***For low-salt diet:***
- 1/4 cup (60 mL) contains 1 mg of sodium
Omit salt; use sprinkle of salt substitute. Be sure to use grated lemon rind for extra flavor.

# Banana Drop Cookies

- Makes 50 cookies
- 1 cookie contains 51 Calories (P1, F3, C5), 10 mg of cholesterol if made with egg, no cholesterol if made with egg substitute
- 1 cookie = 1/4 cup of fruit + 1/2 teaspoon of fat (1/2 fruit exchange + 1/2 fat exchange)

**Margarine**    1/4 cup (56.5 grams); use corn-oil, soybean-oil or safflower-oil margarine
**Brown-type granular sugar substitute**    8 tablespoons (48 grams); or substitute equal to 1 cup (195 grams) of sugar
**Very ripe bananas**    1-1/2 cups (333 grams), mashed
**Eggs**    2 large (114 grams); or 4 ounces (120 mL) of liquid egg substitute
**Plain low-fat yogurt**    1/4 cup (60 mL)
**Butter flavoring**    10 drops
**Oat flour**    2/3 cup (40 grams); see page 25
**Unbleached flour**    3/4 cup (87 grams), sifted; or 3/4 cup (95 grams) whole-wheat flour, sifted
**Salt**    1/2 teaspoon (3 grams)
**Double-acting baking powder**    2 tablespoons (24 grams)
**Walnuts**    1/2 cup (60 grams), chopped
**Vanilla**    1-1/2 teaspoons (7.5 mL)
**Black walnut flavoring**    1 teaspoon (5 mL)

Cream margarine, sugar substitute and bananas until light and fluffy. Beat eggs, yogurt and butter flavoring. Add egg mixture to creamed batter; stir until well mixed. Sift dry ingredients together and add them to the batter gradually, beating until all lumps are gone. Add walnuts and flavorings; mix well. Drop by teaspoonfuls or small melon scoop onto nonstick baking sheet or sheet sprayed with nonstick coating. Bake at 375°F (191°C) about 15 minutes, until edges turn brown. Cool on a rack. Store in a tight container in a cool place, or freeze.

**Suggestions:**
Be sure the bananas are almost black on the outside, or the cookies will need extra sweetening.

### Natural sweetening directions:
- 1 cookie contains 55 Calories (P1, F3, C6)
- 1 cookie = 1/2 teaspoon of fat + 1/4 cup of fruit (1/2 fat exchange + 1/2 fruit exchange)

### For low-salt diet:
- 1 cookie contains 8 mg of sodium
Omit salt; use 1/2 teaspoon (2 grams) of salt substitute. Use salt-free margarine. Use 2 tablespoons (24 grams) of sodium-free baking powder.

# Wilma's Holiday Orange Cookies

- Makes 60 cookies
- 2 cookies contain 72 Calories (P1, F4, C8), no cholesterol if made with egg substitute
- 2 cookies = 1/2 cup of fruit + 1 teaspoon of fat (1 fruit exchange + 1 fat exchange)

**Unbleached or whole-wheat flour**    2 cups (232 or 254 grams), sifted
**Walnuts**    1/2 cup (60 grams), chopped
**Raisins**    1/3 cup (48 grams)
**Orange juice**    1/2 cup (120 mL)
**Orange rind**    1 rounded tablespoon (4.5 grams), grated
**Soft-type margarine**    1/2 cup (113 grams); use corn-oil, soybean-oil or safflower-oil margarine
**Salt**    1/2 teaspoon (3 grams)
**Cinnamon**    1/2 teaspoon (1.5 grams)
**Brown-type granular sugar substitute**    1/3 cup (32 grams); or substitute equal to 2/3 cup (130 grams) of sugar
**Warm water**    1/4 cup (60 mL) or more
**Egg**    1 medium (50 grams); or 2 ounces of liquid egg substitute
**Double-acting baking powder**    2-1/2 teaspoons (10 grams)
**Vanilla**    1/2 teaspoon (2.5 mL)

Cream margarine, egg and grated rind until fluffy. Combine dry ingredients and stir to coat nuts and raisins with flour. Combine liquid ingredients and add alternately with dry mixture, stirring after each addition. If consistency is too thick for a good drop cookie, add warm water, 1 tablespoon (15 mL) at a time. Drop by rounded teaspoons on a nonstick cookie sheet, or one sprayed with a nonstick coating. Bake at 375°F (191°C) 18 to 20 minutes, until edges are slightly browned.

### Natural sweetening directions:
*This recipe is not for hypoglycemics.*
- Makes 64 cookies
- 3 cookies contain 122 Calories (P2, F6, C15), 12 mg of cholesterol
- 3 cookies = 1 slice of bread + 1 teaspoon of fat (1 bread exchange + 1 fat exchange)
Omit sugar substitute, warm water and orange juice; use 1/3 cup + 1 tablespoon (110 mL) frozen concentrated orange juice and 1/3 cup (80 mL) concentrated apple juice plus 1 tablespoon (15 mL) lemon juice. Increase flour to 2-1/3 cups (270 or 296 grams).

### For low-salt diet:
- 1 cookie contains 4 mg of sodium
Omit salt, baking powder and margarine; use salt substitute, salt-free baking powder and salt-free margarine.

# Oatmeal Hermits

- Makes 36 large cookies
- 1 cookie contains 75 Calories (P2, F3, C10), 7 mg of cholesterol if made with egg, no cholesterol if made with egg substitute
- 1 cookie = 1/2 teaspoon of fat + 1/2 cup of fruit (1/2 fat exchange + 1 fruit exchange)

---

**Margarine**   1/3 cup (75 grams); use corn-oil, soybean-oil or safflower-oil margarine
**Brown-type granular sugar substitute**   1/2 cup (48 grams); or substitute equal to 1 cup (195 grams) of sugar
**Plain low-fat yogurt**   1/3 cup (80 mL)
**Egg**   1 large (57 grams); or 2 ounces (60 mL) of liquid egg substitute
**Quick-cooking oatmeal**   2/3 cup (48 grams)
**Unbleached or whole-wheat flour**   2/3 cup (84 or 91 grams), unsifted
**Double-acting baking powder**   2/3 teaspoon (2.7 grams)
**Salt**   1/4 teaspoon (1.5 grams)
**Cinnamon**   1/2 teaspoon (1.5 grams)
**Nutmeg**   1/4 teaspoon (.8 gram)
**Ground cloves**   1/8 teaspoon (.4 gram)
**Raisins**   4 tablespoons (36 grams), cut in half and soaked in hot water and drained
**Vanilla**   2/3 teaspoon (3.3 mL)
**Walnuts**   12 halves (66 grams), chopped

Cream margarine with sugar substitute until fluffy. Add yogurt and egg; mix well. Combine dry ingredients; add gradually to creamed mixture. Drain raisins well; add raisins, vanilla and nuts to creamed mixture. Beat to ensure even mixing of nuts and raisins. Drop by teaspoonfuls onto nonstick baking sheet or sheet sprayed with nonstick coating. Bake at 375°F (191°C) 12 to 14 minutes, until edges are browned. Cool on a rack; store in tight container in cool place, or freeze.

*Suggestions:*
Make a batch of these and use for lunches and snacks. They will keep fresh longer than most dietetic cookies.

---

*Natural sweetening directions:*
*This recipe is not for hypoglycemics.*
- Makes 40 cookies
- 1 cookie contains 79 Calories (P2, F3, C11), no change in cholesterol or sodium
- 1 cookie = 1/2 cup of fruit + 1/2 teaspoon of fat (1 fruit exchange + 1/2 fat exchange)
Omit sugar substitute; replace with 1/2 cup + 2 tablespoons (100 grams) of date sugar. Increase vanilla to 1-1/2 teaspoons (7.5 mL) and add 1-1/2 teaspoons (7.5 mL) of lemon juice. Increase salt to 1/2 teaspoon (3 grams).

*For low-salt diet:*
- 1 cookie contains 6 mg of sodium
Omit salt; use 1/4 teaspoon (1 gram) of salt substitute. Use salt-free margarine. Use 1 teaspoon (4 grams) of sodium-free baking powder.

169

# Soft Ginger Drops

- Makes 60 cookies
- 2 cookies contain 84 Calories (P2, F2, C10), 8 mg of cholesterol if made with egg, no cholesterol if made with egg substitute
- 2 cookies = 1/2 cup of fruit + 1 teaspoon of fat (1 fruit exchange + 1 fat exchange)

**Margarine**   1/2 cup (113 grams); use corn-oil, soybean-oil or safflower-oil margarine
**Brown-type granular sugar substitute**   1 cup (96 grams); or substitute equal to 2 cups (390 grams) of sugar
**Egg**   1 large (57 grams) + 2 egg whites (66 grams); or 4 ounces (120 mL) of liquid egg substitute
**Strong coffee**   3/4 cup (180 mL); use decaffeinated if you prefer.
**Plain low-fat yogurt**   1/4 cup (60 mL)
**Double-acting baking powder**   3/4 teaspoon (3 grams)
**Cinnamon**   1 teaspoon (3 grams)
**Ground cloves**   1 teaspoon (3 grams)
**Ginger**   1-1/2 teaspoons (4.5 grams)
**Salt**   1 teaspoon (6 grams)
**Baking soda**   3/4 teaspoon (3 grams)
**Unbleached or whole-wheat flour**   3-1/8 cups (362.5 or 397 grams), sifted

Cream margarine with sugar substitute until light and fluffy. Beat egg lightly; add to creamed mixture. Combine coffee and yogurt. Sift dry ingredients together. Add liquid and dry ingredients alternately to creamed mixture, beating thoroughly after each addition. Drop by rounded teaspoonfuls onto a nonstick baking sheet or sheet sprayed with nonstick coating. Bake at 375°F (191°C) 18 to 20 minutes, until edges are browned. Cool on a rack; store in tight container in cool place, or freeze.

*Natural sweetening directions:*
*This recipe is not for hypoglycemics.*
- 2 cookies contain 100 Calories (P2, F4, C14), no change in cholesterol or sodium
- 2 cookies = 1 slice of bread + 1 teaspoon of fat (1 bread exchange + 1 fat exchange)
Omit sugar substitute; replace with 3/4 cup (120 grams) of date sugar. Increase ginger to 1-3/4 teaspoons (5.3 grams). Bake 16 to 18 minutes.

*For low-salt diet:*
- 1 cookie contains 5.5 mg of sodium
Omit salt; use 1 teaspoon (4 grams) of salt substitute. Omit both regular baking powder and baking soda; replace with 1-3/4 teaspoons (7 grams) of sodium-free baking powder. Use salt-free margarine. Increase ginger to 1-3/4 teaspoons (5.3 grams).

# Granola Cookies

- Makes 64 cookies
- 3 cookies contain 85 Calories (P2, F5, C8), 24 mg of cholesterol if made with eggs, no cholesterol if made with egg substitute
- 3 cookies = 1/2 cup of fruit + 1 teaspoon of fat (1 fruit exchange + 1 fat exchange)

**Margarine**   1/3 cup (75 grams); use corn-oil, soybean-oil or safflower-oil margarine
**Brown-type granular sugar substitute**   6 tablespoons (36 grams); or substitute equal to 3/4 cup (146 grams) of sugar
**Egg**   2 large (114 grams); or 4 ounces (120 mL) of liquid egg substitute
**Plain low-fat yogurt**   1/2 cup (120 mL)
**Vanilla**   1-1/2 teaspoons (7.5 mL)
**Black walnut flavoring**   2/3 teaspoon (3.3 mL)
**Double-acting baking powder**   1 teaspoon (4 grams)
**Salt**   2/3 teaspoon (4 grams)
**Whole-wheat flour**   1 cup (127 grams), sifted twice
**Dietetic granola**   1 cup (98 grams); see recipe on page 235

Cream margarine and sugar substitute; add beaten eggs and yogurt; mix well. Add both flavorings; mix. Combine baking powder, salt and flour; stir thoroughly into first mixture. Add granola; mix in thoroughly. Drop by teaspoonfuls onto a nonstick baking sheet or sheet sprayed with nonstick coating. Bake at 375°F (191°C) about 15 minutes, until edges are light brown. Cool on a rack. Store in a tight container in cool place.

**Suggestions:**
Don't give away the secret of the ingredients and you will puzzle those who eat the cookies. The taste is excellent, the texture quite chewy.

### Natural sweetening directions:
*This recipe is not for hypoglycemics.*
- 3 cookies contain 101 Calories (P3, F5, C11), no change in cholesterol or sodium
- 3 cookies = 1/2 ounce of meat + 1/2 cup of fruit + 1/2 teaspoon of fat (1/2 meat exchange + 1 fruit exchange + 1/2 fat exchange)

Omit sugar substitute; use 8 tablespoons (80 grams) of date sugar and increase black walnut flavoring to 1 teaspoon (5 mL).

### For low-salt diet:
- 1 cookie contains 7 mg of sodium

Omit salt; use 2/3 teaspoon (2.5 grams) of salt substitute. Use salt-free margarine. Use 1-1/2 teaspoons (6 grams) of sodium-free baking powder. Follow low-salt instructions for granola; see recipe on page 235.

# Crunchy Peanut Butter Cookies

- Makes 60 cookies
- 2 cookies contain 92 Calories (P4, F4, C10), 9 mg of cholesterol, no cholesterol if made with egg substitute
- 2 cookies = 1/2 ounce of meat + 1/2 cup of fruit + 1/2 teaspoon of fat (1/2 meat exchange + 1 fruit exchange + 1/2 fat exchange)

**Whole-wheat flour**   2-1/2 cups (317.5 grams), sifted twice
**Double-acting baking powder**   3 teaspoons (12 grams)
**Baking soda**   1/2 teaspoon (2 grams)
**Powdered buttermilk**   1/3 cup (25 grams) plus enough water to make 1 cup (240 mL) of buttermilk
**Salt**   3/4 teaspoon (4.5 grams)
**Egg**   1 medium (50 grams), well-beaten
**Brown-type granular sugar substitute**   2/3 cup (64 grams); or substitute equal to 1-1/3 cups (260 grams) of sugar
**Lemon juice**   1-1/2 teaspoons (7.5 mL)
**Crunchy peanut butter**   1 cup (251 grams), old-fashioned
**Vanilla**   1/2 teaspoon (2.5 mL)

Cream beaten eggs, lemon juice and peanut butter. Sift together all dry ingredients. Add water to egg/peanut butter mixture, stirring well. Gradually add this to dry mixture, beating after each addition. Divide into three parts; form each into a 2-inch-wide (5 cm) roll. Wrap in waxed paper and chill for at least 1 hour. Cut cookies 1/3-inch (.8 cm) thick, one roll at a time. Place cookies on a nonstick cookie sheet, or one that has been sprayed with a nonstick coating. Bake at 375°F (191°C) for 12 to 15 minutes, until edges of cookies are lightly browned. Cool on a rack.

### Natural sweetening directions:
*This recipe is not for hypoglycemics.*
- 2 cookies contain 100 Calories (P4, F4, C12), no change in cholesterol or sodium
- 2 cookies = 1/2 ounce of meat + 1/2 cup of fruit + 1/2 teaspoon of fat (1/2 meat exchange + 1 fruit exchange + 1/2 fat exchange)

Omit sugar substitute and water; use 2/3 cup (160 mL) concentrated apple juice plus 3 tablespoons (30 grams) of date sugar. Increase lemon juice to 1 tablespoon (15 mL).

### For low-salt diet:
- 2 cookies contain 9 mg of sodium

Use salt-free baking powder and replace baking soda with equal amount of potassium bicarbonate. Use salt-free, old-fashioned crunchy-style peanut butter.

# Sugarless Mincemeat Cookies

- Makes 50 cookies
- 2 cookies contain 71 Calories (P1, F3, C10), 6 mg of cholesterol if made with egg, no cholesterol if made with egg substitute
- 2 cookies = 1/2 cup of fruit + 1/2 teaspoon of fat (1 fruit exchange + 1/2 fat exchange)

**Margarine**   1/3 cup (75 grams); use corn-oil, soybean-oil or safflower-oil margarine
**Brown-type granular sugar substitute**   1/2 cup (48 grams); or substitute equal to 1 cup (195 grams) of sugar
**Plain low-fat yogurt**   1/3 cup (80 mL)
**Egg**   1 medium (50 grams), well beaten; or 2 ounces (60 mL) of liquid egg substitute
**Whole-wheat flour**   1 cup + 2 tablespoons (146.2 grams), sifted twice
**Double-acting baking powder**   2/3 teaspoon (2.7 grams)
**Salt**   1/4 teaspoon (1.5 grams)
**Vanilla**   1/2 teaspoon (2.5 mL)
**Sugarless mincemeat**   1 cup (146 grams); see recipe on page 187

Cream margarine, sugar substitute and yogurt until smooth. Beat in vanilla and egg. Sift together flour, baking powder and salt. Add mincemeat to first mixture, stirring to blend. Gradually add flour, mixing well. Drop cookies by rounded teaspoonfuls on a nonstick cookie sheet, or one that has been sprayed with a nonstick coating. Bake at 375°F (191°C) for 12 minutes, until lightly browned. Cool on a rack. Freeze if you are planning to keep these longer than a few days.

*Natural sweetening directions:*
*This recipe is not for hypoglycemics.*
- 2 cookies contain 79 Calories (P1, F3, C12), 5 mg of sodium if made with egg
- 2 cookies = 1/2 cup of fruit + 1/2 teaspoon of fat (1 fruit exchange + 1/2 fat exchange)
Omit sugar substitute; replace with 1/2 cup + 2 tablespoons (100 grams) of date sugar, plus 1 teaspoon (5 mL) lemon juice.

*For low-salt diet:*
- 1 cookie contains 3 mg of sodium if made with egg, 6 mg or more if made with egg substitute
Omit salt and baking powder; replace with equal amounts of salt substitute and salt-free baking powder.

# Sue's Applesauce Brownies

- Makes 16 squares
- 1 square contains 138 Calories (P3, F10, C9), no cholesterol if made with egg substitute
- 1 square = 1/2 ounce of meat + 1/2 cup of fruit + 1-1/2 teaspoons of fat (1/2 meat exchange + 1 fruit exchange + 1-1/2 fat exchanges)

**Soft margarine**   1/2 cup (113 grams)
**Baking chocolate**   2 squares (56 grams)
**Brown-type granular sugar substitute**   3/4 cup (72 grams); or substitute equal to 1-1/2 cups (292.5 grams) of sugar
**Eggs**   2 medium (100 grams), well-beaten; or 4 ounces (120 mL) of liquid egg substitute
**Unsweetened applesauce**   3/4 cup (192 grams)
**Vanilla**   1-1/4 teaspoons (6.3 mL)
**Whole-wheat flour**   1 cup (127 grams), sifted twice
**Double-acting baking powder**   1-1/4 teaspoons (5 grams)
**Baking soda**   1/4 teaspoon (1 gram)
**Salt**   1/2 teaspoon (3 grams)
**Walnuts**   1/2 cup (60 grams), chopped

Melt chocolate and margarine over low heat; let cool. Beat together eggs and sweetening, then add cooled chocolate mixture. Sift together dry ingredients; add vanilla to applesauce. Alternately add dry ingredients and applesauce to cooled chocolate mixture, beating after each addition. Mix nuts into last addition of flour and add last; mix well. Pour batter into a nonstick pan, or one that has been sprayed with a nonstick coating; level top with a spatula. Bake at 350°F (177°C) for 25 minutes. Cool on a rack. Cut into 16 squares, or slices, if baked in a loaf pan.

## Natural sweetening directions:
*This recipe is not for hypoglycemics.*
- 1 square contains 183 Calories (P3, F11, C18), 8 mg of sodium
- 1 square = 1/2 slice of bread + 1/2 ounce of meat + 1/2 cup of fruit + 1-1/2 teaspoons of fat (1/2 bread exchange + 1/2 meat exchange + 1 fruit exchange + 1-1/2 fat exchanges)

Omit sugar substitute; use 1 cup (160 grams) of date sugar. Increase vanilla to 1-1/2 teaspoons (7.5 mL) and increase applesauce to 1 cup (259 grams).

## For low-salt diet:
- 1 square contains 9 mg of sodium

Omit salt, baking powder and soda; replace with equal amounts of salt substitute, salt-free baking powder and potassium bicarbonate.

# Cream Cheese Cookies

- Makes 36 cookies
- 2 cookies contain 90 Calories (P2, F6, C7), 14 mg of cholesterol if made with egg, no cholesterol if made with egg substitute
- 2 cookies = 1/2 cup of fruit + 1 teaspoon of fat (1 fruit exchange + 1 fat exchange)

**Brown-type granular sugar substitute**   1/2 cup (48 grams); or substitute equal to 1 cup (195 grams) of sugar
**Margarine**   1/2 cup (113 grams); use corn-oil, soybean-oil or safflower-oil margarine
**Low-Calorie cream cheese**   2 ounces (56 grams), at room temperature
**Vanilla**   1/2 teaspoon (2.5 mL)
**Almond extract**   1/2 teaspoon (2.5 mL)
**Egg yolk**   1 (20 grams); or 2-1/2 teaspoons (12.5 mL) of liquid egg substitute + 1 teaspoon (5 mL) oil
**Baking soda**   generous pinch
**Salt**   generous pinch
**Whole-wheat flour**   1-1/2 cups (190.5 grams), sifted twice
**Lemon rind**   1/2 teaspoon (.8 gram)

Cream together margarine and sugar substitute. Gradually add cream cheese, egg, lemon rind and flavorings. Combine dry ingredients; sift into first mixture. Form into two rolls; wrap in waxed paper and chill for 2 hours or more. Slice cookies 1/3-inch (.8 cm) thick; place on a nonstick cookie sheet or one that has been sprayed with a nonstick coating. Bake at 350°F (177°C) for 18 to 20 minutes, until edges are lightly browned. Cool on a rack.

### Natural sweetening directions:
*This recipe is not for hypoglycemics.*
- 2 cookies contain 110 Calories (P2, F6, C12), no change in cholesterol or sodium
- 2 cookies = 1/2 cup of fruit + 1 teaspoon of fat (1 fruit exchange + 1 fat exchange)
Omit sugar substitute; replace with 2/3 cup (107 grams) of date sugar. Increase vanilla to 3/4 teaspoon (3.8 mL) and lemon rind to 3/4 teaspoon (1.2 grams).

### For low-salt diet:
- 2 cookies contain 3 mg of sodium
Omit soda and salt, use salt-free margarine. Use equal amounts of salt substitute and potassium bicarbonate.

175

# They're So Good! Cookies

- Makes 48 cookies
- 2 cookies contain 116 Calories (P2, F8, C9), no cholesterol if made with egg substitute
- 2 cookies = 1/2 cup of fruit + 1-1/2 teaspoons of fat (1 fruit exchange + 1-1/2 fat exchanges)

**Soft-type margarine**   1/2 cup (113 grams); use corn-oil, soybean-oil or safflower-oil margarine
**Brown-type granular sugar substitute**   1/4 cup (24 grams); or substitute equal to 1/2 cup (97.5 grams) of sugar
**Egg**   1 large (57 grams); or 2-1/2 ounces (75 mL) of liquid egg substitute
**Concentrated apple juice**   1 tablespoon (15 mL)
**Whole-wheat flour**   1-1/4 cups (159 grams), sifted twice
**Dates**   1/2 cup (87 grams), chopped fine
**Unsweetened coconut**   3/4 cup (71 grams)
**Vanilla**   2 teaspoons (10 mL)
**Lemon rind**   1/2 teaspoon (.8 gram), grated
**Double-acting baking powder**   1 teaspoon (4 grams)
**Salt**   1/2 teaspoon (3 grams)

Cream margarine; add beaten egg, lemon rind, apple juice, vanilla and sugar substitute. Sift together dry ingredients. Add dates to this mixture, using your fingers to separate them into small pieces. Add nuts and coconut to this mixture, then gradually add all to first mixture, mixing well after each addition. Divide the dough into half. Form each into rolls about 2-1/2 inches (6.25 cm) in diameter. Roll in waxed paper and chill for at least 2 hours, overnight is even better. Slice cookies 1/3-inch (.8 cm) thick and place on a greased or nonstick cookie sheet. Bake at 350°F (177°C) for 12 to 15 minutes, until edges are slightly browned. Cool on a rack.

### Natural sweetening directions:
- 2 cookies contain 120 Calories (P2, F8, C10), no change in cholesterol or sodium
- 2 cookies = 1/2 cup of fruit + 1-1/2 teaspoons of fat (1 fruit exchange + 1-1/2 fat exchanges)

Omit sugar substitute; replace with 1/4 cup (40 grams) of date sugar.

### For low-salt diet:
- 2 cookies contain 4 mg of sodium

Omit salt and baking powder; use equal amounts of salt substitute and salt-free baking powder.

# Pie Crust

***This recipe is not for hypoglycemics.***
• Makes two 8-inch (20 cm) double-crust pies, or 3 pie shells

***Single crust only:***
• 1/8 portion contains 102 Calories (P2, F6, C10), no cholesterol
• 1/8 portion = 2/3 slice of bread + 1 teaspoon of fat (2/3 bread exchange + 1 fat exchange)

***Double crust only:***
• 1/8 portion contains 153 Calories (P3, F9, C15), no cholesterol
• 1/8 portion = 1 slice of bread + 2 teaspoons of fat (1 bread exchange + 2 fat exchanges)

**Unbleached flour**   3 cups (348 grams), sifted
**Salt**   1 teaspoon (6 grams)
**Margarine**   3/4 cup (170 grams); use corn-oil, soybean-oil or safflower-oil margarine
**Cold water**   2/3 cup (160 mL)

Sift flour and salt together. With pastry blender, cut margarine into flour until fat is like coarse crumbs. Work in water gradually, adding only enough to make mixture stick together. The amount will vary with room temperature. Form dough into balls, 3 equal balls for one-crust pies, 2 large and 2 smaller for double-crust pies. Wrap in plastic wrap or waxed paper; refrigerate for 15 to 20 minutes. Using pastry cloth and rolling-pin cover to avoid using too much flour, roll crusts out on lightly floured board; roll into thin circle about the size of the pie plate. Fit crust into plate, rolling edge a bit to be sure it is not stretched too thin.

**For shell only:** Flute edge or firm with a fork. Bake at 450°F (232°C) for about 15 minutes.

**For filled pie:** Place filling in bottom shell; spread evenly. If you wish, fruit may be heaped slightly in center of pie. Roll out top crust from smaller ball of dough; cut slits about 2 inches (5 cm) in from edge to let steam escape during baking. Moisten edge of lower shell; put on top crust to overlap all around; flute edges together or press with fork. Trim all around with sharp knife. Bake at 450°F (232°C) for 15 minutes, then follow individual recipe.

**For frozen pie:** Bake 20 minutes at 450°F (232°C), then 40 to 60 minutes at 375°F (191°C), until center of pie crust is lightly browned.

***Natural sweetening directions:***
• Not needed.

***For low-salt diet:***
• 1/8 portion of pie crust contains 1 mg of sodium
Omit salt; use 1 teaspoon (4 grams) of salt substitute. Use salt-free margarine.

# Whole-Wheat Flour Substitution

If using whole-wheat flour in pie shells, sift twice *before* you measure the amount needed. Sift again when adding to recipe. This will give you a lighter flour and also remove the coarse bran which makes a sugar-free recipe much heavier. DO NOT SKIP THIS STEP!

When using only one pie crust, you may subtract the following from any 2-crust pie recipe in this book:
- 81 Calories (P1, F5, C8), 6 mg of sodium
- 1/2 slice of bread + 1 teaspoon of fat (1/2 bread exchange + 1 fat exchange)

**Note:** *Nutritional values given for the pie recipes include the pie crust. Hypoglycemics use whole-wheat flour only.*

# Whole-Wheat Pastry / *Single and Double Crust*

- Makes crust for a 9-inch (22.5 cm) pie

## Single Crust

- 1/8 portion contains 97 Calories (P2, F5, C11), no cholesterol
- 1/8 portion = 2/3 slice of bread + 1 teaspoon of fat (2/3 bread exchange + 1 fat exchange)

**Whole-wheat flour**   1 cup (127 grams), sifted twice
**Margarine**   1/3 cup (75 grams); use corn-oil, soybean-oil or safflower-oil margarine
**Salt**   1/3 teaspoon (2 grams)
**Cold water**   1/4 cup (60 mL)

## Double Crust

- 1/8 portion contains 148 Calories (P3, F8, C16), no cholesterol
- 1/8 portion = 1 slice of bread + 1-1/2 teaspoons of fat (1 bread exchange + 1-1/2 fat exchanges)

**Whole-wheat flour**   1-1/2 cups (190.5 grams), sifted twice
**Margarine**   2/3 cup (150 grams); use corn-oil, soybean-oil or safflower-oil margarine
**Salt**   1/2 teaspoon (3 grams)
**Cold water**   1/3 cup+ (90 mL)

Sift flour and salt into mixing bowl. Cut in margarine with a pastry blender until mixture resembles coarse corn meal. Gradually add cold water until dough forms a ball. Wrap in wax paper and chill 20 to 30 minutes. Roll out on a lightly floured board, or use a pastry cloth. Fit crust into 9-inch (22.5 cm) pie plate, folding in edges along the rim; trim off any extra crust. Flute edges along the rim. If using as a shell, prick crust all over with a fork to prevent bubbles from forming. Bake at 450°F (232°C) for 12 to 15 minutes, until crust is lightly browned. If using for baked filling, fill crust with filling and bake as directed in the filling recipe.

***Natural sweetening directions:***
- Not needed.

***For low-salt diet:***
- Single crust: 1/8 portion contains 3 mg of sodium
- Double crust: 1/8 portion contains 5 mg of sodium
Omit salt; replace with equal amount of salt substitute, if desired.

# One-Crust Pie or How to Save Calories and Still Enjoy Pie!

- Makes top or bottom crust for an 8- or 9-inch (20 or 22.5 cm) pie
- 1/8 portion contains 106 Calories (P2, F6, C11), no cholesterol
- 1/8 portion = 2/3 slice of bread + 1 teaspoon of fat (2/3 bread exchange + 1 fat exchange)

**Unbleached or whole-wheat flour**     1 cup (116 or 127 grams), sifted.
   *Note: Hypoglycemics use whole-wheat flour only.*
**Margarine**     1/3 cup (75 grams); use corn-oil, soybean-oil or safflower-oil
   margarine
**Salt**     1/3 teaspoon (2 grams)
**Cold water**     1/4 cup (60 mL)

Sift flour and salt into a mixing bowl. Cut in margarine with a pastry blender until mixture resembles coarse corn meal. Gradually add cold water until dough forms a ball when pressed together. Wrap dough in wax paper and chill at least 30 minutes. Roll out on a lightly floured board, or a pastry cloth, to fit an 8- or 9-inch (20 or 22.5 cm) pie plate. Trim and flute edges on bottom for a shell. To use as a top crust, cover pie filling and turn edges under and flute or press to seal in the filling. (When making a pie without a bottom crust, use a nonstick pie plate, or spray plate liberally with nonstick coating before pouring in the filling.) Cut steam holes in top crust, and put pie plate on a metal baking sheet to catch any drips and to help spread the heat evenly. Bake on the middle shelf of the oven decreasing the time by 5 to 10 minutes. The pie will be done when the middle of the crust is well done. Cool on a rack and slice and serve as usual.

***Natural sweetening directions:***
- Not needed.

***For low-salt diet:***
- 1/8 portion contains 6 mg of sodium
Omit salt; use 1/3 teaspoon (1.3 grams) of salt substitute. Use salt-free margarine.

# Mock Graham Cracker Crust

- Makes crust for a 9-inch (22.5 cm) pie
- 1/6 portion contains 136 Calories (P2, F8, C14), no cholesterol
- 1/6 portion = 1 slice of bread + 1-1/2 teaspoons of fat (1 bread exchange + 1-1/2 fat exchanges)

**Whole-wheat bread crumbs**   3/4 cup (112 grams), made from 4 slices of whole-grain bread
**Date sugar**   3 tablespoons (30 grams)
**Melted margarine**   4 tablespoons (60 mL); use corn-oil, soybean-oil or safflower-oil margarine
**Salt**   sprinkle

Bake 4 slices of whole-grain bread in a 200°F (93°C) oven until they are very hard and like Melba toast in texture; bread will not crumb if it is not dry enough. When bread is cool, use a blender or food processor to crumb or crush slices with a rolling pin. Sieve to remove any large pieces and crumb until all are very fine. Place crumbs in a mixing bowl, add date sugar, salt and melted margarine. (*Do not* use soft-type margarine!) Mix well and put into a pie plate, reserving about 3 tablespoons for topping if you wish. Press crumbs against side of pie plate and along the bottom, making it as even as you can. Press firmly to form crust. Chill to harden.

**Natural sweetening directions:**
- Not needed.

**For low-salt diet:**
- 1/6 portion contains 15 mg of sodium; regular recipe contains 109 mg of sodium
- 1/8 portion contains 12 mg of sodium; regular recipe contains 82 mg of sodium
Omit salt; use salt substitute. Use salt-free whole-wheat bread and salt-free margarine.

# Apple-Raisin Pie

- Makes filling for two 8-inch (20 cm) double-crust pies
- 1/8 portion contains 226 Calories (P4, F10, C30), no cholesterol
- 1/8 portion = 1 slice of bread + 3/4 cup of fruit + 2 teaspoons of fat (1 bread exchange + 1-1/2 fruit exchanges + 2 fat exchanges)

*Top-crust-only pie:*
- 1/8 portion contains 175 Calories (P3, F7, C25), no cholesterol
- 1/8 portion = 1 slice of bread + 1/2 cup of fruit + 1-1/2 teaspoons of fat (1 bread exchange + 1 fruit exchange + 1-1/2 fat exchanges)

**Pie crust**   1 recipe for each pie
**Raisins**   4 tablespoons (36 grams), soaked in hot water and drained
**Apples**   6 large sliced thin, 6 generous cups (1.4 Kg)
**Lemon juice**   2 to 4 tablespoons (30 to 60 mL). Use larger amount with sweeter apples
**Brown-type granular sugar substitute**   6 to 8 tablespoons (36 to 48 grams); or substitute equal to 3/4 to 1 cup (146 to 195 grams) of sugar
**Unbleached or whole-wheat flour**   1/4 cup (29 or 32 grams), sifted
**Cinnamon**   1/2 teaspoon (1.5 grams)
**Nutmeg**   1/4 teaspoon (.8 gram)
**Soft-type margarine**   1 tablespoon (14 grams); use corn-oil, soybean-oil or safflower-oil margarine
**Salt**   sprinkle

*Optional:*
**Ginger**   1/8 to 1/4 teaspoon (.4 to .8 gram)

Prepare pie crust; refrigerate. Soak raisins in hot water. Peel and slice apples thin; pour lemon juice on them. Combine dry ingredients in bowl; sift them over apples so all are covered; let stand at least 10 minutes, stirring occasionally to keep slices covered evenly. Roll out bottom crusts, according to directions. Drain raisins; combine with apples; divide fruit mixture into equal parts. Fill each shell with half of mixture. Divide margarine into 2 equal parts; from each part, dab about 6 tiny pieces on top of fruit mixture so it will melt into fruit as evenly as possible. Roll out top crusts and put on pie as directed in recipe, cutting air vents and sealing edges. Bake at 450°F (232°C) for 15 minutes, then at 375°F (191°C) for 40 to 50 minutes, until center of pie is nicely browned. Cool on rack. Do not cut until fairly cool, or filling will be runny.

**Suggestions:**
Second pie may be frozen, unbaked, for later use.

### Natural sweetening directions:
*This recipe is not for hypoglycemics.*
- 1/8 portion contains 246 Calories (P4, F10, C35), no cholesterol, 3 mg of sodium
- 1/8 portion = 1 slice of bread + 3/4 cup of fruit + 2 teaspoons of fat (1 bread exchange + 1-1/2 fruit exchanges + 2 fat exchanges)

Omit sugar substitute; use 8 to 9 tablespoons (80 to 90 grams) of date sugar. Add 1/4 teaspoon (.4 gram) of grated lemon rind. Use the 4 tablespoons (60 mL) of lemon juice.

### For low-salt diet:
- 1/8 portion contains 3.5 mg of sodium

Omit salt; use sprinkle of salt substitute. Use salt-free margarine. Make pie crust according to low-salt directions.

# Cheese Pie

- Makes one 8-inch (20 cm) pie filling
- 1/8 portion contains 195 Calories (P13, F11, C11), 101 mg of cholesterol if made with eggs; 2 mg of cholesterol if made with egg substitute
- 1/8 portion = 2 ounces of meat + 1/2 cup of fruit + 1 teaspoon of fat (2 meat exchanges + 1 fruit exchange + 1 fat exchange)

**Pie shell**   1 unbaked
**Eggs**   3 large (171 grams); or 6 ounces (180 mL) of liquid egg substitute
**Skim milk**   3 tablespoons (45 mL)
**Cottage cheese**   1 pint (470 mL)
**Unbleached flour**   1 tablespoon (8 grams)
**Brown-type granular sugar substitute**   1/2 cup (48 grams); or substitute equal to 1 cup (195 grams) of sugar
**Salt**   1/8 teaspoon (.8 gram)
**Vanilla**   1/2 teaspoon (2.5 mL)
**Lemon rind**   1/2 teaspoon (.8 gram), grated
**Cinnamon**   sprinkle

Make pie shell. Beat eggs well; add milk. Put cottage cheese and 1/2 egg mixture into blender; blend for 1 minute. Add blended mixture to remainder of egg; add flour, sugar substitute, salt, vanilla and lemon rind; mix well. Pour into pie shell; sprinkle generously with cinnamon. Bake at 475°F (246°C) for 10 minutes, then at 375°F (191°C) about 35 minutes, until filling is set (test with silver knife blade). Cool on rack. Do not cut while still very warm, or it may be soft and runny.

### Natural sweetening directions:
- 1/8 portion contains 251 Calories (P12, F11, C25)
- 1/8 portion = 1 slice of bread + 1-1/2 ounces of meat + 1 teaspoon of fat (1 bread exchange + 1-1/2 meat exchanges + 1 fat exchange)

Omit sugar substitute; add 6 tablespoons (96 grams) dietetic applesauce plus 6 tablespoons (60 grams) of date sugar. Increase vanilla to 3/4 teaspoon (3.8 mL) and lemon rind to 3/4 teaspoon (1.2 grams). Increase flour to 1-1/2 tablespoons (12 grams).

### For low-salt diet:
Do not use on 400-mg sodium or 1-gram salt diets. This recipe cannot be made low in salt because of the high natural sodium content of the eggs, milk and cottage cheese.
- 1/8 portion contains 188 mg of sodium

# Cherry Tarts

- Makes 8 tarts
- 1/2 tart contains 155 Calories (P2, F7, C21), no cholesterol
- 1/2 tart = 1/2 slice of bread + 1/2 cup of fruit + 1-1/2 teaspoons of fat (1/2 bread exchange + 1 fruit exchange + 1-1/2 fat exchanges)

**Pie crust**  single-crust recipe, page 179 or 180
**Red pie cherries**  2-1/2 cups or #2 can (538 grams)
**Cornstarch**  2-1/2 tablespoons (20 grams)
**Margarine**  2 teaspoons (9.3 grams); use corn-oil, soybean-oil or safflower-oil margarine
**Salt**  sprinkle
**Brown-type granular sugar substitute**  1/2 cup (48 grams); or substitute equal to 1 cup (195 grams) of sugar
**Almond extract**  1/2 to 3/4 teaspoon (2.5 to 3.8 mL)

Make pie crust, roll thin; cut out tart shells and fit into pans; prick shells (especially the edges) with fork. Bake at 425°F (218°C) 10 to 12 minutes, until lightly browned; allow to cool. Drain cherries, saving liquid. Mix cornstarch, margarine, salt and sugar substitute with cherry liquid. Cook slowly, stirring constantly, until thick. Remove from heat; add almond extract and cherries; cool slightly. Pour cooled fruit mixture into cooled shells; allow to set at least 2 hours before serving. For faster thickening, let set in refrigerator.

*Suggestions:*
If Calorie and fat allowances permit, serve with a tablespoon (8 grams) of vanilla ice cream (see recipe page 193) for topping.

---

*Natural sweetening directions:*
*This recipe is not for hypoglycemics*
- 1/2 tart contains 175 Calories (P2, F7, C26)
- 1/2 tart = 1 slice of bread + 1/2 cup of fruit + 1-1/2 teaspoons of fat (1 bread exchange + 1 fruit exchange + 1-1/2 fat exchanges)

Omit sugar substitute; use 1/2 cup (80 grams) of date sugar. Use only 6 ounces (180 mL) of cherry liquid. Add 1/4 cup (60 mL) white grape juice. Increase cornstarch to 3 tablespoons (24 grams). Use 3/4 teaspoon (3.8 mL) almond extract. Add cherries to the thickened mixture prior to removing from the heat. Allow to heat through to absorb the sweetness. Add almond extract after removing from the heat.

*For low-salt diet:*
- 1 tart contains 3 mg of sodium
Omit sprinkle of salt; use salt substitute. Use salt-free margarine. Make pie crust according to low-salt directions.

# Berry Pie

- Makes one 8-inch (20 cm) pie filling
- 1/8 portion contains 219 Calories (P4, F11, C26), no cholesterol
- 1/8 portion = 1 slice of bread + 1/2 cup of fruit + 2 teaspoons of fat (1 bread exchange + 1 fruit exchange + 2 fat exchanges)

*With top crust only:*
- 1/8 portion contains 138 Calories (P3, F6, C18)
- 1/8 portion = 1/2 slice of bread + 1/2 cup of fruit + 1 teaspoon of fat (1/2 bread exchange + 1 fruit exchange + 1 fat exchange)

**Pie crust**   1 recipe, single or double crust
**Berries**   3 cups (432 grams) **strawberries, raspberries, boysenberries** or **blueberries**
**Lemon juice**   1 to 2 tablespoons (15 to 30 mL), depending on sweetness of the berries
**Brown-type granular sugar substitute**   1/4 cup (24 grams); or substitute equal to 1/2 cup (97.5 grams) of sugar
**Salt**   2 sprinkles
**Unbleached or whole-wheat flour**   3 tablespoons (24 or 29 grams), sifted
**Soft-type margarine**   1 tablespoon (14 grams); use corn-oil, soybean-oil or safflower-oil margarine

*For boysenberry pie:* Add 1/4 teaspoon (1.3 mL) **lemon extract** or 1 teaspoon (1.5 grams) **grated lemon rind**
*For blueberry pie:* Add 1/4 teaspoon (.8 gram) **nutmeg**

Make pie crust; refrigerate. Wash and sort berries. Pour lemon juice over berries, mixing to cover them evenly. Sift together over berries sugar substitute, salt and flour; let stand about 10 minutes, stirring occasionally to keep berries covered. Roll out bottom crust; place in pie plate. Spread berry mixture evenly in bottom crust. Dab margarine over fruit. Roll out top crust, make steam vents, place and seal. Bake at 425°F (218°C) for 15 minutes, then at 350°F (177°C) until middle of crust is lightly browned, 45 to 50 minutes. Cool on rack. Do not cut until cold, or it will be runny.

**Suggestions:**
You may combine apples with berries for a good variation. Such combinations may require added spices, such as nutmeg or cinnamon. Use half of each fruit and adjust the flavoring accordingly.

*Natural sweetening directions:*
- This recipe does not adapt well to natural sweetening.

*For low-salt diet:*
- 1/8 portion contains 3.5 mg of sodium
Omit salt; use 2 sprinkles of salt substitute. Use salt-free margarine. Make crust according to salt-free directions.

# Lemon Pie or Pudding

- Makes 3 cups (720 mL), enough for an 8-inch (20 cm) pie

*Pie, including crust:*

- 1/8 portion contains 183 Calories (P5, F11, C16), 63 mg of cholesterol if made with eggs; no cholesterol if made with egg substitute
- 1/8 portion = 1 slice of bread + 1/2 ounce of meat + 1-1/2 teaspoons of fat (1 bread exchange + 1/2 meat exchange + 1-1/2 fat exchanges)

*Filling only:*

- 1/2 cup (120 mL) contains 102 Calories (P4, F6, C8), 84 mg of cholesterol if made with eggs, no cholesterol if made with egg substitute
- 1/2 cup = 1/2 ounce of meat + 1/2 cup of fruit + 1/2 teaspoon of fat (1/2 meat exchange + 1 fruit exchange + 1/2 fat exchange)

---

**Pie shell**   1 baked and cooled
**Cornstarch**   1/4 cup (32 grams)
**Water**   1-1/4 cups (300 mL)
**Salt**   2 sprinkles
**Lemon juice**   1/4 cup + 1 tablespoon (75 mL)
**Eggs**   2 large (114 grams); or 4 ounces (120 mL) of liquid egg substitute
**Margarine**   2 tablespoons (28 grams); use corn-oil, soybean-oil or safflower-oil margarine
**Granular sugar substitute**   4-1/2 teaspoons (9 grams); or substitute equal to 3 tablespoons (36.5 grams) of sugar
**Diet applesauce**   1/2 cup (128 grams), artificially sweetened
**Lemon rind**   up to 1 tablespoon (4.5 grams)
**Egg whites**   2 (66 grams)

Make shell for pie. Mix flour with water to make smooth paste; add salt. Cook in double boiler, stirring constantly, until slightly thick. Remove from heat; add lemon juice; cool slightly; add beaten eggs, stirring well to prevent curdling. Add remaining ingredients, except lemon rind and egg whites. Return to heat in double boiler; cook, covered, about 10 minutes. Remove from heat; add lemon rind; set aside to cool. Beat egg whites until very stiff; fold into cooked mixture, being gentle so the whites keep their lightness. Pour into baked pie shell; put into freezer to set firm. For pudding, spoon into parfait glasses and refrigerate until firm. Top with small sprigs of mint for garnish (optional).

---

*Natural sweetening directions:*
This recipe is not for hypoglycemics.
*With pie crust:*
- 1/8 portion contains 203 Calories (P5, F11, C21), no change in cholesterol or sodium
- 1/8 portion = 2/3 slice of bread + 1/2 ounce of meat + 1/2 cup of fruit + 1-1/2 teaspoons of fat (2/3 bread exchange + 1/2 meat exchange + 1 fruit exchange + 1-1/2 fat exchanges)
*Filling only:*
- 1/2 cup (120 mL) contains 122 Calories (P4, F6, C13)
- 1/2 cup = 1/2 ounce of meat + 3/4 cup of fruit + 1/2 teaspoon of fat (1/2 meat exchange + 1-1/2 fruit exchanges + 1/2 fat exchange)
Omit sugar substitute; use unsweetened applesauce. Reduce water to 1/2 cup (120 mL). Add 3/4 cup (180 mL) apple or white grape juice. Increase lemon juice to 6 tablespoons (90 mL).

*For low-salt diet:*
*With crust:*
- 1/8 portion contains 52.5 mg of sodium
*Filling only:*
- 1/2 cup (120 mL) contains 60 mg of sodium
Omit salt; use 2 sprinkles of salt substitute. Use salt-free margarine. Make crust according to salt-free directions.

# Mincemeat Pie

*This recipe is not for hypoglycemics.*
- Makes two 8-inch (20 cm) pie fillings
- 1/8 portion contains 233 Calories (P4, F9, C34), no cholesterol
- 1/8 portion = 1 slice of bread + 1 cup of fruit + 2 teaspoons of fat (1 bread exchange + 2 fruit exchanges + 2 fat exchanges)

*With top crust only:*
- 1/8 portion contains 182 Calories (P2, F6, C30), no cholesterol
- 1/8 portion = 1 slice of bread + 3/4 cup of fruit + 1 teaspoon of fat (1 bread exchange + 1-1/2 fruit exchanges + 1 fat exchange)

*Mincemeat:*

**Apple pulp**   3 cups (777 grams); made from 5 medium-large apples, coarse-ground
**Seedless raisins**   1 cup (269 grams), coarse-ground
**Lemon**   1/2 large (79 grams), including skin, coarse-ground; remove seeds
**Currants**   1 cup (162 grams)
**Cinnamon**   2 teaspoons (6 grams)
**Cloves**   3/4 teaspoon (2.3 grams)
**Nutmeg**   3/4 teaspoon (2.3 grams)
**Salt**   1/2 teaspoon (3 grams)
**Unbleached or whole-wheat flour**   2 tablespoons (16 or 19.2 grams)
**Brown-type granular sugar substitute**   1/3 to 1/2 cup (32 to 48 grams); or substitute equal to 2/3 to 1 cup (130 to 195 grams) of sugar
**Brandy**   1/3 cup (80 mL) or 1-1/2 teaspoons (7.5 mL) **rum flavoring**

*Optional:*
**Allspice**   3/4 teaspoon (2.3 grams)
**Pie crust**   2 recipes, single or double-crust

Quarter and core apples, but do not peel. Grind apples, raisins and lemon with coarse blade. Add other dry ingredients and mix well. Stir in brandy or rum flavoring, let stand at least 1 hour. This improves with age, so make it a day ahead and refrigerate. Divide filling in half and spread evenly on bottom crusts. Seal with top crusts. Bake at 475°F (246°C) for 15 minutes, then at 375°F (191°C) about 50 minutes, until center of top crust is browned. Do not cut until cool.

*Suggestions:*
If you like mincemeat less spicy, cut spice amounts by a third or a half. The alcohol in the brandy evaporates during cooking and does not have to be counted. This mincemeat can also be used in cookies; see recipe on page 173.

*Natural sweetening directions:*
*This recipe is not for hypoglycemics.*
- 1/8 portion contains 253 Calories (P3, F9, C40), no cholesterol
- 1/8 portion = 2 slices of bread + 1/2 cup of fruit + 2 teaspoons of fat (2 bread exchanges + 1 fruit exchange + 2 fat exchanges)

*With top crust only:*
- 1/8 portion contains 198 Calories (P2, F6, C35), no cholesterol
- 1/8 portion = 1 slice of bread + 3/4 cup of fruit + 1 teaspoon of fat (1 bread exchange + 1-1/2 fruit exchanges + 1 fat exchange)

*Mincemeat only:*
- 1/8 portion (about 3 ounces (85.5 grams), scant 1/2 cup) contains 100 Calories (P0, F0, C25), no cholesterol, 41 mg of sodium

*For low-salt diet:*
*Do not use on 400-mg or 1-gram salt diets.*
- 1/8 portion contains 42 mg of sodium
Omit salt; use 1/2 teaspoon (2 grams) of salt substitute. Make crust according to salt-free directions.

# Miniature Party Tarts

- Makes 18 tarts
- 1 tart contains 136 Calories (P2, F8, C14), 18 mg of cholesterol if made with egg; none if made with egg substitute
- 1 tart = 1 slice of bread + 1-1/2 teaspoons of fat (1 bread exchange + 1-1/2 fat exchanges)

### Crust:
**Nuefchatel cream cheese**    3 ounces (85.5 grams), at room temperature
**Margarine**    1/2 cup (113 grams); use corn-oil, soybean-oil or safflower-oil margarine
**Unbleached or whole-wheat flour**    1 cup (116 or 127 grams), sifted

### Filling:
**Egg**    1 large (57 grams); or 2 ounces (60 mL) of liquid egg substitute
**Dates**    1/2 cup (87 grams), chopped fine
**Walnuts**    1/3 cup (40 grams), chopped
**Melted margarine**    1 tablespoon (15 mL); use corn-oil, soybean-oil or safflower-oil margarine
**Water**    3/4 to 1 cup (180 to 240 mL). Use more to make a softer filling
**Salt**    sprinkle
**Vanilla**    1 tablespoon (15 mL)
**Lemon juice**    1 tablespoon (15 mL)
**Lemon rind**    1/4 to 1/2 teaspoon (.4 to .8 gram), grated
**Whole-wheat bread crumbs**    1/4 cup (20 grams)

Place cream cheese and margarine in a bowl and warm to room temperature. Cream together until smooth and completely blended. Stir in flour. Chill. Divide into 18 parts, about 1 rounded tablespoon each. Press into miniature tart tins, spreading dough evenly up the sides. Rechill until the filling is ready.

Place dates, nuts and 1 tablespoon (14 grams) of margarine with the water, salt, egg and crumbs in a saucepan. Stir to dissolve. Simmer over low heat for 5 minutes. Remove from the heat and add remaining ingredients; stir to mix. Cool slightly. Fill tart shells with about 1 rounded tablespoon (40 grams) of filling. Bake at 350°F (177°C) for 17 minutes, then at 275°F (137°C) for 20 minutes longer. Remove from tart shells to cool.

### Natural sweetening directions:
- Not needed.

### For low-salt diet:
- 1 tart contains 25 mg of sodium
Omit salt. Use salt-free margarine.

# Peach Custard Pie

- Makes filling for one 8-inch (20 cm) pie
- 1/8 portion contains 147 Calories (P4, F7, C17), 32 mg of cholesterol if made with egg; 1 mg of cholesterol if made with egg substitute
- 1/8 portion = 1 slice of bread + 1-1/2 teaspoons of fat (1 bread exchange + 1-1/2 fat exchanges)

**Pie shell**   1 unbaked
**Fresh peaches**   1-1/2 cups (265.5 grams), sliced; or drained dietetic peaches (349.5 grams)
**Brown-type granular sugar substitute**   2-1/2 tablespoons (15 grams); or substitute equal to 1/3 cup (65 grams) of sugar
**Unbleached or whole-wheat flour**   1 tablespoon (8 or 9.6 grams), sifted; or 1 tablespoon (8.5 grams) quick-cooking tapioca
**Skim milk**   1 cup (240 mL)
**Egg**   1 large (57 grams) plus 1 egg white (33 grams); or 3 ounces (90 mL) of liquid egg substitute
**Salt**   1/4 teaspoon (1.5 grams)
**Almond extract**   1/4 teaspoon (1.3 mL)
**Vanilla**   1/4 teaspoon (1.3 mL)
**Nutmeg**   sprinkle
**Cinnamon**   sprinkle

Make pie shell according to recipe. (If using frozen pie shell, allow to stand at room temperature while preparing filling to prevent sogginess.) Peel and slice fresh peaches, or drain canned slices. For fresh peaches or unsweetened slices, sprinkle with 1-1/2 tablespoons (9 grams) of sugar substitute and mix well. Add flour to milk; let stand at least 10 minutes. Add beaten egg or egg substitute to milk mixture. Add salt, extracts, and 1 tablespoon (6 grams) of sugar substitute. Arrange peaches evenly in shell; sprinkle lightly with nutmeg and cinnamon. Cover peaches with egg/milk mixture; sprinkle top with spices, as before. Bake at 425°F (218°C) about 45 minutes, until custard is set and fruit seems to separate slightly from custard. Cool on rack. Do not cut until cool, or it will be too soft.

***Suggestions:***
Substitute 3/4 cup (150 grams) sliced bananas, or other canned fruit for the peaches, using the spices that best complement that fruit.

***Natural sweetening directions:***
*This recipe is not for hypoglycemics.*
- 1/8 portion contains 167 Calories (P5, F7, C21), no change in cholesterol or sodium
- 1/8 portion = 2/3 slice of bread + 1/2 ounce of meat + 1/2 cup of fruit + 1 teaspoon of fat (2/3 bread exchange + 1/2 meat exchange + 1 fruit exchange + 1 fat exchange)
Omit sugar substitute and skim milk; use 1/2 cup (120 mL) evaporated skim milk plus 1/2 cup (120 mL) white grape juice plus 1-1/2 tablespoons (15 grams) of date sugar.

***For low-salt diet:***
- 1/8 portion contains 42 mg of sodium
Omit salt; use 1/4 teaspoon (1 gram) of salt substitute. Make crust according to salt-free directions.

# Pumpkin Pie or Custard

- Makes two 8-inch (20 cm) pie fillings, or 8 servings of custard
- 1/8 pie contains 133 Calories (P4, F7, C17), 32 mg of cholesterol if made with eggs; 2 mg of cholesterol if made with egg substitute
- 1/8 pie = 1 slice of bread + 1-1/2 teaspoons of fat (1 bread exchange + 1-1/2 fat exchanges)

*Custard:*
- 1/2 cup (120 mL) of custard contains 49 Calories (P3, F1, C7), 37 mg of cholesterol if made with eggs; 2 mg of cholesterol if made with egg substitute
- 1/2 cup of custard = 1/2 ounce of meat + 1/2 cup of fruit (1/2 meat exchange + 1 fruit exchange)

**Hubbard squash**   1-1/2 cups (366 grams), cooked; or use pumpkin or pureed carrots. *Note: Squash makes a sweeter, better pie. May use frozen squash, allowing to thaw completely before using.*
**Eggs**   2 large (114 grams); or 4 ounces (120 mL) of liquid egg substitute
**Evaporated skim milk**   1-1/2 cups (360 mL)
**Whole-wheat flour**   1/4 cup (32 grams), sifted
**Brown-type granular sugar substitute**   4 tablespoons (24 grams); or substitute equal to 1/2 cup (97.5 grams) of sugar. *Note: Use 6 tablespoons of sugar substitute (36 grams) with pumpkin or carrots.*
**Ginger**   1/2 teaspoon (1.5 grams)
**Cinnamon**   1/2 teaspoon (1.5 grams)
**Nutmeg**   1/2 teaspoon (1.5 grams)
**Cloves or allspice**   1/4 teaspoon (.8 gram)
**Salt**   1/4 teaspoon (1.5 grams)
**Vanilla**   1/3 teaspoon (1.7 mL)

*Optional:*
**Pie shells**   2 unbaked

Make pie shells. Add well-beaten eggs to squash; mix well. Stir in milk. Combine dry ingredients; add to mixture. Add vanilla. For pie, pour into unbaked shells; bake at 425°F (218°C) for 15 minutes, then at 350°F (177°C) for 45 minutes. A silver knife blade will come out clean if filling is done. For custard, spray baking dish with nonstick coating; pour in custard. Place dish in pan of hot water and bake at 350°F (177°C) for about 1 hour. Test with knife blade; cool on rack and don't serve until lukewarm.

*Natural sweetening directions:*
- 1/8 pie contains 157 Calories (P4, F7, C23), no change in cholesterol or sodium
- 1/8 pie = 1 slice of bread + 1/2 ounce of meat + 1/2 cup of fruit + 1 teaspoon of fat (1 bread exchange + 1/2 meat exchange + 1 fruit exchange + 1 fat exchange)
Omit sugar substitute; replace with 5-1/2 tablespoons (55 grams) of date sugar, plus 1 teaspoon (5 mL) of lemon juice. Increase vanilla to 2/3 teaspoon (3.3 mL) and salt to 1/2 teaspoon (3 grams).
*Custard:*
- 1/2 cup (120 mL) of custard contains 73 Calories (P3, F1, C13), no change in cholesterol or sodium
- 1/2 cup of custard = 1 slice of bread

*For low-salt diet:*
- 1/8 portion contains 45 mg of sodium
Omit salt; use 1/4 teaspoon (1 gram) of salt substitute. Make pie crust according to salt-free directions.

# Rhubarb Pie

- Makes filling for one 8-inch (20 cm) pie
- 1/8 portion contains 211 Calories (P4, F11, C24), no cholesterol
- 1/8 portion = 1 slice of bread + 1/2 cup of fruit + 2 teaspoons of fat (1 bread exchange + 1 fruit exchange + 2 fat exchanges)

**With top crust only:**
- 1/8 pie contains 130 Calories (P3, F6, C16)
- 1/8 portion = 1/2 slice of bread + 1/2 cup of fruit + 1 teaspoon of fat (1/2 bread exchange + 1 fruit exchange + 1 fat exchange)

---

**Pie crust**   1 recipe, single or double crust
**Rhubarb**   3-1/2 cups (588 grams), sliced 1/2-inch thick
**Apples**   1-1/2 cups (187.5 grams), peeled and diced
**Unbleached or whole-wheat flour** or **quick-cooking tapioca**   1-1/2 tablespoons (12 or 14 or 12.8 grams)
**Lemon juice**   2 tablespoons (30 mL)
**Salt**   sprinkle
**Granular sugar substitute**   1/2 cup (48 grams); or substitute equal to 1-1/2 cups (292.5 grams) of sugar; use more if you like it sweet
**Margarine**   1 tablespoon (14 grams); use corn-oil, soybean-oil or safflower-oil margarine
**Red food coloring**   5 to 6 drops

---

Make pie crust. Dice rhubarb; add 1/3 cup (80 mL) of water; cover and cook until slightly soft. Drain in colander and save liquid. Dice apples small; add 3/4 cup (180 mL) water; cover and simmer until slightly soft; remove from heat. Add red food coloring to make apples as red as the rhubarb. Drain apples in colander; add liquid to rhubarb liquid. Add flour, lemon juice, salt and sugar substitute to liquid; mix well. Add to fruit, stir to blend; set aside. Roll out bottom crust as directed; spoon in filling; smooth out. Dab margarine onto fruit as evenly as possible. Add top crust. Bake at 475°F (246°C) for 15 minutes, then at 375°F (191°C) about 45 minutes, until center of top crust is well browned. Cool on a rack. Do not cut until well cooled, or filling will be runny.

---

**Natural sweetening directions:**
*This recipe is not for hypoglycemics.*
- 1/8 portion contains 243 Calories (P4, F11, C32), no cholesterol; 4 mg of sodium
- 1/8 portion = 2 slices of bread + 2 teaspoons of fat *or* 1 slice of bread + 3/4 cup of fruit (2 bread exchanges + 2 fat exchanges *or* 1 bread exchange + 1-1/2 fruit exchanges)
- 1/10 portion contains 197 Calories (P4, F9, C25), 3 mg of sodium
- 1/10 portion = 1 slice of bread + 1/2 cup of fruit + 2 teaspoons of fat (1 bread exchange + 1 fruit exchange + 2 fat exchanges)

Omit sugar substitute; replace with 3-1/2 tablespoons (35 grams) date sugar. Increase red food coloring to 6 to 8 drops (2 grams) to disguise the color of the date sugar. Omit water when cooking rhubarb and apples. Replace with equal volume apple juice. Increase lemon juice to 3 tablespoons (45 mL).

**For low-salt diet:**
- 1/8 portion contains 5 mg of sodium

Omit salt; use salt substitute. Use salt-free margarine. Make crust according to salt-free directions.

# Buttermilk Iced Dessert

- Makes 8 servings, 1/2 cup (120 mL) each
- 1 serving contains 40 Calories (P4, F0, C6), 1 mg of cholesterol
- 1 serving = 1/2 cup of nonfat milk (1/2 milk exchange)

**Buttermilk**   3 cups (720 mL)
**Lemon juice**   1/2 cup (120 mL)
**Lemon rind**   1 teaspoon (1.5 grams), grated
**Granular sugar substitute**   1/2 cup (48 grams); or substitute equal to 1 cup
   (195 grams) of sugar
**Egg whites**   2 (66 grams)
**Salt**   1/8 teaspoon (.8 gram)
**Yellow food coloring**   few drops

Combine buttermilk, lemon juice and rind
and sugar substitute; taste to be sure it is
sweet enough. It is meant to be rather
tart. Put in freezer and allow to chill until
almost set. Remove from freezer; add egg
whites and salt. Beat with rotary beater or
mixer until very fluffy; add food coloring
for a pale lemon color. Freeze in covered
plastic container. Remove from freezer at
least 15 minutes before serving.

### Natural sweetening directions:
*This recipe is not for hypoglycemics.*
- Makes 10 servings, 1/2 cup (120 mL) each
- 1 serving contains 68 Calories (P3, F0, C14)
- 1 serving = 1 slice of bread (1 bread exchange)
Omit sugar substitute. Use 1/4 cup (64 grams) dietetic applesauce, plus 2/3 cup (107 grams) date sugar.

### For low-salt diet:
*This recipe cannot be made low in salt because of the natural sodium in the buttermilk and egg whites.*

192

# Basic Vanilla Ice Cream

- Makes 10 servings, 1/2 cup (120 mL) each
- 1 serving contains 154 Calories (P3, F10, C13), 26 mg of cholesterol if made with egg; 1 mg of cholesterol if made with egg substitute
- 1 serving = 1/2 ounce of meat + 1-1/2 teaspoons of fat + 1/2 cup of fruit (1/2 meat exchange + 1-1/2 fat exchanges + 1 fruit exchange)

**Skim milk**   2 cups (480 mL). *Note: If there is no cholesterol restriction, use 2-1/2 cups (600 mL) of half-and-half instead of milk, oil and butter flavoring, and skip the blender step. Calories and replacements are the same, except for the cholesterol content.*
**Corn or soybean oil**   1/2 cup (120 mL)
**Butter flavoring**   16 drops
**Plain gelatin**   1 tablespoon (7 grams)
**Water**   1/2 cup (120 mL)
**Egg**   1 large (57 grams); or use 2 ounces (60 mL) of liquid egg substitute
**Granular sugar substitute**   1/2 cup (48 grams); or substitute equal to 1 cup (195 grams) of sugar
**Vanilla**   2 teaspoons (10 mL)
**Salt**   1/2 teaspoon (3 grams)

Put milk, oil and butter flavoring in blender; blend at top speed for 2 minutes to emulsify fat into milk. Add gelatin to water; heat gently to dissolve. Add to milk. Beat egg and add sugar substitute, vanilla and salt; combine with milk mixture; stir well. Place in electric ice cream freezer and mix until almost hard according to instructions for your freezer. Put into covered plastic container and place in freezer to set until hard. Remove from freezer at least 15 minutes before serving.

*Suggestions:*
You can vary this recipe by adding chopped fresh fruit or various flavorings. Add 1 tablespoon (15 mL) of unsweetened chocolate extract to 1/3 of the recipe, then streak it through the ice cream. No extra Calories need be counted for the chocolate.

### Natural sweetening directions:
*This recipe is not for hypoglycemics.*
- 1 serving contains 174 Calories (P3, F10, C18), no change in cholesterol or sodium
- 1 serving = 1/2 slice of bread + 1/2 cup of fruit + 2 teaspoons of fat (1/2 bread exchange + 1 fruit exchange + 2 fat exchanges)

Omit sugar substitute and skim milk; use 1 cup (240 mL) evaporated skim milk, plus 2/3 cup (160 mL) white grape juice and 1/3 cup (80 mL) concentrated apple juice. Increase vanilla to 1 tablespoon (15 mL).

### For low-salt diet:
- 1 serving contains 35 mg of sodium

Omit salt; use 1/2 teaspoon (2 grams) of salt substitute.

# Coffee Ice Cream

- Makes about 5 cups (1.2 L)
- 1/2 cup (120 mL) contains 154 Calories (P3, F10, C13), 22 mg of cholesterol if made with egg; 1 mg of cholesterol if made with egg substitute
- 1/2 cup = 1/2 ounce of meat + 1/2 cup of fruit + 1-1/2 teaspoons of fat (1/2 meat exchange + 1 fruit exchange + 1-1/2 fat exchanges)

**Skim milk**    2 cups (480 mL). *Note: With no cholesterol restriction, use 2-1/2 cups (600 mL) of half-and-half in place of the skim milk, oil and butter flavoring; skip the blender step.*
**Corn or soybean oil**    1/2 cup (120 mL)
**Butter flavoring**    16 drops
**Plain gelatin**    1 tablespoon (7 grams)
**Water**    1/2 cup (120 mL)
**Egg**    1 large (57 grams); or use 2 ounces (60 mL) of liquid egg substitute
**Granular sugar substitute**    1/2 cup (48 grams); or substitute equal to 1 cup (195 grams) of sugar
**Instant coffee granules**    3-1/2 teaspoons (11.2 grams); decaffeinated if you prefer. *Note: Hypoglycemics must use decaffeinated coffee.*
**Salt**    1/3 teaspoon (2 grams)
**Vanilla**    1 teaspoon (5 mL)

Put milk, oil and butter flavoring into blender; blend at top speed for 2 minutes to emulsify fat into milk. Dissolve gelatin in water; heat gently to dissolve completely; add to milk mixture. Beat egg well; add sugar substitute, coffee, salt and vanilla; mix well; add to milk mixture.

Place in ice cream freezer and mix until firm, following instructions for your freezer. When very firm, store in freezer. Be sure container is airtight to help prevent formation of crystals. Remove from freezer at least 15 minutes before serving.

*Natural sweetening directions:*
- This recipe does not adapt well to natural sweetening.

*For low-salt diet:*
- 1/2 cup (120 mL) contains 35 mg of sodium
Omit salt; use 1/3 teaspoon (1.3 grams) of salt substitute.

# Maple Nut Ice Cream

- Makes about 5-1/2 cups (1.25 L)
- 1/2 cup (120 mL) contains 172 Calories (P3, F12, C13), 22 mg of cholesterol if made with egg; 1 mg of cholesterol if made with egg substitute
- 1/2 cup = 1/2 cup of fruit + 1/2 ounce of meat + 2 teaspoons of fat (1 fruit exchange + 1/2 meat exchange + 2 fat exchanges)

**Skim milk**   2 cups (480 mL). *Note: With no cholesterol restriction, use 2-1/2 cups (600 mL) of half-and-half in place of the skim milk, oil and butter flavoring; skip the blender step.*
**Corn or soybean oil**   1/2 cup (120 mL)
**Butter flavoring**   16 drops
**Plain gelatin**   1 tablespoon (7 grams)
**Water**   1/2 cup (120 mL)
**Egg**   1 large (57 grams), well-beaten; or use 2 ounces (60 mL) of liquid egg substitute
**Granular sugar substitute**   1/2 cup (48 grams); or substitute equal to 1 cup (195 grams) of sugar
**Vanilla**   2/3 teaspoon (3.3 mL)
**Maple flavoring**   2-1/2 teaspoons (12.5 mL)
**Salt**   1/2 teaspoon (3 grams)
**Walnuts**   1/2 cup (60 grams), chopped

Put milk, oil and butter flavoring in blender; blend at top speed for 2 minutes to emulsify fat into milk. Add gelatin to water; heat gently to dissolve. Add all ingredients except nuts to the milk; stir well. Put in electric freezer and mix according to directions for your freezer, until almost firm. Add nuts; continue to freeze until very hard. Store in freezer in covered plastic containers. Remove from freezer at least 15 minutes before serving.

### Natural sweetening directions:
*This recipe is not for hypoglycemics.*
- 1/2 cup (120 mL) contains 188 Calories (P3, F12, C17)
- 1/2 cup = 1/2 slice of bread + 1/2 cup of fruit + 1/2 ounce of meat + 2 teaspoons of fat (1/2 bread exchange + 1 fruit exchange + 1/2 meat exchange + 2 fat exchanges)

Omit sugar substitute and skim milk. Use 1 cup (240 mL) evaporated skim milk, plus 3/4 cup (180 mL) white grape juice and 1/4 cup (60 mL) concentrated apple juice. Increase vanilla to 1 teaspoon (5 mL).

### For low-salt diet:
- 1/2 cup (120 mL) contains 35 mg of sodium

Omit salt; use 1/2 teaspoon (2 grams) of salt substitute.

# Raspberry Royal Ice Cream

- Makes 12 servings, 1/2 cup (120 mL) each
- 1 serving contains 145 Calories (P3, F9, C13), 24 mg of cholesterol if made with egg; 1 mg of cholesterol if made with egg substitute
- 1 serving = 1/2 cup of fruit + 1/2 ounce of meat + 1-1/2 teaspoons of fat (1 fruit exchange + 1/2 meat exchange + 1-1/2 fat exchanges)

**Skim milk**   2 cups (480 mL). *Note: With no cholesterol restriction, use 2-1/2 cups (600 mL) of half-and-half in place of the skim milk, oil and butter flavoring; skip the blender step.*

**Corn oil**   1/2 cup (120 mL)

**Butter flavoring**   16 drops

**Plain gelatin**   1 tablespoon (7 grams)

**Water**   1/2 cup (120 mL)

**Egg**   1 large (57 grams), well-beaten; or use 2 ounces (60 mL) of liquid egg substitute

**Granular sugar substitute**   1/2 cup (48 grams); or substitute equal to 1 cup (195 grams) of sugar

**Vanilla**   1-1/2 teaspoons (7.5 mL)

**Salt**   1/4 teaspoon (1.5 grams)

**Raspberries**   1-1/2 cups (216 grams)

Put milk, oil and butter flavoring in blender; blend at top speed for 2 minutes to emulsify fat into milk. Add gelatin to water; heat gently to dissolve. Add gelatin mixture to milk; add other ingredients except fruit. Mash half the berries; add to milk mixture. Put in ice cream freezer and freeze until almost hard. Add whole berries; continue to freeze until hard. Store in covered plastic containers in freezer. Remove from freezer at least 15 minutes before serving.

**Suggestions:**
Instead of raspberries, use strawberries, or blueberries with 2 sprinkles of nutmeg.

**Natural sweetening directions:**
- This recipe does not adapt well to natural sweetening.

**For low-salt diet:**
- 1 serving contains 30 mg of sodium
Omit salt; use 1/4 teaspoon (1 gram) of salt substitute.

# Pineapple Mint Frozen Yogurt

- Makes 5 servings, 1/2 cup (120 mL) each
- 1 serving contains 61 Calories (P1, F1, C12), 3 mg of cholesterol
- 1 serving = 2/3 slice of bread *or* 1/2 cup of fruit (2/3 bread exchange *or* 1 fruit exchange)

**Crushed pineapple**   8 ounces (224 grams), juice-packed. Drain pineapple and save juice
**Plain yogurt**   8 ounces (240 mL)
**Concentrated apple juice**   1/3 cup (80 mL)
**Lemon juice**   1-1/2 teaspoons (7.5 mL)
**Vanilla**   1/2 teaspoon (2.5 mL)
**Salt**   sprinkle
**Mint extract**   1/4 teaspoon (1.3 mL)
**Green food coloring**   4 to 6 drops

Combine pineapple juice, apple and lemon juice with yogurt in a saucepan; heat for 2 to 3 minutes to dissolve yogurt; stir to mix well. Cool; place in a mixing bowl. Add pineapple, mint extract and food coloring to tint mint green. Mix well. Pour into a freezing tray; freeze until very thick, but not set hard. Remove from freezer, place in a mixing bowl and beat with electric mixer or by hand until smooth and fluffy. Return to freezing container, cover and freeze about 4 hours, until mixture is set hard. Let stand at room temperature at least 10 minutes before serving.

*Natural sweetening directions:*
- Not needed, as recipe is naturally sweetened.

*For low-salt diet:*
- 1 serving contains 26 mg of sodium
Omit salt; use sprinkle of salt substitute if desired.

# Fruit Popsicles

- Makes 6 popsicles
- 1 popsicle contains 40 Calories (P0, F0, C10), no cholesterol
- 1 popsicle = 1/2 cup of fruit (1 fruit exchange)

**Unsweetened pineapple juice**   2 cups (480 mL)
**Dietetic lemon-lime soda pop**   2 cups (480 mL)
**Lemon rind**   1/2 teaspoon (.8 gram), grated

*Optional:*
**Granular sugar substitute**   up to 1 tablespoon (6 grams)

Combine pineapple juice and dietetic pop; add lemon rind and sugar substitute to taste; stir well to remove carbonation in the soft drink. Pour into popsicle molds, about 3/4 cup (180 mL) per mold; freeze.

**Suggestions:**
Use other juice/pop combinations, such as raspberry soda with diet lemonade (no food value there at all!), or root beer with apple juice. Use your imagination and experiment. You might come up with the flavor discovery of the century.

### Natural sweetening directions:
*This recipe is not for hypoglycemics.*
- 1 popsicle contains 60 Calories (P0, F0, C15)
- 1 popsicle = 1 slice of bread *or* 3/4 cup of fruit (1 bread exchange *or* 1-1/2 fruit exchanges)
Omit dietetic pop and sugar substitute; replace with 1 cup (240 mL) water plus 1 cup (240 mL) concentrated apple juice and 4 tablespoons (60 mL) lemon juice.

### For low-salt diet:
- 1 popsicle contains 16 mg of sodium
- This recipe is fairly low in salt, as the only sodium comes from the dietetic pop.

# Mock Orange Sherbet

- Makes 4 servings, 1/2 cup (120 mL) each
- 1 serving contains 24 Calories (P2, F0, C4), no cholesterol
- 1 serving = 1/4 cup of fruit (1/2 fruit exchange)

**Plain gelatin**   1 tablespoon (7 grams)
**Water**   1-1/2 cups (360 mL)
**Lemon juice**   2 teaspoons (10 mL)
**Lemon or orange rind**   1-1/2 to 2 teaspoons (2.3 to 3 grams), grated
**Frozen orange juice concentrate**   1/2 cup (120 mL)
**Granular sugar substitute**   1-1/2 teaspoons (3 grams); or substitute equal to
    1 tablespoon (12.2 grams) of sugar
**Salt**   sprinkle

Dissolve gelatin in water; heat gently to complete dissolving. Add lemon juice and rind (use less to make it less lemony), orange juice, sugar substitute and salt. Mix well. Pour into loaf pan and allow to set in refrigerator or freezer until firm. Slice and serve as a frozen sherbert, or in parfait dishes as a gelatin dessert. (Allow frozen sherbert to stand at room temperature for 15 minutes before trying to cut it.)

*Suggestions:*
You can make miniature Dixie Cups from this sherbert and freeze them for summer treats. Use colorful cups to make them attractive as well as tasty.

*Natural sweetening directions:*
- 1 serving contains 36 Calories (P2, F0, C7)
- 1 serving = 1/3 cup of fruit (2/3 fruit exchange)
Omit sugar substitute. Reduce water to 1 cup (240 mL). Add 1/2 cup (120 mL) apple juice and increase lemon juice to 3-1/2 teaspoons (17.5 mL). Use 2 teaspoons (3 grams) grated lemon or orange rind.

*For low-salt diet:*
- 1 serving contains 4 mg of sodium
Omit salt; use sprinkle of salt substitute.

# Vanilla Iced Milk

- Makes 6 servings, 1/2 cup (120 mL) each
- 1 serving contains 64 Calories (P8, F0, C8), 3 mg of cholesterol
- 1 serving = 1 ounce of meat + 1/2 cup of fruit (1 lean meat exchange + 1 fruit exchange or 3/4 milk exchange only)

**Skim milk**   2 cups (480 mL)
**Skim milk powder**   2/3 cup (50 grams)
**Plain gelatin**   1 tablespoon (7 grams)
**Granular sugar substitute**   3 tablespoons (18 grams); or substitute equal to 6 tablespoons (73.2 grams) of sugar
**Egg whites**   2 (66 grams)
**Lemon rind**   1 tablespoon (4.5 grams)
**Lemon juice**   3 tablespoons (45 mL)
**Vanilla**   1 tablespoon (15 mL)

In saucepan, dissolve milk powder in liquid milk; beat until smooth. Add gelatin; stir; heat gently, stirring constantly to dissolve gelatin. Remove from heat; add sugar substitute. Pour into freezer tray; freeze until frozen about 1 inch in from edges. Into mixer bowl put egg whites, lemon rind and juice, and vanilla; add milk mixture; beat at high speed for 2 minutes, until light and fluffy. Store in covered plastic container in freezer. Remove 15 minutes before serving.

### Natural sweetening directions:
- 1 serving contains 92 Calories (P8, F0, C15), no change in cholesterol or sodium
- 1 serving = 1/4 cup of fruit + 1 cup of milk (1/2 fruit exchange + 1 milk exchange)

Omit sugar substitute and skim milk; replace with 1 cup (240 mL) of evaporated skim milk plus 1 cup (240 mL) white grape juice plus 1/3 cup (80 mL) water. Heat the water to dissolve the gelatin. Add to milk mixture and follow directions as given. Increase vanilla to 4 teaspoons (20 mL) and grated lemon rind to 3-1/2 teaspoons (5 grams).

### For low-salt diet:
*Do not use on 400-mg or 1-gram salt diets. This recipe cannot be made low in salt, because of the natural sodium in the milk.*
- 1 serving contains 95 mg of sodium

# Easy Strawberry Sherbet

- Makes 2 servings, 1 cup (240 mL) each
- 1 serving contains 78 Calories (P4, F2, C11), 3 mg of cholesterol
- 1 serving = 1/4 cup of fruit + 1/2 cup of milk (1/2 fruit exchange + 1/2 milk exchange)

**Skim** or **2% milk**    1 cup (240 mL)
**Vanilla**    1/4 teaspoon (1.3 mL)
**Liquid sweetener**    1/4 teaspoon (1.3 mL); use more for sour berries; or substitute equal to 1 teaspoon of sugar
**Frozen unsweetened strawberries**    1 cup (253 grams)
**Salt**    sprinkle

Place liquids and salt in blender, then gradually add frozen berries, until all is well blended. Pour into two parfait glasses and serve. This recipe will keep for a little while in the freezer, but does not freeze well for later eating.

*Suggestions:*
This is also good made with equal amounts of raspberries or blueberries. Just increase the sweetening slightly if you use these berries.

*Natural sweetening directions:*
- 1 serving contains 86 Calories (P4, F2, C13), no change in cholesterol or sodium
- 1 serving = 1 slice of bread + 1/2 cup of milk *or* 1/2 ounce of meat + 2/3 cup of fruit (1 bread exchange + 1/2 milk exchange *or* 1/2 meat exchange + 1-1/4 fruit exchanges)

Omit liquid sweetener. Add 1-1/2 tablespoons (22.5 mL) white grape juice.

*For low-salt diet:*
- 1 serving contains 63 mg of sodium

Omit salt.

# Dieter's Delicious Cheesecake

- Makes filling for 9-inch (22.5 cm) pie

*Without crust:*
- 1/8 portion contains 138 Calories (P3, F10, C9), 25 mg of cholesterol
- 1/8 portion = 1/2 ounce of meat + 1/2 cup of fruit + 1-1/2 teaspoons of fat
  (1/2 meat exchange + 1 fruit exchange + 1-1/2 fat exchanges)

*With Mock Graham Cracker Crust (see recipe on page 181):*
- 1/8 portion contains 240 Calories (P4, F16, C20), 25 mg of cholesterol, 107 mg of
  sodium; 40 mg of sodium if made with salt-free crust
- 1/8 portion = 1/2 slice of bread + 1/2 cup of fruit + 1/2 ounce of meat +
  2-1/2 teaspoons of fat (1/2 bread exchange + 1 fruit exchange + 1/2 meat
  exchange + 2-1/2 fat exchanges)

---

**Plain gelatin**    1 tablespoon (7 grams)
**Apple juice**    1-1/2 cups (360 mL)
**Neufchatel cream cheese**    8 ounces (227 grams), at room temperature
**Vanilla**    1-1/2 teaspoons (7.5 mL)
**Lemon rind**    1 teaspoon (1.5 grams), grated
**Fresh orange sections** or **drained diet-pack mandarin orange sections**    1 cup
  (194 grams)

---

Heat apple juice to boiling; add gelatin and stir to dissolve completely. With blender or electric mixer, blend in cream cheese, vanilla and lemon rind. Cool.

*Without crust:*
 Spray pie plate with nonstick coating. Cover bottom with orange slices and cover with cooled cheese mixture. Sprinkle top with cinnamon if desired. Chill or freeze to set.

*With crust:*
Place orange slices on the crust and follow directions as given.

---

*Natural sweetening directions:*
- Not needed.

*For low-salt diet:*
- 1/8 portion contains 25 mg of sodium
- No changes needed.

# Coffee Jelly

- Makes 4 servings, 1/2 cup (120 mL) each
- 1 serving contains 8 Calories (P2, F0, C0), no cholesterol
- No replacements necessary.

**Plain gelatin**   1 tablespoon (7 grams)
**Cold water**   1/4 cup (60 mL)
**Coffee**   1-3/4 cups (420 mL), strong; use decaffeinated if you prefer.
  *Note: Hypoglycemics must use decaffeinated coffee.*
**Granular sugar substitute**   1 tablespoon (18 grams); or substitute equal to
  2 tablespoons (24.4 grams) of sugar
**Vanilla**   1/2 teaspoon (2.5 mL)
**Salt**   sprinkle

*Optional:*
**Cinnamon**   sprinkle

Dissolve gelatin in 1/4 cup (60 mL) cold water; heat gently to dissolve completely. Add coffee, sugar substitute, vanilla, salt and cinnamon; mix well. Pour into molds or bowl; refrigerate to set.

**Suggestions:**
If your diet allows, serve this with 1 tablespoon of diet ice cream (8 grams) as a topping; use regular ice cream or whipped cream for nondieters. As a variation, use 1 cup (240 mL) of double-strength instant coffee and 3/4 cup (180 mL) of juice from dietetic canned peaches or pears; omit vanilla and use slightly more cinnamon. This too can be used, up to 1/2 cup (120 mL) at a time, without replacement.

**Natural sweetening directions:**
- 1 serving contains 20 Calories (P0, F0, C5)
- 1 serving = 1/4 cup of fruit (1/2 fruit exchange)
Omit sugar substitute and water. Reduce coffee to 1-1/2 cups (360 mL). Add 3/4 cup (180 mL) of apple juice. Increase vanilla to 3/4 teaspoon (3.8 mL).

**For low-salt diet:**
- 1 serving contains 3 mg of sodium
Omit salt; use sprinkle of salt substitute. Use the cinnamon as it helps compensate for the lack of salt.

# Lemon Whip

- Makes 6 servings, 1/2 cup (120 mL) each
- 1 serving contains 24 Calories (P2, F0, C4), no cholesterol
- 1 serving = 1/4 cup of fruit (1/2 fruit exchange)

**Plain gelatin**   1 tablespoon (7 grams)
**Water**   3/4 cup (180 mL)
**Diet applesauce**   1/2 cup (128 grams)
**Salt**   2 sprinkles
**Lemon juice**   7 tablespoons (105 mL)
**Lemon rind**   1 tablespoon (4.5 grams), grated
**Yellow food coloring**   3 to 4 drops
**Granular sugar substitute**   1/4 cup (24 grams); or substitute equal to 1/2 cup
   (97.5 grams) of sugar
**Egg white**   1 (33 grams), chilled

Dissolve gelatin in water; warm gently to dissolve completely. Add applesauce, salt, lemon juice and rind; mix well. Add enough food coloring to give lemon color. Taste; add sugar substitute to suit; if applesauce is fairly sweet, you will need as little as 2 teaspoons (4 grams) (equivalent to 1-1/2 tablespoons (18.3 grams) of sugar). Chill until thick and syrupy. Beat chilled egg white until very stiff; fold into chilled gelatin, using wire whip. Pile into parfait or sherbet glasses; chill until set; serve, perhaps with a thin twist of lemon on top for color.

**Suggestions:**
Do not get this too sweet, or it will lose some of its appeal. The lemon rind flavor develops as it stands and will be considerably stronger the day after the dish is made.

**Natural sweetening directions:**
- 1 serving contains 48 Calories (P2, F0, C10)
- 1 serving = 1/2 cup of fruit (1 fruit exchange)

Omit sugar substitute. Increase diet applesauce to 3/4 cup (194.3 grams). Omit water; replace with 3/4 cup (180 mL) apple juice. Add additional food coloring if desired.

**For low-salt diet:**
- 1 serving contains 4 mg of sodium

Omit salt; use 2 sprinkles of salt substitute.

# Fruited Gelatin

- Makes 5 servings, 1/2 cup (120 mL) each
- 1 serving contains 44 Calories (P1, F0, C10), no cholesterol
- 1 serving = 1/2 cup of fruit (1 fruit exchange)

**Plain gelatin**   1 tablespoon (7 grams)
**Water**   1 cup (240 mL)
**Diet-pack peaches**   1/2 cup (109 grams), drained and diced
**Diet-pack pineapple chunks**   1/2 cup (101 grams), drained
**Juice**   1/2 cup (120 mL), from peaches and pineapple
**Lemon juice**   1-1/2 tablespoons (22.5 mL)
**Granular sugar substitute**   1-1/2 teaspoons (3 grams); or substitute equal to
   1 tablespoon (12.2 grams) of sugar
**Salt**   sprinkle
**Red food coloring**   as needed

*Optional:*
**Lemon rind**   1/2 teaspoon (.8 gram)

Add gelatin to water; let stand a few minutes, then heat gently to complete dissolving; set aside to cool. Slice or dice fruit into bite-size pieces. To 1/2 cup (120 mL) combined peach and pineapple juices, add lemon juice and rind, sugar substitute, salt and food coloring to make a cherry color. Add juice to gelatin; add more coloring if needed to make color deep enough. Add diced fruit; pour into large mold or 5 individual molds; chill.

*Suggestions:*
To change the appearance of this dessert, use pears in place of peaches and green food coloring instead of red, perhaps with 1/4 to 1/2 teaspoon (1.3 to 2.5 mL) of spearmint extract for flavor.

---

### Natural sweetening directions:
- 1 serving contains 52 Calories (P1, F0, C12)
- 1 serving = 1/2 cup of fruit (1 fruit exchange)

Omit sugar substitute. Reduce water to 3/4 cup (180 mL). Add 1/4 cup (60 mL) apple juice. Increase lemon juice to 2 tablespoons (30 mL) and use lemon rind.

### For low-salt diet:
- 1 serving contains 3 mg of sodium

Omit salt; use sprinkle of salt substitute.

# Raspberry Mold

- Makes 6 servings, 3/4 cup (180 mL) each
- 1 serving contains 48 Calories (P2, F0, C10), no cholesterol
- 1 serving = 1/2 cup of fruit (1 fruit exchange)

**Plain gelatin**   1 tablespoon (7 grams)
**Water**   1/3 cup (80 mL)
**Orange juice**   2/3 cup (160 mL)
**Lemon juice**   1 tablespoon (15 mL)
**Granular sugar substitute**   3 tablespoons (18 grams); or substitute equal to
   6 tablespoons (73.2 grams) of sugar
**Salt**   sprinkle
**Raspberries**   1 cup (218 grams), pureed
**Red food coloring**   4 drops
**Raspberries**   1 cup (144 grams)

Add gelatin to water; let stand, then heat gently to dissolve completely. Add juices, sugar substitute, salt and berry puree; stir to mix well; add food coloring to get a pleasing pink. Chill until fairly thick. Pour half of chilled mixture into a mold (5-cup (1.2 L or larger); distribute berries over gelatin as evenly as possible; pour on remaining gelatin mixture and smooth out to fill mold evenly; chill until firm.

**Suggestions:**
Strawberries are good for this dish, and are less seedy. You can make this in winter with frozen berries. If using frozen whole berries, do not thaw before adding. Serve on a bed of washed maple, apple or other leaves.

### Natural sweetening directions:
*This recipe is not for hypoglycemics.*
- 1 serving contains 68 Calories (P3, F0, C14), no cholesterol
- 1 serving = 1 slice of bread or 3/4 cup of fruit (1 bread exchange or 1-1/2 fruit exchanges)
Omit water; replace with 1/3 cup (80 mL) concentrated apple juice. Reduce orange juice to 1/4 cup (60 mL). Add another 1/2 tablespoon (7.5 mL) of lemon juice. Increase red food coloring to 6 to 8 drops.

### For low-salt diet:
- 1 serving contains 3 mg of sodium
Omit salt; use sprinkle of salt substitute.

# Homemade Diet Gelatin

- Makes 2 cups (480 mL)
- 1/2 cup (120 mL) contains 8 Calories (P2, F0, C0), no cholesterol
- No replacements are necessary

**Plain gelatin**    1 tablespoon (7 grams)
**Unsweetened flavored drink mix**    scant 1/2 teaspoon (1.6 to 2 grams)
**Boiling water**    1 cup (240 mL)
**Cold water**    1 cup (240 mL)
**Lemon juice**    1 to 2 tablespoons (15 to 30 mL)
**Liquid sugar substitute**    3/4 to 1 teaspoon (3.8 to 5 mL); or substitute equal to
    4 teaspoons (16.2 grams) of sugar
**Salt**    sprinkle

Place gelatin and drink mix in a mixing
bowl. Pour boiling water over and stir to
dissolve. Add cold water and remaining
ingredients. Mix well. Chill until firm.

### Natural sweetening directions:
**With drink mix:**
- 1/2 cup (120 mL) contains 24 Calories (P2, F0, C4)
- 1/2 cup = 1/4 cup fruit (1/2 fruit exchange)
Omit sugar substitute and cold water; replace with 1/4 cup (60 mL) each apple and pineapple juice, plus
1/2 cup (120 mL) cold water. Use lemon and salt as indicated.
**Without drink mix:**
- 1/2 cup (120 mL) contains 64 Calories (P2, F0, C14)
- 1/2 cup = 1 slice of bread or 3/4 cup of fruit (1 bread exchange or 1-1/2 fruit exchanges)
Use 1/2 cup (120 mL) concentrated orange juice, 1/4 cup (60 mL) pineapple juice, plus 1/4 cup (60 mL) cold
water. Use lemon and salt as indicated.

### For low-salt diet:
- 1/2 cup (120 mL) contains 7 mg of sodium
Omit salt.

# Rod's Orange Yogurt Chiffon

- Makes 6 servings, 1/2 cup (120 mL) each
- 1 serving contains 69 Calories (P4, F1, C11), 3 mg of cholesterol
- 1 serving = 1/2 ounce of meat + 1/2 cup of fruit (1/2 meat exchange + 1 fruit exchange)

**Plain gelatin**   1 tablespoon (7 grams)
**Concentrated apple juice**   1/2 cup (120 mL)
**Boiling water**   1/4 cup (60 mL)
**Lemon juice**   1 teaspoon (5 mL)
**Frozen orange juice concentrate**   3 ounces (90 mL)
**Orange rind**   1/4 teaspoon (.4 gram), grated
**Plain yogurt**   1 cup (240 mL)

*Optional:*
**Walnuts**   1-1/2 teaspoons (3.8 grams), chopped for topping

*Meringue:*
**Egg whites**   2 (66 grams)
**Liquid sugar substitute**   3/8 teaspoon (1.8 mL); or substitute equal to 1-1/2 teaspoons (6 grams) of sugar
**Cream of tartar**   1/8 teaspoon (.5 gram)
**Salt**   sprinkle

Combine apple juice and boiling water. Add gelatin, stirring to dissolve completely. Cool slightly. Add orange juice concentrate to yogurt, then gelatin mixture, stirring until smooth. Place meringue ingredients in a separate bowl. Beat with mixer until firm. Fold in 1/4 of the beaten whites into the orange mixture; gradually fold in the remainder of the meringue. Pour into parfait glasses and top with walnuts. Chill until firm.

*Natural sweetening directions:*
- 1 serving contains 73 Calories (P4, F1, C12), no change in cholesterol or sodium
- 1 serving = 1/2 ounce of meat + 1/2 cup of fruit (1/2 meat exchange + 1 fruit exchange)
Omit liquid sweetener in meringue; replace with 1 teaspoon (5 mL) white grape juice and 1 tablespoon (16 grams) sieved dietetic applesauce. This will be slightly less sweet than the original recipe.

*For low-salt diet:*
- 1 serving contains 36 mg of sodium
Omit salt; use sprinkle of salt substitute.

# Berry Parfait

- Makes 4 servings
- 1 serving contains 66 Calories (P2, F2, C10), 2 mg of cholesterol
- 1 serving = 1/2 ounce of meat + 1/2 cup of fruit (1/2 meat exchange + 1 fruit exchange)

**Fresh berries**   1 cup (144 grams). Use strawberries, raspberries or boysenberries
**Skim milk**   1 cup (240 mL)
**Cornstarch**   2 tablespoons (16 grams)
**Melted margarine**   2 teaspoons (10 mL); use corn-oil, soybean-oil or safflower-oil margarine
**Salt**   1/8 teaspoon (.8 gram)
**Brown-type granular sugar substitute**   1-1/2 tablespoons (9 grams); or substitute equal to 3 tablespoons (36.6 grams) of sugar
**Vanilla or almond extract**   1/8 teaspoon (.6 mL)

Slice 1/2 cup (77 grams) of berries; puree 1/2 cup (109 grams) of berries; keep out 4 small, perfect berries for garnish. Add cornstarch to milk; stir well; add melted margarine. Add other ingredients; stir to mix completely. Cook in double boiler, stirring constantly, until fairly thick.

Remove from heat; add pureed berries and sugar substitute to taste; cool. Put sliced berries in bottom of 4 parfait glasses; spoon in cooked and cooled mixture; top each with a whole berry. Serve very cold.

### Natural sweetening directions:
*This recipe is not for hypoglycemics.*
- 1 serving contains 130 Calories (P2, F2, C26), no change in cholesterol or sodium
- 1 serving = 1 slice of bread + 1/2 cup of fruit + 1/2 teaspoon of fat (1 bread exchange + 1 fruit exchange + 1/2 fat exchange)

Omit sugar substitute; replace with 2 tablespoons (20 grams) of date sugar plus 2 tablespoons (30 mL) concentrated apple juice. Increase vanilla or almond extract to 1/4 teaspoon (1.3 mL).

### For low-salt diet:
- 1 serving contains 52 mg of sodium

Omit salt; use 1/8 teaspoon (.5 gram) of salt substitute. Use salt-free margarine.

# Semisweet Chocolate Pudding / *Plain and With Raisins*

- Makes 4 servings

*Plain:*
- 1 serving contains 85 Calories (P3, F4, C9), no cholesterol
- 1 serving = 1/2 cup of fruit + 1 teaspoon of fat (1 fruit exchange + 1 fat exchange)

*With raisins:*
- 1 serving contains 105 Calories (P3, F4, C14), no cholesterol
- 1 serving = 1 slice of bread + 1 teaspoon of fat (1 bread exchange + 1 fat exchange)

---

**Cocoa**   1-3/4 to 2 tablespoons (9.6 to 11 grams), to taste
**Cornstarch**   2-1/2 tablespoons (20 grams)
**Instant coffee**   1/8 teaspoon (.4 gram), decaffeinated if preferred.
   *Note: Hypoglycemics must use decaffeinated coffee.*
**Salt**   1/8 teaspoon (.8 gram)
**Water**   1 cup (240 mL)
**Hot skim milk**   1 cup (240 mL)
**Margarine**   1 tablespoon (14 grams); use corn-oil, soybean-oil or safflower-oil margarine
**Brown-type granular sugar substitute**   1/2 cup (48 grams); or substitute equal to 1 cup (195 grams) of sugar
**Vanilla**   2 teaspoons (10 mL)
**Cinnamon**   1/8 teaspoon (.4 gram)
**Unsweetened chocolate extract**   1/3 teaspoon (1.7 mL)

*Optional:*
**Raisins**   2 tablespoons (18 grams), soaked for 20 minutes in hot milk, then drained.

Mix cocoa, cornstarch, coffee granules, salt and water in top of double boiler; add milk. Cook, stirring frequently, until it starts to thicken. Add margarine; continue cooking and stirring until thick. Remove from heat; add raisins. Add sugar substitute, vanilla, cinnamon and chocolate extract; mix well. Pour into 4 serving dishes. Allow to cool before serving.

**Suggestions:**
For nondieters, serve with a topping of whipped cream or vanilla ice cream. For dieters, serve plain or with skim milk.

---

**Natural sweetening directions:**
*This recipe is not for hypoglycemics.*
- 1 serving contains 168 Calories (P3, F4, C30), no cholesterol
- 1 serving = 1 slice of bread + 1 teaspoon of fat + 3/4 cup of fruit (1 bread exchange + 1 fat exchange + 1-1/2 fruit exchanges)
Omit sugar substitute and water; replace with 1 cup (240 mL) white grape juice plus 3 tablespoons (30 grams) of date sugar. Increase coffee to 1/4 teaspoon (.8 gram) and increase vanilla to 2-1/2 teaspoons (12.5 mL).

**For low-salt diet:**
- 1 serving contains 36 mg of sodium
Omit salt; use 1/8 teaspoon (.5 gram) of salt substitute. Use salt-free margarine. Use plain old-fashioned or breakfast cocoa, not Dutch-processed cocoa.

# Fruit Cocktail Pudding

- Makes 3 servings
- 1 serving contains 36 Calories (P0, F0, C9), no cholesterol
- 1 serving = 1/2 cup of fruit (1 fruit exchange)

**Dietetic fruit cocktail**   2 cups (492 grams)
**Cornstarch**   1-1/2 tablespoons (12 grams)
**Salt**   1/8 teaspoon (.8 gram)
**Lemon juice**   1 tablespoon (15 mL)
**Lemon rind**   1/3 teaspoon (.5 gram), grated

Drain fruit cocktail, saving juice; add water to juice to make total of 2/3 cup (160 mL) of liquid. Mix cornstarch, salt and lemon juice into liquid. Cook slowly, stirring frequently, until thick. Remove from heat; add fruit cocktail and lemon rind. Cool before serving.

**Suggestions:**
This pudding, layered alternately with Vanilla Cornstarch Pudding (see recipe on page 217) in parfait glasses, makes an excellent dessert. If combining in equal parts, 1 serving equals 1 slice of bread.

### Natural sweetening directions:
- 1 serving contains 44 Calories (P0, F0, C11)
- 1 serving = 1/2 cup of fruit (1 fruit exchange)

Omit diet-sweetened fruit cocktail; replace with water-packed fruit cocktail; or make your own with 1 cup (241 grams) water-packed peaches, 1/2 cup each pears (113 grams) and pineapple (101 grams). Drain liquid as directed, but use 1/3 cup (80 mL) pineapple juice and make up with the liquid from the other fruits.

### For low-salt diet:
- 1 serving contains 7 mg of sodium

Omit salt; use 1/8 teaspoon (.5 gram) of salt substitute.

211

# Rice-Plus Pudding

- Makes 6 servings
- 1 serving contains 83 Calories (P3, F3, C11), 32 mg of cholesterol if made with egg, 1 mg of cholesterol if made with egg substitute
- 1 serving = 1/2 ounce of meat + 1/2 cup of fruit (1/2 meat exchange + 1 fruit exchange)

**Cooked brown rice**   1 cup (180 grams); from 1/3 cup (66 grams) raw rice
**Egg**   1 large (57 grams); or 2 ounces (60 mL) of liquid egg substitute
**Skim milk**   1 cup (240 mL)
**Dates**   2 (16 grams), chopped
**Walnuts**   8 halves (44 grams), chopped
**Raisins**   2 tablespoons (18 grams), cut in half
**Granular sugar substitute**   2-1/2 tablespoons (15 grams); or substitute equal to 5 tablespoons (61 grams) of sugar
**Cinnamon**   1/2 teaspoon (1.5 grams)
**Nutmeg**   1/8 teaspoon (.4 gram)
**Salt**   1/4 teaspoon (1.5 grams)
**Water**   1/2 cup (120 mL)

Cook 1/3 cup (66 grams) of rice until tender; drain and set aside. Beat egg; add to milk. Chop dates, nuts and raisins. Add dry ingredients to milk/egg mixture; add water; add rice; mix well. Put into lightly oiled baking dish; put dish in pan of hot water; bake at 325°F (163°C) about 1 hour, until browned on top. Divide into 6 equal portions.

**Suggestions:**
Use 4 tablespoons (36 grams) of raisins instead of half dates and half raisins.

### Natural sweetening directions:
- 1 serving contains 97 Calories (P3, F3, C14)
- 1 serving = 1 slice of bread + 1/2 teaspoon of fat (1 bread exchange + 1/2 fat exchange)
Omit sugar substitute. Use 1/4 cup (64 grams) diet applesauce plus 1-1/2 tablespoons (15 grams) of date sugar. Add 1/4 teaspoon (.4 gram) grated lemon rind.

### For low-salt diet:
- 1 serving contains 48 mg of sodium
Omit salt; use 1/4 teaspoon (1 gram) of salt substitute. Do not cook the rice in salted water.

# Double Chocolate Tapioca Pudding

- Makes 6 servings, 1/2 cup (120 mL) each
- 1 serving contains 69 Calories (P4, F1, C11), 37 mg of cholesterol if made with egg, 1 mg of cholesterol if made with egg substitute
- 1 serving = 1/2 ounce of meat + 1/2 cup of fruit (1/2 meat exchange + 1 fruit exchange)

**Quick-cooking tapioca**   3 tablespoons (25.5 grams)
**Breakfast cocoa**   1-1/2 tablespoons (8.3 grams)
**Salt**   1/8 teaspoon (.8 gram)
**Skim milk**   2 cups (480 mL)
**Water**   3/4 cup (180 mL)
**Egg**   1 large (57 grams), well beaten; or 2 ounces (60 mL) of liquid egg substitute
**Brown-type granular sugar substitute**   4-1/2 tablespoons (27 grams); or substitute equal to 9 tablespoons (109.8 grams) of sugar
**Vanilla**   1-1/4 teaspoons (6.3 mL)
**Unsweetened chocolate extract**   1/2 teaspoon (2.5 mL)

*Optional:*
**Instant coffee granules**   1/8 teaspoon (.4 gram), for mocha taste.
   *Note: Hypoglycemics must use decaffeinated coffee.*

Put tapioca, cocoa, instant coffee and salt into top of double boiler. Add milk, water and beaten egg; stir well. Let stand at least 15 minutes to moisten tapioca. Bring slowly to boil, stirring frequently; boil for 1 minute. Remove from heat; add sugar substitute, vanilla and chocolate extract. Mix well. Pour equal portions into 6 serving dishes; cool before serving.

**Suggestions:**
For nondieters, top with whipped cream or vanilla ice cream.

*Natural sweetening directions:*
- This recipe does not adapt well to natural sweetening.

*For low-salt diet:*
*Do not use on 400-mg sodium or 1-gram salt diets.*
- 1 serving contains 70 mg of sodium
Omit salt; use 1/8 teaspoon (.5 gram) of salt substitute. Use plain or breakfast cocoa, not Dutch-process cocoa.

# Marbled Berry-Tapioca Pudding

- Makes 6 servings, 1/2 cup (120 mL) each
- 1 serving contains 76 Calories (P5, F1, C12), 37 mg of cholesterol if made with egg, 1 mg of cholesterol if made with egg substitute
- 1 serving = 1/2 ounce of meat + 1/2 cup of fruit (1/2 meat exchange + 1 fruit exchange)

**Quick-cooking tapioca**   3 tablespoons (25.5 grams)
**Egg**   1 large (57 grams) beaten; or 2 ounces (60 mL) of liquid egg substitute
**Skim milk**   2-3/4 cups (660 mL)
**Granular sugar substitute**   2-1/2 tablespoons (15 grams); or substitute equal to 1/3 cup (65 grams) of sugar
**Vanilla**   1/4 teaspoon (1.3 mL)
**Salt**   1/2 teaspoon (3 grams)
**Dietetic berry jam**   3 tablespoons (54 grams)

In top of double boiler put tapioca, beaten egg and milk; stir; let stand at least 15 minutes to moisten tapioca. Heat to boiling point, stirring constantly; boil for 1 minute; remove from heat. Add sugar substitute, vanilla and salt; stir well; drop berry jam on by spoonfuls, then use a knife to streak jam through the pudding. Spoon equally into 6 individual serving dishes. Cool before serving.

### Natural sweetening directions:
- This recipe does not adapt well to natural sweetening.

### For low-salt diet:
*Do not use on 400-mg sodium or 1-gram salt diets. This recipe cannot be made low in sodium.*
- 1 serving contains 85 mg of sodium
Omit salt; use 1/4 teaspoon (1 gram) of salt substitute.

# Peanut Butter-Tapioca Pudding

- Makes 6 servings, 1/2 cup (120 mL) each
- 1 serving contains 155 Calories (P8, F7, C15), 40 mg of cholesterol if made with egg, 4 mg of cholesterol if made with egg substitute
- 1 serving = 1 slice of bread + 1 ounce of meat + 1 teaspoon of fat (1 bread exchange + 1 meat exchange + 1 fat exchange)

**Quick-cooking tapioca**   3 tablespoons (25.5 grams)
**Egg**   1 large (57 grams) beaten; or 2 ounces (60 mL) of liquid egg substitute
**Skim milk**   2-3/4 cups (660 mL)
**Old-fashioned peanut butter**   5 tablespoons (80 grams)
**Granular sugar substitute**   2-1/2 tablespoons (15 grams); or substitute equal to 1/3 cup (65 grams) of sugar
**Salt**   1/4 teaspoon (1.5 grams)
**Vanilla**   1/2 teaspoon (2.5 mL)

*Optional:*
**Nutmeg**   sprinkle

In top of double boiler put tapioca, beaten egg and milk; stir well; allow to stand at least 15 minutes to moisten tapioca. Heat to boiling, stirring often to prevent sticking; boil 1 minute; remove from heat. Add peanut butter; stir well; add sugar substitute and flavorings; stir again. Portion equally into 6 individual serving dishes; cool before serving.

**Suggestions:**
Peanut-butter lovers will prefer this dish with crunchy-style peanut butter. Be sure to use the old-fashioned style, with no sugar or corn syrup.

**Natural sweetening directions:**
*This recipe is not for hypoglycemics.*
- 1 serving contains 167 Calories (P8, F7, C18)
- 1 serving = 1/2 slice of bread + 1 ounce of meat + 1 teaspoon of fat + 1/2 cup of fruit (1/2 bread exchange + 1 meat exchange + 1 fat exchange + 1 fruit exchange)

Omit sugar substitute; replace with 2-1/2 tablespoons (25 grams) of date sugar. Increase vanilla to 3/4 teaspoon (3.8 mL).

**For low-salt diet:**
*Do not use on 400-mg sodium or 1-gram salt diets. This recipe cannot be made low in sodium because of the high natural sodium content of egg or egg substitute and milk.*
- 1 serving contains 90 mg of sodium

Omit salt; use 1/3 teaspoon (1.3 grams) of salt substitute. Use salt-free peanut butter.

# Tapioca Cream

- Makes 4 servings
- 1 serving contains 68 Calories (P5, F0, C12), 3 mg of cholesterol if made with egg white; 77 Calories (P5, F1, C12), no cholesterol if made with egg substitute
- 1 serving = 1/2 ounce of meat + 1/2 cup of fruit (1/2 meat exchange + 1 fruit exchange)

**Skim milk**   2 cups (480 mL)
**Quick-cooking tapioca**   3 tablespoons (25.5 grams)
**Butter flavoring**   4 drops
**Egg white**   1 (33 grams); or 1 ounce (30 mL) of liquid egg substitute
**Salt**   1/4 teaspoon (1.5 grams)
**Granular sugar substitute**   2-1/2 tablespoons (15 grams); or substitute equal to 1/3 cup (65 grams) of sugar
**Vanilla**   1 teaspoon (5 mL)

Soak tapioca in 1/2 cup (120 mL) of milk. Scald remaining milk; cool slightly. Add butter flavoring and tapioca to warm milk; add egg substitute, if using. Cook in double boiler, stirring constantly until fairly thick; remove from heat (the mixture will thicken more as it cools). Add salt, sugar substitute and vanilla; mix well. If using egg white, beat until stiff and fold into tapioca mixture. Cool and serve.

**Suggestions:**
Add 1/2 cup (101 grams) diet-pack diced pineapple to tapioca just before serving. Makes 5 servings. No change in food values.

**Natural sweetening directions:**
*This recipe is not for hypoglycemics.*
- 1 serving contains 92 Calories (P5, F0, C18), no cholesterol if made with egg substitute
- 1 serving = 1/2 slice of bread + 1/2 ounce of meat + 1/2 cup of fruit (1/2 bread exchange + 1/2 meat exchange + 1 fruit exchange)

Omit sugar substitute; replace with 2-1/2 tablespoons (25 grams) of date sugar. Increase vanilla to 1-1/4 teaspoons (6.3 mL). *Note:* This will be light brown and have a different — but good! — flavor from the pudding made with sugar substitute.

**For low-salt diet:**
- 1 serving contains 76 mg of sodium

Omit salt; use 1/4 teaspoon (1 gram) of salt substitute.

# Vanilla Cornstarch Pudding

- Makes 4 servings
- 1 serving contains 74 Calories (P5, F3, C12), 65 mg of cholesterol if made with egg, 2 mg of cholesterol if made with egg substitute
- 1 serving = 1/2 ounce of meat + 1/2 cup of fruit (1/2 meat exchange + 1 fruit exchange)

**Skim milk**　2 cups (480 mL)
**Cornstarch**　3-1/2 tablespoons (28 grams)
**Salt**　1/4 teaspoon (1.5 grams)
**Egg**　1 large (57 grams); or 2 ounces (60 mL) of liquid egg substitute
**Butter flavoring**　6 drops
**Margarine**　1 teaspoon (4.7 grams); use corn-oil, soybean-oil or safflower-oil margarine
**Granular sugar substitute**　1-1/2 tablespoons (9 grams); or substitute equal to 1/4 cup (48.8 grams) of sugar
**Vanilla**　1 teaspoon (5 mL)

Add enough milk to cornstarch to make smooth paste; stir in rest of milk. Add salt; cook in double boiler, stirring frequently, until it starts to thicken; cover; turn down heat; let cook for about 10 minutes. Remove from heat; cool slightly. Add part of mixture to beaten egg, beating well to avoid lumps; add butter flavoring and margarine; return to cooking pot; cook about 2 minutes longer. Remove from heat; add sugar substitute and vanilla. Divide into 5 equal servings; chill.

**Suggestions:**
Add sliced banana for banana-cream pudding or pie filling. Or add drained fruit cocktail, mixed in or as topping. Allow extra food value for added fruit.

**Natural sweetening directions:**
- 1 serving contains 107 Calories (P5, F3, C15), no change in cholesterol or sodium
- 1 serving = 1 slice of bread + 1/2 ounce of meat (1 bread exchange + 1/2 meat exchange)
Omit sugar substitute; replace with 1-1/2 tablespoons (15 grams) of date sugar. Increase vanilla to 1-1/4 teaspoons (6.3 mL).

**For low-salt diet:**
- 1 serving contains 82 mg of sodium
Omit salt; use 1/4 teaspoon (1 gram) of salt substitute. Use salt-free margarine.

217

# Apple Pie Pudding / *Everything but the crust!*

- Makes 6 servings, 1/2 cup (120 mL) each
- 1 serving contains 46 Calories (P0, F2, C7), no cholesterol
- 1 serving = 1/3 cup of fruit + 1/2 teaspoon of fat (2/3 fruit exchange + 1/2 fat exchange)

***With raisins:***
- Makes 7 servings
- 1 serving contains 66 Calories (P2, F2, C10)
- 1 serving = 1/2 cup of fruit + 1/2 teaspoon of fat (1 fruit exchange + 1/2 fat exchange)

**Apples**  2 cups (250 grams), peeled and sliced in chunks
**Water**  1-1/2 cups (360 mL)
**Lemon juice**  1 to 2 tablespoons (15 to 30 mL)
**Unbleached or whole-wheat flour**  1-1/2 tablespoons (12 or 14.4 grams), sifted
**Brown-type granular sugar substitute**  2 tablespoons (12 grams); or substitute equal to 1/4 cup (48.8 grams) of sugar
**Cinnamon**  1/2 teaspoon + (1.5 grams)
**Nutmeg**  1/4 teaspoon + (.8 gram)
**Ginger**  1/8 teaspoon + (.4 gram)
**Salt**  sprinkle
**Margarine**  1 tablespoon (14 grams); use corn-oil, soybean-oil or safflower-oil margarine
**Lemon rind**  1/4 teaspoon (.4 gram), grated

*Optional:*
**Raisins**  4 tablespoons (36 grams)

Cook apples in water until softened, but still in chunks. Drain, and set liquid aside to cool. Mix dry ingredients, using more spices if you prefer a stronger flavor; stir into cooled fruit liquid. Cook over low heat until mixture is thick and clear, indicating the starch is cooked. Remove from heat, add margarine, lemon rind and apples. Cool and serve.

***With raisins:***
Soak 4 tablespoons (36 grams) raisins in the water before cooking apples. Increase water to 1-3/4 cups (420 mL) and simmer for 5 minutes so some of the raisin sweetening will go into the liquid. Add apples and follow directions as given.

### Natural sweetening directions:
*Plain:*
- 1 serving contains 66 Calories (P0, F2, C12)
- 1 serving = 1/2 cup of fruit + 1/2 teaspoon of fat (1 fruit exchange + 1/2 fat exchange)

***With raisins:***
- 1 serving contains 78 Calories (P0, F2, C15)
- 1 serving = 1 slice of bread + 1/2 teaspoon of fat (1 bread exchange + 1/2 fat exchange)

Omit sugar substitute; use 3 tablespoons (30 grams) of date sugar. Increase lemon rind to 1/3 teaspoon (.5 gram).

### For low-salt diet:
- 1 serving plain or with raisins contains 2 mg of sodium

Omit salt and use equal amount of salt substitute. Use salt-free margarine.

# Spreads and Snacks

The snack foods are often not allowed on diets, and finding interesting sandwich spreads for the dieter is always a problem. The recipes given here are low in cholesterol and moderate in Calories. Don't be dismayed by the combinations of ingredients. Try them — you may find you really like them.

# Tasty Party Dip

- Makes 1-1/2 cups (360 mL)
- 3 tablespoons (45 mL) contain 29 Calories (P4, F1, C1), no cholesterol
- 3 tablespoons = 1/2 ounce of meat (1/2 meat exchange)
- You may use 1-1/2 tablespoons (22.5 mL) without substitution.

**Mock sour cream**   1-1/2 cups (360 mL); see recipe on page 239
**Garlic**   1/2 teaspoon (.5 gram), minced
**Fresh parsley**   1/2 teaspoon (.8 gram), diced
**Dry mustard**   1/4 teaspoon (.8 gram), or 6 drops Worcestershire sauce
**Horseradish**   1/2 teaspoon (2.5 grams)
**Tabasco**   3 to 4 drops
**Thyme**   pinch
**Salt**   to taste

*Optional:*
**Lemon juice**   1 tablespoon (15 mL)

Make Mock Sour Cream. Mix other ingredients except lemon juice, together; stir gently into Mock Sour Cream. Taste; add salt to taste; thin with lemon juice if needed.

**Suggestions:**
This dip is delicious served on a tray with a variety of raw vegetables for dipping. It is especially good with raw cauliflower, turnips or rutabagas. Experiment!

**Natural sweetening directions:**
- Not needed.

**For low-salt diet:**
- 1 tablespoon (15 mL) contains 40 mg of sodium
Omit salt; use salt substitute to taste. Make Mock Sour Cream according to low-salt directions.

# Cheese and Pickle Spread

- Makes 1 to 2 servings
- 1/2 recipe contains 80 Calories (P5, F5, C2), 12 mg of cholesterol
- 1/2 recipe = 1 ounce of meat (1 meat exchange)

**Low-fat cheese**   2 ounces (57 grams), 5% butterfat or less
**Extended mayonnaise**   1 tablespoon (15 mL); see recipe on page 85
**Dill pickle**   1 to 2 tablespoons (9 to 18 grams), minced

*Optional:*
**Dill weed**   sprinkle

Allow cheese to soften to room temperature; with large spoon or spatula, mash into an even, soft pile. Add mayonnaise, pickle and dill weed; cream well. Spread on bread or crackers.

*Suggestions:*
Bread that has been spread may become soggy, so keep refrigerated until eaten. If leftover spread weeps, recream.

*Natural sweetening directions:*
- Not needed.

*For low-salt diet:*
*This recipe cannot be made low in salt.*

# Chicken / Turkey Salad Spread

- Makes 1 or 2 servings
- 1/2 recipe contains 73 Calories (P7, F5, C0), 32 mg of cholesterol
- 1/2 recipe = 1 ounce of meat (1 meat exchange)

**Chicken or turkey**   2 ounces (57 grams), without skin, chopped or coarse-ground
**Celery**   1 tablespoon (7.5 grams), diced
**Chives**   1/2 teaspoon (.5 gram), minced
**Green pepper or pimento**   1/2 teaspoon (1.5 or 2 grams), diced
**Mayonnaise**   1 teaspoon (5 mL)
**Plain low-fat yogurt**   1 tablespoon (15 mL)
**Cider vinegar**   1/4 teaspoon (1.3 mL)
**Salt, pepper and paprika**   sprinkle of each

Put meat into mixing bowl; add vegetables; mix well. Combine mayonnaise, yogurt, vinegar and seasonings; add to first mixture; mix thoroughly. Taste; add seasonings to suit.

*Natural sweetening directions:*
- Not needed.

*For low-salt diet:*
- 1/2 recipe contains 24 mg of sodium
Omit salt; use sprinkle of salt substitute. Cook chicken or turkey without salt. Use salt-free mayonnaise.

# Fish Salad Spread

- Makes 1 to 2 servings
- 1/2 recipe contains 85 Calories (P7, F6, C1), 30 mg of cholesterol
- 1/2 recipe = 1 ounce of meat (1 meat exchange)

**Water-packed tuna or flaked white fish, such as halibut or sole**    2 ounces
  (57 grams)
**Celery**    1 teaspoon (2.5 grams), chopped fine
**Onion**    1/2 teaspoon (1.7 grams), minced
**Dill pickle**    1 teaspoon (3 grams), minced
**Extended mayonnaise**    1 tablespoon (15 mL); see recipe on page 85
**Pepper**    sprinkle
**Cider vinegar**    1/2 to 1 teaspoon (2.5 to 5 mL), to taste

Flake tuna in mixing bowl; add vegetables and mayonnaise. Add pepper and 1/2 teaspoon (2.5 mL) of vinegar; mix well; taste; add more vinegar and seasonings if desired. Spread on bread or crackers.

*Suggestions:*
You will want to add more spices if you use a bland white fish. Try adding a sprinkle of garlic powder and a pinch of sweet basil for variety.

*Natural sweetening directions:*
- Not needed.

*For low-salt diet:*
- 1/2 recipe contains 20 mg of sodium

Use salt-free water-packed tuna, or fresh fish cooked without salt. Omit pickle; use sprinkle of dill weed. Use mayonnaise extended by salt-free directions.

# Herbed Cheese Spread / Dip

- Makes 1-1/4 cups (300 mL)
- 1 tablespoon (15 mL) contains 31 Calories (P1, F3, C0), 10 mg of cholesterol
- 1 tablespoon = 1/2 teaspoon of fat (1/2 fat exchange)

*Dip:*
- 1 tablespoon contains 31 Calories (P1, F3, C0), 10 mg of cholesterol, 28 mg of sodium
- 1 tablespoon = 1/2 teaspoon of fat (1/2 fat exchange)

**Neufchatel cream cheese**   8 ounces (224 grams), at room temperature
**Plain yogurt**   2 tablespoons (30 mL)
**Concentrated apple juice**   1-1/2 teaspoons (7.5 mL)
**Lemon rind**   1/8 teaspoon (.2 gram), grated
**Bouquet garni herb mix**   1 teaspoon (3 grams)

*Optional:*
**Salt**   1/4 teaspoon (1.5 grams)

Leave cheese at room temperature for about an hour before mixing. Place in a bowl, cream in yogurt, apple juice and other ingredients. Cover and chill before serving.

**Dip:**
Increase yogurt to 4-1/2 tablespoons (67.5 mL). Increase bouquet garni to 1-1/4 teaspoons (3.8 grams).

*Suggestions:*
This is excellent on hot toast, crackers or matzos.

**Natural sweetening directions:**
- Not needed.

**For low-salt diet:**
- 1 tablespoon (15 mL) of spread contains 30 mg of sodium
- 1 tablespoon (15 mL) of dip contains 28 mg of sodium
Omit salt.

# Jane's Favorite Spread

- Makes 1 serving
- 1 serving contains 60 Calories (P8, F3, C4), 6 mg of cholesterol
- 1 serving = 1 ounce of meat + 1/4 cup of fruit (1 meat exchange + 1/2 fruit exchange)

**Low-fat cottage cheese**   1/4 cup (59 grams)
**Dietetic berry jam or jelly**   2 teaspoons (12 grams)
**Lemon rind**   sprinkle

*Optional:*
**Cinnamon**   sprinkle

In sieve or colander, wash cottage cheese in cold water to remove any fat or liquid. Dry cottage cheese on paper towel. Mix cheese with jam; add lemon rind. Spread on bread, crackers or hot toast. Top with a light sprinkle of cinnamon if you wish.

*Suggestions:*
Make this spread just before using it; it does not hold well.

### Natural sweetening directions:
- No change in food values.
- Use jam made by natural sweetening directions; see recipes on pages 249-261.

### For low-salt diet:
*Do not use on 400-mg sodium or 1-gram salt diets. This recipe cannot be made low in sodium because of the natural sodium in cottage cheese.*
- 1 serving contains about 128 mg of sodium

# Low-Cholesterol Egg Salad Spread

- Makes 3 portions
- 1 portion contains 105 Calories (P7, F8, C0), 8 mg of cholesterol
- 1 portion = 1 ounce of meat + 1/2 teaspoon of fat (1 meat exchange + 1/2 fat exchange)

**Liquid egg substitute**   2/3 cup (160 mL)
**Egg**   1 large (57 grams), hard-cooked
**Extended mayonnaise**   1 tablespoon (15 mL); see recipe on page 85
**Prepared mustard**   1/4 teaspoon (1.2 mL)
**Cider vinegar**   1/2 teaspoon (2.5 mL)
**Onion**   1/3 teaspoon (1 gram), minced fine
**Salt**   1/4 teaspoon (1.5 grams)
**Pepper**   1/8 teaspoon (.5 gram)

Into top of double boiler sprayed with nonstick coating, put egg substitute; place over boiling water; cook for 5 minutes; turn off heat and let stand for 5 minutes; remove from heat; allow to cool slightly. Turn out egg substitute into small mixing bowl; mince with fork until evenly broken and fairly fine; add hard-cooked egg white (discard yolk); mince to same consistency. Add mayonnaise, mustard, vinegar, onion and seasonings. Mix thoroughly; taste; add more seasonings if you wish. Divide into 3 equal portions and use as spread.

*Suggestions:*
If you have enough fat allowance, add minced stuffed olives into this for a change. Do not use olives if diet limits salt or sodium intake.

*Natural sweetening directions:*
- Not needed.

*For low-salt diet:*
*Do not use on a low-sodium diet.*
- 1 portion contains 137 mg of sodium
Omit salt; use 1/4 teaspoon (1 gram) of salt substitute. Omit prepared mustard; use 1/16 teaspoon (.2 gram) of dry mustard dissolved in the vinegar; add a few drops of water to make a paste, which will blend with the other ingredients. Use salt-free mayonnaise, extended according to salt-free directions.

# Peanut Butter Spread

- Makes 2 servings
- 1 serving contains 143 Calories (P6, F12, C6), 2 mg of cholesterol
- 1 serving = 1 ounce of meat + 1/4 cup of fruit + 1 teaspoon of fat (1 meat exchange + 1/2 fruit exchange + 1 fat exchange)

**Old-fashioned peanut butter**   3 tablespoons (48 grams)
**Plain low-fat yogurt**   2 tablespoons (30 mL)
**Liquid sweetener**   1 to 3 drops
**Nutmeg**   1 or 2 sprinkles

In small bowl, mix peanut butter and yogurt; cream with spoon or spatula until smooth. Add sweetener and spice; blend thoroughly. Spread on crackers or bread.

**Suggestions:**
This spread keeps well, so may be made ahead of time. It makes an excellent stuffing for celery.

***Natural sweetening directions:***
- No change in nutritional values.
Omit liquid sweetener; add 1/8 teaspoon (.4 gram) of date sugar. Omit nutmeg.

***For low-salt diet:***
- 1 serving contains 10 mg of sodium
Use salt-free peanut butter.

# Smoky Cheese Spread

- Makes 2 servings
- 1 serving contains 107 Calories (P6, F8, C2), 12 mg of cholesterol
- 1 serving = 1 ounce of meat + 1/2 teaspoon of fat (1 meat exchange + 1/2 fat exchange)

**Low-fat cheese**   2 ounces (57 grams), 5% butterfat or less
**Extended mayonnaise**   1 tablespoon (15 mL); see recipe on page 85
**Plain low-fat yogurt**   1 tablespoon (15 mL)
**Garlic powder**   sprinkle
**Imitation bacon bits**   1 teaspoon (4 grams)

Allow cheese to soften to room temperature; with large spoon or spatula, mash into an even, soft pile. Add mayonnaise, yogurt and garlic powder; cream thoroughly. Stir in imitation bacon bits. Taste; add more seasonings if you wish. Spread on bread or crackers.

**Suggestions:**
Because this is a soft spread, it is best refrigerated until eaten.

***Natural sweetening directions:***
- Not needed.

***For low-salt diet:***
*This recipe cannot be made low in salt.*

# Vegetable Nibblers

- Makes 2 quarts of vegetables (1.92 L)
- 1 cup (240 mL) contains 32 Calories (P1, F0, C7), no cholesterol
- 1 cup = 1/2 slice of bread *or* 1 vegetable serving (1/2 bread exchange *or* 1 vegetable exchange)

### *Marinade:*
**Water**    4 cups (960 mL)
**Granular sugar substitute**    1/4 cup (24 grams); or substitute equal to 1/2 cup (97.5 grams) of sugar
**White vinegar**    1/2 cup (120 mL)
**Salt**    1/4 cup (72 grams)

### *Vegetables:*
**Celery sticks**
**Carrot sticks**
**Cauliflower buds**
**Green pepper sections**
**Small onions, or onion slices**
**Tomato wedges**
**Turnip or rutabaga slices**
**Celery root slices**
**Raw mushroom slices**
**Other raw vegetables to suit your taste**

Prepare marinade; mix well to dissolve all solids. Pour over raw vegetables; let stand overnight in refrigerator. Serve in marinade, or drain and serve.

### *Suggestions:*
This is an excellent nibbling food for the cocktail hour, low-Calorie and appetizing. The marinade may be saved and used a second time. Be sure to keep refrigerated.

### *Natural sweetening directions:*
- 3/4 cup (180 mL) contains 36 Calories (P1, F0, C8), no cholesterol
- 3/4 cup = 1 vegetable serving (1 vegetable exchange)

Omit sugar substitute; replace with 1/2 cup (120 mL) apple juice plus 1/2 cup (120 mL) white grape juice and 1 tablespoon (15 mL) lemon juice. Reduce water to 3 cups (720 mL).

### *For low-salt diet:*
- 1/2 cup (120 mL) contains 6 to 12 mg of sodium, depending upon vegetables used.

Omit salt; use salt substitute. Omit celery sticks and turnip slices; use fewer carrot sticks, which are high in sodium.

# High-Calorie Granola Snack Mix

- Makes 12-1/2 cups
- 1/3 cup contains 231 Calories (P9, F15, C15), no cholesterol
- 1/3 cup = 1 slice of bread + 1 ounce of meat + 2-1/2 teaspoons of fat (1 bread exchange + 1 meat exchange + 2-1/2 fat exchanges)

**Oatmeal**    4 cups (288 grams), not instant
**Four-grain cereal, or other mixture of uncooked grains**    2 cups (174 grams)
**Wheat germ**    1/2 cup (48 grams)
**Sesame seeds**    6 tablespoons (54 grams)
**Unsalted, hulled sunflower seeds**    1 cup (145 grams)
**Unsalted dry-roasted peanuts**    1 cup (144 grams)
**Pecan or walnuts**    1 cup (105 or 119 grams), broken in pieces
**Margarine**    2/3 cup (150 grams); use corn-oil, soybean-oil or safflower-oil margarine
**Raisins**    1-1/2 cups (216 grams)

*Optional:*
**Brown-type granular sugar substitute**    1/2 cup (48 grams); or substitute equal to 1 cup (195 grams) of sugar

Combine all ingredients except margarine and sugar substitute in a large bowl. Melt margarine; dribble over dry mixture, stirring to coat evenly. Sprinkle sugar substitute over this mixture and stir well. Spread flat on a baking sheet and bake at 300°F (149°C) for 30 minutes, stirring two or three times to allow for even browning. Cool well before placing in an airtight container. Store in a cool place, or package and freeze in small amounts to be used as needed.

### Natural sweetening directions:
*If made with date sugar, this recipe is not for hypoglycemics.*
**With date sugar:**
- 1/3 cup contains 239 Calories (P9, F15, C17), no cholesterol
- 1/3 cup = 1 slice of bread + 1 ounce of meat + 2-1/2 teaspoons of fat (1 bread exchange + 1 meat exchange + 2-1/2 fat exchanges)

Omit sugar substitute; use 2/3 cup (107 grams) of date sugar. Or omit sweetening entirely; this granola is quite tasty without any added sweetening.

### For low-salt diet:
- 1/3 cup contains 6 mg of sodium

Use all salt-free nuts and salt-free margarine.

# Holiday Snack Mix

- Makes 10 cups
- 1/2 cup contains 121 Calories (P2, F9, C8), no cholesterol
- 1/2 cup = 1/2 slice of bread + 2 teaspoons of fat (1/2 bread exchange + 2 fat exchanges)

**Miniature shredded wheat biscuits**    3 cups (105 grams)
**Puffed wheat or rice**    3 cups (45 grams)
**Thin pretzels**    3 cups (150 grams)
**Walnuts**    1 cup (120 grams), broken into quarters or eighths
**Melted margarine**    2/3 cup (160 mL); use corn-oil, soybean-oil or safflower-oil margarine
**Onion powder**    1/2 teaspoon (.8 gram)
**Garlic powder**    1/3 teaspoon (1 gram)
**Worcestershire sauce**    1 teaspoon (5 mL)

*Optional:*
**Salt**    1/2 teaspoon (3 grams)

Combine cereals, pretzels and nuts in a large bowl. Melt margarine and add all seasonings. Pour margarine mix over cereals; stir well to coat all pieces. Spread on baking sheet; put into oven at 200°F (93°C) for about 20 minutes; stir every 5 minutes to brown evenly. Cool; store in airtight container in cool place. Will keep well for about 2 weeks.

*Suggestions:*
You may vary the ingredients, but only the dry cereals listed are completely sugar-free and fat-free. If you want more margarine, double the amount and allow twice as much fat — 3 teaspoons (15 mL) of fat per 1/2 cup of mix.

*Natural sweetening directions:*
- Not needed.

*For low-salt diet:*
- 1/2 cup contains 3 mg of sodium
Omit salt; use 1/2 teaspoon (2 grams) of salt substitute. Use salt-free margarine. Omit pretzels; use 4-1/2 cups (157.5 grams) of miniature shredded wheat and 4-1/2 cups (67.5 grams) of puffed wheat, or 3 cups each shredded wheat (105 grams), puffed wheat (45 grams) and puffed rice (45 grams).

# Emergency Snack Mix
## *(For Hypoglycemics and Diabetics)*

- Makes 1 serving, 3 tablespoons
- 3 tablespoons contain 184 Calories (P7, F12, C12), no cholesterol
- 3 tablespoons = 1 ounce of meat + 1/2 cup of fruit + 1-1/2 teaspoons of fat
  (1 meat exchange + 1 fruit exchange + 1-1/2 fat exchanges)

**Dry-roasted peanuts**    1 tablespoon (9 grams)
**Unsalted roasted sunflower seeds**    1 tablespoon (9 grams)
**Raisins**    1 tablespoon (9 grams)

Measure out nuts, seeds and raisins into a
plastic bag. Fasten and carry with you for
emergency feedings.

*Natural sweetening directions:*
- Not needed.

*For low-salt diet:*
- 3 tablespoons contain 6 mg of sodium
- Be sure that the peanuts and sunflower seeds are salt-free.

# Odds and Ends
### Recipes that are out of the usual!

# Tasty Corn Chips / *Taco, Too!*

- Makes 120 1-inch squares
- 10 contain 95 Calories (P3, F3, C14), no cholesterol
- 10 = 1 slice of bread + 1/2 teaspoon of fat (1 bread exchange + 1/2 fat exchange)

**Boiling water**   1 cup (240 mL)
**Margarine**   3 tablespoons (42 grams); use corn-oil, soybean-oil or safflower-oil
   margarine
**Tabasco**   1 teaspoon (5 mL)
**Garlic powder**   1/2 teaspoon (1.5 grams)
**Yellow corn meal**   1 cup (122 grams), coarse-ground
**Whole-wheat flour**   3/4 cup (102.8 grams), unsifted
**Gluten flour**   1/4 cup (36 grams)
**Baking soda**   1/3 to 1/2 teaspoon (1.3 to 2 grams)
**Salt**   3/4 teaspoon (4.5 grams)

*Optional:*
**Salt**   for tops
**Taco flavoring**   1 teaspoon (4 grams) + some for sprinkling on top

Combine water, margarine, Tabasco and garlic powder in a bowl. Place all other ingredients in a mixing bowl, and mix well. Add water mixture and stir until dough forms a ball. Knead on a lightly floured board for 5 minutes. Divide dough into three or four parts. Roll each part as thin as possible. Place each on a greased baking sheet and reroll. Prick with a fork, then cut into 1-inch squares; you can then cut these into 2 triangles. Bake at 375°F (191°C) about 15 minutes, until chips are golden brown. Cool slightly before taking off the baking sheets. Store in loosely covered containers in a dry place.

***Natural sweetening directions:***
- Not needed.

***For low-salt diet:***
- 10 chips contain 10 mg of sodium
Omit salt, baking soda and regular margarine; replace with equal amounts of salt substitute, potassium bicarbonate and salt-free margarine.

# Lemon Ginger Drink

- Makes 3 servings, poured over crushed ice
- 1 serving contains 32 Calories (P0, F0, C8), no cholesterol
- 1 serving = 1/2 cup of fruit (1 fruit exchange)

**Orange juice**    1/2 cup (120 mL), or 1/3 cup (80 mL) unsweetened pineapple juice
**Lemon juice**    1/2 cup (120 mL)
**Granular sugar substitute**    1-1/2 tablespoons (9 grams); or substitute equal to
    3 tablespoons (36.6 grams) of sugar
**Diet Ginger Ale**    2 cups (480 mL)
**Crushed ice cubes**
**Slices of lemon, orange or sprig of mint**

Combine orange juice and lemon juice. Add sugar substitute; stir well. Combine with Ginger Ale; mix gently to avoid losing the carbonation. Pour over crushed ice in tall glasses; garnish with slice of fruit.

**Suggestions:**
This can be made a little ahead of time, but not long. A sprig of peppermint or spearmint, if available, will give a faint mint flavor.

*Natural sweetening directions:*
- This recipe does not adapt well to natural sweetening.

*For low-salt diet:*
*This recipe cannot be made lower in salt because of the dietetic Ginger Ale.*
- 1 serving contains 34 mg of sodium

# Fruit Squares

- Makes 25 squares
- 2 squares contain 91 Calories (P3, F3, C13), no cholesterol
- 2 squares = 1 slice of bread + 1 teaspoon of fat (1 bread exchange + 1 fat exchange)

**Dried fruit**   6 ounces (171 grams); use apples, apricots, peaches and pears, or prunes
**Water**   2 cups (480 mL)
**Cornstarch or instant flour**   1 tablespoon (8 grams)
**Lemon juice**   1 tablespoon (15 mL)
**Salt**   1/8 teaspoon (.8 gram)
**Plain gelatin**   2 tablespoons (14 grams)
**Lemon extract or rind**   1/4 teaspoon (1.3 mL or .4 gram)
**Walnuts**   1/2 cup (60 grams), chopped into eighths
**Granular sugar substitute**   1-1/2 teaspoons (3 grams); or substitute equal to 1 tablespoon (12.2 grams) of sugar

Cook dried fruit in water until tender; add a little more water if it gets too dry to prevent sticking and scorching. Puree in food mill to remove any skins or fibers. Add cornstarch, lemon juice, salt and enough water to prevent sticking. Cook slowly until the cornstarch is cooked and the color clears, stirring often. Dissolve gelatin in hot mixture; stir well to blend. Remove from heat; add lemon, walnuts and sugar substitute. Mix well; pour into 8- or 9-inch-square (20 or 22.5 cm) pan lined with wax paper or foil. Cool until firm. Cut into 25 parts, 5 each way in the pan.

*Optional:* Sift 1 tablespoon (8 grams) of cornstarch over squares to keep them from sticking together; turn them to cover all sides.

*Suggestions:*
You can vary these greatly by changing the fruit used. Equal parts of apple, apricot and pear make a very good combination. Prunes make the least attractive color. It is better to use prunes by themselves or with apple only.

*Natural sweetening directions:*
- 1 square contains 95 Calories (P3, F3, C14), no cholesterol, no change in sodium
- 1 square = 1 slice of bread + 1/2 teaspoon of fat (1 bread exchange + 1/2 fat exchange)
Omit sugar substitute. Reduce water to 1-1/2 cups (360 mL). Add 1/3 cup (80 mL) white grape juice. Increase lemon juice to 1-1/2 tablespoons (22.5 mL)

*For low-salt diet:*
- 1 square contains 2 mg of sodium
Omit salt; use 1/8 teaspoon (.5 gram) of salt substitute.

234

# Christine's Dietetic Granola

- Makes 9 cups
- 1/4 cup contains 130 Calories (P4, F6, C15), no cholesterol
- 1/4 cup = 1 slice of bread + 1 teaspoon of fat (1 bread exchange + 1 fat exchange)

**Oatmeal**   4 cups (288 grams), not instant
**4-grain cereal**   2 cups (174 grams)
**Wheat germ**   1/2 cup (48 grams)
**Sesame seeds**   3 tablespoons (27 grams)
**Sunflower kernels**   1/2 cup (72.5 grams)
**Pecan chips**   1-5/8 ounces (46.3 grams)
**Walnut or almond chips**   1-5/8 ounces (46.3 grams)
**Salt**   1/2 teaspoon (3 grams)
**Margarine**   1/3 cup (75 grams); use corn-oil, soybean-oil or safflower-oil margarine
**Brown-type granular sugar substitute**   1/3 cup (32 grams); or substitute equal to 2/3 cup (130 grams) of sugar
**Raisins**   3/4 cup (108 grams)

Combine dry ingredients except sugar substitute and raisins. Melt margarine and dribble over dry ingredients; mix well. Sprinkle sugar substitute over all; mix again; add raisins. Spread on baking pan; bake at 300°F (149°C) 20 to 25 minutes, stirring every 5 minutes until slightly browned. Remove from oven and let cool; stir occasionally to speed cooling. Pack in covered containers and store in cool place.

*Suggestions:*
The raisins will be quite different in texture if you add them after baking, rather than before. See Granola Cookie recipe, page 171, for a very special cookie made from this mixture.

*Natural sweetening directions:*
- 1/4 cup contains 150 Calories (P4, F6, C20)
- 1/4 cup = 1 slice of bread + 1/4 cup of fruit + 1 teaspoon of fat (1 bread exchange + 1/2 fruit exchange + 1 fat exchange)

Omit sugar substitute; replace with 1/3 cup (53 grams) date sugar.

*For low-salt diet:*
- 1/4 cup contains 3 mg of sodium

Omit salt; use 1/2 teaspoon (2 grams) of salt substitute. Use salt-free margarine.

# Homemade Noodles

- Makes 10 ounces (285 grams)
- 1 ounce (28.5 grams) contains 57 Calories (P3, F1, C9), 25 mg of cholesterol
- 1 ounce = 1/2 slice of bread + 1/3 ounce of lean meat (1/2 bread exchange + 1/3 lean meat exchange)

**Whole-wheat flour**  1 cup + 1 tablespoon (146.6 grams), unsifted
**Soy flour**  1 tablespoon (7 grams)
**Salt**  1/4 teaspoon (1.5 grams)
**Egg**  1 large (57 grams). *Note: Do not use egg substitute as it will not bind satisfactorily.*
**Cold water**  2 tablespoons (30 mL)

Combine flour and salt in a mixing bowl. Mix the egg with the water. Make a well in the flour, then gradually pour in the egg/water, working with your fingers to mix. Knead on floured board or in the bowl until gluten has developed as in bread dough — at least 5 minutes. When texture is elastic, cover and let rest for 15 to 20 minutes before rolling out. Or you can refrigerate dough and roll out later.

Divide dough into two or more smaller balls; roll out on lightly floured pastry cloth, as thin as possible. Turn pastry often to get as even a spread as possible, about 1/16th (.16 cm) of an inch. Cut into four strips and stack on top of each other. Slice noodles as thin as you wish. This will make four strips at a time and save time. Allow noodles to dry on a cookie sheet before storing. You can speed drying time by laying noodles on a cookie sheet and placing them in the oven at 150°F (65°C), with the door open.

When cooking, add 1 teaspoon (5 mL) of oil to the water to prevent the noodles from sticking together.

***Natural sweetening directions:***
- Not needed.

***For low-salt diet:***
- 1 ounce (28.5 grams) contains 6 mg of sodium
Omit salt; replace with equal amount of salt substitute.

# Grated Fruit Rind

• No substitution required. Calories negligible.

**Citrus fruit**    1 or 2 lemons or oranges, 1 grapefruit, or all three mixed

Using fine grater, grate rinds onto nonstick cookie sheet; spread over sheet, avoiding large clumps. Place on top rack of oven preheated to 200°F (93°C); turn heat control to 150°F (65°C); leave in oven for 1-1/2 hours, or until completely dry; remove and let cool. Crush any lumps with bottom of tumbler or rolling pin covered with wax paper. Store in airtight container. Do not leave in bright sunlight or some color will be lost. Refrigeration not needed.

*Suggestions:*
Most, if not all, dried fruit rind on the market has been sugared. Read the label and you will see that dextrose is a principal ingredient. Make your own to have something you can use — and save money. Use slightly more orange than lemon rind for a less bitter flavor; use grapefruit rind in the same proportion as lemon. You will not usually notice the difference in a recipe. About 3 tablespoons (13.5 grams) of wet ingredients yield 1-1/2 tablespoons (4.5 grams) of dry material. Use about half the volume of fresh called for in a recipe. If you wish, add a small amount of liquid to the dry rind and allow to remoisten before using.

*Natural sweetening directions:*
• Not needed.

*For low-salt diet:*
• Sodium content is less than 1 mg per tablespoon. No changes are required.

# How to Make Your Own Peanut Butter

- Makes 2 cups (502 grams)
- 1 tablespoon contains 52 Calories (P2.5, F4, C1.5); 2 tablespoons contain 104 Calories (P5, F8, C3)
- 2 tablespoons = 1 ounce of lean meat + 1/2 vegetable serving + 1 teaspoon of fat (1 lean meat exchange + 1/2 vegetable exchange + 1 fat exchange)

**Raw or dry-roasted peanuts**   2 cups (288 grams), shelled
**Peanut or vegetable oil**   1 to 2 tablespoons (15 to 30 mL)
**Salt**   1/2 teaspoon (3 grams)

If using raw peanuts, spread on a baking sheet with sides. Roast at 325°F (163°C) for 20 to 25 minutes, until they are lightly browned. Taste to be sure they are roasted enough. Cool before trying to make into peanut butter. Grind peanuts until they are quite fine, about 1/2 cup (72 grams) at a time in the blender or food processor. Mix with oil and salt, using the lesser amount of oil and adding more if needed to get a butter-like consistency. Blend or process about 1/3 of the recipe at a time until all is evenly mixed. Store in a jar and refrigerate to keep fresh. Note: Oil will not separate out from nuts when peanut butter is kept cool.

*Suggestions:*
Other nuts can be used to make butter. Use oil as necessary, usually not more than 1 tablespoon (15 mL) per cup. A few drops of hot water will also help thin the butter if necessary. The following food values are based on using salt-free nuts. All equal 1 fat exchange.

- **Almonds:** 1 tablespoon contains 61 Calories (P2, F5, C2), .4 mg of sodium
- **Cashews:** 1 tablespoon contains 48 Calories (P1, F4, C2), 1.2 mg of sodium
- **Filberts:** 1 tablespoon contains 53 Calories (P1, F5, C1), .2 mg of sodium
- **Pecans:** 1 tablespoon contains 53 Calories (P1, F5, C1), 0 mg of sodium
- **English walnuts:** 1 tablespoon contains 44 Calories (P1, F4, C1), .1 mg of sodium

*Natural sweetening directions:*
- Not needed.

*For low-salt diet:*
- 2 tablespoons contain less than 1 mg of sodium
Omit salt; use 1/2 teaspoon (2 grams) of salt substitute. Be sure to use raw or salt-free dry-roasted peanuts, not just the regular dry-roasted ones, as they pick up salt in processing, although none extra is added after they are cooked.

# Mock Sour Cream

- Makes 1-1/2 cups (360 mL)
- 3 tablespoons (45 mL) contain 29 Calories (P4, F1, C1), 1 mg of cholesterol
- You may use 1-1/2 tablespoons (22.5 mL) without substitution
- 3 tablespoons = 1/2 ounce of meat (1/2 meat exchange)

**Liquid pectin**   4 to 6 tablespoons (60 to 90 mL)
**Low-fat cottage cheese**   1 cup (235 grams)
**Lemon juice**   2 tablespoons (30 mL)
**Skim milk**   1 tablespoon (15 mL)

Put 4 tablespoons (60 mL) of pectin and other ingredients into a blender; blend at high speed for 1 minute. Check for smoothness; if some graininess still shows, add 2 tablespoons (30 mL) of pectin and blend 1 minute longer at highest speed. Store covered in refrigerator. Will usually keep about 10 days without separating.

*Suggestions:*
Use as a sour cream substitute on baked potato or in stroganoff, or as a dip for raw vegetables (see Tasty Party Dip recipe, page 220).

Use with sugar substitute for fruit dressing (1/4 teaspoon (1.3 mL) of liquid sugar substitute, 1/2 teaspoon (1.5 grams) of celery seed and 1/2 cup (120 mL) of Mock Sour Cream with 1/2 teaspoon (2.5 mL) lemon juice to thin).

Use with 2 teaspoons (8 grams) of imitation bacon bits and 1 teaspoon (1 gram) of chopped chives for fancier baked potato dressing.

*Natural sweetening directions:*
- Not needed.

*For low-salt diet:*
- 1 tablespoon (15 mL) contains 31 mg of sodium

Wash cottage cheese with cold water until water runs clear to remove salt added in processing. Use unsalted cottage cheese, if you can find it. It has about 1/3 less sodium.

# Imitation Half-and-Half

- Makes 2-1/2 cups (600 mL)
- 2 tablespoons (30 mL) contain 70 Calories (P1, F6, C3), 3 mg of cholesterol
- 2 tablespoons = 1/4 slice of bread + 1 teaspoon of fat (1/4 bread exchange + 1 fat exchange)

**Skim milk**  2 cups (480 mL)
**Corn or soybean oil**  4 ounces (120 mL)
**Butter flavoring**  16 drops
**Salt**  sprinkle

Place all ingredients in the blender and blend at top speed for 2 minutes to emulsify oil with the milk. Refrigerate to keep stable. Note: Be sure oil is fresh, so there is no taste of rancid oil. To prevent oil from becoming rancid, refrigerate after opening.

### Natural sweetening directions:
- Not needed.

### For low-salt diet:
- 1 ounce (30 mL) contains 14 mg of sodium
Omit salt; use sprinkle of salt substitute.

# Salt-Free Herb Seasoning Mix

- 1 teaspoon contains 0 Calories (P0, F0, C0), no cholesterol
- 1 teaspoon contains less than 1 mg of sodium

**Sweet basil**  1 tablespoon (9 grams), dried
**Savory**  2 teaspoons (6 grams), dried
**Celery seed**  2 teaspoons (6 grams)
**Sage**  2 teaspoons (6 grams)
**Thyme**  1 teaspoon (3 grams)
**Marjoram**  1 teaspoon (3 grams)
**Coarse black pepper**  1 teaspoon (4 grams)

Combine all ingredients and mix well. Store in a covered jar and keep in a cool, dark place.

### Suggestions:
This is good on almost anything! It is excellent on salads, fish, poultry and seafood. If kept cool and out of the light, it will keep for several months without losing its flavor.

240

# Sodium-Free Baking Powder

- Makes 8-1/2 tablespoons (93.5 grams)
- 1 tablespoon weighs 11 grams

**Potassium bicarbonate**    2-1/2 tablespoons (27.5 grams)
**Cream of tartar**    4-2/3 tablespoons (53 grams)
**Cornstarch**    1-1/3 tablespoons (10 grams)

Mix well. Place in a container with a tight
lid and store in a dry place.

# Homemade Egg Substitute

- Makes substitute for 2 eggs
- 1/2 recipe contains 76 Calories (P7, F4, C3), no cholesterol; without added salt,
    99 mg of sodium
- 1/2 recipe with lecithin contains 81 Calories (P7, F4.5, C3)
- 1/2 recipe = 1/4 slice of bread + 1 ounce of meat (1/4 bread exchange + 1 meat
    exchange)

**Egg whites**    3 medium (99 mL)
**Powdered skim milk**    1-1/2 tablespoons (10.5 grams)
**Oil or melted margarine**    2 teaspoons (10 mL); use corn, soybean or safflower oil
**Yellow food coloring**    4 drops

*Optional:*
**Salt**    sprinkle
**Lecithin**    1/4 teaspoon (1 gram)

Place all ingredients in a blender and mix
on low speed until smooth. Scramble, or
use in cooking as replacement for eggs.
The lecithin will keep the ingredients
from separating too quickly. Divide in half
to replace 1 egg.

# Canning, Freezing and Pickling

Because the cost of dietetic foods is so high, those who have the time and inclination can save a lot of money by doing their own processing when the fruit and vegetables are ripe and available at a good price.

There are three ways to can fruit: with sugar substitute, in unsweetened fruit juice, or in water, without added sweetening. There are recipes for all three methods in this chapter. Try canning some each way, then decide which way you prefer. If you use fruit juice for sweetening, you will have to reduce the portion allowed for diabetics and hypoglycemics. This is true for all foods processed with fruit juice rather than with artificial sweetening. Amounts allowed are indicated in each recipe.

*Note:* Fruits canned in juice will taste more like fresh fruit than if canned with sugar. They will be sweeter than the raw fruit, but much less sweet than those prepared with sugar syrup.

It is best to process fruits in small jars so you don't have to eat lots of one kind before it spoils. Care must be taken that the canning is done properly because spoilage can take place if the lid is not sealed or if there is any air leak.

Because the danger of botulism from home-canned vegetables is so high, we suggest you freeze all vegetables other than tomatoes; see directions on page 264. Always discard any jar or can of processed food if it looks the least bit suspicious or questionable.

## Canning Fruit
### Preparation of Fruit

**Be sure fruit is ripe enough to eat.** Pick it over to be sure all pieces are firm and unbruised; for best results, use only fruit that is at its peak. Wash in cold water to remove any dust or dirt. Drain on several layers of paper towels to remove excess water.

For soft fruits, peel, core or remove pits. Dipping fruit in boiling water for a minute makes it easier to remove the peel. When peeled, drop the fruit into a solution that contains 3 tablespoons (45 mL) of lemon juice per quart (960 mL) of water to prevent it from browning until you can get it into jars.

For berries, pick them over and remove any stems or overripe fruit. To can whole berries, prick each with a fork to allow liquid to penetrate the berries during cooking.

### Preparation of Syrup

It is much better to under-sweeten than to use too much sweetener. More sugar substitute can be added to opened jar just before you use it. Add sweetening to taste. Allow the fruit to stand in the syrup 15 to 20 minutes before tasting so the flavor will penetrate the fruit. Longer standing time gives an even better penetration, especially for thick pieces of fruit. If the syrup is to be made ahead, store it in a sterilized jar in the refrigerator and then reboil it just before using. Check the labels of the sweetening products to be sure they are the following strength:

*Granular:* The label states that it is to be used in equal amounts with sugar. If less volume is recommended, reduce amounts used in the syrup.

*Liquid:* 1 tablespoon (15 mL) = 1/2 cup (97.5 grams) of sugar.

*To make 1 cup syrup,* put suggested amount of sweetener in cup, fill with boiling water.

| | Light sweetening | Medium sweetening | Extra-heavy sweetening |
|---|---|---|---|
| Granular-type sweetener | 1 teaspoon (2 grams) | 2 teaspoons (4 grams) | 3 teaspoons (6 grams) |
| Liquid-type sweetener | 1/3 teaspoon (1.7 mL) | 1/2 teaspoon (2.5 mL) | 2/3 teaspoon (3.3 mL) |

## Preparation of Jars and Lids

Be sure jars are clean and lids are the proper type for the jars. Fill canning boiler with water, add jars and fill with water until tops are completely covered. Boil for at least 5 minutes; start timing after water comes to a vigorous boil. Boil lids and rings in a separate pan, covering with water and timing the same as for jars.

Drain jars, pack with fruit to within 1 inch of top. Fill with hot syrup. Use tongs to remove lids from hot water. Place on jars and fasten down with rings. Be careful that no fruit gets on the rims or the lid will fail to seal when processed.

## Canning Directions

Only acidic fruits — apples, apricots, berries, peaches, pears, pineapple, plums, rhubarb and tomatoes — can be processed in a boiling water bath. ALL OTHERS MUST BE PRESSURE-COOKED for safety.

Fill boiler with boiling water to almost jar height. Place a rack in the boiler so the jars will not sit directly on the bottom of the pan. Place jars (with lids screwed down tight) on rack, leaving 2 inches between jars. Add more boiling water to cover the tops of the jars by at least 1 inch. Process by cooking 25 minutes from the time the water reboils after adding jars. Add more boiling water if needed to keep jar tops well covered.

Remove jars from boiler with tongs. Cool in upright position for 12 hours.

Then check for seal by tapping jar lids with a metal spoon. You will get a ringing note from properly sealed jars. If the sound is dull and hollow, reprocess or use immediately. Store jars of fruit in a 45°F to 60°F (7°C to 16°C), dark place to avoid color fading and prevent spoilage. Fruits canned without sugar tend to fade in color, but this does not affect the taste or change the food value.

Before canning a large batch, do a small amount open-kettle to see if you like the flavor. Take 1 cup (240 mL) of fruit with 1/4 cup (60 mL) of the fruit syrup you think you want to use. Cover and simmer for 10 to 15 minutes until the fruit is tender; taste.

## Tricks to Improve Flavor

When canning pitted fruits, leave a few pits in the fruit so that each jar has one or two. The oil in the pit will give an almond flavor to the fruit.

Add a sprinkle of salt or salt substitute to each jar before you put the lid on. This helps bring out the natural sweetness of the fruit.

Combine fruits to make interesting mixtures, such as apple slices, apricots and plums.

***For low-salt diet:***

Omit sprinkle of salt when

processing. All natural fruit is low in sodium. Canning does not alter the sodium content, so fruit may be eaten without concern about the sodium content.

## Canning Directions With Sugar Substitute

Follow the Canning Directions (opposite) and process all in sterile jars in a boiling water bath for 25 minutes after water returns to boiling with jars in the canner.

**Applesauce:** Make open-kettle as directed (opposite). Put into sterile jars, process as directed. You can also add cinnamon, nutmeg, and ginger along with grated lemon rind to suit your taste.

**Apple slices:** Use light or medium syrup. Add 1-1/2 teaspoons (7.5 mL) lemon juice and 1/4 to 1/2 stick cinnamon, or 1/4 to 1/2 teaspoon (.8 to 1.5 grams) ground cinnamon per pint. Process as directed.

**Apricots:** Use light or medium syrup. To peel, drop fruit into boiling water for 1 minute; the skins will come off easily, if the fruit is ripe. To can with the skins on, prick each piece of fruit several times to prevent it from bursting when cooked. Halve and remove pits; leave at least one pit per jar to give added flavor to the fruit. Use 1 teaspoon (5 mL) lemon juice per quart of fruit. Process as directed.

**Berries:** Pack cleaned and dry berries into jars, add medium syrup and 1 teaspoon (5 mL) lemon juice per quart. You can add red food coloring 1/4 teaspoon (1.3 mL) per pint to replace the color lost in cooking; process as directed.

**Cherries:** Use light or medium syrup for dark sweet cherries; medium or extra-heavy syrup for light cherries. Pit cherries, saving a few pits to place in the jars for flavor. Use 1 teaspoon (5 mL) lemon juice per pint. Mix dark and light cherries for a delightful flavor and more color in the fruit syrup. Pack into sterile jars and process as directed.

**Peaches:** Use light or medium syrup. Dip into boiling water for 1 minute to loosen skins. Peel, slice and pack into sterile jars. Leave at least one pit per jar for added flavor. Use 1 teaspoon (5 mL) lemon juice per quart. Process as directed.

**Pears:** Use light or medium syrup. Dip into boiling water for 1 minute to loosen skins. Peel, core, and either slice or halve. Pack into sterile jars, adding a few whole cloves for flavor, if desired. Add 1-1/2 teaspoons (7.5 mL) lemon juice per quart. Process as directed.

**Prune plums:** Use light or medium syrup. Cut in halves or quarters or prick skins to prevent fruit from bursting when cooked whole. Remove pits. Pack in sterile jars, adding 1 teaspoon (5 mL) lemon juice per quart and process as directed.

## Canning with Fruit Juice

You can use regular or concentrated apple juice, white grape juice, pineapple juice or a combination such as apple/pear or orange/pineapple.

---

To make 1 cup (240 mL) of the following fruit syrups, put suggested amount of juices in measuring cup, add enough boiling water to fill total:

**Very light syrups:**
- 1/3 cup (80 mL) apple juice
    + 1 teaspoon (5 mL) lemon juice
- 1/4 cup (60 mL) white grape juice
    + 1 teaspoon (5 mL) lemon juice
- 1/3 cup (80 mL) pineapple juice
    + 1 teaspoon (5 mL) lemon juice

**Medium syrups:**
- 2/3 cup (160 mL) apple juice
    + 1 teaspoon (5 mL) lemon juice
- 1/2 cup (120 mL) white grape juice
    + 1 teaspoon (5 mL) lemon juice
- 2/3 cup (160 mL) pineapple juice
    + 1 teaspoon (5 mL) lemon juice

---

Pack the fruit into sterile jars, using your fingers to pack it tightly — don't squeeze too much! Leave 1 inch at the top to allow for expansion during processing. Use the following amounts of syrup per container:
- 1/4 cup (60 mL) per 1/2 pint (240 mL)
- 1/2 cup (120 mL) per pint (480 mL)
- 1 cup (240 mL) per quart (960 mL)

Fill the jar with syrup and run a knife along the sides to break up any air pockets and to completely fill the jar with syrup. Put on sterile lids and process as directed.

**Apple slices:**
- Use medium syrup.
- 1/3 cup (80 mL) contains 40 Calories (P0, F0, C10); 1/3 cup = 1 fruit exchange

**Berries:**
- Use medium syrup; white grape juice is best.
- 1/2 cup (120 mL) contains 40 Calories (P0, F0, C10); = 1 fruit exchange

**Dark sweet cherries:**
- Use very light syrup; white grape juice is best.
- 8 cherries + 1-1/2 tablespoons (22.5 mL) of syrup contain 40 Calories (P0, F0, C10);
- 8 cherries + 1-1/2 tablespoons of syrup = 1 fruit exchange

**Light sweet cherries:**
- Use medium syrup; white grape or pineapple juice is best.
- 6 cherries + 1 tablespoon (15 mL) of syrup contain 40 Calories (P0, F0, C10); = 1 fruit exchange

**Peaches:**
- Use medium syrup; white grape or pineapple juice is best.
- 1/3 cup (80 mL) contains 40 Calories (P0, F0, C10); = 1 fruit exchange

**Pears:**
- Slice into eighths to fit more into the jar.
- Use medium syrup; apple, white grape or pineapple juice are all good.
- 1/4 cup (60 mL) contains 40 Calories (P0, F0, C10); = 1 fruit exchange

**Purple plums:**
- Cut into halves or quarters.
- Use medium syrup; either apple or white grape juice is good.
- 1/3 cup (80 mL) contains 40 Calories (P0, F0, C10); = 1 fruit exchange

### For low-salt diet:

All fruit is low in sodium. Adding the syrup as directed will not increase the sodium content. All canned fruits are below 2 mg of sodium per 1/2 cup (120 mL).

## Freezing Fruit

### Preparation of Fruit

Use only completely ripe fruit! Pick over fruit to be sure all is firm and unbruised. Wash in cold water to remove any dust or dirt. Drain on several layers of paper towels to absorb all water left on fruit.

Peel, core or remove pits of soft fruits. You may want to dip fruit to be peeled in boiling water for 1 minute to make it easier to remove the skin. When fruit is peeled, drop it into a solution that contains 3 tablespoons (45 mL) of lemon juice per quart of water. If you wish, you can add sugar substitute to this liquid and use it for freezing the fruit. See amounts in canning section, page 243.

Berries need only be picked over to remove stems and bruised fruit. (Canning berries changes the texture but freezing does not.) When drained of wash water, pack berries into containers and place in freezer. If whole strawberries are packed, prick each with a fork before freezing. This is supposed to release any trapped air and to give a finer end product. Do not add anything to berries. Sweeten when thawed, when you are ready to eat them.

### Preparation of Syrup for Soft Fruits

Bring water to boil. Remove from heat and add sugar substitute (see chart, page 243) or combine juice and water (see canning chart, page 246), increasing lemon juice as directed. When syrup is cooled, add 3 tablespoons (45 mL) of lemon juice per quart (960 mL). Do not reheat or the blanching action of the lemon juice will be destroyed.

Cool syrup until very well chilled. It can be made the day before and kept in a sterile container in the refrigerator.

Additional instructions for freezing fruit begin on page 263.

### Packing Fruit

Use a container large enough to hold the amount of fruit to be eaten at one meal, or two meals at the most. (Frozen fruit loses much of its appetizing qualities when left too long after being thawed.)

Prepare liquid according to directions given on pages 243 or 246.

Pack fruit into containers leaving 1 to 1-1/2 inches of space at the top for expansion. In the case of soft fruits, cover with prepared syrup, again leaving space at the top. If the soft fruit will not stay below the liquid, use a piece of crumpled wax paper in the top of the container. This can be left in and discarded when the fruit is thawed. Cover with lid; sharp-freeze.

*Note:* Apple slices, cherries, peaches and pears will give a superior frozen product if you blanch them before you put them into the syrup. (You may use the blanching liquid to make syrup so it saves any juice

which comes out in blanching.) To blanch, use a steamer basket so fruit is not in direct contact with the boiling water for best results. Process for about 1-1/2 minutes of steam from the time blanching liquid boils after adding fruit.

### For low-salt diet:

These fruits are low in sodium as packed.

# Jams, Jellies and Relishes

Most people find the dietetic jams on the market too expensive, and often they don't find their favorite varieties at all. Also, most contain fructose (fruit sugar) so they must be limited by the diabetic and hypoglycemic.

The recipes given here are easy to make, and the unusual combinations make meals more appetizing.

Texture of cooked jams is generally superior to frozen jams when made with sugar substitute. (Large ice crystals tend to form in the sugarless frozen jam, which makes the fruit less tender.)

## Natural Sweetening for Jams and Relishes

It is difficult to reduce the volume of fruit juice sufficiently to use it for sweetening jam. Concentrated apple juice can be used as it is purchased, but white grape juice has to be boiled down to reduce the volume and concentrate the sweetening. Date sugar gives a flavor that is not too acceptable with most fruits. Combinations of these prove best for many of the fruits. Also, to compensate for the added liquid, you may have to add gelatin to some of the recipes.

***Important note:*** Preserves made with natural sweetening will not be as sweet as those made with sugar. If you have been using sugar regularly, these will not taste sweet enough to you. After you have stopped using sugar for several weeks they will taste just right.

### Frozen Jams

If you are making only a small batch of jam at a time, or if you don't want to bother with the canning process, frozen jams are your answer.

Jam made without sugar cannot be frozen and used without thawing. (The sugar crystals keep it soft in regular freezer jam.) However, you can thaw these overnight in the refrigerator and continue to use them for several weeks without danger of spoiling, provided you keep them cold and don't allow them to stand at room temperature.

### For low-salt diet:

Sodium content is negligible; no changes are required; 5 tablespoons (75 mL) contain 1 mg of sodium.

# Basic Recipe for Cooked Jam

- Makes 9-1/2 cups (2.28 L)
- 1 tablespoon (15 mL) may be eaten without replacement (no exchange).
- Equipment needed: At least a 5-quart (5 L) kettle big enough to allow about 3 quarts (2.9 L) of contents to come to a rolling boil.
- Canning jars and lids that can be processed to seal.
- Water bath deep enough to cover jars completely during boiling process.

**Fresh fruit**    10 cups (1.3 to 1.5 Kg), with stems and pits removed
**Powdered pectin**    1/2 package (28.4 grams)
**Glycerine**    4 tablespoons (60 mL). *Note: This is USP-grade glycerine (drugstore). Glycerine is not digested, but merely thickens the jam as it precipitates the gel. If no glycerine is used, sugarless jams will not thicken.*
**Lemon juice**    2 to 3 tablespoons (30 to 45 mL)
**Liquid sugar substitute**    2-1/2 to 4 tablespoons (37.5 to 60 mL), to taste; or substitute equal to 2/3 to 1-1/4 cups (130 to 243.8 grams) of sugar
**Salt**    sprinkle

Sort and cut fruit; put in large kettle with 1 tablespoon (15 mL) of water per cup of cut fruit; bring to boil; cover; simmer until soft. Time will vary from 8 to 10 minutes for berries to 15 minutes for plums. Add pectin, glycerine and lemon juice; stir well; bring to a full, rolling boil; boil for exactly 1 minute; remove from heat; add sugar substitute to taste. Pack into sterile jars, leaving 3/4 to 1 inch at top for expansion; sprinkle with salt. Put on sterilized lids and rings; tighten. Put into boiling water bath so jars are completely covered through processing. Process for 20 minutes after water returns to boiling, or longer, if you like jam very soft. Cool; check seals, as on canned fruit; store in cool place.

### Natural sweetening directions:
- Makes 11 cups (2.64 L)
- 1 tablespoon (15 mL) may be eaten without replacement.
- 1 tablespoon (15 mL) contains 8 Calories (P0, F0, C2)
- 5 tablespoons (75 mL) contain 50 Calories (P0, F0, C10)
- 5 tablespoons = 1 fruit exchange

Omit sugar substitute. Simmer 2 cups (480 mL) concentrated apple juice to reduce to 1 cup (240 mL). Omit water. Increase pectin to 1 package (56.7 grams) and glycerine to 6 tablespoons (90 mL). Increase lemon juice to 5 tablespoons (75 mL). Add 5 tablespoons (50 grams) date sugar before adding the pectin. Stir well to completely dissolve. Cook 20 minutes.

### For low-salt diet:
- Sodium content is negligible; no changes are required
- 5 tablespoons (75 mL) contain 1 mg of sodium

# Apple-Berry Jam

- Makes 9-1/2 cups to 10 cups (2.28 to 2.4 L)
- 1 tablespoon (15 mL) may be eaten without replacement
- 1 tablespoon (15 mL) contains 6 Calories
- 6 tablespoons (90 mL) contain 40 Calories (P0, F0, C10), no cholesterol
- 6 tablespoons = 1/2 cup of fruit (1 fruit exchange)

**Berries**    5 cups (720 grams). Use strawberries, raspberries or boysenberries, mashed or chopped.
**Apples**    5 cups (625 grams), peeled and sliced; yellow transparents are best
**Powdered pectin**    1/2 package (28.4 grams)
**Glycerine**    4 tablespoons (60 mL).
**Lemon juice**    3 to 5 tablespoons (45 to 75 mL), depending on the sweetness of the apples
**Liquid sugar substitute**    2-1/2 to 4 tablespoons (37.5 to 60 mL), to taste; or substitute equal to 2/3 to 1-1/4 cups (130 to 243.8 grams) of sugar
**Salt**    sprinkle

Wash, sort and measure fruit; put into large kettle; add 1 tablespoon (15 mL) of water for each cup of fruit, more if fruit is not juicy. Bring to a boil; turn heat down; cover kettle. Simmer until fruit is soft, 8 to 12 minutes or up to 15 minutes if apples were firm. Remove from heat; add pectin, glycerine and lemon juice — 5 tablespoons (75 mL) if apples are sweet, 3 tablespoons (45 mL) for tart apples; stir until well dissolved. Return to heat; bring to a full, rolling boil; boil for exactly 1 minute. Remove from heat; add 1/2 of the sweetener or less; taste; add more if needed, remembering that it will taste sweeter when cool. Pour into sterile jars, leaving 3/4 to 1 inch at top for expansion; sprinkle with salt; put on caps and rings; tighten. Put into boiling water bath so jars are completely covered through processing; process for 20 minutes after water returns to boiling. Add water as needed to keep jars well covered. Cool; check seals as on canned fruit; store in a cool place.

*Suggestions:*
This jam can be made with slices of apples and whole berries for a conserve, or mashed and blended for the usual jam appearance.

*Natural sweetening directions:*
- 1 teaspoon (5 mL) may be eaten without replacement
- 1 tablespoon (15 mL) contains 12 Calories (P0, F0, C3)
- 3 tablespoons (45 mL) contain 36 Calories (P0, F0, C9)
- 3 tablespoons = 1 fruit exchange

Simmer 1 cup (240 mL) concentrated apple juice and 1 cup (240 mL) white grape juice to reduce to 1 cup (240 mL) total, and add to the fruit. Omit sugar substitute. Increase pectin to 1 package (56.7 grams) and glycerine to 6 tablespoons (90 mL). Use 5 to 7 tablespoons (75 to 105 mL) lemon juice, depending upon the sweetness of the apples; use more for sweeter apples.

*For low-salt diet:*
- 3 tablespoons (45 mL) contain 1 mg of sodium

Omit salt; use sprinkle of salt substitute.

251

# Apple Butter

- Makes about 6 cups (1.4 L)
- 1 teaspoon may be eaten without replacement
- 3 tablespoons (45 mL) contain 36 Calories (P0, F0, C9), no cholesterol
- 3 tablespoons = 1/2 cup of fruit (1 fruit exchange)

**Apples**   6 cups (750 grams), diced
**Apple juice or cider**   6 cups (1.4 L)
**Lemon juice**   6 tablespoons (90 mL)
**Cinnamon**   1 tablespoon (9 grams)
**Nutmeg**   1 teaspoon (3 grams)
**Ground cloves**   1 teaspoon (3 grams)
**Salt**   1/8 teaspoon (.8 gram)
**Brown-type granular sugar substitute**   8 to 10 teaspoons (16 to 20 grams); or
   substitute equal to 6 tablespoons (73.2 grams) of sugar

Peel and core apples; remove stems and blossom ends; put in large kettle; add apple juice and lemon juice; cook over low heat until volume is reduced to about half; if not thick, cook to consistency of applesauce. Add spices and salt; mix to blend well; heat about 1 minute. Taste; if sweet enough, omit sugar substitute; if not, add up to 10 teaspoons (20 grams) — a little at a time. Freeze in small, tight containers, or put into sterilized canning jars and process as for cooked jams (see recipe on page 250).

*Suggestions:*
You may want to vary the amounts of spices used. If you add smaller amounts, taste and then adjust at the end of the cooking.

### Natural sweetening directions:
- 1 teaspoon (5 mL) may be eaten without replacement
- 1 teaspoon (5 mL) contains 5 Calories
- 2-1/2 tablespoons (37.5 mL) contain 40 Calories (P0, F0, C10)
- 2-1/2 tablespoons = 1 fruit exchange

Omit sugar substitute. Reduce apple juice to 4-3/4 cups (1.1 L). Add 1-1/4 cups (300 mL) concentrated apple juice. Increase the lemon juice to 7 tablespoons (105 mL).

### For low-salt diet:
- 2-1/2 tablespoons (37.5 mL) contain less than 1 mg of sodium

Omit salt; use 1/8 teaspoon (.5 gram) of salt substitute.

# Apricot-Lemon Jam

- Makes 9-1/2 cups (2.28 L)
- i tablespoon (15 mL) may be eaten without replacement
- 4 tablespoons (60 mL) contain 10 Calories (P0, F0, C10), no cholesterol
- 4 tablespoons = 1/2 cup of fruit (1 fruit exchange)

**Fresh apricots**   9 cups (1.4 Kg), quartered
**Lemon**   1 large (158 grams), sliced paper thin
**Lemon juice**   2 to 3 tablespoons (30 to 45 mL)
**Powdered pectin**   1 package (56.7 grams)
**Glycerine**   6 tablespoons (90 mL)
**Salt**   sprinkle
**Granular sugar substitute**   4 tablespoons (24 grams); or substitute equal to
   1/2 cup (97.5 grams) of sugar
**Almond extract**   1/4 to 1/2 teaspoon (1.3 to 2.5 mL)
**Plain gelatin**   1 tablespoon (7 grams) dissolved in 1/4 cup (60 mL) of water

Pit and quarter apricots; slice lemons (remove seeds); put apricots, lemon, lemon juice and 2 tablespoons (30 mL) of water into kettle; cook until tender, about 20 minutes. Add pectin, glycerine and salt; stir well; return to heat; bring to full rolling boil; boil exactly 1 minute.

Remove from heat; add sugar substitute and almond extract; taste; add more sugar if desired; add gelatin; stir well. Pack in sterile jars and process for 20 minutes in hot water bath. Cool; check seals; store in cool, dark place.

*Natural sweetening directions:*
- 2 teaspoons (10 mL) may be used without replacement
- 2 teaspoons (10 mL) contain 8 Calories (P0, F0, C2)
- 3-1/3 tablespoons (50 mL) contain 40 Calories (P0, F0, C10)
- 3-1/3 tablespoons = 1 fruit exchange

Omit sugar substitute and water; replace with 1/2 cup (120 mL) concentrated white grape juice, reduced from 1 cup (240 mL). Increase lemon juice to 4 tablespoons (60 mL).

*For low-salt diet:*
- 1 tablespoon (15 mL) contains less than 1 mg of sodium

Omit salt; use sprinkle of salt substitute.

# Grapefruit-Orange Marmalade

- Makes 10 cups (2.4 L)
- 1 tablespoon (15 mL) may be eaten without replacement
- 5 tablespoons (75 mL) contain 40 Calories (P0, F0, C10), no cholesterol
- 5 tablespoons = 1/2 cup of fruit (1 fruit exchange)

**Grapefruit**    3 large (1.2 Kg)
**Oranges**    15 large (2.7 Kg)
**Lemon**    1 large (158 grams)
**Powdered pectin**    1 package (56.7 grams)
**Glycerine**    6 tablespoons (90 mL)
**Salt**    sprinkle
**Liquid sugar substitute**    4 to 5 tablespoons (60 to 75 mL); or substitute equal to
     1 to 1-1/4 cups (195 to 243.8 grams) of sugar
**Plain gelatin**    1 tablespoon (7 grams) dissolved in 1/4 cup (60 mL) of water

Section grapefruit and oranges; retain juice with fruit. Should be 9 cups total (2.16 L). Using coarsest blade, grind 1 grapefruit rind, 2 orange rinds and the whole lemon (remove the seeds), or chop rinds very fine instead of grinding. Add to fruit. Cook until fruit is tender and rind is firm but not hard. Add pectin, glycerine and salt; bring to boil; cook exactly 1 minute at rolling boil; remove from heat. Add sugar substitute to taste (keep it slightly tart); add gelatin; mix well. Pack in sterile jars; process for 20 minutes in hot water bath; cool, check seals. Store in cool, dark place.

**Suggestions:**
You may vary the proportions of the fruit, using less or more grapefruit or lemon. Chop the sectioned fruit if smaller pieces are preferred.

**Natural sweetening directions:**
*This recipe is not for hypoglycemics.*
- 2 teaspoons (10 mL) may be used without replacement
- 2 teaspoons (10 mL) contain 8 Calories (P0, F0, C2)
- 3-1/3 tablespoons (50 mL) contain 40 Calories (P0, F0, C10)
- 3-1/3 tablespoons = 1 fruit exchange
Omit sugar substitute and water; replace with 1 cup (240 mL) concentrated apple juice and 1 cup (240 mL) concentrated white grape juice, reduced from 2 cups (480 mL). Add 2 tablespoons (30 mL) lemon juice in addition to the fresh lemon. Increase the gelatin to 1-1/2 tablespoons (10.5 grams). *Note: This marmalade will be fairly tart.*

**For low-salt diet:**
- Sodium content is less than 1 mg per tablespoon (15 mL)
Omit salt; use salt substitute.

# Mixed Soft Fruit Jam

- Makes 9-1/2 cups (2.28 L)
- 1 tablespoon (15 mL) may be eaten without replacement
- 5 tablespoons (75 mL) contain 40 Calories (P0, F0, C10), no cholesterol
- 5 tablespoons = 1/2 cup of fruit (1 fruit exchange)

**Fruit**   10 cups (1.3 to 1.5 Kg), diced. Use apricots, peaches, pears, or any other combination.
**Water**   10 tablespoons (150 mL)
**Powdered pectin**   1 package (56.7 grams)
**Glycerine**   6 tablespoons (90 mL)
**Salt**   sprinkle
**Lemon juice**   5 tablespoons (75 mL)

*Optional:*
**Liquid sugar substitute**   2 to 3 tablespoons (30 to 45 mL); or substitute equal to 1/2 to 3/4 cup (97.5 to 146 grams) of sugar

Peel and chop fruit; retain any juice and include with total volume. Put fruit into large kettle; add water, more if fruit is not juicy. Bring to boil; cover, lower heat and cook until fruit is soft, 10 to 15 minutes. Remove from heat; add pectin, glycerine, salt and lemon juice; stir well. Return to heat; bring to full rolling boil; boil exactly 1 minute. Remove from heat; add sugar substitute to taste. Pack into sterilized jars, seal and process in hot water bath for 30 minutes after bath returns to boiling. Cool; check seals. Store in cool place.

*Suggestions:*
This jam can be made with the fruit in slices, ground into very small pieces, or chopped as for marmalade. If you like, add 1/4 teaspoon (1.3 mL) of almond extract to each jar just before filling. This will not give a strong almond flavor, but will add to the appeal.

*Natural sweetening directions:*
- 1 tablespoon (15 mL) may be eaten without replacement
- 4 tablespoons (60 mL) contain 40 Calories (P0, F0, C10)
- 4 tablespoons = 1 fruit exchange

Omit sugar substitute and water; replace with 1/2 cup (120 mL) concentrated apple juice or 2/3 cup (160 mL) concentrated white grape juice, reduced from 1-1/3 cups (320 mL). Increase lemon juice to 6 tablespoons (90 mL).

*For low-salt diet:*
- 1 tablespoon (15 mL) contains less than 1 mg of sodium

Omit salt; use sprinkle of salt substitute.

# Plum Jam

- Makes 9-1/2 to 10 cups (2.28 to 2.4 L)
- 1 tablespoon (15 mL) may be eaten without replacement
- 5 tablespoons (75 mL) contain 40 Calories (P0, F0, C10), no cholesterol
- 5 tablespoons = 1/2 cup of fruit (1 fruit exchange)

**Plums**    10 cups (1.6 Kg), ripe, stemmed, pitted and quartered
**Lemon juice**    5 tablespoons (75 mL)
**Powdered pectin**    1 package (56.7 grams)
**Glycerine**    6 tablespoons (90 mL)
**Salt**    sprinkle
**Liquid sugar substitute**    2 to 4 tablespoons (30 to 60 mL); or substitute equal to
   1/2 to 1 cup (97.5 to 195 grams) of sugar

*Optional:*
**Lemon rind**    1-1/2 tablespoons (6.8 grams), grated

Wash and sort plums. Remove stems and pits; cut into quarters. Put into kettle; add 1 tablespoon (15 mL) of water per cup of fruit, or 1-1/2 tablespoons (22.5 mL) if fruit is not juicy. Bring to a boil; lower heat; cover and simmer until fruit is soft, 12 to 14 minutes. Remove from heat; add lemon juice and rind, pectin, glycerine and salt; stir well. Return to heat; bring to full rolling boil; boil for exactly 1 minute. Remove from heat; add sugar substitute to taste. If fruit is very ripe, you may need none. Put into sterilized jars; seal and process for 30 minutes (20 minutes if you want firm fruit) in hot water bath as for cooked jams (see recipe, page 250). Cool; check seals; store in cool, dark place.

**Suggestions:**
For plum preserve, add 1/2 cup (60 grams) of finely chopped (not ground) walnuts and seeded coarse-ground orange to fruit after adding sugar substitute. Five tablespoons (75 mL) equal 1/2 cup of fruit + 1 teaspoon (5 mL) of fat.

**Natural sweetening directions:**
- 2 teaspoons (10 mL) contain 8 Calories (P0, F0, C2) and may be eaten without replacement
- 3-1/3 tablespoons (50 mL) contain 40 Calories (P0, F0, C10)
- 3-1/3 tablespoons = 1 fruit exchange

Omit sugar substitute and water; replace with 1 cup (240 mL) concentrated white grape juice, reduced from 2 cups (480 mL), and add 1 tablespoon (7 grams) gelatin plus 5 tablespoons (50 grams) date sugar. Dissolve gelatin in hot juice, stir in date sugar. Add 1/3 teaspoon (.5 gram) grated lemon rind. **Optional:** Add 10 whole cloves (2 grams).

**For low-salt diet:**
- 1 tablespoon (15 mL) contains less than 1 mg of sodium

Omit salt; use salt substitute.

# Basic Recipe for Frozen Jam

- Makes 10-1/2 cups (2.6 L)
- 1 tablespoon (15 mL) may be eaten without replacement
- 10 tablespoons (150 mL) contain 40 Calories (P0, F0, C10), no cholesterol
- 10 tablespoons = 1 fruit exchange

**Fresh fruit**    10 cups (1.3 to 1.5 Kg), stems and pits removed
**Lemon juice**    2 tablespoons (30 mL)
**Powdered pectin**    1 package (56.7 grams)
**Glycerine**    6 tablespoons (90 mL)
**Salt**    1/8 teaspoon (.8 gram)
**Plain gelatin**    2 tablespoons (14 grams)
**Cold water**    1/2 cup (120 mL)
**Liquid sugar substitute**    3 to 5 tablespoons (45 to 75 mL); or substitute equal to
    3/4 to 1-1/4 cups (146 to 243.8 grams) of sugar

*Equipment needed:*
At least a 3-quart (3 L) kettle, big enough to allow about 1-1/2 quarts (1.5 L) of
    contents to come to a rolling boil.
For freezing, use canning jars with tight lids that can be sterilized, or disposable
    containers.

Mash half the fruit, add lemon juice, pectin, glycerine and salt; bring to a hard boil for 1 minute, stirring constantly. Remove from heat; add remainder of fruit — whole berries, halves or mashed — as you prefer. Add gelatin to water; allow to stand about 5 minutes, then heat gently to completely dissolve; add to berry or fruit mixture. Add sugar substitute to taste; cool. Place slightly cooled mixture in jars or freezer cartons. Leave 3/4 inch at top for fruit to expand when freezing. Cover and place in coldest part of freezer to freeze quickly. Store in freezer; to thaw, place in refrigerator for 24 hours before using. Use within 10 days of thawing to prevent spoiling.

*Note:* The jam will be all hard crystals when frozen. It cannot be used directly from the freezer. In ordinary frozen jam, the sugar and corn syrup keep the ice crystals from becoming solid, so it can be kept semiliquid and can be used directly. This recipe will make a fairly soft jam, but by keeping it in the refrigerator until just before using it, it will be similar in consistency to ordinary freezer jam.

*Natural sweetening directions:*
- 1 tablespoon (15 mL) may be eaten without replacement
- 6 tablespoons (90 mL) contain 36 Calories (P0, F0, C9)
- 6 tablespoons = 1 fruit exchange

Omit sugar substitute and water; replace with 1/2 cup (120 mL) concentrated apple juice, or 2/3 cup (160 mL) concentrated white grape juice — reduced from 1-1/3 cups (320 mL). Heat juice to dissolve the gelatin. Increase lemon juice to 3 tablespoons (45 mL) and add 1/4 to 1/2 teaspoon (.4 to .8 gram) lemon rind; add this last after tasting.
*Note:* Some fruits are higher than others in sugar, so in some cases the Calorie content will be 8 Calories per tablespoon. This may still be used without replacement.

*For low-salt diet:*
- 1 tablespoon (15 mL) contains less than 1 mg of sodium

Omit salt; use 1/8 teaspoon (.5 gram) of salt substitute.

# Easy Berry Jam

- Makes 4 cups (960 mL)
- 1 tablespoon (15 mL) may be eaten without replacement
- 10 tablespoons (150 mL) contain 40 Calories (P0, F0, C10), no cholesterol
- 10 tablespoons = 1 fruit exchange

**Strawberries**   4 cups (680 grams), sliced in half
**Water**   1/2 cup (120 mL)
**Lemon juice**   2 tablespoons (30 mL)
**Plain gelatin**   1-1/2 tablespoons (10.5 grams). *Note: If making raspberry jam, use only 1 tablespoon (7 grams) of gelatin.*
**Salt**   sprinkle
**Liquid sugar substitute**   1 to 1-1/2 teaspoons (5 to 7.5 mL); or substitute equal to 4 to 5 tablespoons (48.8 to 61 grams) of sugar

Place berries, water, lemon juice and salt
in a saucepan. Mash berries to release
juice. Heat to boiling, sprinkle gelatin
over top of hot mixture, stirring well to be
sure it dissolves. Remove from heat and
add liquid sweetener. Pour into small jars,
leaving 3/4 inch at top for expansion.
Cool; refrigerate or freeze for longer
storage.

### Natural sweetening directions:
- 1 tablespoon (15 mL) may be eaten without replacement
- 6-1/2 tablespoons (97.5 mL) contain 40 Calories (P0, F0, C10)
- 6-1/2 tablespoons = 1 fruit exchange
Omit liquid sweetener and water; replace with 1/2 cup (120 mL) concentrated apple juice. Add 1/4 to 1/3 teaspoon (.4 to .5 gram) grated lemon rind.

### For low-salt diet:
- 1 tablespoon (15 mL) contains less than 1 mg of sodium
Omit salt; replace with salt substitute.

# Frozen Strawberry Jam

- Makes 10-1/2 cups (2.52 L)
- 2 tablespoons (30 mL) may be eaten without replacement
- 10 tablespoons (150 mL) contain 40 Calories (P0, F0, C10), no cholesterol
- 10 tablespoons = 1/2 cup of fruit (1 fruit exchange)

**Strawberries**   10 cups (1.4 Kg), washed and hulled
**Lemon juice**   2 tablespoons (30 mL)
**Powdered pectin**   1 package (56.7 grams)
**Glycerine**   6 tablespoons (90 mL)
**Salt**   sprinkle
**Plain or strawberry-flavored dietetic gelatin**   2 tablespoons (14 grams) or
   2 envelopes (17.7 grams)
**Cold water**   1/2 cup (120 mL)
**Liquid sugar substitute**   3 to 4 tablespoons (45 to 60 mL); or 6 to 8 tablespoons
   (36 to 48 grams) granular sugar substitute; or substitute equal to 1 cup
   (195 grams) of sugar

Mash half the berries after cleaning and culling any that are overripe or green; place in a kettle with lemon juice, pectin and glycerine; sprinkle salt on top. Bring to a full rolling boil for 1 minute, stirring constantly. Remove from the heat. Add the remainder of the berries (diced, sliced or whole, as you prefer). Combine gelatin with 1/2 cup (120 mL) of cold water; allow to stand 5 minutes, then heat gently to dissolve. Add to berries; add sugar substitute. Stir well to mix. Allow to cool slightly before packing into jars. Pour into jars or freezer cartons, leaving 3/4 inch for expansion when fruit freezes. Cover. Place on coldest shelf in freezer to allow quick freezing. Store in freezer until time of use. Allow 24 hours thawing time in the refrigerator before using. Use within 10 days of thawing to prevent spoilage.

*Note:* If fruit is not sweet and ripe it will not make good jam. Be sure not to over-sweeten as it is our experience that it tastes sweeter when cold than when warm and first cooked.

### Natural sweetening directions:
- 1 tablespoon (15 mL) may be eaten without replacement
- 6-1/2 tablespoons (97.5 mL) contain 40 Calories (P0, F0, C10)
- 6-1/2 tablespoons = 1 fruit exchange
Omit sugar substitute. Increase lemon juice to 3 tablespoons (45 mL). Omit water; replace with 1 cup (240 mL) concentrated white grape juice, reduced from 2 cups (480 mL)

### For low-salt diet:
- 1 tablespoon (15 mL) contains less than 1 mg of sodium
Omit salt; use salt substitute.

259

# Frozen Boysenberry Jam

- Makes 10-1/2 cups (2.52 L)
- 1 tablespoon (15 mL) may be eaten without replacement
- 7 tablespoons (105 mL) contain 40 Calories (P0, F0, C10), no cholesterol
- 7 tablespoons = 1/2 cup of fruit (1 fruit exchange)

**Boysenberries**  10 cups (1.4 Kg), washed and hulled
**Lemon juice**  3 tablespoons (45 mL)
**Lemon rind**  2 tablespoons (9 grams), grated
**Powdered pectin**  1 package (56.7 grams)
**Glycerine**  6 tablespoons (90 mL)
**Salt**  sprinkle
**Plain gelatin**  2 tablespoons (14 grams)
**Cold water**  1/2 cup (120 mL)
**Liquid sugar substitute**  2 to 4 tablespoons (30 to 60 mL); or substitute equal to
    3/4 to 1-1/4 cups (130 to 243.8 grams) of sugar

Mash or crush half the boysenberries, place in a kettle; add lemon juice, lemon rind, pectin, glycerine and salt. Bring to a full rolling boil for exactly 1 minute, stirring constantly. Remove from heat; add the remainder of the berries (whole or crushed, as you prefer). Add the gelatin to 1/2 cup (120 mL) of cold water; allow to stand 5 minutes, then warm to dissolve completely; add to the berry mixture. Sweeten with sugar substitute to suit your taste. (Remember that the jam will taste sweeter when cold.) Allow to cool slightly before packaging. Pour into jars or freezer containers, leaving 3/4 inch for expansion when the fruit freezes. Cover. Place in coldest area of freezer to allow quick freezing. Keep frozen until ready for use. Place in refrigerator 24 hours before using to thaw slowly. Use within 10 days of thawing to prevent spoiling.

### Natural sweetening directions:
- 1 tablespoon may be eaten without replacement
- 5 tablespoons (75 mL) contain 40 Calories (P0, F0, C10)
- 5 tablespoons = 1 fruit exchange

Omit sugar substitute and water; replace water with 1/2 cup (120 mL) concentrated apple juice, or 2/3 cup (160 mL) concentrated white grape juice, reduced from 1-1/3 cups (320 mL). Heat juice to dissolve gelatin. Increase lemon juice to 4 tablespoons (60 mL).

### For low-salt diet:
- 1 tablespoon (15 mL) contains less than 1 mg of sodium

Omit salt; use sprinkle of salt substitute.

# Lazy Person's Jam

- Makes 4-1/2 cups (1.1 L)
- 1 tablespoon (15 mL) may be used without replacement
- 10 tablespoons (150 mL) contain 40 Calories (P0, F0, C10), no cholesterol
- 10 tablespoons = 1 fruit exchange

**Fruit**   4 cups (600 grams), washed and chopped
**Lemon**   1/4 cup (40 grams), with rind, chopped fine
**Hot water**   1/2 cup (120 mL)
**Plain gelatin**   1 tablespoon (7 grams)
**Liquid sugar substitute**   1 to 1-1/2 teaspoons (5 to 7.5 mL); or substitute equal to
   4 to 6 tablespoons (48.8 to 73.2 grams) of sugar
**Salt**   sprinkle

### Spices:
**with apples, add:**   1/2 teaspoon (1.5 grams) **cinnamon;** 1/4 teaspoon (.8 gram)
   **nutmeg;** 1/8 teaspoon (.4 gram) **ginger**
**with berries, add:**   1 tablespoon (15 mL) **lemon juice**
**with plums, add:**   1/4 to 1/2 teaspoon (.8 to 1.5 grams) **nutmeg**
**with sour fruit, add:**   1/4 cup (40.5 grams) **raisins,** chopped

Place fruit and water in saucepan; cover and simmer about 5 minutes until fruit is barely cooked. Remove from heat; sprinkle with gelatin over fruit, or dissolve gelatin in hot water before adding the fruit; stir to dissolve. Add spices and sweetening. Taste, and adjust sweetening to suit your taste. Pour into small sterile jars, cover and cool. Freeze until needed. The night before you want to use it, thaw it in the refrigerator; it will keep about 10 days without spoiling.

### Natural sweetening directions:
- 1 tablespoon (15 mL) may be used without replacement
- 5 tablespoons (75 mL) contain 40 Calories (P0, F0, C10)
- 5 tablespoons = 1 fruit exchange
Omit water and sugar substitute; replace with 2/3 cup (160 mL) concentrated apple juice or 1 cup (240 mL) concentrated white grape juice, reduced from 2 cups (480 mL). Add 1 tablespoon (15 mL) lemon juice along with the whole lemon.

### For low-salt diet:
- 5 tablespoons (75 mL) contain less than 2 mg of sodium
Omit salt; use sprinkle of salt substitute.

# Fruit Relish

- Makes 2-1/8 cups (510 mL)
- 1 tablespoon (15 mL) may be eaten without replacement
- 10 tablespoons (150 mL) contain 40 Calories (P0, F0, C10), no cholesterol
- 10 tablespoons = 1/2 cup of fruit (1 fruit exchange)

**Sweetened dietetic applesauce**   2 cups (512 grams)
**Prepared horseradish**   2 tablespoons (30 grams)
**Lemon juice**   1 tablespoon (15 mL)
**Salt**   sprinkle

*Optional:*
**Lemon rind**   1/4 teaspoon (.4 gram), grated

Mix well to blend flavors. Pack in jars or containers for freezing, leaving 3/4-inch space for contents to expand when freezing. Cover; freeze in coldest part of freezer. Keep frozen until needed.

**Suggestions:**
This can be made at canning time and frozen for later use or may be made up as wanted during the year. You may color this green or red for special occasions. It is best not to try to freeze it after it has been colored as it may develop an odd appearance and become unappetizing.

**Natural sweetening directions:**
This may be made two ways:
*With apple juice:*
- 1 tablespoon (15 mL) may be eaten without replacement
- 5 tablespoons (75 mL) contain 40 Calories (P0, F0, C10)
- 5 tablespoons = 1 fruit exchange
Use unsweetened applesauce. Add 1/4 cup (60 mL) concentrated apple juice. Increase lemon juice to 1-1/2 tablespoons (22.5 mL) and add 1/4 tablespoon (1.8 grams) gelatin for thickening (dissolve in hot apple juice before adding).
*With date sugar:*
- 1 tablespoon (15 mL) may be eaten without replacement
- 6-1/2 tablespoons (97.5 mL) contain 40 Calories (P0, F0, C10)
- 6-1/2 tablespoons = 1 fruit exchange
Use unsweetened applesauce. Add 1-1/2 tablespoons (15 grams) date sugar to applesauce and heat to dissolve. Add 1/4 teaspoon (1.3 mL) additional lemon juice to help dissolve the sugar.

**For low-salt diet:**
- 1 tablespoon (15 mL) contains less than 1 mg of sodium
Omit salt; use salt substitute.

# Freezing Fruits and Vegetables Diet-Style

For those who must limit their sugar or salt, home freezing is the answer. Fruits and vegetables can be frozen without adding either item. (Brine is used in commercial processing, so the salt content of the grocers' frozen vegetables is 100% to 150% higher than the raw food, even if no additional salt is added in packaging. Frozen fruits are almost always packed in sugar syrup, but you can pack them at home without this addition.) The following section gives simple directions for this preparation — try them and save yourself money and add variety to your diet meals.

## Freezing Fruits

Use only tree-ripened fruit, just as you would like to eat it raw. Wash, dry on paper towels, or use a lettuce spinner to remove surplus water. Place individual pieces on cookie sheet and sharp-freeze until hard. Then pack in plastic bags, place in tightly covered containers and place in freezer until wanted. *Note:* Pack only enough for one meal in each container as frozen food is best when used immediately after thawing.

*The following fruits can be frozen without any additions:*

**Blueberries**   (blanch with steam for 30 to 60 seconds to keep skins tender: chill)
**Boysenberries**
**Cranberries**
**Currants**
**Himalayan blackberries**
**Loganberries**
**Melons**
**Pineapple**
**Raspberries**
**Rhubarb**
**Strawberries**   (prick with fork to allow air release before freezing)
**Sweet cherries, pitted**

*The following fruits are best frozen after dipping in lemon solution:*

**Apple slices**
**Pitted Plums**

Use only tree-ripened fruit. Wash and dry well; then dip in solution of 1-1/2 tablespoons (22.5 mL) lemon juice (or

1/8 teaspoon (.6 mL) ascorbic acid) in 2 cups (480 mL) water. Drain, freeze on cookie sheets until hard. Package in tightly covered containers, freeze until needed.

263

*The following fruits are best frozen in syrup:*
- Apricots
- Nectarines
- Peaches

Use only tree-ripened fruit. Wash well. If peeling, dip into boiling water for 1 minute, then in cold water. Skin will slip off, if the fruit is really ripe. Pack into plastic bags and cover with syrup to ensure all fruit is away from air. Seal, pack in covered plastic containers, and freeze until needed. Thaw in original containers, as directed below.

## Syrup for freezing fruit:

Use any of the syrups in the canning section, using either sugar substitute or fruit juice for sweetening. With either, increase the lemon juice to 2 teaspoons (10 mL) per cup syrup to prevent browning. (Do not boil syrup after you have added the lemon juice or the anti-browning action will be destroyed.)

*Thawing Frozen Fruit:*

Thaw in original container. The best way is to put the container in the refrigerator and allow the fruit to thaw overnight. If thawed faster, the fruit will be mushy and its appearance much less attractive. When using frozen berries or other frozen fruit in fruit cup or other mixed fruit dishes, don't thaw first! You will like the texture of frozen berries or other fruits when mixed with the soft canned fruit.

Don't discard the liquid that comes off your frozen fruit — eat it as part of the food. If fruit was frozen in a fruit juice syrup, diabetics and hypoglycemics should eat slightly

smaller portions. Adding 1/4 cup (60 mL) of medium syrup will add 2.5 grams carbohydrate per cup fruit (1/4 fruit exchange).

## Freezing Vegetables:

All vegetables need blanching before being frozen to stop the ripening action, which toughens them. They must then be chilled well to stop the cooking process, drained and sharp-frozen. If you take the time to do it properly, the result will be choice vegetables for your winter meals.

*You can freeze the following vegetables with good results:*
- Asparagus
- Beans, all types
- Broccoli
- Brussels sprouts
- Carrots
- Cauliflower
- Celery, diced
- Corn, whole kernel
- Greens (Chard, Kale, Spinach, etc.)
- Mushrooms
- Okra
- Peas, black-eyed
- Peas, green
- Peppers, red and green
- Winter squash (acorn, hubbard, etc.)
- Mixed vegetables (do separately, combine before freezing)

Use only tender, young vegetables in top condition.

All vegetables must be processed in small amounts. Do not try to steam-blanch or parboil more than 3 cups — about 1 pound (454 grams) at a time. Water can be reused three times before you need to start with fresh. Use basket and tight-fitting lid on pan for either type of processing. When time is up, cool in cold water, then ice water to really chill the vegetables. Place in lettuce spinner to remove surplus water before packing in tight containers and freezing, or freeze on cookie sheets until hard, then pack for permanent storage. Prepare as for cooking and either parboil or steam-blanch according to the following:

## Vegetable Parboiling Chart

| Vegetable | Minutes to parboil | Minutes to chill in ice water |
|---|---|---|
| Asparagus thin spears | 3 | 5 to 7 |
| medium spears | 5 to 6 | 5 to 7 |
| Beans, green & yellow | 2 | 5 |
| limas, shelled | 1-1/2 | 4 to 5 |
| Broccoli, florets (or cut stems) | 3 to 5 | 5 to 7 |
| Brussels sprouts | 4 | 8 to 10 |
| Carrots, sliced/diced | 3 | 5 |
| Cauliflower, florets | 3 | 5 |
| Celery, diced | 2 | 6 to 9 min. (over, not in water) |
| Greens | 2 to 2-1/2 | 3 to 4 |
| Mushrooms, whole or halved* | 2 to 3 | 5 |
| Okra | 2 to 2-1/2 | 5 |
| Peas, black-eyed | 2 | 5 |
| Peapods | 1/2 to 1 | 5 |
| Peppers, green or red, seeded | 2 | 5 |

## Vegetable Steaming Chart

| Vegetable | Minutes to parboil | Minutes to chill in ice water |
|---|---|---|
| Broccoli, florets or split stems | 3 to 5 | 5 |
| Cauliflower, florets | 3 | 4 to 5 |
| Corn, whole kernel | 3 | 15 min. (over, not in water) |
| Peas, green | 2 to 2-1/2 | 5 |
| Turnips, Rutabaga, diced/sliced | 1-1/2 to 2 | 5 |

*Mushrooms may be frozen raw, without any processing. This will make them less tender than if parboiled before freezing.

## Freezing Pumpkin, Winter Squash and Sweet Potato:
*These vegetables must be completely cooked before freezing:*
**Pumpkin and Winter Squash:**

Remove seeds, cut into 2- to 3-inch (5 to 7.5 cm) pieces. Place on a flat baking dish with the skin side down. Add 1-1/2 cups (360 mL) water, cover with foil, bake at 325°F (163°C), until very tender. Drain off any liquid; remove skins and puree in food mill to remove any seeds or strings. When cool, pack in plastic bags inside freezing containers; freeze until wanted. *Note:* these vegetables can also be canned after cooking. Place in sterile jars with sealing lids and process in pressure cooker for 90 minutes at 10 pounds pressure.

**Sweet Potatoes and Yams:**

Bake or boil sweet potatoes or yams until very tender. Remove from heat; cool, peel and remove any eyes that do not come off with skin. Puree in food mill to remove any strings or hard pieces. When cool, pack in plastic bags, place in freezer containers; freeze until wanted.

*WARNING:* We do not recommend canning vegetables at home unless you use a pressure cooker. The danger of botulism from improperly processed vegetables is very great. Freezing vegetables, provided they are kept at desirable temperatures, eliminates this danger.

## Pickles and Seasoning Sauces

When these items are made with sugar substitute they have very little food value. Accordingly, they can be used in reasonable amounts without giving up anything else. Pickles made with fruit juice for sweetening must be used in small amounts (or not at all) by hypoglycemics. Amounts allowed and the diabetic equivalents are given on each recipe.

Some of these recipes are listed as ingredients in other recipes in the various chapters of this cookbook. For example, the Tomato Sauce is used in the Spaghetti Sauce; the Ketchup is the basis for the Barbecued Salmon recipe. So if you think that you have no interest in these items, it will be a limiting factor in making other things in the book.

If you don't want to try making pickles or sauces because you don't want to have to can them, you can make them open-kettle (in a large nonaluminum pan, uncovered) and cook for the recommended time after heating to a boil. They can then be put into clean containers and frozen until used. Sauces will be excellent made this way. Pickles do not freeze well — they get soft. If you don't mind soft pickles, then do them this way, too.

Many of these recipes cannot be made salt-free or even low in salt, due to the use of salt solution in making pickles. Substituting potassium chloride for sodium chloride results in a very strong and somewhat bitter pickle. We do not recommend that you try this. However, if you use the salt substitute we recommended on page 19, you can make pickles that are satisfactory. Use salt substitute in equal amounts to salt.

# Bread and Butter Pickles

- Makes 4 pints (1.8 L)
- 1/4 cup (60 mL) may be used without replacement
- 1/4 cup (60 mL) contains 8 Calories (P0, F0, C2), no cholesterol

**Cucumbers**   9 large or 12 medium (2.8 Kg)
**Onions**   2 small or 8 pickling size (240 grams)
**Coarse pickling salt**   1/4 cup (72 grams)
**Cider vinegar**   1 cup (240 mL)
**Granular sugar substitute**   10 tablespoons (60 grams); or substitute equal to
    1-1/4 cups (243.8 grams) of sugar
**Celery seed**   1/2 teaspoon (1.5 grams)
**Pepper**   1 teaspoon (4 grams)
**Tumeric powder**   scant 1/2 teaspoon (1.5 grams)
**Whole mustard seed**   2/3 teaspoon (2 grams)

Score cucumbers lengthwise all around with tines of sharp fork. Slice into medium slices (5 to 6 per inch or less), discarding the hard ends. Slice onions equally thin or even thinner. Combine cucumber and onion slices and cover with coarse salt; mix so all slices are covered; allow to sit for 1/2 hour to remove excess moisture. Discard the liquid that comes off. Combine vinegar, sugar substitute and seasonings in a nonaluminum kettle; add the cucumber and onion slices. Heat to boiling; boil for about 5 minutes until the slices look a little transparent. Pack immediately in hot sterilized jars leaving 1 inch at the top for expansion; seal with sterilized lids. Process in water bath 20 minutes after water returns to boiling. Store in cool, dark area until you wish to use them.

*Suggestions:*
You can pickle other vegetables in this type of liquid. Cucumbers, cauliflower, celery, carrots and green peppers all make fine pickles. Leave the pieces larger and process for a little longer (25 to 30 minutes) to be sure the vinegar has penetrated the vegetables thoroughly.

*Natural sweetening directions:*
- 1/4 cup (60 mL) contains 32 Calories (P0, F0, C8)
- 1/4 cup = 1 vegetable serving (1 vegetable exchange)
Omit sugar substitute. Increase vinegar to 1-1/3 cups (320 mL). Add 3 cups (720 mL) concentrated white grape juice, reduced from 6 cups (1.4 L). Add juice to vinegar and seasonings, simmer 5 minutes to further reduce volume before adding vegetables.

*For low-salt diet:*
- 1/4 cup (60 mL) contains 8 mg of sodium
Omit salt; use 1 cup (192 grams) of recommended salt substitute.

267

# Christine's Mustard Pickles

- Makes 8 quarts (7.6 L)
- 1/4 cup (60 mL) may be eaten without replacement
- 1/4 cup (60 mL) contains 16 Calories (P1, F0, C3), no cholesterol
- 1/4 cup = 1/2 vegetable serving (1/2 vegetable exchange)

**Cucumbers**  2 quarts of tiny, 2 inches or smaller (840 grams)
**Pearl onions**  2 quarts tiny white (880 grams)
**Green beans**  2 quarts (840 grams), ends trimmed, and beans cut in half or thirds
**Green tomatoes**  2 quarts (1.5 Kg), quartered
**Cauliflower**  2 heads (1.7 Kg), cut into 1-inch buds
**Green peppers**  6 small (360 grams), coarsely chopped
**Coarse pickling salt**  1/4 cup (72 grams)
**Tumeric powder**  3 tablespoons (28.4 grams)
**Whole mustard seed**  2 tablespoons (18 grams)
**Celery seed**  2 tablespoons (18 grams)
**Cloves**  1/2 tablespoon (4.5 grams)
**Whole allspice**  1 tablespoon (9 grams)
**Dry mustard**  2/3 cup (96 grams)
**Cider vinegar**  to completely cover vegetables
**Whole-wheat flour**  1/2 cup (68.5 grams), unsifted
**Granular sugar substitute**  3/4 to 1 cup (72 to 96 grams); or substitute equal to
   2 cups (390 grams) of sugar

*Optional:*
**White cabbage**  1 small head (545 grams), coarsely chopped

Place chopped vegetables in nonaluminum kettle and cover with pickling salt, mix well so salt covers all the vegetables. Place a plate over the vegetables so they stay down in the kettle and allow to stand 24 hours. Drain and discard the liquid that comes off. Place vegetables and seasonings, with vinegar to cover, over heat and bring to a boil. Boil for 5 minutes, or until vegetables are soft but not mushy. Leave a little crisp, if you prefer them chewy. Drain off liquid and save. Make a thin paste with flour, sugar substitute and a little water. Add to the liquid and cook until it is slightly thick. Add vegetables to thickened liquid. Heat through. Pack in sterilized jars while still very hot leaving 1 inch for expansion. Seal with sterilized lids. Process 15 minutes in boiling water bath to ensure seal. Cool. Store in cool, dark place.

### Suggestions:
You can pickle almost any vegetable in this vinegar mixture. Try zucchini or broccoli. It makes excellent yellow wax bean pickles mixed with small onions.

### Natural sweetening directions:
- 1/4 cup (60 mL) contains 28 Calories (P1, F0, C6)
- 1/4 cup = 1 vegetable serving (1 vegetable exchange)
Omit sugar substitute. Add 2 cups (480 mL) concentrated apple juice to 2 cups (480 mL) vinegar and simmer for 5 to 8 minutes to reduce in volume before adding the vegetables. Add additional vinegar to completely cover the vegetables before cooking. When making flour paste, increase flour to 3/4 cup (102.8 grams) and use 1/4 cup (60 mL) lemon juice instead of water, and add 1/3 cup (53 grams) of date sugar for sweeter pickles.

### For low-salt diet:
*This recipe cannot be made low in salt.*

268

# Celery Chutney

- Makes 3 pints (1.4 L)
- 2 tablespoons (30 mL) may be eaten without replacement
- 2 tablespoons (30 mL) contain 16 Calories (P0, F0, C4), no cholesterol
- 2 tablespoons = 1/2 vegetable serving (1/2 vegetable exchange)

**Celery**   3 cups (360 grams), diced fine
**Tomatoes**   6 cups (1.1 Kg), chopped. *Note: If you use canned tomatoes, use only 1 teaspoon (6 grams) of salt.*
**Green pepper**   1/4 (32.5 grams), diced fine
**Onion**   1 medium (150 grams), diced
**Garlic**   1 clove (2 grams), diced
**Cider vinegar**   1/2 cup (120 mL)
**Brown-type granular sugar substitute**   1/3 cup (32 grams); or substitute equal to 2/3 cup (130 grams) of sugar
**Salt**   1 tablespoon (18 grams). Use only 1 teaspoon (6 grams) with canned tomatoes.
**Pepper**   1/2 teaspoon (2 grams)
**Celery seed**   1 teaspoon (3 grams)

Sterilize the jars and keep them hot. Combine chopped vegetables in large nonaluminum kettle; add vinegar and other ingredients. Mix well. Simmer over low heat until the volume is reduced and the mix looks quite thick. Do not allow chutney to cool but pack it in hot jars while it is boiling hot, leaving 1 inch for expansion. Top with sterilized lids and tighten rings firmly. Process in water bath (water must cover jars completely) for 15 minutes to sterilize and seal the jars. Cool. Store in cool, dark place until you wish to use them. Refrigerate after opening to prevent spoiling.

*Suggestions:*
This is particularly good with cold meat or cold fish. Use it to give color and interest to a meal of leftovers.

*Natural sweetening directions:*
- Makes 3-1/2 pints (1.6 L)
- 1 tablespoon (15 mL) contains 12 Calories (P0, F0, C3)
- 3 tablespoons (45 mL) = 1/2 slice of bread (1/2 bread exchange)
Omit sugar substitute. Add 1 cup (240 mL) concentrated apple juice and 1 tablespoon (15 mL) lemon juice.

*For low-salt diet:*
*This recipe cannot be made low in salt because of the natural high salt content of the celery.*

# Barbecue Sauce

- Makes 2-1/2 cups (600 mL)
- 1 tablespoon (15 mL) may be eaten without replacement
- 1/2 cup (120 mL) contains 36 Calories (P2, F0, C7), no cholesterol
- 1/2 cup = 1/2 slice of bread (1/2 bread exchange)

**Tomato sauce**    1 pint (.47 L). See recipe on page 274, or make the recipe below.
**Cider vinegar**    1/2 cup (120 mL)
**Worcestershire sauce**    1/2 teaspoon (2.5 mL)

### For hot barbecue sauce add:
**Tabasco**    1/2 teaspoon (2.5 mL)
**Cayenne powder**    1/4 to 1/2 teaspoon (1 to 2 grams)

### Tomato sauce:
**Tomato puree**    2 cups (480 mL)
**Granular sugar substitute**    1 tablespoon (6 grams); or substitute equal to 2 tablespoons (24.4 grams) of sugar
**Onion powder**    1/4 teaspoon (.8 gram)
**Allspice**    1/16 teaspoon (.2 gram)
**Garlic powder**    1/16 teaspoon (:2 gram)

Mix all ingredients and stir to blend well.
Taste, then add salt and pepper to suit.
Use to baste barbecued or baked meat,
fish or poultry.

### Natural sweetening directions:
- 1 tablespoon (15 mL) may be eaten without replacement
- 1/2 cup (120 mL) contains 40 Calories (P2, F0, C8)
- 1/2 cup = 1/2 slice of bread (1/2 bread exchange)
Omit sugar substitute. Add 1/4 cup (60 mL) white grape juice, or 1/3 cup (80 mL) apple juice plus 2 tablespoons (30 mL) lemon juice.

### For low-salt diet:
- 2 tablespoons (30 mL) contain 14 mg of sodium
Make Tomato Sauce according to low-salt directions, page 274. Use only tomato puree that is labeled salt-free. Omit Worcestershire sauce; use salt-free soy sauce.

# Spanish Barbecue Sauce

- Makes 1-1/2 pints (720 mL)
- 2 tablespoons (30 mL) may be eaten without replacement
- 1/4 cup (60 mL) contains 16 Calories (P0, F0, C4), no cholesterol
- 1/4 cup = 1/2 vegetable serving (1/2 vegetable exchange)

**Green pepper**    1/4 cup (37.5 grams), chopped
**Tomatoes**    1 quart (760 grams)
**Onion**    1/3 cup (53 grams), finely chopped
**Dry mustard**    1/2 teaspoon (1.5 grams)
**Salt**    1 teaspoon (6 grams)
**Granular sugar substitute**    1 tablespoon (6 grams); or substitute equal to
    2 tablespoons (24.4 grams) of sugar
**Tabasco**    1/16 to 1/8 teaspoon (.3 to .6 mL), to taste
**Cayenne**    several sprinkles

Puree green pepper and tomatoes in food mill or food processor, or grind in meat grinder. Put all ingredients into large nonaluminum kettle; simmer about 15 minutes, until mixture begins to look thick. If sauce is not to be used soon, pack into sterilized jars, leaving 1 inch for expansion. Cover with sterilized lids, and process for 15 minutes in boiling water bath (see instructions for canning fruit, page 244).

*Suggestions:*
This sauce may be used as a topping for meat, for meat balls or with other dishes. It is very hot, so a little goes a long way. For a milder sauce, cut the cayenne and Tabasco to half or less.

*Natural sweetening directions:*
- Makes 2 pints (960 mL)
- 2 tablespoons (30 mL) may be eaten without replacement
- 2 tablespoons (30 mL) contain 8 Calories (P0, F0, C2)

Omit sugar substitute. Add 3/4 cup (180 mL) white grape juice plus 6 tablespoons (90 mL) vinegar and 2 tablespoons (30 mL) lemon juice. Simmer 5 minutes longer to achieve desired thickness.

*For low-salt diet:*
- 1 tablespoon (15 mL) contains 2 mg of sodium

Omit salt; use 1 teaspoon (4 grams) of salt substitute. Use only 6 drops of Tabasco.

# Ketchup

- Makes 3-1/2 pints (1.6 L)
- 2 tablespoons (30 mL) may be eaten without replacement
- 1/4 cup (60 mL) contains 16 Calories (P0, F0, C4), no cholesterol
- 1/4 cup = 1/2 vegetable serving (1/2 vegetable exchange)

**Tomatoes**   8 cups (1.5 Kg); use fresh, peeled and quartered, or drained canned tomatoes.
**Onions**   2 medium (300 grams), chopped
**Green pepper**   1 (130 grams), chopped
**Garlic**   4 small cloves (8 grams), minced
**Celery**   2 large stalks (140 grams), diced
**Cider vinegar**   1 cup (240 mL)
**Granular sugar substitute**   1/2 cup (48 grams); or substitute equal to 1 cup (195 grams) of sugar
**Ground cloves**   1/2 teaspoon (1.5 grams)
**Dry mustard**   1 teaspoon (3 grams)
**Cinnamon**   1 teaspoon (3 grams)
**Mace**   1/2 teaspoon (1.5 grams)
**Allspice**   1 teaspoon (3 grams)
**Salt**   1 tablespoon (18 grams)
**Pepper**   1/2 teaspoon (2 grams)

*Optional:*
**Tabasco**   1/4 teaspoon (1.3 mL)

Prepare vegetables; combine all ingredients in large nonaluminum kettle. Cook slowly over low heat until vegetables are very soft; do not allow to boil. Remove from heat; put through food mill or blend to break up any hard fibers. Return to heat and bring to boiling point. Bottle in sterilized jars, leaving 1 inch for expansion; seal with sterilized lids; process in hot water bath for 15 minutes (see instructions for canning fruit, page 244). Store in cool, dark place to prevent color loss.

**Suggestions:**
You may want to use less spice than the recipe calls for. As given, this makes a spicy, hot ketchup.

### Natural sweetening directions:
- 1 tablespoon (15 mL) may be eaten without replacement
- 3 tablespoons (45 mL) contain 24 Calories (P0, F0, C6), no cholesterol
- 3 tablespoons = 1/2 fruit exchange

Omit sugar substitute. Add 2 cups (480 mL) concentrated white grape juice, reduced from 4 cups (960 mL). Add 1 tablespoon (15 mL) lemon juice.

### For low-salt diet:
- 1 tablespoon (15 mL) contains 1 mg of sodium

Omit salt; use 1 tablespoon (12 grams) of salt substitute. Use fresh or diet-pack tomatoes.

# Cucumber Ketchup

- Makes 6-1/2 cups (1.56 L)
- 1 tablespoon (15 mL) may be used without replacement
- 1 tablespoon (15 mL) contains 5 Calories
- 1/2 cup (120 mL) contains 40 Calories (P1, F0, C9), no cholesterol
- 1/2 cup = 1/2 cup of fruit (1 fruit exchange)

**Cucumbers**   2 medium large (55 grams)
**Apples**   2 large (460 grams), tart
**Onion**   1 medium (150 grams)
**Horseradish**   1 to 2 tablespoons (15 to 30 grams), grated
**Liquid sugar substitute**   1-1/4 teaspoons (6.25 mL)
**Lemon juice**   2 teaspoons (10 mL)
**Cider vinegar**   1 cup (240 mL)
**Salt**   1-1/2 teaspoons (9 grams)
**Pepper**   1/2 teaspoon (2 grams)
**Paprika**   1/2 teaspoon (2.5 grams)

Cut off the ends of the cucumbers; quarter apples and remove cores, stems and blossom ends. Grind cucumbers, apples and onion in meat grinder using coarse blade. Place in a nonaluminum kettle. Add remaining ingredients, except liquid sugar substitute, and bring to a boil; reduce heat and cook for 8 minutes. Add sugar substitute, and cook for another 2 or 3 minutes, until vegetables are tender. Taste, and adjust seasonings if desired. Remember, it will taste sweeter when it is cool. Pour into hot sterile jars, leaving 3/4 inch at the top for expansion. Cap with hot sterile lids and process in boiling water bath for 15 minutes after water returns to boiling, or for 15 minutes in a pressure cooker at 10 pounds pressure. Store jars in a cool, dark place to prevent color fading.

*Natural sweetening directions:*
- 7 tablespoons (105 mL) contain 40 Calories (P1, F0, C9)
- 7 tablespoons = 1/2 cup of fruit (1 fruit exchange)

*For low-salt diet:*
- 1 tablespoon (15 mL) contains 1 mg of sodium
Omit salt; use 1 teaspoon (4 grams) of salt substitute. Increase lemon juice to 2-1/2 teaspoons (12.5 mL). Use only 1 tablespoon (15 grams) of horseradish.

# Tomato Sauce

- Makes 3 pints (1.4 L)
- 2 tablespoons (30 mL) may be eaten without replacement
- 1/4 cup (60 mL) contains 16 Calories (P0, F0, C4), no cholesterol
- 1/4 cup = 1/2 vegetable serving (1/2 vegetable exchange)

**Tomatoes**   8 cups (1.5 Kg), peeled and quartered; or tomato puree
**Onions**   2 medium (300 grams), chopped
**Green pepper**   1 (130 grams), chopped
**Garlic**   1 large clove (3 grams), minced
**Cider vinegar**   2/3 cup (180 mL)
**Allspice**   1/2 teaspoon (1.5 grams)
**Salt**   1 tablespoon (18 grams)
**Pepper**   1/4 teaspoon (1 gram)
**Granular sugar substitute**   1/2 cup (48 grams); or substitute equal to 1 cup
   (195 grams) of sugar

Prepare vegetables; combine in large nonaluminum kettle; add all ingredients except sugar substitute and tomato puree (if used). Cook over low heat until all vegetables are very soft and volume is reduced about 1/3; remove from heat; add sugar substitute. Put through food mill to remove seeds and any other firm material. Return to heat; add tomato puree (if used) and bring to boil. Pack in sterilized jars, leaving 1 inch for expansion; seal with sterilized lids; process for 15 minutes in hot water bath (see canning instructions on page 244). Cool; store in cool, dark place.

### Natural sweetening directions:
- Makes 3-1/2 pints (1.6 L)
- 1 tablespoon (15 mL) may be eaten without replacement
- 2 tablespoons (30 mL) contain 18 Calories (P0, F0, C6)
- 2 tablespoons = 1 vegetable serving (1 vegetable exchange)

Omit sugar substitute; use 1-1/2 cups (360 mL) concentrated white grape juice, reduced from 3 cups (720 mL), plus 2 tablespoons (30 mL) lemon juice.

### For low-salt diet:
- 1 tablespoon (15 mL) contains .5 mg of sodium

Omit salt; use 1 tablespoon (12 grams) of salt substitute. Use fresh or diet-pack tomatoes, or salt-free tomato puree.

# 5 Eating Out

One of the worst problems with trying to stick to a diet is the temptation offered when you have to eat away from home. It can be discouraging and alarming to read a menu and find nothing on it that you should be eating.

This chapter is meant to start you thinking about how to cope without getting into too much trouble. If you are new to special dieting, it will show you how to plan; even old hands may find new ideas. One meal off the diet will not cause serious problems for most people. However, once you allow yourself to break the routine, it becomes easier to do it another time. If you need to be on a diet for medical

reasons, then you should try to stick to it carefully unless the circumstances are most unusual.

Read the suggestions carefully. Try the meal replacements and practice until the items are familiar to you. Then try the next time you are away from home. We predict that your choices will be wise and close to what you should be having for that meal —and you will be very pleased with yourself for having learned to eat away from home without too much difficulty.

If you're on a low-salt diet, you will be sure to get more salt than you should have unless you pick very carefully. Even at best there are

sources of sodium that you may not know about. Plan on being very careful for the following several days to make up for the extra salt in restaurant food.

## General Rules for Eating Out

Menus in restaurants aren't planned to fit a diet. If you try, often you can find items that will fit your needs both in type of food and size of portion — unless you're on a low-salt diet. It is not usually possible to follow a restricted-salt menu in a restaurant. Picking foods that require a minimum of preparation (baked potato, broiled meat, poultry or fish), avoiding canned vegetables and asking that no salt be added in cooking gives the best results. If you continually eat in the same places, they will probably try harder to fix the food as you request.

Fast-food restaurants usually don't have many items suitable for diets. Their foods are high in salt, fat and refined starches as well as sugars. If there is no other choice in restaurants, avoid the milk shakes and desserts and do your best.

For other than low-salt diets, try to replace each item of your normal meal with what is available on the menu. If you use the items from the replacement lists that follow this chapter, you should do quite well. But eating out is not ideal, and you will do better at home or where the cook understands your diet restriction.

### *Replacements*

Here's how to figure a whole meal easily.

1. Write down your meal plan. Leave space alongside for replacements.

2. Take each item and look it up in the groups given in the replacement lists. Pick something you would probably find in a restaurant and write it down beside what you would normally have.

3. Consider what else you have picked for replacement so you have an appetizing meal — and when you are done, congratulate yourself on not letting dieting be dull.

While this doesn't look the same, your body will get just about the same nourishment from the two meals. Depending on your choice, you

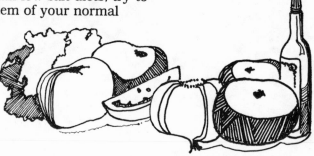

276

| Sample Diet Plan | |
|---|---|
| *Diet Plan* | *Replacement* |
| 3 meat servings | 1 slice of roast beef (lean only) |
| 2 starch servings | 1/2 of a large baked potato and 3 ounces of dry wine, or 1 roll |
| 1 to 2 vegetable servings | green salad with oil and vinegar dressing, and frozen peas |
| 1 fruit serving | 2/3 of a roll or 1/3 more baked potato |
| 1 fat serving | oil in salad dressing |

may not be as satisfied because the replacement isn't as bulky. (For a low-cholesterol replacement, a poultry or fish entree is your best choice.)

### Practice

Write down a favorite restaurant meal — one that you often ate in predieting days. Now try to see how much of it you can eat on your diet. Try to replace with similar items if possible.

You may be pleasantly surprised to find that you can eat almost everything except the dessert. You may have to take meat home in a doggie bag and eat it for lunch the next day, but many people do. In fact, some restaurants have people bags —and call them that.

## Banquets and Dinner Parties

There you are, captive for a meal. Do you make a big scene and show all around that you are dieting? Or do you try to be selective and follow your pattern as well as you can with what is available? For the least fuss, try the following:

If you can find out ahead of time what the menu will be, replacement will be much easier. Then plan ahead at home as explained under the general rules for eating out. You will have to skip sweet salads, such as gelatin, the dessert and gravy. Make up for these with additional bread or starchy vegetables to fill the holes in your diet pattern. (Nobody will think you are on a special diet if you eat both the bread and potato. What they won't know is that one replaces your usual dessert of fruit.)

If you don't know the menu, it is much harder to plan. Perhaps ahead of the main dish you can ask the waitress what is coming. If you find the dessert is fresh fruit — a welcome but rare occasion — you can save for it. If it is the usual sweet, gooey dish, plan to have more starch at the earlier courses and skip the dessert.

277

Again, use the substitutions given in the replacement lists.

If you can't find out anything ahead, then assume the worst and act as if you knew you could not eat the dessert. Eat the main course as both entree and dessert. If they bring you dessert, put it aside and ignore it or even offer it to a neighboring diner. (Since they saw you eating all that starch, they will just think you are full and don't want it.) Avoid making yourself conspicuous. Your table companions aren't interested in your diet and it gets old very quickly as a main subject of conversation.

If you plan to have a drink, remember that 1 ounce of alcohol (or 3 ounces of dry wine) replaces 1 serving of starch. You probably can't have both a before-dinner drink and dry wine with dinner. Choose what you want and then don't fudge and have both. Some diets totally forbid the use of alcohol, and if your doctor says that you can't have any, then don't. Chances are there is a sound medical reason and drinking could delay your recovery of good health.

Do the best you can and then don't worry about it.

## Drive-Ins

*Drive-ins are not for low-sodium dieters.*

The only place you can find to eat is a drive-in . . . or you like to eat at drive-ins . . . or all the others want to go to a drive-in to eat. Whatever the

---

### 1981
### DIABETIC FOOD EXCHANGE LIST FOR
### McDONALD'S® RESTAURANTS

This information for foods served at McDonald's is provided to assist persons following diabetic diets. Based on a nutritional analysis conducted by Raltech Scientific Services in Madison, food exchange conversions were prepared by the American Diabetes Association, Northern Illinois Affiliate, Inc. Values listed are drawn from the publication *Exchange Lists for Menu Planning* (1976). Persons wishing the nutrient values of McDonald's foods or additional copies of this list may write to McDonald's Corporation, Public Policy Dept., Oak Brook, IL 60521.

| | Exchange Units | Calories | Cholesterol (mg) |
|---|---|---|---|
| Hamburger | 2 breads, 1½ high fat meats | 255 | 25 |
| Cheeseburger | 2 breads, 2 high fat meats | 307 | 27 |
| Quarter Pounder® (wt. before cooking ¼ lb.) | 2 breads, 3 high fat meats | 424 | 67 |
| Quarter Pounder with Cheese | 2 breads, 3½ high fat meats | 524 | 96 |
| Big Mac® | 2½ breads, 3 high fat meats, 2 fats | 563 | 86 |
| Filet-O-Fish® | 2½ breads, 2 lean meats, 3 fats | 432 | 47 |
| French Fries (regular) | 2 breads, 2 fats | 220 | 9 |
| Egg McMuffin® | 2 breads, 2 medium fat meats | 327 | 229 |
| Pork Sausage Patties | 1 high fat meat, 2 fats | 206 | 43 |
| English Muffin (buttered) | 2 breads, 1 fat | 186 | 13 |
| Hash Browns | 1 bread, 1 fat | 125 | 7 |
| Scrambled Eggs | 2 medium fat meats, 1 fat | 180 | 349 |
| * Hot Cakes with Butter & Syrup | 3 fruits, 4 breads, 2 fats | 500 | 47 |
| Orange Juice-6 oz. | 2 fruits | 85 | 0 |
| Grapefruit Juice-6 oz. | 2 fruits | 75 | 0 |
| * Danish | | | |
| * Apple Pie | 1½ fruits, 1 bread, 3 fats | 253 | 12 |
| * Cherry Pie | 1½ fruits, 1 bread, 3 fats | 260 | 13 |
| * McDonaldland® Cookies | 3 breads, 2 fats | 308 | 10 |
| * Chocolaty Chip Cookies | 3 breads, 2 fats | 342 | 18 |
| * Chocolate Shake | 1 whole milk, 1 fruit, 3 breads | 383 | 30 |
| * Vanilla Shake | 1 whole milk, 2 fruits, 2 breads | 352 | 31 |
| * Strawberry Shake | 1 whole milk, 1 fruit, 3 breads | 362 | 32 |
| * Sundaes | | | |
| Hot Fudge | ½ whole milk, 1 fruit, 2 breads, 1 fat | 310 | 18 |
| Strawberry | ½ whole milk, 1 fruit, 2 breads, 2 fats | 289 | 20 |
| Carmel | ½ whole milk, 1 fruit, 2 breads, 1 fat | 328 | 26 |
| * Ice Cream w/sugar cone | 2 breads, 1 fat | 170 | 19 |
| * Ice Cream w/cake cone | 2 breads, 1 fat | 185 | 24 |

*These items contain large portions of carbohydrate derived from sugar. Persons with diabetes are strongly discouraged from eating such items, since such carbohydrate is quickly absorbed resulting in an abrupt peaking of the blood sugar. McDonald's Danish is not a standard item because specifications are determined on a local basis. They are also high in carbohydrate derived from sugar.

Many McDonald's serve low fat 2% milk.

Additional information about diabetes and exchange list diets is available from the American Diabetes Association, 2 Park Avenue, New York, New York 10016.

McD 8179                                          © 1981  McDonald's Corporation

reason you are there, and now what can you eat? Following is a suggested replacement meal. For other replacement values, check the replacement lists that begin on page 281. If you eat out often, it's handy to have this information with you. McDonald's has even prepared its own diabetic exchange list. Copies are available from McDonald's Corporation, Public Policy Department, Oak Brook, Illinois 60521.

| Your Usual Meal | Your Drive-In Choice |
|---|---|
| 2 slices of bread | Hamburger bun (both halves) |
| 2 ounces of low-fat meat | Fish square (if too large, leave some uneaten) |
| 1 fruit serving | 2/3 of a small bag of potato chips or 1/3 of a cup of French fries Coffee, tea, diet pop |
| 2 fat servings | 1 teaspoon of tartar sauce and fat in the potatoes |

## Picnics

What can you take on a picnic and still follow your diet? Recipes for the following items are all in this cookbook. They will keep without refrigeration for a reasonable time, and most are items that the whole family will eat without complaining.

### Main Dishes and Salads
Meat Loaf Sandwiches
Chicken Italienne or Chicken Bavarian
Patrick's Shrimp Dish (very good cold)
Three-Bean Salad with Tuna or Chicken
Hot Potato Salad (good cold, too)
Coleslaw or Sauerkraut Slaw
Cabbage Fruit Salad
Onion and Carrot Puree (good cold)

Vegetable Potpourri
Tomato Madrilene Soup (good chilled)
Chicken Salad with Green Grapes
Ginger Baked Chicken
Turkey Loaf sandwiches

### Desserts
Crunchy Banana Bread
Fruit Betty, Fruited Gelatin
Raisin-Applesauce Cake
Fruit Medley
Apple-Raisin Pie
Berry Pie
Rhubarb Pie
Cookies, Sue's Applesauce Brownies
Homemade Graham Crackers
Ann Meerkerk's Zucchini Bread
Date-Nut Cake

279

## Travel Meals
### By Car
Travel by car requires only a little planning ahead.

Take along a small ice chest. Prepare your own breakfast and lunch and eat only your dinner meal out. If it happens that at lunch time there is a nice restaurant on the road, stop and eat there. If all that is available is a greasy spoon, find a park and picnic.

Low-fat cheese or cottage cheese can be satisfactory breakfast items. They are the easiest things to carry, provided you have an ice chest, and will allow you to have the protein at breakfast that will stick with you through the morning.

### By Airplane
If you can eat on the ground before boarding the plane, it will simplify things aboard. Then you can skip or pick items from the meal served without too much hunger.

It is possible to order special diet meals on an airplane if you notify the airline about 24 hours ahead of time. However, airlines often offer a choice of meat or fish/poultry, so you could select the one you should have without making a special order. Avoid the breading and sauces; eat only the meat. Then you won't have to allow any extra for the cooking method. Use the methods suggested under "Banquets and Dinner Parties," page 277.

### By Bus
Most bus meal-stops are not fancy. You may have to fall back on the drive-in menu selection. Try not to take a long trip without making a stop for a night's sleep and some more appropriate meals. For the first day you can pack a lunch from the picnic items. Beyond that you are on your own; do the best you can.

**Note:** Hypoglycemics should carry packages of the Emergency Snack Mix (see recipe on page 230) with them in case they can not get meals on time.

### Rule
The real success is when you manage to follow your diet under difficult circumstances. Then you can be proud of yourself! Give yourself a treat (not food!) to reward your inner person.

# 6 Tables

## Table 1 / *Restaurant Food Replacements*

Each food listed here is measured not in Calories but in equivalent servings of bread, meat, fruit or fat. This is done so that you can easily make trades between the restaurant menu and your usual diet. Choose either the food listed to the left or the equivalent serving of bread, meat, fruit or fat listed at the right. With a little juggling, you should be able to assemble a restaurant meal that won't wreck your diet.

All food values are approximate.

***Note:*** Much of the carbohydrate in bulky raw vegetables is not digestible and need not be counted. In a salad, however, there will usually be at least 1 teaspoon of salad dressing (1 fat serving) and as much as 1/4 cup or more. This is indicated by a †.

### Breakfast Foods

Don't eat pastry, sweet rolls, butterhorns or doughnuts. Do use dietetic syrup (in reasonable amounts) on the French toast, pancakes and waffles.

| | |
|---|---|
| Grapefruit half | 1/4 of a large cantaloupe<br>small glass of fruit juice<br>1 fruit serving<br>2/3 bread serving |
| Cereal, unsweetened, 1/2 cup | 1 bread serving |
| Scrambled eggs (usually 2 eggs) | 2 meat servings |
| Omelette (usually 3 eggs) | 3 meat servings |
| Bacon, 1 crisp slice | 1 fat serving |
| Canadian bacon, 2 thin slices | 1 meat serving |
| Sausage, 2 small links | 1 meat + 3 fat servings |

| French toast, 1 slice | 1 bread + 1/2 meat serving |
|---|---|
| Pancake, 3-inch | 1 bread serving |
| Waffle, 3-1/2-inch square | 1 bread serving |
| Fruit muffin, 1 small | 1 bread + 1 fruit serving |

## Beverages

| Black coffee or tea | free; no replacement needed |
|---|---|
| Whole milk (4% fat), 8 ounces | 1 bread + 1 meat + 1 fat serving |
| Skim or buttermilk, 8 ounces | 1 bread + 1 meat serving |
| Beer (3.2%), 8 ounces (7 grams of alcohol) | dry wine, 3 ounces (11 grams of alcohol)<br>whiskey, gin, vodka, 1 ounce (12 grams of alcohol)<br>1 bread serving |

## Bread and Cereal

| Bread, 1 slice | 1 medium roll<br>5 salted crackers<br>1 small potato<br>1/2 cup of rice or noodles<br>1 bread serving |
|---|---|
| Cereal (unsweetened) or starch, 1/2 cup | 1 bread serving |
| Salted crackers, 5 | 1 bread serving |
| French toast, 1 slice | 1 bread + 1/2 meat serving |
| Pancake, 3-inch | 1 bread serving |
| Waffle, 3-1/2-inch square | 1 bread serving |
| Fruit muffin, 1 small | 1 bread + 1 fruit serving |

## Soup

| Thin, watery, 6-ounce cup | 1/2 bread serving |
|---|---|
| Average, 6-ounce cup | 1 bread serving |
| Thick, 6-ounce cup | 1-1/4 to 1-1/2 bread servings |
| "Meaty" thick soup, 6-ounce cup | 1 meat + 1 bread serving |

## Salad

| | |
|---|---|
| Raw mixed vegetables†, 1 cup | free except for dressing; no replacement needed |
| Cottage cheese and fruit (1/2 cup of cottage cheese and 2 pieces of sweetened, canned fruit) | 2 meat + 2 fruit servings |
| Starchy (potato, macaroni), 1 cup | 2 bread + fat allowance for salad dressing† |
| Meaty (chicken, seafood), 1 cup | 3 to 4 meat servings + fat allowance for salad dressing† |
| Salad dressing†, 1 tablespoon | oil or mayonnaise, 1 teaspoon 1 fat serving |

## Meats

### Fish:

| | |
|---|---|
| 1 ounce | 1 meat serving |
| 1 medium fish steak (4 ounces) | 3 to 4 meat servings |

### Poultry:

| | |
|---|---|
| 1 ounce | 1 meat serving |
| 1/2 chicken breast (4 ounces) | 1 chicken drumstick and 1 thigh 3 to 4 meat servings |

### Beef, pork, lamb, veal:

| | |
|---|---|
| 1 ounce | 1 meat serving |
| 2 ounces | 1 small meat patty 1 small chop 2 eggs 1/2 cup of creamed cottage cheese 2 meat servings |
| 4 ounces | 1 large meat patty center of lean rib steak 1 cup of cottage cheese 4 meat servings |

283

| *Casserole:* | |
|---|---|
| Meaty, 1 cup | 1 bread + 2 to 3 meat servings |
| Starchy, 1 cup | 1-1/2 bread + 1 to 2 meat servings |
| *Breakfast meat:* | |
| Bacon, 1 crisp slice | 1 fat serving |
| Canadian bacon, 2 thin slices | 1 meat serving |
| Sausage, 2 small links | 1 meat + 3 fat servings |

## Eggs and Cheese

| | |
|---|---|
| Egg, 1 medium | 1 meat serving |
| Eggs, scrambled (usually 2 eggs) | 2 meat servings |
| Omelette (usually 3 eggs) | 3 meat servings |
| Cottage cheese, 1/4 cup | low-fat cheese, 1 slice (1 ounce) 1 meat serving |

## Vegetarian Entrees

| | |
|---|---|
| Macaroni & Cheese, 1 cup | 1 meat serving + 1-1/2 bread servings |
| Baked beans (may be too sweet), 1 cup | 2 meat servings + 1 bread serving |
| Tofu, 3 ounces | 1 meat serving |

## Vegetables

| | |
|---|---|
| Bulky vegetables (cauliflower, celery, tomato, cucumber, etc.) raw†, 1 cup | cooked, 1/2 cup free except for dressing; no replacement needed |
| Semistarchy vegetables (beets, carrots, mixed vegetables, onions, rutabagas, turnips), raw or cooked, 1/2 cup | 1/2 bread serving |
| Starchy vegetables (beans, potatoes, etc.), cooked, 1/2 cup | Corn, 1/3 cup Parsnips, 2/3 cup |

| Green peas, 1/2 cup<br>Pumpkin, winter squash, 1/2 cup<br>Yams, sweet potatoes, 1/4 cup | 1 bread serving |
|---|---|

## Fruit Dishes

| Grapefruit half | 1/4 of a large cantaloupe<br>small glass of fruit juice, 1/2 cup<br>   (except grape or prune juice,<br>   1/4 cup)<br>1 fruit serving<br>2/3 bread serving |
|---|---|
| Bulky fruit<br>  (melon, berries), 1 cup | 1 fruit serving<br>2/3 bread serving |
| Average fruit (apples, apricots,<br>  grapefruit, oranges, peaches, pears,<br>  plums), 1/2 cup | 1 fruit serving<br>2/3 bread serving |
| Sweet fruit (bananas, cherries, dried<br>  fruits, grapes), 1/4 cup | 1 fruit serving<br>2/3 bread serving |

## Desserts

   Unless fresh fruit is available, skip dessert and have more starch with the main course.

| Fruit, 1 serving | 2/3 bread serving |
|---|---|
| Dietetic gelatin | free; no replacement needed |

## Fats

| Salad dressing†, 1 tablespoon | oil or mayonnaise†, 1 teaspoon<br>Reduced-Calorie mayonnaise, 1-1/2 to<br>  2 teaspoons<br>Reduced salad dressing*, 1-1/2 to 2<br>  teaspoons<br>margarine, 1 teaspoon<br>6 peanuts<br>5 olives<br>4 walnut halves<br>1 fat serving |
|---|---|

*Watch for sugar in salad dressing

## Drive-in Food*

Hot dogs and hamburgers are both high in fat and high in cholesterol. Fish and chicken on the other hand, are low in cholesterol and moderate in fat. Each half of a hamburger bun is 1 bread serving; if you can eat your hamburger, chicken or fish sandwich without the lid, you can save one bread serving. And since hot dogs are never as large as hot dog buns, the value given in this table is based on the assumption that you'll only eat the 2/3 of the bun that the hot dog fills.

Also, the tomatoes and pickles† are free, as long as the pickles aren't sweet. Also, watch out for sweet relish!

| | |
|---|---|
| Hot dog, 1 large | 1 bread + 1-1/2 to 2 meat servings |
| Hamburger (on a bun), regular size | 2 bread + 2 meat servings |
| Hamburger deluxe (on a bun), 1/4 pound, with tomato and pickle† | 2 bread + 4 meat servings |
| Fish sandwich | 2 bread + 3 meat servings |
| Chicken sandwich | 2 bread + 3 meat servings |
| Potato chips, 1 small bag (1 cup) | 1 bread + 1 to 2 fat servings |
| Potato chips, 2/3 of a small bag | 1 fruit + 1 fat serving |
| French fries, 1/2 cup | 1 bread + 2 fat servings |
| French fries, 1/3 cup | 1 fruit + 1 fat serving |
| Pizza, 1 wedge | 1 bread + 1 meat serving |
| Coleslaw, 1/2 cup | 1 bulky vegetable† (free) + 1 to 2 fat servings (fat is in dressing) |

*Note: Some drive-in chains have lists of their foods giving Calories, protein, fat, carbohydrates and diabetic exchanges. Ask to see if these are available from your favorite fast-food restaurants. For example, McDonald's diabetic exchange list is reprinted with permission on page 278.

# Table II / *Average Food Values*

All food values are approximate.
*Cal = Calories.

P, F and C = protein, fat and carbohydrate, in grams. These values are expressed in a similar way in recipes throughout the book.

†Much of the carbohydrate in bulky raw vegetables is not digestible and need not be counted. In a salad, however, there will usually be at least 1 teaspoon of salad dressing (1 fat serving) and perhaps much more.

| Food and Amount | Cal | P | F | C |
|---|---|---|---|---|
| **Beverages** | | | | |
| Coffee (without sugar) | 7 to 9 | 0 | 0 | 1 |
| Tea (without sugar) | 0 | 0 | 0 | 0 |
| Milk, 8 ounces: | | | | |
| Skim | 84 | 9 | 0 | 12 |
| 2%-fat | 125 | 8 | 5 | 12 |
| Whole (4%-fat) | 170 | 8 | 10 | 12 |
| Buttermilk | 84 | 9 | 0 | 12 |
| Beer (3.2%), 8 ounces (7 grams of alcohol) | 81 | 1 | 0 | 8 |
| Wine, dry red or white, 3 ounces (11 grams of alcohol) | 81 | 0 | 0 | 1 |
| Whiskey, gin or vodka, 1 ounce (12 grams of alcohol) | 80 | 0 | 0 | 0 |
| **Salad** | | | | |
| Raw mixed vegetables†, 1 cup | 12 to 28 | 1 to 2 | 0 | 3 to 5 |
| Cottage cheese and fruit (1/2 cup of cottage cheese and 2 pieces of canned fruit): | | | | |
| Unsweetened fruit at home | 154 | 15 | 6 | 10 |
| Sweetened fruit in restaurant | 194 | 15 | 6 | 20 |
| Starchy (potato, macaroni—includes 1 tablespoon of salad dressing†), 1 cup | 271 | 4 | 15 | 30 |

Food Values*

287

| Food and Amount | Cal | Food Values* | | |
|---|---|---|---|---|
| | | P | F | C |
| Meaty (chicken, seafood—includes 1 tablespoon of salad dressing†), 1 cup | 313 | 16 | 21 | 15 |
| Salad dressing†, 1 tablespoon in each cup of potato, macaroni, chicken or seafood salad | 135 | 0 | 15 | 0 |

## Bread and Cereal

| | | | | |
|---|---|---|---|---|
| Bread, 1 slice | 68 | 2 | 0 | 15 |
| Roll, 1 medium | 68 | 2 | 0 | 15 |
| Salted crackers, 5 | 68 | 2 | 0 | 15 |
| Cereal or starch, 1/2 cup | 68 | 2 | 0 | 15 |
| French toast, 1 slice | 107 | 5 | 3 | 15 |
| Pancake, 3-inch | 72 | 3 | 2 | 13 |
| Waffle, 3-1/2-inch square | 84 | 3 | 3 | 15 |
| Fruit muffin, 1 small | 135 | 3 | 4 | 22 |

## Soup

| | | | | |
|---|---|---|---|---|
| Thin, watery, 6-ounce cup | 54 | 1 | 2 | 8 |
| Average, 6-ounce cup | 86 | 2 | 2 | 15 |
| Thick, 6-ounce cup | 93 to 136 | 3 to 5 | 1 to 4 | 18 to 20 |

## Meats

*Fish:*

| | | | | |
|---|---|---|---|---|
| 1 ounce | 55 | 7 | 3 | 0 |
| Fish steak, 1 medium (4 ounces) | 220 | 28 | 12 | 0 |

*Poultry:*

| | | | | |
|---|---|---|---|---|
| 1 ounce | 55 | 7 | 3 | 0 |
| Chicken breast, 1/2 large (4 ounces) | 220 | 28 | 12 | 0 |
| Chicken, 1 drumstick and 1 thigh | 220 | 28 | 12 | 0 |

| Food and Amount | | Food Values* | | |
| --- | --- | --- | --- | --- |
| | Cal | P | F | C |
| *Beef, pork, lamb, veal:* | | | | |
| 1 ounce very lean | 55 | 7 | 3 | 0 |
| 1 ounce, average fat | 73 | 7 | 5 | 0 |
| 2 ounces (1 average meat patty or 1 small chop) | 146 | 14 | 10 | 0 |
| 4 ounces (1 large meat patty or center of lean rib steak) | 292 | 28 | 20 | 0 |
| *Casserole:* | | | | |
| Meaty, 1 cup | 214 | 16 | 10 | 15 |
| Starchy, 1 cup | 177 | 10 | 5 | 23 |
| *Breakfast meat:* | | | | |
| Bacon, 1 crisp slice | 45 | 0 | 5 | 0 |
| Canadian bacon, 2 thin slices | 73 | 7 | 5 | 0 |
| Sausage, 1 small link | 104 | 3½ | 10 | 0 |

## Eggs and Cheese

| | | | | |
| --- | --- | --- | --- | --- |
| Egg, 1 medium | 73 | 7 | 5 | 0 |
| Cottage cheese, 1/4 cup | 55 | 7 | 3 | 0 |
| Low-fat cheese, 1 slice (1 ounce) | 55 to 66 | 7 | 3 to 5 | 0 |

## Vegetables

| | | | | |
| --- | --- | --- | --- | --- |
| Bulky vegetables (cauliflower, celery, tomato, cucumber, etc.), raw†, 1 cup, or cooked, 1/2 cup | 12 to 28 | 1 to 2 | 0 0 | 3 to 5 |
| Semistarchy vegetables, (beets, carrots, green peas, mixed vegetables, onions, rutabagas, turnips, winter squash), raw or cooked, 1/2 cup | 36 | 2 | 0 | 7 |
| Starchy vegetables (beans, potatoes, etc.), cooked, 1/2 cup | 68 | 2 | 0 | 15 |

| Food and Amount | Cal | P | Food Values* F | C |
|---|---|---|---|---|
| Corn, 1/3 cup | 68 | 2 | 0 | 15 |
| Parsnips, 2/3 cup | 68 | 2 | 0 | 15 |

## Fruit Dishes

| | | | | |
|---|---|---|---|---|
| Use fresh fruit if possible, or unsweetened diet-pack fruit. | | | | |
| Grapefruit half | 40 | 0 | 0 | 10 |
| 1/4 of a large cantaloupe | 40 | 0 | 0 | 10 |
| Fruit juice, 1/2 cup (except grape or prune juice, 1/4 cup) | 40 | 0 | 0 | 10 |
| Bulky fruit (melon, berries), 1 cup | 40 | 0 | 0 | 10 |
| Average fruit (apples, apricots, grapefruit, oranges, peaches, pears, plums), 1/2 cup | 40 | 0 | 0 | 10 |
| Sweet fruit (bananas, cherries, dried fruits, grapes), 1/4 cup | 40 | 0 | 0 | 10 |

## Desserts

| | | | | |
|---|---|---|---|---|
| Unless fresh fruit is available, skip dessert and have more starch with the main course. | | | | |
| Fruit, 1 serving | 40 | 0 | 0 | 10 |
| Dietetic gelatin, 1/2 cup | 8 | 2 | 0 | 0 |

## Fats

| | | | | |
|---|---|---|---|---|
| Diluted fats (French or Italian salad dressing†), 1 tablespoon | 45 | 0 | 5 | 0 |
| Concentrated fats (oil†, mayonnaise†, margarine), 1 teaspoon | 45 | 0 | 5 | 0 |
| Nuts (6 peanuts, 5 olives or 4 walnut halves) | 45 | 0 | 5 | 0 |

# Table III / *Food Replacements for Diabetics*

If you are a diabetic on insulin or for some other reason need to eat an exact amount of carbohydrate (even if you feel nauseated), this table will show you how to replace the available carbohydrate* in foods left uneaten.

All food values are approximate.

*1 ounce of milk is equivalent to 1 scant ounce of grapefruit or orange juice or 3/4 ounce of apple juice.

†Much of the carbohydrate in bulky raw vegetables is not digestible and need not be counted. In a salad, however, there will usually be at least 1 teaspoon of salad dressing (1 fat serving) and perhaps much more.

*Approximately 50% of your diet's protein is converted to glucose, but at a slow rate. However, this must be counted in when balancing with insulin. Approximately 10% of your diet's fat may end up in glucose, but it is converted very slowly. It still has to be counted when balancing with insulin. This is why you have to replace uneaten meat and fat with a carbohydrate.

| Food and Amount | Grams of carbohydrate | Ounces of milk or juice to replace carbohydrate* | | |
| --- | --- | --- | --- | --- |
| | | *Milk* | *Orange* | *Apple* |
| **Beverages** | | | | |
| Black coffee or tea | 0 | 0 | 0 | 0 |
| Milk, 8 ounces | 12 | 8 | 7 | 6 |
| **Bread and Cereal** | | | | |
| Bread, 1 slice | 15 | 8 | 7 | 6 |
| Roll, 1 medium | 15 | 8 | 7 | 6 |
| Salted crackers, 5 | 15 | 8 | 7 | 6 |
| Cereal or starch, 1/2 cup | 15 | 8 | 7 | 6 |
| **Soup** | | | | |
| Thin, watery, 6-ounce cup | 8 | 4 | 3 | 2 |
| Average, 6-ounce cup | 15 | 8 | 5 | 4 |
| Thick, 6-ounce cup | 20 | Too variable to calculate | | |
| Meaty, thick, 6-ounce cup | 20 | 10 | 8 | 7 |

| Food and Amount | Grams of carbohydrate | Ounces of milk or juice to replace carbohydrate* | | |
|---|---|---|---|---|
| | | *Milk* | *Orange* | *Apple* |

## Salad

| Food and Amount | Grams of carbohydrate | Milk | Orange | Apple |
|---|---|---|---|---|
| Raw mixed vegetables†, 1 cup (Free except for dressing; no replacement needed.) | 5 | 0 | 0 | 0 |
| Starchy (potato, macaroni), 1 cup | 30 | 16 | 11 | 8 |
| Meaty (chicken, seafood), 1 cup | 15 | 12 | 8 | 6 |
| Salad dressing†, 1 tablespoon | 0 | 0 | 0 | 0 |
| Oil or margarine†, 1 teaspoon | 0 | 0 | 0 | 0 |

## Meats

*Fish:*

| Food and Amount | Grams of carbohydrate | Milk | Orange | Apple |
|---|---|---|---|---|
| 1 ounce | 0 | 2 | 1 | 1 |
| 1 medium fish steak (4 ounces) | 0 | 7½ | 5 | 4 |

*Poultry:*

| Food and Amount | Grams of carbohydrate | Milk | Orange | Apple |
|---|---|---|---|---|
| 1 ounce | 0 | 2 | 1 | 1 |
| 1/2 large chicken breast (4 ounces) | 0 | 7½ | 5 | 4 |
| 1 chicken drumstick and 1 thigh | 0 | 7½ | 5 | 5 |

*Beef, pork, lamb, veal:*

| Food and Amount | Grams of carbohydrate | Milk | Orange | Apple |
|---|---|---|---|---|
| 1 ounce | 0 | 1 | 1 | 1 |
| 2 ounces (1 small meat patty or 1 small chop) | 0 | 4 | 2 | 2 |
| 4 ounces (1 large meat patty or center of lean rib steak) | 0 | 8 | 4 | 4 |

*Casserole:*

| Food and Amount | Grams of carbohydrate | Milk | Orange | Apple |
|---|---|---|---|---|
| Meaty, 1 cup | 15 | 10 | 8 | 6 |
| Starchy, 1 cup | 23 | 13 | 9 | 7 |

*Breakfast meat:*

| Food and Amount | Grams of carbohydrate | Milk | Orange | Apple |
|---|---|---|---|---|
| Bacon, 1 crisp slice | 0 | 0 | 0 | 0 |

| Food and Amount | Grams of carbohydrate | Ounces of milk or juice to replace carbohydrate* | | |
|---|---|---|---|---|
| | | *Milk* | *Orange* | *Apple* |
| Canadian bacon, 2 thin slices | 0 | 2 | 1 | 1 |
| Sausage, 1 small link | 0 | 2 | 1 | 1 |

## Eggs and Cheese

| | | | | |
|---|---|---|---|---|
| Egg, 1 medium | 0 | 2 | 1 | 1 |
| Cottage cheese, 1/4 cup | | 2 | 1 | 1 |
| Low-fat cheese, 1 slice (1 ounce) | 0 | 2 | 1 | 1 |

## Vegetables

| | | | | |
|---|---|---|---|---|
| Very bulky vegetables (Chicory, Chinese cabbage, endive, escarole, lettuce, parsley, radishes, watercress) | 0 | 0 | 0 | 0 |
| Bulky vegetables (asparagus, bean sprouts, beets, broccoli, Brussels sprouts, cabbage, carrots, cauliflower, celery, cucumbers, eggplant, green pepper, greens [beet, chard, collards, dandelion, kale, mustard, spinach, turnip], mushrooms, okra, onions, rhubarb, rutabaga, sauerkraut, string beans [green and yellow], summer squash, tomatoes, tomato juice, turnips, vegetable juice cocktail, zucchini), raw†, 1 cup, or cooked, 1/2 cup | 5 | 2½ | 1⅔ | 1⅓ |

| Food and Amount | Grams of carbohydrate | Ounces of milk or juice to replace carbohydrate* | | |
|---|---|---|---|---|
| | | *Milk* | *Orange* | *Apple* |
| Semistarchy vegetables, (beets, carrots, mixed vegetables, onions, rutabagas, turnips), raw or cooked, 1/2 cup | 7 | 3½ | 2½ | 2 |
| Starchy vegetables, cooked: | | | | |
| Beans, potatoes, etc., 1/2 cup | 15 | 7 | 5 | 4 |
| Corn, 1/3 cup | 15 | 7 | 5 | 4 |
| Lima beans, 1/2 cup | 15 | 7 | 5 | 4 |
| Parsnips, 2/3 cup | 15 | 7 | 5 | 4 |
| Peas, green (canned or frozen), 1/2 cup | 15 | 7 | 5 | 4 |
| Pumpkin, 3/4 cup | 15 | 7 | 5 | 4 |
| Winter squash, 1/2 cup | 15 | 7 | 5 | 4 |
| Yams, sweet potato, 1/4 cup | 15 | 7 | 5 | 4 |

## Fruit Dishes

| Food and Amount | Grams of carbohydrate | Milk | Orange | Apple |
|---|---|---|---|---|
| Grapefruit half | 10 | 3½ | 3 | 2½ |
| 1/4 of a large cantaloupe | 10 | 3½ | 3 | 2½ |
| Small glass of fruit juice, 1/2 cup (except grape or prune, 1/4 cup) | 10 | 3½ | 3 | 2½ |
| Bulky fruit (melon, berries), 1 cup | 10 | 3½ | 3 | 2½ |
| Average fruit (apples, apricots, grapefruit, oranges, peaches, pears, plums), 1/2 cup | 10 | 3½ | 3 | 2½ |
| Sweet fruit (bananas, cherries dried fruits, grapes), 1/4 cup | 10 | 3½ | 3 | 2½ |

| Food and Amount | Grams of carbohydrate | Ounces of milk or juice to replace carbohydrate* | | |
|---|---|---|---|---|
| | | *Milk* | *Orange* | *Apple* |
| **Desserts** | | | | |
| Fruit, 1 serving | 10 | 3½ | 3 | 2½ |
| Dietetic gelatin, 1/2 cup | 0 | 0 | 0 | 0 |
| **Fats** | | | | |
| Diluted fats (French or Italian salad dressing†), 1 tablespoon | 0 | 0 | 0 | 0 |
| Concentrated fats (oil†, mayonnaise†, margarine), 1 teaspoon | 0 | 0 | 0 | 0 |
| Nuts (6 peanuts, 5 olives or 4 walnut halves) | 0 | 0 | 0 | 0 |

# Table IV / *Measurement Equivalents* (approximate)

| Tablespoons | Teaspoons | Ounces | Grams | Milliliters* | Cups |
|---|---|---|---|---|---|
| 1/3 tbs. | 1 tsp. | 1/6 oz. | 5 gr. | 5 mL | — |
| 1 tbs. | 3 tsp. | 1/2 oz. | 15 gr. | 15 mL | — |
| 2 tbs. | 6 tsp. | 1 oz. | 30 gr. | 30 mL | 1/8 c. |
| 4 tbs. | 12 tsp. | 2 oz. | 60 gr. | 60 mL | 1/4 c. |
| 6-2/3 tbs. | 20 tsp. | 3-1/3 oz. | 100 gr. | 100 mL | scant 1/2 c. |
| 8 tbs. | 24 tsp. | 4 oz. | 120 gr. | 120 mL | 1/2 c. |
| 16 tbs. | 48 tsp. | 8 oz. | 240 gr. | 240 mL | 1 c. |

*Note: For materials similar to water.

# Bibliography

Analytical data. Crescent Manufacturing Company, Seattle, Wash., 1974.

Analytical data. Prepared by Washington State Heart Association and Northwest Lipid Research Center, Seattle, Wash., 1974.

Analytical data. Shasta Beverages, Seattle, Wash., 1974.

*Average Weight of a Measured Cup of Various Foods.* Agricultural Research Service 61-6, U.S. Department of Agriculture. U.S. Government Printing Office, Washington, D.C., 1969.

*Code of Federal Regulations: #21 Food and Drugs, Parts 1 to 119.* Office of the Federal Register, National Archives and Records Service, General Services Administration. U.S. Government Printing Office, Washington, D.C., 1972.

*Conversion Factors and Weights and Measures for Agricultural Commodities and Their Products.* Statistical Bulletin #362, Economic Research Service, U.S. Department of Agriculture. U.S. Government Printing Office, Washington, D.C., 1965.

Feeley, R.M., Criner, P.E., and Watt, B.K., "Cholesterol Content of foods." *Journal of the American Dietetic Association* 61:134, 1972.

*Food Values of Portions Commonly Used, Bowes and Church* (13th edition). Revised by C.F. Church and H.N. Church. J.P. Lippincott Co., Philadelphia, 1979.

Goddard, V.R., and Goddall, L. *Fatty Acids in Food Fats.* Home Economics Research Report #7, U.S. Department of Agriculture. U.S. Government Printing Office, Washington, D.C., 1959.

*Heinz Handbook of Nutrition.* McGraw-Hill Book Company, New York, 1959.

McCance, R.A., and Widdowson, E.M. *Chemical Composition of Foods.* Chemical Publishing Co., Brooklyn, 1947.

Mattice, Marjorie R. *Bridges' Food and Beverage Analyses* (3rd edition). Lea and Febiger, Philadelphia, 1950.

*Nutritive Value of American Foods, in Common Units.* Agricultural Handbook No. 456, U.S. Department of Agriculture. U.S. Government Printing Office, Washington, D.C., 1975.

Product data from manufacturers as shown on product labels. Margarines — Fleischmann's, Mazola and Saffola. Sweeteners — Sugar Twin, Sweet & Low and Sucaryl. Instant flour — Wondra. Liquid egg substitutes — Egg Beaters and Second Nature.

*Sodium-Restricted diets: The Rationale, Complications and Practical Aspects of Their Use.* Natural Resources Council, Pub. #325. National Academy of Sciences, Washington, D.C., 1954.

Stansby, M.E., "Composition of Fish." Fishery Leaflet #116, U.S. Fish & Wildlife Service. U.S. Government Printing Office, Washington, D.C., 1953.

Watt, B.K., and Merrill, A.L. *Composition of Foods — Raw, Processed, and Prepared* (revised). U.S. Department of Agriculture Handbook #8. U.S. Government Printing Office, Washington, D.C., 1963.

# Index